# The
# African American
## Encyclopedia

### Second Edition

# The
# African American
## Encyclopedia

## Second Edition

### Volume 3
### Com-Fed

*Editor, First Edition*
**Michael W. Williams**

*Consulting Editor, Supplement to First Edition*
**Kibibi Voloria Mack**

**Advisory Board, Second Edition**

**Barbara Bair**
*Duke University*

**Carl L. Bankston III**
*Tulane University*

**David Bradley**
*City University of New York*

**Shelley Fisher Fishkin**
*University of Texas, Austin*

**Wendy Sacket**
*Coast College*

*Managing Editor, Second Edition*
**R. Kent Rasmussen**

**Marshall Cavendish**
New York • London • Toronto • Sydney

Project Editor: McCrea Adams
Production Editor: Cindy Beres
Assistant Editor: Andrea Miller
Research Supervisor: Jeffry Jensen
Photograph Editor: Philip Bader
Page Layout: William Zimmerman

Marshall Cavendish Corporation
99 White Plains Road
Tarrytown, New York 10591-9001

© 2001 Marshall Cavendish Corporation
Printed in the United States of America
09  08  07  06  05  04  03  02  01        5  4  3  2  1

**Library of Congress Cataloging-in-Publication Data**

The African American encyclopedia.—2nd ed. / managing editor, R. Kent Rasmussen.
        p. cm.
Includes bibliographical references and index.
1. Afro-Americans—Encyclopedias. I. Rasmussen, R. Kent.
E185 .A253   2001
973'.0496073'003—dc21
ISBN 0-7614-7208-8 (set)                                      00-031526
ISBN 0-7614-7211-8 (volume 3)                                 CIP

∞ This paper meets the requirements of ANSI/NISO Z39.48-1992 (R1997)
Permanence of Paper for Publications and Documents in Libraries and Archives

# Contents

# The
# African American
## Encyclopedia

**Second Edition**

**Community and culture:** African Americans in the United States meet the sociological criteria to be classified as a "community." However, there is no unanimity of opinion as to whether this community is sufficiently functional so that its culture is protected from the interests of competing—and more dominant—American communities. The African American community is distinctive partly because it is maintained as a social unit by power structures that are external to it. Its culture therefore is sometimes termed a "subculture" because it is evaluated in relation to a dominant Eurocentric main culture.

*Social Institutions*

The African American community is a social system that includes interrelated activities, and these activities are expressed through social institutions that meet African American needs. The adequacy of the institutions' responses, however, is always partly determined by the dominant society's impact on the institutions. Communities function through their institutions to accomplish specific tasks such as production and distribution of goods, socialization, social control, social participation, and mutual support. For the African American community, none of these tasks is performed exclusively internally; each is affected decisively by more dominant social units.

Certainly, needs for social participation and mutual support are often met through FAMILY LIFE, church participation, and African American social organizations, but production, socialization, and social control are far more influenced by external communities. It is clear that the economic system under which African Americans live is not their construction, that the educational system in which they are included promulgates Eurocentric ideas, and that the legal and criminal justice system is not controlled by their community. The African American community's institutions, though they often meet people's needs, are never isolated from the larger social environment; further, these institutions are often what could be called "allowed structures"—they exist partly because more dominant communities perceive their continuance as beneficial. Conversely, if African American institutions are considered threatening by the power structures of dominant groups, they may be directly challenged.

The BLACK PANTHER PARTY is a prime example. Several of its leaders were killed or felt compelled to leave the United States, and the organization disintegrated in the 1970's. Subordinate communities, including the African American community, have found it difficult, if not impossible, to maintain high-profile institutions that directly conflict with the perceived needs and values of more powerful groups.

*Cultural Categories*

The culture produced by the African American social unit is not monolithic. It can be divided into three categories. First, there are cultural universals common to both African Americans and other groups, ideas and habits that are usual to adult members of the larger American society. To what extent these universals are externally imposed is debated. Insofar as African American culture is produced within a non-African environment and in a Eurocentrically dominated context, the African American is a recipient of other cultural influences. African Americans, however, also share cultural ideas and habits with others because they are functional in given times and places. African American INVENTORS, for example, have not necessarily had their new concepts and products imposed on them. The inventions may have occurred out of recognizable needs of both the African American community and others.

Second, African American culture has specialties and traits that are exclusive to that community. This is the case for all social groups that are distinctive from others: The total population of a multiethnic society neither produces nor continues all specialties of particular groups. African Americans have produced religious practices, vocabulary, and dress styles peculiar to themselves. Specialty components of African American culture often have been short-lived. The development of technology and mass communication in American society disperses a community's distinctive cultural characteristics more easily and makes them more likely to became part of the larger community's culture. This is recognized and resented when African Americans complain that their linguistic phrases or music forms have been exploited and used by others. Few sociologists claim that the United States of the late twentieth century is a true "melting pot," but most find evidence of appropriation of African American cultural forms by external groups.

The third aspect of African American culture is its alternatives—those cultural components shared by some individuals in the group but not by all. Cultural alternatives may be distinctively African American, since others do not appear to produce them, but they may be shared by very small segments of the community and may not be representative of the community as a whole. The NATION OF ISLAM is a case in point. Membership in the group is minuscule compared with the total African American population, yet no other ethnic community is a participant in this religion. It clearly is an alternative only for African Americans and a product of African American cultural innovators, but it is unrepresentative of religious beliefs and practices of the black community.

### The Black Community as a Subculture

The universals, specialties, and alternatives found within African American culture help to address whether it is appropriately consid-ered a subculture. Even its specialties are transmitted to external groups, and its alternatives may be allowed by external power structures. The term "subculture" has something of a pejorative connotation. Subcultures are those values, attitudes, behavior modes, and lifestyles of a group that are distinct from but always in relation to more dominant cultures. The prefix "sub" implies a culture that is not dominant, not independent, and perhaps not as significant as the dominant culture. African American culture is certainly interrelated with mainstream white culture in the United States. Although it is not dominant, it can be perceived as often innovative and influential beyond its group and sometimes it is determinate of external-group cultural trends.

A strong case can be made that the religion of SANTERÍA, for example, although dependent on West African (Yoruba) practices for its origins, has had an impact on whites in CUBA and on Cuban Americans. No matter how closely associated with black slaves or how closely suppressed by white political authority, the religion has enjoyed a larger social acceptance than a "sub" categorizing of it implies. Melville HERSKOVITS's work (*The Myth of the Negro Past*, 1941) clearly shows how African cultures in the Caribbean and Brazil as well as in the United States had "survivals" that eluded repression. The dominant social group's inability to erase others' cultural products makes the term "subculture" imprecise.

In summary, a subordinate group such as African Americans may be so culturally influential in the larger society that some of its cultural contributions exceed traditional descriptions such as "subcultural." For example, the musical products of Berry GORDY, Jr.'s MOTOWN record comany in the 1960's and early 1970's suggest that in some fields, times, and places, African Americans have, in fact dominated the larger society's cultural production.

## Cultural Security

The continuing historical and contemporary issue that confronts African Americans as an ethnic-minority social unit is how the black community can be further empowered so that its culture is more secure. The question is not only an abstract theoretical concern: It is also existentially faced each moment that African Americans share a geographical region, political process, economic system, or social institution dominated by other groups.

One of the most influential responses to the issue was made by social historian W. E. B. Du Bois in his classic work *The Souls of Black Folk: Essays and Sketches* (1903). Du Bois's perspective was important intellectually mostly because it reflected the ways in which black Americans actually lived. He claimed that a dual or double consciousness must be employed if the community is to be functional and its culture continued. African Americans are both African and American simultaneously, and there is a necessary though uneasy joining of these identities. Historian Oscar Handlin was specific about the dual identities for ethnic-minority communities, generally in the United States, claiming political and economic unity among groups with cultural diversity.

Each of these analyses can be challenged. Handlin's interpretation of cultural diversity as a positive contribution that leads toward a cultural melting pot is debatable. Du Bois was his own critic. In his later life, he abandoned the idea of dual consciousness when he acknowledged that nonblack Americans would never accept the empowering of the African American community or allow its culture to flourish without their control of it.

Community empowerment has been attempted by African Americans historically by a variety of means that include such differing approaches as identifying with, adopting, or "parroting" majority group culture at one extreme and rejecting Eurocentric cultural values through the back-to-Africa movement of Marcus GARVEY at the other. The responses have correlated closely with the historical situations in which black Americans have found themselves. In the United States, this "situational ethic" has at least allowed black Americans to survive as a social unit and to continue distinctive cultural production.

## History of Assimilation

The processes of ASSIMILATION and then absorption were not intended for the black slaves brought to the United States. There was a cultural ACCOMMODATION that existed between blacks and whites during the era of SLAVERY; that is, there was some realization of the distinctions between the two groups that existed and would persist. There were also events that contradicted accommodation. In GEORGIA and SOUTH CAROLINA particularly, slave insurrections or revolts were common; more frequently, slaves resisted cultural impositions by using acceptable religious practices to mask unacceptable social and political acts. Christian spirituals, for example, were sung to advise, warn, and gather slaves who needed protection against slave masters and to aid in slave escapes.

Cultural accommodation was severely tested as African Americans moved to cities. Attempts by white southerners to keep them a subordinate caste were less successful after URBANIZATION. The attempt by white northerners to keep African Americans outside the industrial organizations of large northern urban centers was unsuccessful. Urbanization of African Americans in the eighteenth and nineteenth centuries was limited, but those who moved to cities were a greater threat to previous cultural accommodations than were those who remained in rural areas.

Migration, after 1876, and urbanization, particularly after the nineteenth century, have been the dominant features of black social and cultural change in the United States. They are wholly interrelated, as African American migration has been primarily to American cities. Some scholars contend that the migrations caused black folk culture to be disrupted, changed rural peasants into a landless proletariat in the cities, or increased African American family disunity. The problems encountered, however, must be balanced with the possibilities. Migration and urbanization made African Americans less isolated, allowed communication among them that led to increased ethnic group power, and allowed creation of a larger African American middle-class culture. City life appeared to place far more emphasis on achieved status than on the ascribed status so important to rural life. To some extent, this meant that urbanized African Americans could achieve merit on a more individual basis. This achievement process, however, must be understood as limited by the ethnic ascription from which African Americans could not escape as a subordinated people in the United States.

### Twentieth-Century Urbanization

The relocation of African Americans to both western and northern cities during the twentieth century is one of the most important events in American history, not only for the black community but also for other urbanized social groups. The movement, widely called the GREAT MIGRATION, was so thorough, involved so many, and happened so quickly that both rural and urban life were changed radically across the United States. In 1910, 73 percent of the African American population was rural, with 91 percent living in the South. By 1960, 73 percent lived in cities, and only 60 percent in the South.

The important point about black urbanization is not only that the process was massive and uprooting: It was also a process that reorganized American society. In spite of the resegregation of urbanized African Americans since WORLD WAR II, black political and economic power were enhanced by this movement. Since the 1960's, the majority of large urban centers in the United States have elected African American MAYORS; among these cities are New York, Los Angeles, Chicago, Atlanta, Birmingham, Detroit, and Philadelphia. This political change has been complemented by election of black police chiefs, school superintendents, city council members, and others who at least symbolically represent black social power.

Simultaneously, urbanization allowed the development of African American institutions that represent economic power, such as the multicollege Clark ATLANTA UNIVERSITY complex, black-owned banks in most southern as well as northern cities, and major personal products and music corporations in Chicago and Detroit. Traditional black businesses such as funeral homes and hair salons have increased in size, diversified in their offerings, and sometimes opened several branches. Religion has its largest congregations and its most affluent adherents, as well as increased economic and political impact, in urban centers. Even though American cities have continued in their ethnic segregation, geographical separations have not decreased African American community empowerment. They have in some cases concentrated it through bloc voting and through establishing institutions within ethnic enclaves that can flourish in a friendly environment. Unofficial but actual resegregation of African Americans allowed some subordinate group dominance, especially within central cities.

In the late 1980's, there was some reversal of the earlier urban migration among blacks. Some African Americans returned from the Northeast to the South, for example, making cities such as Atlanta recipients of northern populations. Southern urban centers benefited from reinforcement of black middle classes, since professionals were an important component of the reverse migrations.

There has also been a more limited movement from northern and western cities to rural and small-town locales in the South. This has been explained mostly by "push" factors, such as the desire to leave high-crime areas or an attempt to find less expensive housing. None of the reverse migrations, however, is comparable to the massive rural-to-city and South-to-North movements that had occurred previously. Although there is significance to the changes, it is not clear that they represent any trend.

*Political Power*
The urbanization of African Americans was a key component in the black community's development of a critical mass that could express political power. To political scientists, this "critical mass" is a number of people in a given place sufficient to determine political decisions and reflect group interests. As African Americans created large populations in northern and other cities, political leverage helped to transform the power relations between African Americans and other ethnic communities. The transformation is distinct from earlier rural black history, during which dispersed people were unable to form political power blocs that could alter the sociopolitical environment.

During RECONSTRUCTION, African Americans held national elective as well as state and local offices, but the effects of this participation were short-lived. When federal troops were removed from the South in 1877, unprotected and widely dispersed African Americans were unable to prevent the return of domination by southern whites. The NATIONAL ASSOCIATION FOR THE ADVANCEMENT OF COLORED PEOPLE (NAACP), organized in 1909, successfully re-enfranchised large numbers of African American VOTERS. The impact of this effort was not realized, however, until an urbanized critical mass was established, especially after 1915.

One result of the urbanization process was a shift in party affiliation by a majority of African Americans. Allegiance to the REPUBLICAN PARTY, associated with Abraham Lincoln and emancipation, was replaced by attraction to the DEMOCRATIC PARTY, with its policies and programs that were less hostile to African Americans. By 1928 the Democrats sought African American votes overtly. Following Franklin D. Roosevelt's victories in 1932 and 1936, the black community was one direct beneficiary of New Deal programs aimed at lower-class and underclass communities.

Nationally, the voting power of African Americans has been significant in presidential elections, including the 1940 Roosevelt victory, the 1948 win by Harry S Truman over Thomas Dewey, and the John F. Kennedy victory in 1960. The last of those contests was won by only 112,827 votes. Estimates indicate between 70 and 80 percent of African American votes cast for Kennedy, with black voters providing winning margins in key states such as Illinois and Texas.

Black political culture, however, has not been limited to participation in the larger society's official political processes. Many African Americans have argued that their voting power has not reaped significant benefits. Therefore, the African American community has developed confrontational political strategies while simultaneously guarding the hard-earned right to vote.

*Political Culture*
The African American shift to the Democratic Party failed to empower the black community in some significant ways. Institutionalized racism continued, residential segregation increased, and black as well as white politicians attempted to manipulate African American voters for personal rather than black communal gain. RACE RIOTS in the 1940's were the result of white police killings of blacks, and some African Americans were murdered

while attempting to desegregate social institutions.

Confrontational politics, always a possibility since the early slave revolts in the 1700's, enjoyed a resurgence after 1955 and the MONTGOMERY BUS BOYCOTT. Legal forms of social protest were considered insufficient even by mainstream African American political leaders such as the Rev. Martin Luther KING, Jr., and new organizations were formed that were external to the white-dominated political parties. The STUDENT NONVIOLENT COORDINATING COMMITTEE (SNCC) and the CONGRESS OF RACIAL EQUALITY (CORE) initiated direct action against segregated institutions in the 1960's. The Black Panther Party attempted black community self-defense against white police brutality in the 1960's and early 1970's. MALCOLM X increasingly symbolized African American ideas about self-determination.

The ethic of self-determination had its logical consequence in the formation of institutions that attempted to function apart from Eurocentric systems in the United States. The most important of these, in terms of ideological influences on the African American community, was the Nation of Islam. The Nation, through its longtime leader Elijah MUHAMMAD, devised a theology of black purity as well as black institutional alternatives in education, business, and religion. It became an example of a political culture that rejected even a confrontation with nonblacks: Its policy was to separate from unredeemable social and political institutions dominated by whites.

### The Family

The family remains the basic social unit in the structure of the African American community. The importance of family is implied in language often used by African Americans to describe relationships external to families; for example the use of "brother" to mean "friend," and "family" to describe a church congregation. Family culture can be evaluated both as

the result of necessary exploration and as strength-allowing options. The African American's family ethic is influenced by the history of slavery. The disruption and disorganization that occurred destroyed traditional kinship ties and created a caste system from which modern black families have not fully escaped. It is doubtful that sociologists E. Franklin FRAZIER and Daniel Patrick Moynihan were correct, however, when they implied that modern characteristics of black families can be attributed largely to the slave era. Instead, trends in African American family structures and functions also closely follow nonblack trends, or at least correlate with them.

Monogamy remains a norm among black families in the United States. Variations from monogamy such as serial monogamy or common-law marriage are more common in lower socioeconomic classes. Increasingly, however, more casual living arrangements among unmarried couples have become accepted across class lines, in both the black and white communities. African Americans also share with other ethnic groups a variety of household patterns that include husband and wife, the nuclear family, and the attenuated nuclear family, which has one of the marital partners absent. What appears distinctive about African American family life and makes it different from Anglo American family styles is that black kinship networks still tend to be more extensive and cohesive than are similar bonds among whites. Census data show that a higher percentage of black families take in relatives and include them as part of their households. There are practical economic and social reasons for this, and they have existed since slavery. This EXTENDED FAMILY style, however, is neither as pervasive nor as necessary among middle-class African Americans as it once was. (Comparatively, it has nearly disappeared among middle-class whites in the United States.)

Attention focused on the African American

family has questioned the functionality of the female-headed household. This social phenomenon also is not distinctive to African Americans, although its increase among them has been more rapid than among non-Hispanic whites. Data suggest a strong correlation between high percentages of female-headed households and lower income groups. The increasing incidence of poor female-headed families is addressed somewhat by the extended kinship mode of adaptation: In the black community, other women may be present in the household to help both economically and in child rearing. In addition, non-family men living outside the household often assist.

The debate as to whether these arrangements indicate a matriarchal form of family life is unresolved. What is certain is that differing arrangements are responses to varieties of social circumstances, and as responses, they have some sort of functionality. It is also clear that in the absence of institutional racism, African Americans might not engage in some of the family relations that have been established.

*The Black Church*

The other major social institution in the African American community is the church. It, too, represents a mode of accommodating to external group power. Although the mainstream black religious denominations may not exert the social and political power that they did a generation ago, they remain the only national organizations that enjoy broad community allegiance.

A trend developed in the late twentieth century toward leaving one religious organization for another. This process often includes a variety of experiences among established denominations, smaller sects, and non-Christian cults. There is also a reinvigoration of traditional Protestant thought by younger experimental theologians, who are committed to relating Protestant theology either to African American nationalism or to pan-Africanism. Further, many African American congregations are committed to the practical acts of addressing immediate social needs. The mentoring of young black men is one example; disaster relief for victims of riots or hurricanes is another. Again, as in political culture and family culture, the African American community shows both considerable diversity and some unity in its religious functions.

The African American church has a history of being a political, social, and economic center as well as a theological instructor. Clergy still promulgate political points of view and are key political organizers in many areas. The church remains for many parishioners a center for socializing as well as for encouraging specific socialization processes among the young. Most churches act as economic welfare centers through their distribution of material goods and economic services.

Black religious institutions can afford to function in these ways, since they are the most self-determining of African American organizations. Both historically and contemporarily, white power structures have exerted less dominance over these institutions than over any other major social institutions in the black community. The diminishing of religious influence is discernible, however. One indicator is the increasing number of black political leaders who are not clergy. Another is the variety of professions open to and chosen by educated African Americans, who historically were limited largely either to teaching or to the ministry.

The African American community functions so that it can produce a culture that both adjusts to the cultures of more powerful communities and is sufficiently distinctive to continue black values. African Americans have social systems and institutions that legitimately make "community" an appropriate and descriptive term for the social unit. The community's culture is functional mostly because it varies between sharing universals with others, offering specialties for its own groups, and allowing alternatives for some members.

—*William T. Osborne*

*See also:* Afrocentricity; African cultural transformations; African heritage; Black English; Hairstyles; Historically black colleges; Politics and government; Religion; Single-parent households; Slang and street language.

Suggested Readings:

Adell, Sandra. *African American Culture*. Detroit: Gale Research, 1996.

Asante, Molefi K., and Mark T. Mattson. *The Historical and Cultural Atlas of African Americans*. New York: Macmillan, 1991.

Barboza, Steven. *The African American Book of Values: Classic Moral Stories*. New York: Doubleday, 1998.

Blackwell, James E. *The Black Community: Diversity and Unity*. 2d ed. New York: Harper & Row, 1985.

Cone, James H. *A Black Theology of Liberation*. New York: J. B. Lippincott, 1970.

Fanon, Frantz. *The Wretched of the Earth*. New York: Grove Press, 1963.

Frazier, E. Franklin. *Black Bourgeoisie*. Glencoe, Ill.: Free Press, 1957.

Horton, James O., and Lois E. Horton, eds. *A History of the African American People: The History, Traditions, and Culture of African Americans*. Detroit: Wayne State University Press, 1997.

Myrdal, Gunnar. *An American Dilemma: The Negro Problem and Modern Democracy*. New York: Harper & Brothers, 1944.

Salzman, Jack, David L. Smith, and Cornel West, eds. *Encyclopedia of African-American Culture and History*. New York: Simon & Schuster Macmillan, 1996.

Smith, C. Carter, ed. *The African-American Experience on File*. New York: Facts On File, 1999.

**Comprehensive Employment and Training Act of 1973:** Federal legislation concerning job training. When the national economy has been unable to generate jobs for all those who need and desire work, the federal government has tried a variety of approaches. One of these was the Comprehensive Employment and Training Act, or CETA, passed in 1973. This law directed the Department of Labor and other federal agencies to provide job-training programs and, where possible, jobs to the hard-core unemployed. African Americans were disproportionately represented in this category, and CETA programs were directed toward them. CETA provided steady, if low-paying, jobs and internships for many African Americans during the 1970's and financed a number of community action programs and institutions through paying for their employees. Many financially strapped cities used CETA-paid employees for needed work.

CETA replaced the Manpower Development and Training Act (MDTA) of 1962 and reflected a different approach to job training and unemployment. The MDTA, the most significant of the MANPOWER PROGRAMS, paid for government training programs. Aid to the unemployed or unskilled workers enrolled in MDTA programs came from the federal government. CETA, on the other hand, directed money toward communities, which then provided programs. Communities thus had much more discretion in how funds were used.

Despite their positive aspects in dealing with unemployment, CETA programs ultimately were stifled by America's stagnant economy during the 1970's. A growing conservative movement also put this type of government activity into disfavor. CETA programs were vulnerable to critics who claimed that they were wasteful, ineffective, and prone to corruption. The failure of the American economy to grow significantly in the 1970's resulted in CETA programs making only small dents in the unemployment rate.

In 1981, the year President Ronald Reagan took office, CETA was allowed to expire. The following year it was replaced by the Job Training Partnership Act (JTPA). The JTPA decentralized training even further, providing funds to private employers who trained workers. *See also:* Civil rights and congressional legislation; Employment and unemployment.

**Compromise of 1850:** Political agreement that settled issues related to the admission of CALIFORNIA to the United States as a free state. The cession of lands to the United States by MEXICO after the MEXICAN-AMERICAN WAR and the discovery of gold in California exacerbated tension over the future of SLAVERY in the western territories. When California's application to join the union as a free state threatened to upset the power balance in the Senate between fifteen slave and fifteen free states,

Henry Clay of Kentucky, then seventy-two years of age, proposed a compromise that incorporated many of the issues of the day.

Clay had been responsible for leading the nation into the MISSOURI COMPROMISE OF 1820 and past the nullification crisis of 1832. His proposals in January, 1850, held the union together for another decade. His comprehensive plan resolved that California would be admitted as a free state, that land ceded by Mexico would be divided into the territories of NEW MEXICO and UTAH, with no conditions concerning slavery, that TEXAS would settle its border dispute with New Mexico in return for partial federal assumption of Texas debt, that the District of Columbia would abolish the slave trade while keeping slavery, that Congress would stop interfering in the interstate slave trade, and that a stronger FUGITIVE SLAVE LAW would be enacted.

The last great debate by the "great triumvi-

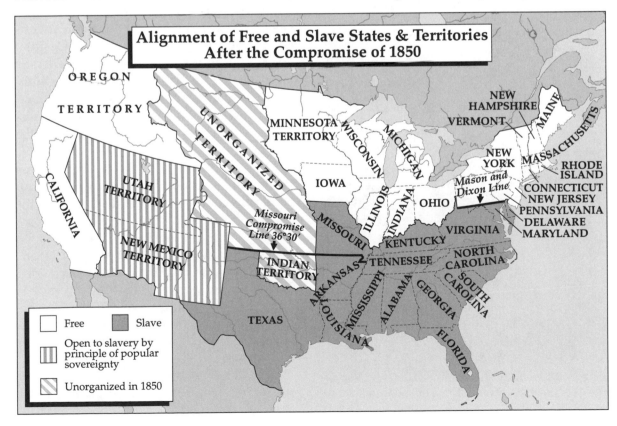

601

rate"—Clay, Daniel Webster, and John C. Calhoun—rang through the Senate. Calhoun warned that the North was usurping all the nation's power and must stop or risk civil war. Webster's famous "seventh of March" speech called for both sides to give up extremism and to preserve the union. Clay offered an omnibus bill that called for acceptance of all of his proposals as a group instead of a vote on each one. Instead, Stephen Douglas of Illinois called for a separate vote on each issue and skillfully arranged for majority coalitions on each proposal.

By September 15, 1850, Congress had hammered out the Compromise of 1850, which was almost identical to Clay's plan. California entered the union as a free state; Texas received federal debt relief in exchange for its present-day boundary (an adjustment that included 33,333 square miles more than Clay had suggested); the newly created territories of New Mexico and Utah would decide the is-

Illinois senator Stephen A. Douglas, principal architect of the Compromise of 1850. *(Library of Congress)*

sue of slavery by vote, or popular sovereignty; a new Fugitive Slave Law replaced the 1793 one; and the slave trade was abolished in the District of Columbia. Most Americans welcomed the compromise as a respite from growing sectional antagonism. It raised serious issues, however, and was no more than a temporary solution to the dispute over slavery. The new Fugitive Slave Law made northerners firmer in their insistence that slavery not be expanded into the territories, since escape from slavery had become more difficult. Similar issues would be faced in the drafting of the KANSAS-NEBRASKA ACT in 1854.

**Compromise of 1877:** Political bargain that resolved the disputed 1876 presidential election and ended the RECONSTRUCTION era.

Conflict over electoral votes left the outcome of the 1876 U.S. presidential election in doubt. Although Democratic candidate Samuel J. Tilden clearly had won the popular vote, he received only 184 undisputed electoral votes, one vote short of the 185 needed to claim the White House. Republican Rutherford B. Hayes received only 165 electoral votes; however, if he received all 20 of the disputed electoral votes he would become the new president.

One contested vote from Oregon was quickly determined to belong to Hayes, but politicians could not resolve disputes over the remaining nineteen votes, which were from South Carolina, Florida, and Louisiana. In each state there were at least two boards, one Republican and one Democrat, which claimed to have the authority to declare the victor in the state's election; in each state the Democratic board gave the electoral votes to Tilden, while the Republican board declared Hayes the winner.

The U.S. Constitution provided no guidance as to how to resolve the disputes over the electoral votes, so Congress appointed a fif-

President Rutherford B. Hayes, the chief beneficiary of the Compromise of 1877. *(Library of Congress)*

teen-member commission to handle the matter. Efforts were made to have seven Democrats, seven Republicans, and a neutral judge on the panel, but in the end Republicans held a majority. The commission awarded all the votes to Hayes. The Senate, which was controlled by Republicans, approved the committee's decision, but the Democrat-controlled House rejected it. House members conducted a filibuster, preventing any count of the electoral votes. The situation remained deadlocked into February, 1877, sparking concerns that a president would not be selected before March 4, the inauguration date.

On February 26, southern Democrats met with Hayes's representatives at the Wormley House, a hotel in Washington, D.C. The Democrats agreed to support Hayes on the condition that he recall federal troops stationed in the South. Such a move would lead to the collapse of the only remaining Republican governments in the region, those in South Carolina and Louisiana, and would mark the end of Reconstruction.

The Wormley House agreement, which became known as the Compromise of 1877, confirmed the end of Reconstruction, which would have happened no matter who was elected. Hayes probably received support from southern Democrats because he agreed to measures regarding economic growth in the South, especially construction of the Texas & Pacific Railroad. Northern Democrats gave Hayes their approval because they feared that reversing the commission's decision for Hayes might lead to further political conflict.

The resolution of the disputed election revealed that both northerners and southerners wanted to abandon Reconstruction. For African Americans, this meant that they would receive no help from the North as they struggled to protect their civil and political rights and as they tried to expand economic opportunities. In the years after the Compromise of 1877, African Americans witnessed the erosion of the political power they had gained during Reconstruction and a continuation of violence and repression at the hands of racist southerners.

—*Thomas Clarkin*

*See also:* Democratic Party; Electoral politics; Politics and government; Republican Party.

Suggested Readings:

Foner, Eric, and Olivia Mahoney. *America's Reconstruction: People and Politics After the Civil War.* New York: HarperCollins, 1995.

_____. *Reconstruction: America's Unfinished Revolution, 1863-1877.* New York: Harper & Row, 1988.

Polakoff, Keith. *The Politics of Inertia the Election of 1876 and the End of Reconstruction.* Baton Rouge: Louisiana State University Press, 1973.

Richter, William L. *The ABC-CLIO Companion to American Reconstruction, 1862-1877.* Santa Barbara, Calif.: ABC-CLIO, 1996.

Trefousse, Hans L. *Historical Dictionary of Reconstruction*. New York: Greenwood Press, 1991.

Woodward, C. Vann. *Reunion and Reaction: The Compromise of 1877 and the End of Reconstruction*. Boston: Little, Brown, 1966.

**Confederacy:** The eleven Southern slave-holding states that fought against the Union in the CIVIL WAR (1861-1865).

In November, 1860, Republican candidate Abraham Lincoln was elected president of the United States. Southern leaders were unwilling to accept Lincoln's election because of the Republican Party's strong stand against the further spread of SLAVERY into the western territories. Southern states therefore began seceding (withdrawing) from the United States.

*Founding of the Confederacy*
The first state to secede was SOUTH CAROLINA, on December 20, 1860. By early February, 1861, six more states had seceded: MISSISSIPPI, FLORIDA, ALABAMA, GEORGIA, LOUISIANA, and TEXAS. One week later, delegates from these seven states formed the Confederacy—in full, the Confederate States of America—at Montgomery, Alabama. Jefferson Davis of Mississippi and Alexander Stephens from Georgia were elected provisional (later permanent) president and vice president by the delegates.

The Civil War began in April, 1861, after South Carolina troops attacked a Union fort, Fort Sumter, in the Charleston, South Carolina, harbor. The Confederate constitution was ratified by late April, 1861. It was similar to the U.S. Constitution, although it had some notable differences, including a guarantee of slavery. By June 8, four additional states, VIRGINIA, ARKANSAS, NORTH CAROLINA, and TENNESSEE, had joined the Confederacy. It was these eleven states that fought against the Union in the Civil War. Montgomery served as the capi-

Toward the end of the Civil War, the Confederacy began enlisting thousands of African Americans into its army, but only in noncombatant positions. This soldier, named Marlboro, was an officer's servant. *(AP/Wide World Photos)*

tal of the Confederate States of America until the capital was moved to Richmond, Virginia, in July, 1862.

*African Americans and the War Effort*
African Americans were vital to the Confederacy's ability to conduct its military affairs during the Civil War. The South's manpower needs were especially compelling because of the discrepancy between the population sizes of the two belligerents. The North (Union) outnumbered the South (Confederacy) by roughly 23 million to 9 million; the South's 9 million included more than 3.5 million black slaves and 132,000 free African Americans.

Despite their pronounced fear of slave uprisings throughout the war, Southern whites had African Americans work not only at their traditional tasks but also in new and different occupations directly related to the Confederate war effort. Many blacks continued to labor as field hands, planting, nurturing, and harvesting crops. A smaller number assumed working roles in munitions factories and armories or were blacksmiths, shoemakers, or carpenters. Others were attached to the army as cooks, hospital attendants, and, most often, members of labor battalions.

Slaves and free African Americans as well were forced (impressed) to build fortifications for the Confederate military. Elaborate conditions were laid down by the Adjutant and Inspector General's Office in October, 1863, pertaining to conditions of black employment. The owner of impressed slaves was paid twenty dollars monthly for each borrowed slave. In March of the following year, free male African Americans between the ages of eigh-

teen and fifty could be drafted to perform a variety of tasks for the military—virtually anything short of serving as a Confederate soldier. In return, they received rations, clothing, and eleven dollars monthly, the same as white soldiers.

Many slaveowners were unwilling to loan their slaves to the military. They complained about the frequent delays in receiving their twenty-dollar monthly payment and said that slaves were being used beyond the agreed-upon length of time. They were also upset by the impressment of their slaves at times when they were most needed at home. Finally, there was concern over the poor physical condition of the slaves when they were returned to their owners.

By late 1864 and early 1865 the Confederacy was in dire straits. Union general Ulysses Grant was besieging Petersburg, only twenty-five miles south of the Confederate capital at

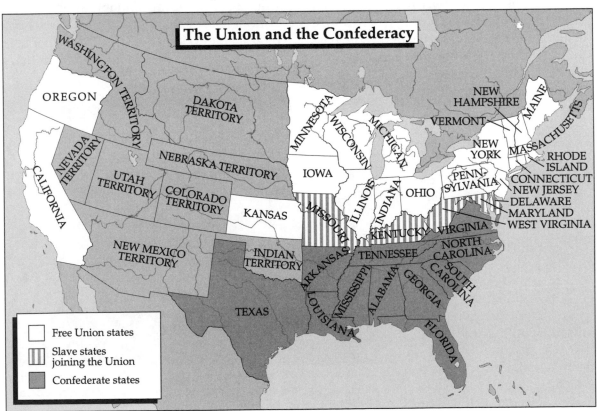

**The Union and the Confederacy**

Free Union states

Slave states joining the Union

Confederate states

Richmond. In addition, Union general William Sherman was executing his devastating march to the sea, and thence from Savannah, Georgia, northward into South and North Carolina. Confederate hope for victory reached its lowest ebb—so low in fact, that a plan was finally presented to enlist not only free African Americans but slaves as well into the Confederate army. There had been scattered earlier examples of free African Americans serving in special military units, but none had experienced combat, nor were the units permanent.

### Need for Black Troops

Gradually the president of the Confederacy, Jefferson Davis, became convinced that military manpower shortages could only be offset by the recruitment of African Americans, including slaves. He argued that unless there was a sufficient number of available white soldiers (he knew there was not), he favored drafting slaves to serve as combat troops. Aware of the need to resort to desperate measures, a few state governors supported the proposal, as did a number of Southern newspapers, including the *Richmond Enquirer.*

Various arguments were presented supporting the enlistment of slaves. Since slaves were enlisted in the Union army to fight against the Confederacy, why should they not be enlisted to fight for the South? It was also argued that since slaves were accustomed to following orders, they should adjust easily to military discipline, and indeed, would ennoble the institution of slavery by demonstrating their willingness to lay down their lives for its continuance. It was re-called that black slaves had fought for American independence during the revolution against the British. Finally, the most telling and obvious argument simply stressed the desperate need for more troops, without which the war would surely be lost. Confederate soldiers, who were most directly affected by the lack of numbers, were ready to welcome additional troops, no matter what their color.

However, opposition to recruiting slaves was clamorous and pervasive. It was difficult for white Southerners to accept the idea that they might owe their independence to slaves. The outcome, they feared, might eventually be the death of slavery and the elevation of blacks' social and political status.

The issue was debated in the Confederate Congress for months before legislation approving black troops was passed on March 13, 1865, less than one month before the end of the war. Approval was attributable in large part to a strongly favorable endorsement for passage by General Robert E. Lee, the most popular, trusted, and revered Confederate military leader.

In 1999 the recently opened Tennessee Civil War Museum presented an exhibit claiming that thousands of black men fought for the Confederacy. *(AP/Wide World Photos)*

*Authorization and War's End*

The legislation authorized President Davis to recruit slaves as soldiers, with the permission of their owners. They were eligible to serve in any military capacity, including combat. Slaves would be assigned to units led by black officers—contrary to the status of African Americans fighting for the Union, who were commanded by white officers. Slaves in the Confederate military were to be compensated at the same pay rate as the white troops and were to receive the same rations and clothing. The initial goal was to recruit 300,000 blacks between eighteen and forty-five years of age. If that number was not reached, Davis was authorized to draft the number of additional black recruits required to reach 300,000, but with no more than 25 percent to be taken from any single Confederate state. The effort was barely underway when the war ended. In practical terms, the Confederacy died on April 9, 1865, when General Lee surrendered to General Grant at Appomattox Court House, Virginia; some prefer the date May 10, 1865, when Davis was captured.

There is no record of African Americans fighting for the Confederacy during the Civil War. However, there are numerous examples of their contributions to the Confederate war effort, both voluntary and forced, in noncombatant service.

*—John Quinn Imholte*

Suggested Readings:

Barrow, Charles K., J. H. Segars, and R. B. Rosenburg, eds. *Forgotten Confederates: An Anthology About Black Southerners.* Atlanta, Ga.: Southern Heritage Press, 1995.

Brewer, James H. *The Confederate Negro: Virginia's Craftsmen and Military Laborers.* Durham, N.C.: Duke University Press, 1969.

Coulter, E. Merton. *The Confederate States of America, 1861-1865.* Baton Rouge: Louisiana State University Press, 1958.

Nieman, Donald G., ed. *The Day of the Jubilee: The Civil War Experience of Black Southerners.* New York: Garland, 1994.

Preisser, Thomas M. "The Virginia Decision to Use Negro Soldiers in the Civil War, 1864-1865." *Virginia Magazine of History and Biography* 83 (January, 1975): 98-113.

Wesley, Charles H. "The Employment of Negroes as Soldiers in the Confederate Army." *Journal of Negro History* 4 (July, 1919): 239-253.

**Congressional Black Caucus:** Body formed in 1971 to combine the power of African American members of Congress.

The two-party system in the United States does not always adequately represent the concerns of minority groups. Although the Democratic and Republican Parties seek to serve the majority of voters, the major parties sometimes establish agendas that ignore the concerns of smaller groups. Congressional caucuses allow disfranchised groups to gain a voice in government and to bring a sense of unity to diverse opinions within the traditional party structure. Thus, the most important function of a caucus is to create alliances, agreements, and compromises with majority groups that can form the basis for policy and action.

*Early History*

The Congressional Black Caucus was the first group of African American legislators since the Reconstruction period following the Civil War to join in a national effort to promote black causes. Its origins can be traced to the late 1960's, when Congressman Charles Diggs of Michigan formed the Democratic Select Committee. He envisioned this group as a way of bringing black representatives together to discuss issues of concern to African American voters. Although at first the committee met infrequently, the nine black members of Congress joined forces in 1969 to oppose the nomination of Clement Haynsworth to the U.S. SUPREME COURT. Also in that year, they conducted an unofficial public hearing in Chicago on the killings of members of the Chicago BLACK PANTHER PARTY.

In February, 1970, black representatives in Congress sent a letter to President Richard M. Nixon requesting a conference to discuss the plight of black and poor people in the United States. Nixon refused to meet with the committee members, who retaliated by boycotting the president's State of the Union Address. Finally, fourteen months after their initial request and a few weeks after Nixon's address, he agreed to meet with them. The congress members presented the president with some sixty recommendations, which included enforcement of CIVIL RIGHTS laws, replacement of the existing welfare system with a guaranteed annual income of $6,500 for a family of four, a declaration that drug abuse was a national crisis, and withdrawal of American troops from Southeast Asia. The meeting with the president was a turning point in the evolution of the Black Caucus. During a time when the Civil Rights movement seemed to be in a period of decline following the deaths of MALCOLM X in 1965 and Martin Luther KING, Jr., in 1968, the caucus answered a need for African American leadership within the American federal government and became a powerful forum for the expression of black concerns.

*Political Agenda*

The Congressional Black Caucus was formally established in 1971. Initially, the members saw themselves as an extension of the Civil Rights movement and other protest movements of the 1960's and as a unified response to President Nixon's conservative domestic policies. They believed that they were serving as representatives-at-large for the nation's twenty million black people, and they began holding a series of hearings around the country on issues of health, education, racism, Africa, and black enterprise. As the 1972 presidential election approached, Congressman Charles Diggs, then chair of the Black Caucus, issued a call for a national black political convention in the spring of 1972 in Gary, Indiana, to develop a national black agenda before the convening of the Democratic and Republican conventions in the summer of 1972.

The caucus was not the official sponsor of the black convention, a fact that caused problems when convention delegates endorsed two controversial resolutions, one supporting the existence of the state of Israel, and another in support of school busing to achieve integration in public schools. The caucus also drafted a "Black Declaration of Independence" and a "Black Bill of Rights" to add to the agenda proposed by the black convention. The effect of these actions was to create a state of conflict between caucus members. While some members strongly endorsed these proposals, others felt that powerful white liberal, Jewish, and labor interests—groups that some black politicians depended upon for financial support— would be offended by the platform that emerged from the convention.

By the middle of 1972, caucus leaders began to shift their primary focus. While at first members saw themselves as a united voice for black America, the group began, with the election of Representative Louis STOKES of Ohio as chairman, to turn away from collective concerns of African Americans. Stokes believed that if the caucus was to remain productive, it would have to concentrate on increasing the effectiveness of its members as legislators within the political system. Members decided that the best way to accomplish this was to assure that African Americans remained in Congress long enough to gain seniority and win seats on major committees. Because of their small numbers in the House, the individual votes of black representatives were not enough to have a significant impact on legislation. By gaining seniority and assuming chairs of committees, however, they could exert much greater influence. Much of the real work of Congress takes place through committees; if a bill has insufficient committee backing, it has little chance of gaining support on the House floor and eventually becoming law.

### Major Accomplishments

In 1974 Representative Charles RANGEL of New York replaced Louis Stokes as caucus chairman. Also in that year, the caucus organized a nationwide lobbying effort to extend the social programs established by the Economic Opportunity Act of 1964 and to prevent the impoundment of federal funds by President Nixon. Each member of the caucus introduced or sponsored legislation in support of these two important issues. Although their efforts were only partially successful, the united efforts of caucus members served to consolidate their power and influence. In 1974, for example, they voted together on eleven of sixteen key pieces of legislation introduced in the House of Representatives.

Another important achievement was the Black Voter's Participation Network, estab-

lished by Representative Walter E. FAUNTROY of the District of Columbia. The Fauntroy network, which was originally formed as an outgrowth of Fauntroy's efforts on behalf of Martin Luther KING, Jr., to register black voters in the 1960's, consisted of a computerized contact list of African American leaders in southern congressional districts that had black voting-age populations of 20 percent or more. By 1984 the list had grown to include more than fifty thousand names.

The caucus also established several "braintrusts," national networks formed to address major issues such as health, education, energy, minority business, foreign affairs, defense, and criminal justice. One of the first established, and one of the most effective, was the Minority Business Enterprise Braintrust established by Congressman Parren MITCHELL. Mitchell held quarterly braintrust meetings that brought together African American entrepreneurs and business leaders from across the United States to offer recommendations for legislation or changes in federal regulations. A major accomplishment of the

Hearing of the Congressional Black Caucus held in 1971. *(Library of Congress)*

braintrust was Mitchell's success in the passage of legislation that set aside billions of dollars in federal funds to procure government contracts for minority businesses.

In 1976 the Congressional Black Caucus Foundation, an independent, nonprofit public organization, was formed to conduct policy research and to deal with the underrepresentation of black professional staff members in congressional offices and committees. The foundation also supports scholarly research into social and economic problems facing the black community, other minorities, and low-income Americans and provides stipends for research fellows who utilize Congress as a laboratory for the study of American politics.

By building coalitions with women, other ethnic minorities, and special-interest groups such as the Hispanic Caucus and the Congressional Caucus for Women's Issues, the caucus had a great impact on the passage of important legislation. Notable examples include the 1977 Humphrey-Hawkins Full Employment and Balanced Growth Act, the 1977 Public Works Employment Act, the 1982 Martin Luther King, Jr., holiday bill, and the 1986 South African sanctions legislation. Caucus members also provided key votes for passage of minimum wage increases, the Elementary and Secondary Education Act Amendments, congressional budget reform, and the Housing and Community Development Act. By 1984, even though its twenty representatives constituted less than 5 percent of all House members, caucus members chaired five of the twenty-two standing committees and two of the five select congressional committees.

### The 1990's

In 1994 the caucus helped President Bill Clinton pass a $30 billion crime package. After the bill had failed to pass the House of Representatives earlier in the year, President Clinton lobbied members of Congress for another attempt. Congressional Black Caucus chairman Kweisi MFUME (a Maryland Democrat) promised his support and lobbied members of the caucus. Several members opposed to the death penalty refused to vote for the bill, which increased the number of crimes punishable by death from two to sixty. Mfume was able to gain the votes of twenty-seven of the thirty-nine voting members of the caucus, enough votes to ensure the bill's passage. The White House credited Mfume with getting the bill through Congress. During 1994, the caucus also counseled the president on foreign policy, in particular keeping an eye on events in HAITI.

The sweeping Republican victory in the 1994 midterm congressional elections spelled trouble for the Congressional Black Caucus and a number of other special-interest caucuses in Congress. Soon after the Republicans gained a majority of seats in the House of Representatives, they announced their intention to eliminate funding for the twenty-eight legislative service organizations (LSOs), including the Congressional Black Caucus. The LSOs all received office space and funds for the hiring of staff. Committed to reducing the size and budget of the federal government, Republicans charged that the LSOs were a waste of taxpayers' money.

Some members of the Congressional Black Caucus believed that the Republicans were attempting to reduce the clout of minorities in Congress, and Mfume vowed to fight the Republican plan. The Congressional Hispanic Caucus united with the Black Caucus in opposing the funding cuts. The Republican majority prevailed, however, and on January 5, 1995, funding to the LSOs was eliminated.

More troubling even than the loss of funds and office space was the loss of important committee chairmanships. Their majority in the House entitled Republicans to all chairmanships. Members of the Congressional Black Caucus lost a total of three committee chairmanships and seventeen subcommittee chairmanships, resulting in a significant loss of power in the House.

Members of the caucus elected Congressman Donald PAYNE, a Democrat from New Jersey, to succeed Kweisi Mfume as chairman. Payne ran the caucus from his own office while a committee began searching for alternative methods of funding. While admitting that the caucus faced difficulties in the coming years, Payne outlined three goals for the organization to work toward. He declared that the caucus would continue to be a moral force in Congress, would represent the struggling middle class, and would protect the needs of the underclass, most affected by budget cuts. Recognizing the fact that the caucus lacked the power to push major legislation through the Republican-dominated Congress, Payne perceived the caucus's role as preventing the passage of legislation detrimental to the nation's disadvantaged.

The caucus spent the early part of 1995 reorganizing as an unofficial group. Payne vowed that the organization would continue to be a "strong factor" in influencing Democratic Party and House positions. The caucus continued working through the 1990's. At its four-day annual legislative conference in 1998, with its theme "Tools for 2000," topics discussed included the AIDS problem, black farmers, affirmative action, education, capital formation, and drugs. Representative Maxine WATERS, chair of the caucus, stated, "The Congressional Black Caucus will not be deterred from our agenda. . . . We are in a struggle for justice and equality." President Clinton and Vice President Al Gore spoke at the event's awards gala. Crucially important fund-raising events were also held.

In January, 1999, Waters and the (then thirty-eight member) caucus strongly voiced support for President Clinton, appreciative of his support of civil rights efforts, and denounced the impeachment effort then underway against him. During House impeachment hearings in November and December, 1998, Waters and other caucus members—notably John CONYERS, Jr.—often clashed with House Judiciary Chairman Henry Hyde. In 1999 South Carolina Democrat James E. CLYBURN assumed leadership of the Congressional Black Caucus and launched a caucus publication intended to inform voters about issues and about the caucus's efforts.

—Raymond Frey
—Updated by Thomas Clarkin

*See also:* Civil rights and congressional legislation; Congress members; Politics and government.

Suggested Readings:

Barnett, Marguerite R. "The Congressional Black Caucus." In *Congress Against the President: Proceedings of the Academy of Political Science.* Edited by Harvey C. Mansfield, Sr. New York: Academy of Political Science, 1975.

Bositis, David A. *The Congressional Black Caucus in the 103rd Congress.* Washington, D.C.: Joint Center for Political and Economic Studies, 1994.

Brown, Frank D. "The CBC: Past, Present and Future." *Black Enterprise* (September, 1990): 25-28.

Faryna, Stan, Brad Stetson, and Joseph G. Conti, eds. *Black and Right: The Bold New Voice of Black Conservatives in America.* Westport, Conn.: Praeger, 1997.

"How Black Politicians Changed America." *Ebony* 46 (August, 1991): 34.

Ragsdale, Bruce A., and Joel D. Treese. *Black Americans in Congress, 1870-1989.* Washington, D.C.: U.S. Government Printing Office, 1990.

Ruffin, David C., and Frank D. Brown. "Clout on Capitol Hill." *Black Enterprise* (October, 1984): 97-104.

Singh, Robert. *The Congressional Black Caucus: Racial Politics in the U.S. Congress.* Thousand Oaks, Calif.: Sage Publications, 1998.

**Congress members:** Prior to the CIVIL WAR, African Americans in the United States were either slaves, former slaves, or FREE BLACKS who were nevertheless treated like second-class citizens. They were denied, by law or practice, most of the rights of citizenship. No one of known African descent served in the U.S. Congress until after the Civil War.

*Reconstruction to 1900*

After the end of the Civil War in 1865, the lot of African Americans started to improve. With federal troops stationed throughout the former Confederacy, the RECONSTRUCTION era began in the war-torn South. The Reconstruction Act of 1867 gave former slaves the right to vote; any state refusing to comply risked losing its representation in Congress.

During the last quarter of the nineteenth century, twenty-two African Americans served in the U.S. Congress, including thirteen former slaves. The entry into office was not easy: Even after successful campaigns, Congress often debated whether to let them take their seats. Outraged white members of congress used such tactics as unfounded charges of voter fraud, challenges to credentials and citizenship, bribery, and even armed intimidation to dissuade blacks from becoming members of Congress.

Five of the first twenty African Americans elected to the House of Representatives were denied their seats, and ten others had their terms delayed or interrupted. Former slave Josiah Thomas Walls of FLORIDA was unseated twice by opponents. James T. RAPIER of ALABAMA was forced to relinquish his seat to former Confederate general Jeremiah Williams.

Nevertheless, the African American senators and representatives were an impressive group. Among them were seven lawyers, three ministers, a banker, and three college presidents. The first African American senator was Hiram Rhoades REVELS of MISSISSIPPI, who was chosen by the state legislature in 1870 to finish the unexpired term of Confederate leader Jefferson Davis. Revels was a minister who had organized two black regiments in the Union army. Representative Robert SMALLS of SOUTH CAROLINA was a Civil War hero who had been the first African American captain in the Union army. Throughout the 1870's, African Americans took active roles in debates on key CIVIL RIGHTS acts, though they often introduced measures only to see them die in committee or on the chamber floor.

In 1876 the controversial election of President Rutherford B. Hayes over Samuel Tilden led to the removal of federal troops from the South and the end of Reconstruction. White supremacy returned, and white supremacist groups such as the KU KLUX KLAN and the Knights of the White Camellia proliferated. By 1900 eight southern states had passed literacy tests for African American voters. These tests, combined with poll taxes, restrictive registration criteria, and physical intimidation, almost totally purged African Americans from voter lists in many places.

George H. WHITE of North Carolina was the last African American to serve in Congress during the nineteenth century. In his final address to the House in 1901, White predicted that African Americans would someday return to Congress. That prediction would not come true for nearly three decades.

*Twentieth-Century Pioneers: 1928-1970*

In 1928 Oscar DePRIEST was elected to the House from the First Congressional District of ILLINOIS. DePriest was a Republican, as all his African American predecessors in Congress had been. That pattern changed in 1934, when DePriest was defeated in his reelection bid by Democrat Arthur W. MITCHELL. After Mitchell, the vast majority of African American congressmen have been from the DEMOCRATIC PARTY.

CHICAGO's First Congressional District was the only district to send African Americans to

Arthur W. Mitchell, the only African American member of Congress in 1937, defending the appointment of Hugo L. Black to the Supreme Court in the face of charges that Black had been a member of the Ku Klux Klan. *(AP/Wide World Photos)*

Lou Henry Hoover included Oscar DePriest's wife in a gathering of congressional wives at the White House. The incident created such controversy that the Florida and TEXAS state legislatures passed resolutions condemning President Herbert Hoover for inviting an African American woman to a White House social event. In Congress, African Americans were assigned to insignificant committees, excluded from important gatherings, and denied fringe benefits taken for granted by white legislators. Outside the Capitol, they were not welcome in neighborhood restaurants, hotels, or theaters: Powell and actor Hazel SCOTT were turned away from a Washington movie theater, though Scott had starred in the film the theater was showing.

Nevertheless, William Dawson and Adam Clayton Powell, Jr., amassed impressive records during careers that spanned three decades. Dawson became the first African American to chair a committee—the Committee on Government Operations—as well as the first African American vice chairman of the Democratic National Committee. A WORLD WAR I veteran, Dawson was instrumental in defeating the Winstead Amendment of 1951, which would have allowed white military personnel to refuse to serve in integrated units. Powell set a record by sponsoring sixty pieces of legislation through Congress. Powell eventually became chairman of the powerful House Education and Labor Committee, and he passed the Title I Education Act, legislation creating the HEAD START program, the Manpower Development and Training Act, the Vocational Education Act, and the National Defense Education Act.

Powell sought to personify African American politics, but his flamboyance and controversial lifestyle ultimately helped his opponents defeat him. Accused of various abuses, some of which were practices not uncommon in the halls of Congress, Powell was expelled from Congress in 1967. Even so, he was re-

Congress until 1945, when Mitchell's successor, William DAWSON, was joined by Adam Clayton POWELL, Jr., of NEW YORK CITY. Powell was a minister and a gifted orator with a dynamic personality that quickly made him both famous and infamous. In 1946 Powell attached an amendment to the Flanagan School Lunch Bill, making him the first African American successfully to sponsor civil rights legislation. Soon a standard addendum to legislation, the Powell Amendment denied federal funding to any project in which RACIAL DISCRIMINATION was tolerated.

In the middle years of the twentieth century, African American representatives still faced staggering challenges. WASHINGTON, D.C., was a segregated city, and they were widely treated like second-class citizens both in and out of the Capitol. In 1929 First Lady

elected by his constituents with an overwhelming seven-to-one majority. In 1969 the U.S. SUPREME COURT overruled his expulsion, and Powell was given back his congressional seat. However, by then Powell had lost his desire to serve in Congress and hardly attended any sessions. He was defeated in the 1970 primary election.

The practice of GERRY-MANDERING—adjusting voting district lines for a political purpose—kept white congressmen representing predominantly African American areas for term after term. Finally, however, in the 1950's and 1960's, a succession of northern cities sent a stream of African American representatives to Washington. In 1954 Charles C. DIGGS was elected to the House from Detroit. At age thirty-two, he was one of the youngest members of Congress. During Diggs's twenty-six years in office, he fought to integrate the MILITARY and became an authority on U.S. foreign relations in Africa.

Robert C. NIX (senior) of PHILADELPHIA became the fourth member of the African American delegation in 1958. He served in the House for twenty years, becoming chair of the Post Office and Civil Service Committee. Augustus F. HAWKINS was elected in 1963 to represent LOS ANGELES. During his fourteen terms, he was coauthor of the Hawkins-Humphrey Full Employment Act, which helped to create the Peace Corps, VISTA, and Foster Grandparents. In 1964 John R. CONYERS, Jr., was elected to the House from Detroit. He was a leader in the drive for the VOTING RIGHTS ACT OF 1965 and for a national holiday commemorating Martin Luther KING, Jr. Conyers also served on the House committees for both the Water-

## Members of U.S. House of Representatives by Race/Ethnicity

|  | White | Black | Asian, Pacific Islander | Hispanic |
|---|---|---|---|---|
| 97th Congress, 1981 | 409 | 17 | 3 | 6 |
| 98th Congress, 1983 | 402 | 21 | 3 | 8 |
| 99th Congress, 1985 | 401 | 20 | 3 | 10 |
| 100th Congress, 1987 | 397 | 23 | 4 | 11 |
| 101st Congress, 1989 | 394 | 24 | 5 | 10 |
| 102d Congress, 1991 | 396 | 25 | 3 | 11 |
| 103d Congress, 1993 | 376 | 38 | 4 | 17 |
| 104th Congress, 1995 | 374 | 40 | 4 | 17 |

*Sources:* Joint Center for Political and Economic Studies; Library of Congress Congressional Research Service; National Association of Latino Elected and Appointed Officials; U.S. Bureau of the Census.

*Note:* Numbers are for first session of each Congress, beginning January 3.

gate investigation of 1974 and the 1999 impeachment of President Bill Clinton. In 1966 Edward W. BROOKE of MASSACHUSETTS became the first African American elected to the Senate during the twentieth century. By early 2000, only two African Americans had served in the Senate during the century; the second was Carol E. Moseley BRAUN, elected by Illinois voters in 1992. Between 1942 and 1969, fifteen African Americans were elected to Congress, of whom eleven served for more than two decades.

### The Next Generation: 1970 to 2000

By 1969 nine African Americans were in Congress simultaneously. With the election of 1970, that number rose to thirteen, including Shirley CHISHOLM of Brooklyn, New York, the first woman in the delegation; Louis STOKES of Cleveland, the brother of that city's mayor; Ronald DELLUMS of OAKLAND, CALIFORNIA, an ardent opponent of the war in Southeast Asia; William Clay of St. Louis, an advocate for workers' rights; Parren J. MITCHELL of Baltimore, a key figure in the establishment of the African Development Bank; Charles B. RANGEL of New York, victor over the scandal-ridden Powell; and Walter E. FAUNTROY of the District of Columbia, who helped to establish a National Black Leadership Roundtable.

Yvonne Brathwaite BURKE of California and Barbara JORDAN of Texas came to Congress in 1972. Burke worked to enhance opportunities for African American businesses, and Jordan went on to deliver a keynote address for the Democratic National Convention in 1976. Andrew YOUNG, a civil rights activist from ATLANTA, GEORGIA, with personal connections to the late Martin Luther King, Jr., also was elected in 1972. Young was later appointed by President Jimmy Carter as the first African American U.S. ambassador to the United Nations.

Representative William GRAY of PENNSYLVANIA, first elected in 1978, was chosen Democratic Caucus chair in 1985 and became the Democratic House whip in 1989. That same year, Representative George "Mickey" LELAND of Texas was killed in an airplane crash in Ethiopia while leading a delegation to monitor and address that nation's crippling hunger problem. During the mid-1980's, African American legislators sponsored twenty-four bills directed at helping to bring an end to the racist apartheid policies in the Republic of South Africa.

Through the end of the twentieth century, African Americans continued to play a growing role in the U.S. Congress. Their numbers increased, and their influence was enhanced by greater seniority. Other African American members of Congress have included Harold E. FORD of Tennessee; Julian DIXON, Mervyn DYMALLY, and Maxine WATERS of California; Harold WASHINGTON of Illinois; Edolphus TOWNS and Major OWENS of New York; John LEWIS and Cynthia McKINNEY of Georgia;

---

## African Americans in Congress, 1997-1999 Term

*HOUSE OF REPRESENTATIVES*

**Bishop, Sanford D.** Democrat; Georgia (1992).
**Brown, Corrine.** Democrat; Florida (1992).
**Carson, Julia.** Democrat; Indiana (1996).
**Christian-Green, Donna M.** Democrat; Delegate, U.S. Virgin Islands (1996).
**Clay, William.** Democrat; Missouri (1968).
**Clayton, Eva M.** Democrat; North Carolina (1992).
**Clyburn, James E.** Democrat; South Carolina (1992).
**Conyers, John, Jr.** Democrat; Michigan (1964).
**Cummings, Elijah.** Democrat; Maryland (1996).
**Davis, Danny K.** Democrat; Illinois (1996).
**Dellums, Ronald V.** Democrat; California (1970).
**Dixon, Julian C.** Democrat; California (1978).
**Fatta, Chaka.** Democrat; Pennsylvania (1994).
**Flake, Floyd H.** Democrat; New York (1986).
**Hastings, Alcee.** Democrat; Florida (1992).
**Hilliard, Earl F.** Democrat; Alabama (1992).
**Jackson, Jesse L., Jr.** Democrat; Illinois (1995).
**Jefferson, William J.** Democrat; Louisiana (1990).
**Johnson, Eddie Bernice.** Democrat; Texas (1992).
**Kilpatrick, Carolyn Cheeks.** Democrat; Michigan (1997).

**Lee, Sheila Jackson.** Democrat; Texas (1994).
**Lewis, John.** Democrat; Georgia (1980).
**McKinney, Cynthia A.** Democrat; Georgia (1992).
**Meek, Carrie.** Democrat; Florida (1992).
**Millender-McDonald, Juanita.** Democrat; California (1996).
**Norton, Eleanor Holmes.** Democrat; Delegate, District of Columbia (1990).
**Owens, Major.** Democrat; New York (1982).
**Payne, Donald M.** Democrat; New Jersey (1988).
**Rangel, Charles B.** Democrat; New York (1970).
**Rush, Bobby.** Democrat; Illinois (1992).
**Scott, Robert C.** Democrat; Virginia (1992).
**Stokes, Louis.** Democrat; Ohio (1968).
**Thompson, Bennie G.** Democrat; Mississippi (1993).
**Towns, Edolphus.** Democrat; New York (1982).
**Waters, Maxine.** Democrat; California (1990).
**Watt, Melvin L.** Democrat; North Carolina (1992).
**Watts, J. C., Jr.** Republican; Oklahoma (1994).
**Wynn, Albert R.** Democrat; Maryland (1992).

*SENATE*

**Braun, Carol Moseley.** Democrat; Illinois (1992).

---

Alan Wheat of Missouri; Mike Espy of Mississippi; Kweisi Mfume of Maryland; Gary Franks of Connecticut; and Carolyn Kilpatrick of Michigan.

### The Congressional Black Caucus

The early 1970's marked a turning point not only in the number of African Americans in Congress but also in their effectiveness as an organized political unit. In 1969 the small delegation established the Select Democratic Committee, holding hearings on such incidents as the Black Panther raid in Chicago and the killings at Jackson State University in Mississippi.

In 1971 the committee became the Congressional Black Caucus. The caucus lobbied to meet with President Richard M. Nixon to discuss African American interests, but for months the White House ignored the requests. On March 25, 1971, the president received sixty recommendations from the caucus during a two-hour meeting, agreeing to respond by May 17. Nixon's response, on May 18, insisted that programs already in effect were addressing the problems of African Americans. The following week, the caucus issued a "Report to the Nation" outlining its frustrations with the administration. Likewise, after Nixon's 1972 State of the Union Address, the Caucus delivered a "True State of the Union" report to the House, examining such issues as poverty, unemployment, civil rights compliance, education, health, and housing.

In June, 1971, the Congressional Black Caucus sponsored the first of its annual organizing and fundraising dinners. The gala event, in Washington, D.C., brought together some twenty-seven hundred people, including entertainers such as Bill Cosby, civil rights figures such as Coretta Scott King and the Reverend Jesse Jackson, business leaders, educators, and others.

Through the decades, the Congressional Black Caucus became an influential organization in U.S. politics. The caucus began holding a regular Conference of Black Elected Officials in 1972, created a Black Declaration of Independence in 1976, and answered the federal budget of the Reagan administration with an alternative budget proposal in 1981. The caucus also established a political action committee and a foundation for the development of future African American leadership. The caucus faced serious financial struggles after federal funding to it and other legislative service organizations was eliminated in 1995, but the caucus continued.

—*Barry Stewart Mann*

*See also:* Politics and government; Radical Republicans; Republican Party.

Suggested Readings:

Christopher, Maurice. *Black Americans in Congress*. New York: Thomas Y. Crowell, 1976.

Clay, William L. *Just Permanent Interests: Black Americans in Congress 1870-1991*. New York, N.Y.: Amistad Press, 1992.

Gill, LaVerne McCain. *African American Women in Congress: Forming and Transforming History*. New Brunswick, N.J.: Rutgers University Press, 1997.

Ragsdale, Bruce A., and Joel D. Treese. *Black Americans in Congress, 1870-1968*. Washington, D.C.: U.S. Government Printing Office, 1990.

Stone, Chuck. *Black Political Power in America*. Indianapolis: Bobbs-Merrill, 1984.

Swain, Carol M. *Black Faces, Black Interests*. Cambridge, Mass.: Harvard University Press, 1993.

Travis, Dempsey J. *An Autobiography of Black Politics*. Chicago: Urban Research, 1987.

**Congress of Racial Equality:** Also known as CORE, Civil rights group founded in Chicago, Illinois, in 1942. The group's leaders believed in direct action to challenge segregation and discrimination and saw the group as consisting of blacks and whites working together. The organization moved its headquarters to New York City in 1946. Beginning in the 1950's, its membership mushroomed. By 1963 CORE had seventy thousand members, a paid staff of thirty-five, and an annual budget of $700,000. With leaders such as James FARMER, CORE made many contributions to the civil rights crusade.

When students at North Carolina A&T in Greensboro began their SIT-IN movement in 1960 protesting segregation, they called CORE for help, and the agency quickly sent in a corps of field workers who taught students to remain peaceful even if assaulted. After Greensboro, CORE workers continued to visit sit-ins in other areas and to offer guidance.

One of CORE's greatest moments came in 1961, when its leaders decided to sponsor the FREEDOM RIDES that challenged segregated transportation in the South. Although both the Interstate Commerce Commission and the U.S. SUPREME COURT had ruled against segregation of interstate passengers, bus companies in the South refused to comply. CORE's founder, James Farmer, led thirteen freedom riders (including five whites) as they boarded buses and rode into the heart of the South. Many volunteers rallied to the cause, and scores of civil rights crusaders joined in the rides.

The riders faced violent reactions in many places. In Anniston, ALABAMA, for example, a white mob attacked the riders and burned their bus. Another attack came in BIRMINGHAM, ALABAMA, where one rider was hurt so severely that his head required fifty stitches. In MONTGOMERY, ALABAMA, public officials and police helped a mob assault twenty riders. Federal marshals and National Guard troops had to restore order. The riders' courage in the face of assaults riveted public attention in the United States to their cause. Ultimately, the South capitulated to a new ruling in 1961 that all bus companies should integrate.

In 1968 Roy Innis became CORE's national director. *(Library of Congress)*

CORE continued its activist role as civil rights crusaders won even more victories. Sit-in protests, demonstrations, marches, and voter-registration drives continued through the 1960's, and CORE was usually involved, working alongside other groups such as the NATIONAL ASSOCIATION FOR THE ADVANCEMENT OF COLORED PEOPLE (NAACP) and the SOUTHERN CHRISTIAN LEADERSHIP CONFERENCE (SCLC). In the late 1960's, CORE became increasingly militant and became part of the BLACK POWER MOVEMENT. It still assisted in various civil rights campaigns and voter registration drives. However, its power and influence waned, and its funding dwindled. Much of its white membership left. CORE continued, however, and remained active through the 1990's. It engaged in such activities as providing immigration assistance, monitoring racism, sponsoring Martin Luther King, Jr., holiday events, and administering job-training programs.

**Connecticut:** The migration of African Americans to the New England state of Connecticut after the CIVIL WAR was limited. In Connecticut in 1880, 46.8 percent of employed residents engaged in manufacturing and mechanical pursuits requiring special skills that many recently liberated African Americans lacked. Although many runaway slaves had earlier passed through New England heading to CANADA, it was not until 1915 that significant numbers of African Americans immigrated into Connecticut. American industry geared up to supply munitions to the combatants in WORLD WAR I. This created in Connecticut a shortage of people to cultivate and harvest the tobacco crop, important to the state's economy.

*1997 Population: 3,270,000*
*African American Population: 300,000*
*African American Percentage of Total: 9.17*

Connecticut's tobacco farmers looked first to NEW YORK CITY for African Americans to come to Hartford to work. They succeeded in rounding up some two hundred female workers. These women, however, proved unsuitable for the work. Connecticut farmers then turned to the NATIONAL URBAN LEAGUE to help them recruit respectable black workers from the South. These people were brought through NORTH CAROLINA to Hartford and Hazelwood to work long hours but to earn between $11.50 and $14.00 a week during the heaviest season.

Once African Americans entered Connecticut's work force, many were found to be reliable and conscientious. They remained in the state and made their way into many occupations outside farming. WORLD WAR II brought defense industries to Connecticut. African Americans were drawn into such industries, many new ones migrating from the South to join those already there. By the mid-twentieth century, nearly a quarter of a million African Americans lived in Connecticut. Most lived in the major urban centers of Hartford, Bridgeport, New Haven, and New London. The black population reached 273,555 in the 1990 census, with the largest percentage of the state's black men being between twenty-five and thirty-four years old and of its black women being between twenty-five and thirty-nine years old.

—*R. Baird Shuman*

**Conservatives:** During the late 1980's, scholars and journalists began to observe a new political trend within the African American community, a trend toward political conservatism. It involved African American men and women from all regions of the United States and included individuals who were graduates of state universities and Ivy League colleges as well as people who were self-educated. These individuals espoused a belief in self-reliance and individual initiative; they favored less government intervention and sought to encourage community-based approaches to problem solving.

Throughout the 1990's, black conservatives became an increasingly significant presence in the American political landscape. From churches to college campuses to political rallies to academic think tanks, they were recognized as a growing political and intellectual force. Black conservatives have been viewed with suspicion by many African Americans and have been chastised by many white liberals. They have also been praised and revered by some REPUBLICAN PARTY politicians.

### Historical Background

Before 1950, most African American voters were Republicans. Author Zora Neale HURSTON and baseball great Jackie ROBINSON were prominent supporters of the party, and civil rights activist Martin Luther KING, Jr., was once a registered Republican (he later changed his affiliation). Many African Americans saw the Republican Party as being more hospitable to the interests of African Americans, especially because of its historic role in abolishing slavery. When it was founded in the 1850's, the Republican Party was known as the antislavery party. As the first Republican president, Abraham Lincoln was responsible for signing the EMANCIPATION PROCLAMATION, which proclaimed freedom for the slaves in the CONFEDERACY. His determination to reunify the nation guaranteed that slavery as an institution would be overthrown.

For most of the early twentieth century, the Republican Party was perceived as being more sympathetic to the plight of African

Americans than the DEMOCRATIC PARTY. Nevertheless, most African Americans saw the Republican Party as the lesser of two evils. As a Democrat, President Franklin D. Roosevelt managed to make inroads against the large Republican stronghold in the South. The GREAT MIGRATION of African Americans from the rural South to the urban North that had begun in the early decades of the twentieth century had increased the number of registered black voters. By 1964 the majority of African Americans were voting for the Democratic ticket. This shift was evident in the landslide victory for Lyndon B. Johnson that year.

### Beliefs Rooted in Community

Many black scholars and leaders agree that the African American community has a long tradition of being conservative in behavior. African Americans share a tradition of being churchgoers, building cohesive family units through their reliance on extended family and kinship networks, and adhering to other principles that have been identified as conservative. These behaviors were necessary for survival.

Advocates of black conservatism argue that most African Americans adhere to conservative principles but have shunned the label "conservative" because of the negative image associated with the term. Some of the nation's leading African American intellectuals are known for their conservative beliefs. Among them are Walter WILLIAMS, a professor of economics at George Mason University; Thomas SOWELL, a senior fellow at the Hoover Institute at Stanford University; Ann Wortham, a professor of sociology at the University of Missouri; James ROBINSON, a former professor of political science and history at Rutgers University; and Shelby STEELE, professor of English at San Jose State University. Journalist George S. SCHUYLER, who died in 1977, is considered by many to be an influential figure of African American conservatism.

A staunch critic of the New Deal programs of the 1930's and Civil Rights movement of the 1950's and 1960's, Schuyler titled his 1966 autobiography *Black and Conservative*.

## Visibility and Criticism

Conservative African American academics have publicized their views through columns and editorials in national newspapers and upscale magazines, through appearances on radio talk shows, and through political programs broadcast on television networks such as C-SPAN, CNN, and PBS. They have articulated a message that denounces African American dependence on welfare, choosing instead to encourage self-sufficiency in the tradition of African American leader Booker T. WASHINGTON. Their message has attacked liberal government social programs for encouraging a politics of victimization within the black community.

Critics of this conservative message have argued that, unlike Booker T. Washington, these new conservatives have no viable economic program for the community. They also argue that many of these new conservatives are often protégés of white conservative organizations such as the Manhattan Institute, the Heritage Foundation, the Olin Foundation, and other groups that have not been known for their concern in regards to minority issues. As a result, these black conservatives' talk of self-reliance and personal responsibility seems to ring hollow.

## Running for Public Office

Although they have been less visible than their Democratic counterparts, some notable African American politicians have campaigned as Republicans and won elections. Edward BROOKE won election to the U.S. Senate as a representative from Massachusetts in 1966. Brooke was the first African American elected to the Senate since RECONSTRUCTION. His election was seen as a milestone both in U.S. race relations and in the Republican Party's efforts to reach out to African American voters. Although Brooke was reelected in 1972, his liberal views placed him at odds with more conservative colleagues within the Republican Party. Party optimism that Brooke's example would generate more Republican support from black voters faded when other African American candidates who ran on the Republican ticket failed to win election to Congress. After Brooke lost his bid for a third term in 1978, there were no black Republicans in Congress until Gary FRANKS was elected as a representative from CONNECTICUT in 1990.

During much of the 1970's and 1980's, the vast majority of African Americans either dismissed or ignored the Republican Party, claiming the party was hostile and insensitive to the needs of ethnic minorities and poor people. Although notable black candidates did run for state and federal office in the 1980's and 1990's as Republicans—William LUCAS for governor of MICHIGAN in 1986, and Alan Keyes for a U.S. Senate seat from MARYLAND in 1988 and 1992 and for the Republican presidential nomination in 1996 and 2000—they received lukewarm support from both the Republican Party and the voting electorate. This response caused Keyes and many other black observers to lambaste the party and question whether African Americans had any allies in the party.

## Clarence Thomas

One of the most prominent individuals associated with the growing conservatism in the African American community is Clarence THOMAS, confirmed as SUPREME COURT justice in 1991. A federal circuit judge who had served as head of the EQUAL EMPLOYMENT OPPORTUNITY COMMISSION (EEOC) in the Ronald REAGAN ADMINISTRATION, Thomas was nominated by President George Bush to replace retiring African American justice Thurgood MARSHALL on the Court.

Born in rural GEORGIA, Thomas grew up in poverty. Throughout his confirmation hearings, Thomas spoke eloquently and emotionally of growing up without indoor plumbing, being schooled by the local nuns who lived in the area, living under the shadow of racism, and hearing about the humiliation and degradation that his older relatives had endured because of racism. He also spoke of his gratitude for receiving scholarship assistance in the pursuit of higher education, first at Holy Cross College and later at Yale Law School.

During his law school years Thomas became acquainted with John Danforth, who later represented Missouri in the U.S. Senate. As attorney general of Missouri, Danforth hired Thomas to serve as assistant attorney general during Thomas's summer vacations from law school. Thomas later worked as Danforth's legislative assistant when Danforth served in the Senate. These experiences formed the foundation of what became a lifelong friendship between the two men. In the fall of 1991, when Danforth defended Thomas at the Senate hearings on his nomination, Anita HILL, a law professor at the University of Oklahoma who had worked as Thomas's assistant when he was the head of the EEOC, testified at the nomination hearings that Thomas had sexually harassed her during her tenure at the EEOC years earlier.

For an entire week, millions of Americans sat in front of their television sets listening to complex, direct, and graphic testimony from Thomas and Hill as well as from their friends, critics, and colleagues. Thomas's nomination appeared to be in serious jeopardy. Many journalists, professors, and other individuals believed that a turning point in the trial occurred when Thomas confronted the Senate Judiciary Committee, headed by Senator Joseph Biden of Delaware, and decried the hearings as having turned into a "high-tech lynching." Experts say that some of the senators were dumbfounded by such a comment and thus were manipulated into silence.

Numerous critics lambasted Thomas for comparing his situation with the horrors of LYNCHING, charging him with hypocrisy. The comment also prompted some liberals (particularly African Americans) to remark cynically and angrily that Thomas had no grounds for playing the RACE CARD, given his past history. He was on the record as attacking affirmative action, for example, even though he had clearly been a beneficiary of it. The Senate voted 52-48 to confirm Thomas to the U.S. Supreme Court. It was the closest margin for a successful Supreme Court nominee in the nation's history. After taking his seat on the Court, Thomas generally voted in a manner that pleased his conservative supporters and dismayed his liberal detractors. Along with Chief Justice William Rehnquist and Justice Antonin Scalia, Thomas was considered to be part of the Court's right wing.

### A Conservative Renaissance

Since the mid-1990's, African Americans have run as Republican candidates and as conservative politicians at all levels of government. A few of these candidates have been successful, including DELAWARE state senator Margaret Rose Henry, Ohio state treasurer J. Kenneth Blackwell, NEW JERSEY secretary of state Lonna R. Hooks, and NORTH CAROLINA state senator Henry McKoy. Two black Republicans became notable as members of the U.S. House of Representatives: Gary FRANKS of CONNECTICUT and J. C. WATTS of OKLAHOMA. Speaker of the House Newt Gingrich selected Watts to head a task force responsible for encouraging more African Americans to register to vote as Republicans.

More than twenty-four African Americans ran for public office as Republican candidates in the 1994 elections. From coast to coast, they ran on platforms that emphasized lower taxes, school vouchers, strong families, less government interference in local affairs, and tougher laws on crime, among other issues. Some were critical of affirmative action and even called for an end to programs associated with it. Some of these candidates advocated prayer in the schools, supported home schooling, and called for an end to forced busing.

For the most part, African Americans who have run as Republicans have been defeated in their bids for public office. Critics have offered a variety of reasons for this lack of success. Some African Americans believe that the Republican Party, particularly its conservative right wing, has become far too exclusionist. These critics have argued that black Republican candidates would never be successful in winning elections until the party began to acknowledge their presence and invest more money in their election campaigns. Other observers noted that the party seemed obsessed with attacking women's rights, denouncing affirmative action, and opposing civil rights legislation, and that its leading representatives seemed to thrive on engaging in racial politics.

*Conservative Black Media*

Since 1990 a growing number of newspapers, magazines, and talk shows have presented a conservative message to the African American community. Newspapers espousing a conservative message include Detroit's *Michigan Chronicle*, The *Chicago Independent Bulletin*, and The *Atlanta Daily World*. Conservative magazines include *Destiny* (published in Salem, Oregon), *National Minority Politics* (published in Houston, Texas), and *Issues and Views* (published in New York City). The organization *Project 21*, based in Washington, D.C., worked to generate interest in conservative politics among black youth.

The common theme of these publications is a message of personal responsibility, strong families, marital fidelity, free enterprise, limited government, and other traditionally conservative themes. The majority of the publications have a select readership that is loyal and enthusiastic in its support of conservative ideals.

The media field in which many conservative African Americans have managed to make their presence known is talk radio. Echoing the success of white conservative radio hosts such as Rush Limbaugh and G. Gordon Liddy,

---

## Black Conservative Politicians

In November of 1994, twenty-four African Americans ran for office as Republican congressional candidates, up from eleven who ran in 1990 and fifteen who ran in 1992. Fourteen of the black Republicans who ran for Congress in 1994 faced Democratic opponents in majority black districts. Demonstrating the difficulty of generating support for Republican candidates among black voters, the two black Republicans who were elected to Congress—Gary Franks of Connecticut and J. C. Watts of Oklahoma—were elected from majority white districts.

In 1995 only ten African Americans served in state legislatures as Republican politicians. Two black Republicans were elected as state officials—Victoria Buckley as secretary of state for Colorado, and J. Kenneth Blackwell as state treasurer for Ohio.

In the 1996 presidential campaign, several African Americans ran for the Republican presidential nomination. Former federal civil rights commissioner Arthur Fletcher entered the race for a time in 1995. Former State Department official Alan Keyes made a bid for the Republican presidential nomination and published a book articulating his policy concerns, but he was unable to generate widespread support in the face of competition from high-profile and well-financed candidates such as Senate majority leader Bob Dole, political commentator Pat Buchanan, and millionaire publisher Steve Forbes. Retired General Colin Powell was touted as a candidate before announcing his decision not to run.

*Sources: Christian Science Monitor, November 2, 1994, p. 1, and April 18, 1995, p. 18; Los Angeles Times, December 23, 1995, p. A24.*

black conservative radio hosts captured the attention of a considerable segment of the listening public. These radio talk show personalities include Ronald Edwards, Armstrong Williams, and the Reverend Earl Jackson, all of whom broadcast syndicated shows; Larry Elder, Star Parker, and Errol Smith, based in Los Angeles, California; Mason Weaver in San Diego, California; Kenneth Hamblin in Denver, Colorado; James Hereford in Cleveland, Ohio; Marie Kaigler in Detroit, Michigan; Jesse Peterson in Medford, Oregon; and Edward Shannon in Houston, Texas.

Black conservatives populating the airwaves have also included the Reverend Keith Butler, a minister from Detroit, Michigan; Ezola Foster, a schoolteacher and writer from Venice, California, who is president of Black Americans for Family Values; Jackie Cissell, president of the Family Research Council; and Phyllis Berry Myers, a former Reagan administration official who became the producer of the program *A Second Look Live* in Washington, D.C.

These talk show hosts, foundation presidents, and ministers discuss issues that they believe are of interest to the African American community. A common theme is the belief that African Americans are too preoccupied with racism and must rid themselves of this obsession and make an effort to achieve and succeed in spite of it. While they have generated significant sympathy among white listeners, these conservatives have especially garnered

Jacqueline Gordon, communications director of Conservatives for a Better America, at the "Black Conservative Unity Summit" held in New York City in April, 1997, where black conservatives presented a manifesto for the twenty-first century. *(AP/Wide World Photos)*

the attention of many African Americans.

Conservative African Americans have managed to carve their own niche within a segment of American society. Like any group of individuals who claim a particular ideology, they have encountered enthusiastic loyalty as well as considerable disdain from various politicians, magazines, spokespersons, and other observers.

Like other social critics, black conservatives depend on the strength and loyalty of their followers. Many have sought to build on a consensus of opinion within the African American and white communities. In trying to bridge the racial gap, however, many black conservative spokespersons have been criticized as opportunists by the African American community. Moreover, these conservatives have drawn criticism for appearing to surpass their white counterparts in their insensitivity to the needs of the black community. Clearly this perception must change in order for the black conservative movement to gain a larger following among its own people.

—*Elwood David Watson*

Suggested Readings:

Danforth, John C. *Resurrection: The Confirmation of Clarence Thomas*. New York: Viking Press, 1994.

Davison, James, Jr. *Prisoners of Our Past: A Critical Look at Self-Defeating Attitudes in the Black Community*. New York: Carol, 1993.

Eisenstadt, Peter R., ed. *Black Conservatism: Essays in Intellectual and Political History*. New York: Garland, 1999.

Faryna, Stan, Brad Stetson, and Joseph G. Conti, eds. *Black and Right: The Bold New Voice of Black Conservatives in America*. Westport, Conn.: Praeger, 1997.

Foster, Ezola, with Sarah Coleman. *What's Right for All Americans*. Waco, Tex.: WRS, 1995.

Keyes, Alan L. *Masters of the Dream: The Strength and Betrayal of Black America*. New York: William Morrow, 1995.

Loury, Glenn C. *One by One from the Inside Out: Essays and Reviews on Race and Responsibility in America*. New York: Free Press, 1995.

Randolph, Lewis A. "A Historical Analysis and Critique of Contemporary Black Conservatism." *The Western Journal of Black Studies* 19 (Fall, 1995): 149-163.

Robinson, James. *Racism or Attitude? The Ongoing Struggle for Black Liberation and Self-Esteem*. New York: Insight Books, 1995.

Sowell, Thomas. *Race and Culture: A World View*. New York: BasicBooks, 1994.

Williams, Armstrong. *Beyond Blame: How We Can Succeed by Breaking the Dependency Barrier*. New York: Free Press, 1995.

**Constitution, U.S.:** Foundation of law of the United States. In 1776 the Declaration of Independence was signed by fifty-six patriots. It declared the reasons why the American colonies had dissolved their political ties with Great Britain. In lofty terms, the Declaration announced that, "all Men are created equal, that they are endowed by their Creator with certain unalienable Rights, that among these, are Life, Liberty, and the Pursuit of Happiness."

Eleven years later, in May, 1787, fifty-five delegates from the thirteen newly independent American states met in Philadelphia, Pennsylvania, at the Constitutional Convention. They wrote a new charter creating a strong national government for the United States.

The Constitution's seven articles establish the government's legislative, executive, and judicial branches. They also describe the relationship of the states to the federal government, the amendment process, the supremacy of the Constitution and laws of the United States, and the ratification process. The first ten amendments to the Constitution, known as the Bill of Rights, were added in 1791 expressly to protect personal rights against federal government abuses. The Constitution was amended seventeen more times between then and 1992.

*"Other Persons"*

For one-sixth of the population of the United States in 1787—the 697,000 human beings bound in SLAVERY—the U.S. Constitution adopted in Philadelphia that year was hardly the "miracle" that historian Catherine Drinker Bowen later called it. Instead, the Constitution institutionalized slavery. That the framers could not bring themselves to use that word furnishes evidence that they were embarrassed, if not ashamed, by what they had done.

The text of the Constitution explicitly refers to slavery in three places, though not by name.

Article I, section 2, paragraph 3, provides for the apportionment of representatives and direct taxes among the states according to their respective populations. Given the gravity of what it refers to, the formula for determining the relevant population is strangely banal: Begin with "the whole number of free persons" (wording that implies that there are also "unfree" persons), include "those bound to service for a term of years" (that is, indentured servants), exclude "Indians not taxed," and add "three-fifths of all other persons." Tellingly, slaves first appear in the Constitution as "other persons"—not free, but "other" than free. They are defined by their absence of freedom, identified by their contrast with "free persons."

The "three-fifths" clause (counting a slave as only "three-fifths" of a person) contains a deeper humiliation. The entire paragraph deals with the respective power of each state in the House of Representatives and in the electoral college, which selects presidents. Denied all the constitutional rights enjoyed by "free persons," slaves nonetheless served their masters by increasing the voting power of the slave states in the new American government.

The Constitution proceeds to refer to slaves, again not by that term, in two other specific provisions. Article I, section 9, paragraph 1, permits the ending of the slave trade ("Importation of such Persons as any of the States now existing shall think proper to admit") after twenty years, but not before.

The fugitive slave clause—Article IV, section 2, paragraph 3—installs in the United States' founding charter a national obligation to return slaves to their owners: "No Person held to Service or Labour in one State, under the Laws thereof, escaping into another, shall, in Consequence of any Law or Regulation therein, be discharged from such Service or Labour, but shall be delivered up on Claim of the Party to whom such Service or Labour be due."

The inclusion of these three explicit provisions, and the equally important implicit "right to property," which served as the foundation for slavery, was the price paid by the free states to secure the consent of the slave states to the new Constitution. James Madison made it clear in his letter to Thomas Jefferson, reporting on the results of the Constitutional Convention, that, "S. Carolina and Georgia were inflexible on the point of slaves."

Madison and Jefferson got their Constitution, but its duality concealed a conflict that would not go away, despite the naïve hopes of

Preamble and first article of the U.S. Constitution. *(National Archives)*

many of the framers. As historian Don Fehren-bacher wrote: "It is as though the Framers were half-consciously trying to frame two constitutions, one for their own time and the other for the ages, with slavery viewed bifocally—that is, plainly visible at their feet, but disappearing when they lifted their eyes."

### The Bill of Rights

The First Congress, led by Representative James Madison, adopted a Bill of Rights, which was ratified on December 15, 1791. On its face the Bill of Rights cured none of the defects in the Constitution when it came to slavery. Yet the Bill of Rights would ultimately serve as the constitutional basis for a series of groundbreaking U.S. SUPREME COURT decisions guaranteeing equality, due process of law, and integration. African Americans would, in time, enjoy the fruits of the Bill of Rights, including constitutional protection for free speech; free press; religious freedom; the right of association; the right to peaceably assemble; the right to petition the government for redress of grievances; the right to be secure in one's person, house, papers, and effects; the right against unreasonable searches and seizures; the right against double jeopardy; the right against self-incrimination; the right not to be deprived of life, liberty, or property without due process of law; the right to a speedy and public trial before an impartial jury, to be informed of the charges, to confront one's accusers and to have assistance of counsel; the right to be protected from cruel and unusual punishment; and all other rights retained by the people.

### The Perpetuation of Slavery

It would take more than a century, however—indeed, in many ways, almost two centuries—for slaves, former slaves, and African Americans to enjoy the liberties guaranteed by the Bill of Rights. During the formative decades of the new nation, slavery and its complete de-

nial of all constitutional rights, would be ingrained in the economic, social, and political life of the United States. Constitutional change abolishing slavery and guaranteeing equal rights to these "other persons" was unthinkable so long as slavery remained a cornerstone of American life.

The ownership of slaves was not confined to the first generation of American leaders. William Lee Miller makes the point powerfully by observing that "five of the first seven presidents were slaveholders; for thirty-two of the nation's first thirty-six years, forty of its first forty-eight, fifty of its first sixty-four, the nation's president was a slaveholder." Miller also notes that the

> majority of cabinet members and—very important—of justices on the Supreme Court were slaveholders. The slaveholding Chief Justice Roger Taney, appointed by the slaveholding President Andrew Jackson to succeed the slaveholding John Marshall, would serve all the way through the decades before the war into the years of the Civil War itself.

### The Dred Scott Decision

In 1857 Chief Justice Roger Brooke Taney announced the Supreme Court's decision in *Scott v. Sandford*—the DRED SCOTT DECISION—that excluded free blacks from citizenship. Dred Scott was a Missouri slave owned by an army medical officer who took him to live at military posts in Illinois and in federal territory, where slavery had been prohibited by the Missouri Compromise. In 1846 Scott brought suit, claiming he had been emancipated by his residence on free soil. Complicated legal proceedings brought the case to the U.S. Supreme Court.

The majority of the Court held that African Americans, free and slave, were not citizens when the Constitution was written because, in its notorious words, they "had no rights which the white man was bound to respect." Taney treated all blacks as a degraded class of beings who "had been subjugated by the dominant race, and, whether emancipated or not, yet remained subject to their authority." Furthermore, Taney's opinion held that the antislavery provision of the MISSOURI COMPROMISE OF 1820 was unconstitutional.

Dred Scott was manumitted (given his freedom) shortly after the decision that bore his name was decided, but he lived only sixteen months as a free man before dying of tuberculosis. In June, 1862, Congress abolished slavery in all federal territories (the CIVIL WAR had begun in 1861). That same year, Abraham Lincoln's attorney general issued an official opinion holding that, contrary to *Scott v. Sandford*, free men of color born in the United States were citizens of the United States. It took the bloody Civil War, and the three pivotal constitutional amendments that followed, to remove the stain of slavery from the U.S. Constitution.

*The Civil War Amendments*
The word "slavery" first appeared in the Constitution on the occasion of slavery's abolition. The THIRTEENTH AMENDMENT, ratified on December 18, 1865, in thirty-two simple words declared that "neither slavery nor involuntary servitude, except as a punishment for crime whereof the party shall have been duly convicted, shall exist within the United States, or any place subject to their jurisdiction."

The FOURTEENTH AMENDMENT, ratified on July 21, 1868, granted the rights of citizenship to former slaves. It provided that "all persons born or naturalized in the United States, and subject to the jurisdiction thereof, are citizens of the United States and of the State wherein they reside. No State shall make or enforce any law which shall abridge the privileges or immunities of citizens of the United States; nor shall any State deprive any person of life, liberty, or property, without due process of law;

nor deny to any person within its jurisdiction the equal protection of the laws."

Furthermore, the Fourteenth Amendment expressly eliminated the noxious "three-fifths" clause by providing that representatives shall be apportioned among the states by "counting the whole number of persons in each State" (still excluded were "Indians not taxed"). Alleviating one badge of servitude but perpetuating another, even the Fourteenth Amendment referred only to the right of "male inhabitants" to vote.

The FIFTEENTH AMENDMENT, ratified March 30, 1870, guaranteed that the "right of citizens of the United States to vote shall not be denied or abridged by the United States or by any State on account of race, color, or previous condition of servitude." The Civil War Amendments would, in time, prove to be powerful instruments in securing equality, not only for African Americans, in whose interest the Amendments were first adopted, but for all Americans.

The vehicle which gave meaning and power to the Fourteenth Amendment is known as the "incorporation doctrine," under which the guarantees of the Bill of Rights, originally binding only to the federal government, were made applicable to the states by incorporation or absorption into the Fourteenth Amendment. In particular, the Supreme Court on a case-by-case basis interpreted the "privileges and immunities," "due process," and "equal protection" clauses of the Fourteenth Amendment to prohibit state and local governments from abridging fundamental rights protected by the Bill of Rights, including the freedoms protected by the First Amendment, and criminal justice rights protected by the Fourth, Fifth, Sixth, Seventh, and Eighth Amendments.

*From Plessy to Brown*
With the adoption of the Civil War Amendments, the struggle of African Americans for

equality under the Constitution shifted from the abolition of slavery to the removal of its consequences in the realm of civil and political rights. The implementation of BLACK CODES and JIM CROW LAWS and a series of Supreme Court decisions, most notably PLESSY V. FERGUSON (1896), prevented African Americans from fully enjoying their constitutional rights.

It would take another half century for the decision in *Plessy v. Ferguson*, upholding a state law requiring "separate but equal" segregation of whites and blacks in interstate rail travel, to be replaced by the historic 1954 decision in BROWN V. BOARD OF EDUCATION, holding that racial segregation of public school children violated the Fourteenth Amendment's guarantee of equal protection of the laws and the Fifth Amendment's guarantee of due process of law.

*Brown v. Board of Education* has been called the Supreme Court's most important decision of the twentieth century. Speaking for a unanimous Court, Chief Justice Earl Warren announced that given the importance of public education for the individual and for American society, segregation of public school children was unconstitutional. Whereas *Plessy v. Ferguson* had minimized the claim that segregation stamped blacks with a mark of inferiority, *Brown v. Board of Education* supported the argument that segregated schools produced feelings of inferiority in black pupils and interfered with their motivation to learn.

### The Civil Rights Movement

The Court's *Brown v. Board of Education* decision did not order an immediate end to segregated schools; rather, it required that lower courts issue decrees admitting children to schools on a racially nondiscriminatory basis "with all deliberate speed." Nonetheless, the groundbreaking decision was a catalyst for the CIVIL RIGHTS movement, as it placed the U.S. Constitution squarely on the side of African Americans. Bolstered by *Brown* and other

Supreme Court decisions which breathed life into the doctrines of equal protection and due process, Congress passed the Civil Rights Act of 1964 and the VOTING RIGHTS ACT OF 1965.

Armed with the full panoply of First Amendment rights to free speech, free press, free association, and peaceful assembly, the Civil Rights movement spread beyond the issue of education and fought for equality in housing and employment and for full participation in political activities and electoral office. By the last half of the twentieth century, the U.S. Constitution, born as a stranger to African Americans and repaired by the Civil War Amendments, had become a defender of racial equality, a guarantor of justice, and a partner in the struggle for freedom.

—*Stephen F. Rohde*

Suggested Readings:

Bailyn, Bernard. *The Ideological Origins of the American Revolution*. Cambridge, Mass.: Harvard University Press, 1967.

Corwin, Edward S. *The Constitution and What It Means Today*. Princeton, N.J.: Princeton University Press, 1978.

Fehrenbacher, Don E. *Slavery, Law, and Politics: The Dred Scott Case in Historical Perspective*. New York: Oxford University Press, 1981.

Kluger, Richard. *Simple Justice: The History of Brown v. Board of Education and Black Americans' Struggle for Equality*. New York: Alfred A. Knopf, 1975.

Konvitz, Milton R. *A Century of Civil Rights*. New York: Columbia University Press, 1961.

McPherson, James M. *Battle Cry of Freedom*. New York: Oxford University Press, 1988.

Miller, William Lee. *Arguing About Slavery: The Great Battle in the United States Congress*. New York: Alfred A. Knopf, 1996.

**Convict release system and chain gangs:** The convict release system arose after the CIVIL WAR in the South as a means of solving three

Convict laborers strengthening the side of a southern road during the 1890's. *(National Archives)*

problems: a lack of money, a rise in crime, and a surplus of freedmen for whom there was yet no place in the economic system. Instead of being housed in overfilled and inadequately supplied state penitentiaries, state convicts were leased to private individuals or industry in exchange for their upkeep and a nominal fee. Reform movements in the early twentieth century caused the state convict release system to be replaced by a system of chain gangs. Instead of being leased to private individuals, prisoners were forced to work for the county. Under both systems, African Americans were disproportionately affected, and they were abused and exploited.

Part of the increasing need for penitentiary space in the 1870's resulted from new criminal codes passed by southern states that were reasserting themselves after a decade of being ruled by northern military governments. These codes weakened legal rights and also exacted heavy penalties for petty crimes. For example, a law passed in 1874 stated that a person convicted of stealing a pig in MISSISSIPPI could be sentenced to five years in a penitentiary. In a span of three years, largely as a result of such laws, the number of Mississippi state convicts increased by a factor of five. The overwhelming majority of convicts were Afri-

can American. Similar laws had similar effects in other southern states.

The convict release system meant that states, instead of having to raise taxes to pay for prisoner upkeep, simply shifted the responsibility for prisoners to the owners of mining, logging, and turpentine camps, cotton plantations, and railroads. Because these owners paid for the use of the prisoners, the state government actually made a profit. In turn, the owners were eager to use convict labor, which was much cheaper than free labor. Joseph E. Brown, former governor and U.S. senator from GEORGIA, based his industrial empire on convict labor leased from the state for seven cents per person per day.

The system was notoriously corrupt. Like former governor Brown, many of those who wished to lease convicts were powerful and influential. To increase the pool of labor, some judges could be persuaded to convict more African Americans and to sentence them to longer terms. In 1879 African Americans represented 90 percent of Georgia's felony convicts. They also were likely to serve longer sentences, more likely to die in custody, and less likely to be pardoned than were white convicts. Sometimes prisoners were leased out for as many as thirty years, essentially becoming the slaves of whoever leased them. Reports of abuse, brutality, and degradation were common. Prisoners often were not provided with decent living conditions, bedding, clothes, food, or medical facilities. Many states failed to enact laws that would protect prisoners' rights, few guidelines existed for how much the prisoner reasonably could be expected to work, and few if any state inspections were conducted to ensure the prisoners' welfare.

Various reform groups and political parties, including the Greenback-Labor Party and the Populist Party, campaigned to abolish the convict release system. Between 1900 and 1913, it was replaced with the county chain gangs. Under this system, convicts were taken out of the control of private individuals and put under county supervision to work on roads and public works projects. As protection against escape, prisoners wore striped clothes, were chained together, and often rode in cages erected on wagons. Vagrancy laws helped supply the chain gangs with able bodies. Any unemployed person could be convicted of vagrancy and sent to a chain gang. Black people suffered disproportionately from vagrancy laws, as they faced higher rates of unemployment than did white people.

**Conyers, John, Jr.** (b. May 16, 1929, Detroit, Michigan): Politician. Conyers was elected as congressman from the First District of MICHIGAN in 1964. He became a leader in emphasizing legislation to promote full employment, small business priorities, and domestic human resources programs. He also favored the curtailment of what he thought were excessive military budgets. Because of his long service in the House of Representatives, and because of his ability to capture as much as 91 percent of the vote in his district, Conyers was nationally influential in representing issues that are important to African Americans.

Conyers graduated from Wayne State Uni-

Representative John Conyers, Jr., in 1999. *(AP/Wide World Photos)*

versity, which awarded him the B.A. (1957) and J.D. (1958) degrees. Before entering politics, he was a legal assistant to Congressman John Dingell, senior partner in the firm of Conyers, Bell, and Townsend, referee for the Michigan Workmen's Compensation Department, and general counsel for the Trade Union Leadership Council. He was appointed to the National Lawyers Committee for Civil Rights Under Law by President John F. Kennedy in 1963, and later was a cosponsor of the Medicare program proposed by President Lyndon B. Johnson. He consistently supported strong voting rights bills in the House of Representatives, beginning with the VOTING RIGHTS ACT OF 1965.

Conyers was the first African American to serve on the House of Representatives' Judiciary Committee, and he chaired the House Subcommittee on Criminal Justice and was a member of its subcommittee on crime. He also chaired the Government Operations Committee and served on subcommittees for housing and for civil and constitutional rights. He participated in the impeachment inquiry that preceded President Richard M. Nixon's resignation and was the only African American on that panel.

A strong and critical legislator, Conyers challenged national priorities at the federal level. It was partly a result of his influence that housing, voting rights, and employment laws were enacted beginning in 1965. In authoring some of these bills and assertively supporting others, he served the interests of the poor and of ethnic communities. Conyers also wrote several books about the American military and its twentieth-century campaigns.

In the 1990's Conyers repeatedly introduced controversial bills in Congress that would provide REPARATIONS to African Americans descended from slaves, similar to the payments authorized in 1988 for Japanese survivors of WORLD WAR II internment camps. In 1998 Conyers—by then in his seventeenth term in Congress—was active in the congressional hearings on whether to impeach President Bill Clinton. Like other members of the CONGRESSIONAL BLACK CAUCUS, such as caucus chair Maxine WATERS, he supported Clinton and opposed the impeachment proceedings. On the final day of House debate in December, 1998, Conyers was almost scornful of the House Republicans' fight for impeachment. Comparing the Clinton impeachment hearings with the earlier Watergate hearings, he argued that the Republicans were trying to "dress up" charges of perjury "in the clothes of Watergate 'abuse of power' language."
*See also:* Congress Members; Politics and government.

**Cook, Charles "Cookie"** (1914, Chicago, Illinois—August 8, 1991, New York, New York): Tap dancer. As a child, Cook performed VAUDEVILLE theater with Garbage and the Two Cans and, until 1929, with the act Sarah Venable and Her Picks. A "pick" (short for pickaninny) in this case was a black child who danced in the background for a white female singer. The practice was a form of theatrical child labor, but it was one of the few ways a black child could get into show business.

In 1930 Cook joined with tapper Ernest "Brownie" Brown and Ben Bernie's orchestra to perform at the College Inn in Chicago. Four years later, Cook and Brown opened at the COTTON CLUB. Thereafter, their knockabout comic dance routine became a headline act in vaudeville theaters throughout the United States and in Europe. Having watched circus tumblers and studied vaudeville comedians, they combined myriad vernacular dance steps with first-rate acrobatics. The six-foot-tall Cook played the grouchy foil to the four-foot, ten-inch Brown.

The two appeared together in several films, including *52nd Street* (1937), *Toot That Trumpet* (1941), and *Chatter* (1943), as well as on Broadway in *Kiss Me Kate* (1948). They continued to work through the 1960's, even while employment for tap dancers dwindled. Later, the team made occasional reappearances for tap galas and in a video documentary entitled *Cookie's Scrapbook* (1987), in which they reminisce about vaudeville.

Cook taught tap in New York City and continued to perform on his own. With members of the Copasetics, a group of veteran tap dancers, he made the video documentary *Great Feats of Feet* (1967). He appeared in the film *The Cotton Club* (1984), on public television in the *Gershwin Gala*, and in tap programs at the Jacob's Pillow Dance Festival, the Brooklyn Academy of Music, the Newport Jazz Festival, and the 1984 Summer Olympics. He choreographed and performed in a program called *Fancy Feet* at the Smithsonian Institution and made a teaching video with Brenda Bufalino and Kevin Ramsey called the *Video Encyclopedia of Tap Technique* (1990).
*See also:* Dance.

**Cook, Julian Abele, Jr.** (b. June 22, 1930, Washington, D.C.): Federal judge. Cook graduated from Pennsylvania State University with his B.A. degree in 1952. He then served in the U.S. Army Signal Corps until 1954, achieving the rank of first lieutenant before he was honorably discharged. He attended law school at Georgetown University and received his J.D. degree in 1957. Cook began his legal career as a law clerk for Judge Arthur E. Moore from 1957 to 1958. He then went into private practice as an attorney.

Cook's political career began when he served as special assistant attorney general for the state of MICHIGAN in 1968, a post he held for ten years. In 1978 President Jimmy Carter appointed him U.S. district judge for the Eastern District of Michigan. He was promoted to chief judge of the Eastern District in 1989.

During his judicial career, Cook served on the boards of several organizations and was a president and member of the executive board of directors for Child and Family Services of Michigan. In 1988 he was appointed to serve on the Judicial Conference of the U.S. Judicial Ethics Commission. Also in that year, Cook participated as an instructor at Harvard University's Trial Advocacy Workshop. He received several awards and citations for his work with the Oakland County chapter of the NATIONAL ASSOCIATION FOR THE ADVANCEMENT OF COLORED PEOPLE (NAACP) and the Pontiac, Michigan, chapter of the NATIONAL URBAN LEAGUE.
*See also:* Judges.

**Cook, Mercer** (March 30, 1903, Washington, D.C.—October 4, 1987, Washington, D.C.): Educator, author, poet, and political appointee. Cook grew up in WASHINGTON, D.C., in the same neighborhood where bandleader Duke ELLINGTON lived, and graduated from Dunbar High School. His classmates included such notables as critic Sterling BROWN, Judge William H. HASTIE, and Dr. Charles DREW. Cook studied at Amherst College and received his B.A. degree in 1925. After pursuing advanced studies and earning a teacher's diploma at the University of Paris in 1926, Cook returned to the United States and earned his M.A. and Ph.D. degrees from Brown University in 1931 and 1936, respectively.

Cook began his teaching career as assistant professor of romance languages at HOWARD UNIVERSITY in 1927 and taught there until 1936. He moved to ATLANTA UNIVERSITY to take a position as professor of French in 1936. In 1943 he took an assignment to teach English at the University of HAITI for two years before returning to Howard as a full professor in romance languages from 1945 to 1960. After leaving Howard in 1960, he traveled extensively around the world and spent a great deal of time in AFRICA. Cook was appointed by President John F. Kennedy to serve as U.S. ambassador to Nigeria from 1961 to 1964. Cook

Scholar Mercer Cook served as U.S. ambassador to three African nations. *(AP/Wide World Photos)*

was later appointed as an alternate delegate representing the United States in the U.N. General Assembly in 1963. President Lyndon Johnson appointed Cook to serve as U.S. ambassador to Senegal and Gambia from 1965 to 1966.

Upon leaving the foreign service in 1970, Cook returned to Howard University, where he accepted the post of head of the department of romance languages. Cook wrote several books on Haiti and on African authors, and he published English translations of works by Léopold Senghor and Cheikh A. Diop.

**Cook, Samuel DuBois** (b. November 21, 1928, Griffin, Georgia): Educator. Cook received his B.A. from Morehouse College and his Ph.D. from Ohio State University. He was a long-time CIVIL RIGHTS activist and the author of numerous scholarly articles. A specialist in political science, he taught at ATLANTA UNIVERSITY, the University of Illinois, and Duke University; he was named the president of Dillard University in 1975.

**Cooke, Sam** (Samuel Cook; January 22, 1931, Clarksdale, Mississippi—December 11, 1964, Los Angeles, California): GOSPEL singer. Cooke was the first African American gospel star to achieve success in popular music. As a singer and songwriter, Cooke helped to create SOUL MUSIC by combining elements of gospel with secular material. As a music entrepreneur with his own record company, music publishing company, and management firm, he helped other gospel singers and musicians—including Bobby Womack, Johnnie Taylor, and Lou Rawls—cross over to careers in popular music.

There is some disagreement about the date and location of Cooke's birth. Some authorities date his birth to 1931 and give his birthplace as Clarksdale, Mississippi; others have

Sam Cooke. *(AP/Wide World Photos)*

argued that he was born in Chicago about 1934 or 1935. At any rate, Cooke, grew up in Chicago. The son of a minister, he began singing in church. By the early 1950's, as a lead singer of the Soul Stirrers, he had become a major gospel star.

In 1957 Cooke achieved his first popular success with "You Send Me," which reached the number-one position on the popular music charts and sold almost two million copies. He followed up with a series of hits, including "Only Sixteen," "Another Saturday Night," and "Everybody Likes to Cha Cha Cha." His early popular recordings were ballads and novelty tunes meant to appeal to a popular audience. After 1960, however, Cooke began to produce recordings that drew more heavily on gospel and blues and that used African American slang, such as his duet with Lou Rawls, "Bring It on Home to Me," and the posthumously released "A Change Is Gonna Come."

Cooke was shot to death by a Los Angeles motel manager after allegedly attacking her and another woman. His funeral drew two hundred thousand people, testifying to Cooke's status as an important figure in the African American community. Cooke's vocal style was a major influence on Otis Redding, Al Green, and Rod Stewart. In 1986 Cooke was inducted into the Rock and Roll Hall of Fame.

*See also:* Gospel music and spirituals.

**Coolio** (b. Artis Ivey, Jr.; August 1, 1963, Los Angeles, California): Vocalist and rap artist. Coolio was recognized as one of the biggest rap stars of the late 1990's. His lyrics are both poignant and explicit. They express ideas about family, love, respect, and revolution, and they touch on issues such as the acquired immunodeficiency syndrome (AIDS) epidemic.

Coolio first began performing while in high school during the late 1970's. Although he came from an underprivileged background, he never joined a gang or became involved in any serious crime. Instead, he concentrated on building his musical and lyrical skills.

Working with disk jockey Bryan Dobbs, Coolio recorded his debut album, *It Takes a Thief*, in 1994. On the strength of the hit "Fantastic Voyage," the album became an instant success, and it eventually attained platinum status (selling more than one million copies). His follow-up album, *Gangsta's Paradise* (1995), won him a Grammy Award for best rap solo performance. The title song was featured in the film *Dangerous Minds* (1995), in which Coolio also appeared, playing a junkie. The song's chorus was a reworking of Stevie Wonder's 1976 song "Pastime Paradise." The song, album, videos, and many television appearances made Coolio a star. He formed his own management company, Crowbar Manage-

Coolio performing at the California Music Awards in San Francisco in March, 1998. *(AP/Wide World Photos)*

ment. Like his previous two albums, *My Soul*, released in 1997, was a hit; it contained the single "C U When U Get There."

—*Alvin K. Benson*

*See also:* Hip-hop; Youth culture.

**Cooper, Anna Julia Haywood** (August 10, 1858, Raleigh, North Carolina—February 27, 1964, Washington, D.C.): Pioneer in secondary education and civil rights. Cooper was the daughter of a North Carolina slave, George Washington Haywood, and Hannah Stanley Haywood, a free woman. She first attended school in Raleigh, at Saint Augustine's Normal and Collegiate Institute. She apparently was precocious. One account states that she began student-teaching at the age of nine and another at the age of eleven; either account is impressive—and credible, in view of this woman's remarkable achievements.

She studied and student-taught at Saint Augustine's until 1881. In 1877 she married the Reverend George Christopher Cooper, an

EPISCOPAL clergyman and professor of Greek. He died two years later. In 1881 she began studying at Oberlin College, where she earned the A.B. and A.M. degrees in 1884 and 1887, respectively. While she was earning the A.B. degree at Oberlin, she taught classes composed mostly of white students. She did graduate work at La Guilde Internationale in Paris (1911-1912) and at Columbia University (1913-1916) to prepare herself to earn a doctorate from the Sorbonne in Paris (1925).

Cooper's primary work in education and administration came during her fifty years as an instructor and principal of a high school in WASHINGTON, D.C., which was named the Old M Street High and was later renamed Dunbar High School. For many years, Dunbar was the only academic high school for African Americans in the nation's capital. At one time, the graduates of M Street High and Dunbar won more honors at the best universities than African Americans from any other high school in the nation.

A strong advocate of civil rights, Cooper presented a paper entitled "The Negro Problem in America" at the Pan-African Conference in London in 1900. That presentation resulted in her being named to the Pan-African executive committee. Her doctoral dissertation was a discussion of SLAVERY and racial inequality in America. She ran Frelinghuysen University, a school for unemployed African Americans, from her home.
See also: Pan-Africanism.

**Cooper, Julia** (b. 1921?, Fayetteville, North Carolina): Federal JUDGE. Cooper earned her bachelor's degree from HAMPTON INSTITUTE and received her law degree from HOWARD UNIVERSITY. She worked as a criminal lawyer with the Department of Justice and was a civil rights lawyer with the Equal Employment Opportunity Commission, where she served as deputy counsel general. Cooper had twenty years of experience in the legal profession before President Gerald Ford appointed her to the federal bench as an associate judge on the District of Columbia Court of Appeals in 1975.

*Cooper v. Aaron:* U.S. SUPREME COURT case in 1958 involving school desegregation. The Court ruled that BROWN V. BOARD OF EDUCATION (1954) applied to schools nationwide. In this decision, the Court stated that local resistance to desegregation was not a valid reason for suspending attempts to desegregate.
*See also:* Segregation and integration.

**Cornish, Samuel Eli** (1795, Sussex County, Delaware—1858, Brooklyn, New York): Abolitionist, editor, and PRESBYTERIAN cleric. Cornish was born of free parents. Little is known about his early years. In 1815 he began his education in PHILADELPHIA, PENNSYLVANIA, training for the ministry under John Gloucester, pastor of First African Church, Presbyterian. Licensed to preach in 1819, Cornish took up missionary work to slaves on MARYLAND's eastern shore. He helped to organize the New Demeter Street Presbyterian Church in 1821. Ordained in 1822, he became an active itinerant preacher, especially to free blacks in the vicinity of NEW YORK CITY. He also had a more formal relationship with churches in NEWARK, NEW JERSEY, and New York City throughout the 1830's and 1840's. In 1824 he married Jane Livingston, with whom he later had four children.

Although his preaching was a significant contribution to African American cultural life in the first half of the nineteenth century, Cornish is best remembered for his role in founding and maintaining several significant African American newspapers and journals important in the ABOLITIONIST MOVEMENT. In 1827 with John RUSSWURM, he founded the first African American newspaper, FREEDOM'S

JOURNAL. It was reorganized as *The Rights of All* that same year. In mid-1837, Cornish was named editor of *The Colored American*, founded by Philip A. Bell. His editorial work led him to be active in several abolitionist and benevolent societies, such as the AMERICAN ANTI-SLAVERY SOCIETY, the New York City Vigilance Committee, and the American Missionary Society. He was also the founder of the New York Anti-Slavery Society.

Cornish was not a radical. His commitment to broad moral reform and the Christian faith made him skeptical of solutions to the problems of slavery and racism outside the abolitionist mainstream. Typical of his position was a pamphlet he coauthored with Theodore S. Wright: *The Colonization Scheme Considered* (1840). It challenged the idea of repatriation to Africa, and instead asserted a faith in "hard work," "moral uplift," and "civilizing." His reputation was established upon his work for the improvement of conditions for free blacks in the North and his innovative work in helping to establish the BLACK PRESS.
*See also:* Colonization movement.

**Corrigan and Curtis v. Buckley:** U.S. SUPREME COURT case in 1926 involving a restrictive covenant. The court stated unanimously that RESTRICTIVE COVENANTS regarding transactions in private property could not be ruled unconstitutional. The argument for unconstitutionality was based on the Fifth, Thirteenth, and Fourteenth Amendments. The Court also ruled that it did not have jurisdiction in the case. For all practical purposes, SHELLEY V. KRAEMER reversed this decision in 1948, stating that state courts could not enforce restrictive covenants.

**Corrothers, James D.** (July 2, 1869, Cass County, Michigan—February 12, 1917, West Chester, Pennsylvania): Writer, poet, and min-

ister. James David Corrothers had to surmount many barriers in order to make a contribution to African American LITERATURE through his poetry, magazine and newspaper articles, short stories, sketches, and autobiography. Some of his writings were in black dialect and some were not.

A friend of Paul Laurence DUNBAR, Corrothers was inspired by Dunbar's writings. Many of Corrothers's dialect poems were published in magazines and newspapers. For many years, his poems and short stories appeared in several prominent publications. In 1902 he published his first book, *The Black Cat Club*, composed of newspaper sketches, and in 1916 he published his autobiography, *In Spite of the Handicap*.

Corrothers's mother died in childbirth, so he was raised by his paternal grandfather in South Haven, MICHIGAN, where he encountered racial problems while attending public school. Often he was the only black student in his class. He held a number of menial jobs, including working as a janitor at the *Chicago Tribune*, where he subsequently became a staff writer.

Corrothers was an avid reader, appreciating, among others, the works of Alfred, Lord Tennyson and Henry Wadsworth Longfellow. He was a student at Northwestern University from 1890 to 1893. He also studied at Bennett College in Greensboro, North Carolina.

Corrothers decided to leave the newspaper enterprise and enter the ministry. First he became a METHODIST minister in 1894; later he joined the BAPTIST Church, and in 1914 he became affiliated with the PRESBYTERIAN Church. In 1917 he succumbed to a stroke in West Chester, Pennsylvania.

—*Nila M. Bowden*

**Cortez, Jayne** (b. May 10, 1936, Arizona): Poet and performer. Cortez moved with her family to the WATTS area of Los Angeles in 1944. At an early age, she became fascinated with recording the family's folk stories and oral traditions. An avid musician, Cortez drew inspiration for her writing from the musical jam sessions she attended. In 1951 she met JAZZ saxophonist Ornette COLEMAN; the two were soon married, remaining together for seven years.

Appearing in anthologies, collections, and numerous publications, Cortez's work is also available on recordings. Following literature's oral tradition, she intended her poetry to be read aloud. She assembled the jazz group the Firespitters to accompany her in her own performances of her poems. A politically engaged poet, Cortez published through her own Bola Press to ensure artistic control over her work. Among her books are *Festivals and Funerals* (1971), *Firespitter* (1982), *Fragments* (1994), and *Somewhere in Advance of Nowhere* (1996).

**Cosby, Bill** (b. July 12, 1937, Philadelphia, Pennsylvania): Comedian and actor. Bill Cosby was born William Henry Cosby, Jr., in Germantown, a district of North PHILADELPHIA, PENNSYLVANIA. Cosby rose from a life of poverty to become the first African American to obtain a starring role in a weekly television series. He thereafter earned recognition as a major American entertainment figure.

*Youth and Education*
Cosby grew up in the all-black Richard Allen housing projects with his two younger brothers, Russell and Robert. Since his father, a U.S. Navy mess steward, was frequently away from home and eventually did not return, Cosby worked hard shining shoes and delivering groceries to help augment the family income. Cosby credited his mother with being his inspiration for both hard work and humor. "I remember how my mother worked twelve-hour days cleaning other people's houses before coming home to take care of her own

house and kids," he later recalled. He noted that she found time to read to her children from the works of Mark Twain, Jonathan Swift, and the Brothers Grimm and from the Bible. She also passed along her eccentric way of viewing the commonplace.

Another influence, Samuel Russell, Cosby's maternal grandfather, encouraged Cosby to create elaborate tales by rewarding the best stories with a quarter. Thus, as a child, his humor, wit, and charm were already being recognized and fostered. His sixth-grade teacher wrote of Cosby that "William is an alert boy who would rather clown than study." Having scored high on an IQ test, Bill was transferred into a program for gifted students. His employment in food markets and drugstores and his leisure interests in asphalt baseball, two-handed touch football, and the art of mimicry took precedence over academics, and he left school after tenth grade.

In 1956, after brief employment as a shoe repairman, Cosby enlisted in the U.S. Navy. While in the service, he passed an equivalency exam to earn his high school diploma. After being discharged from the Navy in 1961, he enrolled in Temple University on a TRACK-AND-FIELD scholarship. A physical education major, Cosby was a discus and javelin thrower, long jumper, high jumper, and hurdler for the track team, and he played right halfback on the school's football team. His performance on the football field prompted Emlen Tunnell, a scout for the New York Giants and the Green Bay Packers and a former football star, to predict that Cosby had the potential for a career as a professional defensive halfback.

*Beginning a Comedy Career*
Successful appearances as a comedian at coffeehouses in Philadelphia prompted Cosby to take a leave of absence from Temple University in 1962 to perform at the Gaslight Cafe, a coffeehouse in NEW YORK CITY's Greenwich Village. Critical acclaim in New York con-

vinced Cosby to withdraw from Temple and pursue a career in comedy. His tours as a co-median included appearances at the Gate of Horn and Mr. Kelly's in CHICAGO; the Shad-ows Club and the Shoreham Hotel in WASH-INGTON, D.C.; the Fifth Peg in Toronto; the hungry i in San Francisco; the Flamingo in Las Vegas; the Bitter End and Basin Street East in New York; and Harrah's at Lake Tahoe.

### Stand-Up Comedian

Cosby wrote all of his own material and devel-oped a style of humor that became his trade-mark. A tremendous storyteller who drew upon his own childhood experiences and ev-eryday life, Cosby enhanced his delivery with sound effects, gestures, funny faces, and exag-gerated impersonations. At the core of his pre-sentation were keen observations about hu-man nature and the positive values he hopes his vignettes will reflect. Cosby was not inter-ested in performing comedy based on race; he once stated, "I don't think you can bring the races together by joking about the differences between them. I'd rather talk about the simi-larities, about what's universal in their experi-ences."

In 1963 Bill Cosby made his first comedy album, entitled *Bill Cosby Is a Very Funny Fel-low . . . Right!*. Response to the album was en-thusiastic, and the record earned Cosby his first Grammy Award for best comedy album of the year. A second album, *I Started Out as a Child*, won him another Grammy. Subsequent albums led to six more Grammy Awards in the best comedy album category. Among his com-edy albums are *Revenge*; *To Russell, My Brother, with Whom I Slept*; *Why Is There Air? Wonderful-ness*; *It's True, It's True*; *Reunion*; *Bill Cosby . . . Himself*; and *Those of You with or Without Chil-dren, You'll Understand*.

### Television Star

Following a 1965 guest appearance on *The To-night Show*, Cosby was approached by pro-

Bill Cosby. *(Howard Bingham)*

ducer Sheldon Leonard, who wanted to give him a screen test. As a result, Cosby was cast as Alexander Scott in the National Broadcasting Company (NBC) adventure-espionage series *I Spy*. He was teamed with Robert Culp, and the role made Cosby the first black performer to star in a weekly network series. The series pre-miered on September 15, 1965, and remained popular until its final showing in September, 1968. Through those years he won three Emmy Awards. Also in 1968, Cosby played a successful weeklong engagement at the APOLLO THEATER in HARLEM. In 1969 he won his fourth Emmy Award, for his *Bill Cosby Spe-cial*.

In 1969 he returned to NBC portraying a physical-education teacher, Chet Kincaid, on *The Bill Cosby Show*, which ran for three years. In September, 1972, he was back with a one-hour comedy and variety program called *The New Bill Cosby Show*, which lasted through

May of 1973. Overlapping this program was *Fat Albert and the Cosby Kids*, a Saturday-morning cartoon designed to entertain and instruct children by presenting ways to deal with the problems of growing up. This program remained in production through September, 1984, and won the Children's Theater Association Seal of Excellence in 1973. Later, McGraw-Hill distributed shortened versions to schools as teaching tools.

Awarded his B.A. from Temple University, Cosby enrolled part-time in a doctoral program in education at the University of Massachusetts at Amherst. In 1977 he completed his Ed.D. degree, using his television experience to support his 242-page dissertation. During the 1970's, Cosby became a regular guest on the educational children's television programs *Sesame Street* and *The Electric Company*. In addition, his engaging personality became increasingly appealing to advertisers, and he filmed numerous commercials. *Advertising Age* referred to Cosby as the "star presenter of 1978."

### The Cosby Show

Early in 1984, NBC accepted the idea of starring Cosby in a family situation comedy entitled THE COSBY SHOW. Cosby played an upper-middle-class obstetrician named Cliff Huxtable. Demanding artistic control over the show, Cosby insisted that the Huxtables were to be an American family that reflected the best family values—love, respect, mutual support, and understanding. The program was extremely successful; it quickly climbed to number one in the ratings and remained near the top for eight seasons, from 1984 to 1992. It also became an international success and even achieved top ratings in white-ruled South Africa.

### Later Career

After *The Cosby Show* ended its run, Cosby returned to television in the 1990's, first with a revival of Groucho Marx's classic *You Bet Your Life*, which combined interviews with a game show, then with *The Cosby Mysteries*; neither show was successful. In 1996 he began starring in a new comedy show, *Cosby*, which teamed him once again with Phylicia Rashad, who had played his wife in *The Cosby Show*. In the 1990's Cosby also became an outspoken critic of television's stereotypical portrayals of African Americans, arguing that the medium was taking a huge step backward. He made a serious attempt to pool enough investors to buy NBC but could not raise the capital.

In the 1990's Cosby also faced problems and tragedies in his personal life. A woman named Autumn Jackson claimed to be his illegitimate daughter and demanded money; she was accused of extortion, and at her trial she was convicted. Immeasurably worse, Cosby's twenty-seven-year-old son Ennis was murdered in Los Angeles in 1997 by a man attempting to rob him. His killer was arrested and convicted.

### Other Entertainment Credits

Cosby's feature film credits include roles in *Hickey and Boggs* (1972), *Uptown Saturday Night* (1974), *Let's Do It Again* (1975), *Mother, Jugs, and Speed* (1976), *A Piece of the Action* (1977), *California Suite* (1979), *The Devil and Max Devlin* (1981), *Bill Cosby—Himself* (1983), *Leonard Part 6* (1987), and *Ghost Dad* (1990). In addition, Cosby wrote several books, including *The Wit and Wisdom of Fat Albert* (1973), *Bill Cosby's Personal Guide to Power Tennis* (1986), *Fatherhood* (1986), *Time Flies* (1988), and *Love and Marriage* (1989).

Beyond acting and comedy, Cosby developed an interest in music at a young age, notably JAZZ and RHYTHM AND BLUES. He began playing the drums at the age of eleven and eventually was able to exercise his fondness for jazz by sitting in with a number of bands and performers. He often served as master of ceremonies for the Playboy Jazz Festival in

Hollywood and the Kool Jazz Festival in New York. He was named president of the Rhythm and Blues Hall of Fame in 1968.

Cosby's compassion and generosity have often been cited. He frequently came to the aid of those in need by doing benefit performances, and he undertook the role of advocate for education by offering financial support to several black colleges. In 1999 he became part owner of the New Jersey Nets basketball team, drawn in part by the team's commitment to a trust fund benefiting inner-city youth. Among Cosby's many honors was a Kennedy Center Honor in 1998.

—*Mary Krenitsky Perrone*

*See also:* Comedy and humor; Comics, stand-up; Television industry; Television series.

Suggested Readings:

Adler, Bill. *The Cosby Wit: His Life and Humor.* New York: Carroll & Graf, 1986.

Fuller, Linda K. *The Cosby Show: Audiences, Impact, and Implications.* New York: Greenwood Press, 1992.

Kettelkamp, Larry. *Bill Cosby: Family Funny Man.* New York: Wanderer Books, 1987.

Latham, Caroline. *Bill Cosby, for Real.* New York: Tom Doherty Associates, 1985.

Rosenberg, Robert. *Bill Cosby: The Changing Black Image.* Brookfield, Conn.: Millbrook Press, 1991.

Schiffman, Jack. *Uptown: The Story of Harlem's Apollo Theater.* New York: Cowles Books, 1971.

Smith, Ronald L. *Cosby: The Life of a Comedy Legend.* Rev. ed. Amherst, N.Y.: Prometheus Books, 1997.

*Cosby Show, The* (NBC, 1984-1992): Television situation comedy. Bill Cosby was credited with reviving the fading television genre of situation comedy with this highly rated and well-respected series about the day-to-day lives of an upscale African American family.

Phylicia Rashad played the beautiful and understanding Clair Huxtable, a lawyer and wife to loving and patient obstetrician and father Cliff Huxtable. Sabrina Le Beauf, Lisa Bonet, Malcolm-Jamal Warner, Tempest Bledsoe, and Keshia Knight Pulliam were the original cast of Huxtable children, joined in time by various spouses, friends, cousins, and children of their own.

The show's first telecast dealt with son Theo's failure to realize the importance of a college education. Its finale eight years later brought the story full circle with Theo's graduation from college with a degree in psychology. Although some observers criticized the series as an unrealistic portrayal of African Americans, others lauded it as providing a role model for African American achievement and familial love and support.

*See also:* Television series.

Bill Cosby as Dr. Cliff Huxtable. *(AP/Wide World Photos)*

**Cose, Ellis Jonathan** (b. February 20, 1951, Chicago, Illinois): Journalist and cultural critic. Born the son of Raney and Jetta Cameron Cose, Ellis Cose was educated at the University of Illinois at CHICAGO and received his bachelor's degree in 1972. From 1970 to 1977, Cose worked as a reporter and columnist for the *Chicago Sun-Times*. In 1977 he accepted a two-year fellowship at the Joint Center for Political Studies in Washington, D.C., where he served as director of energy policy studies. Cose spent much of his time writing and editing essays on energy and the urban environment; he also worked as a columnist for the *Detroit Free Press*. While in Washington, D.C., Cose completed a master's degree at George Washington University in 1978.

From 1983 to 1986, Cose served as president of the Institute for Journalism Education at the University of California at Berkeley. In 1987 he accepted a fellowship at the Gannett Center for Media Studies at Columbia University. His work there led to the publication of *The Press* (1989). The book examined the internal politics and operation of the Gannett and Knight-Ridder newspaper chains and prominent family-controlled newspapers, such as *The New York Times*, *The Washington Post*, and the *Los Angeles Times*. Cose paid particular attention to the difficulties faced by black newspaper reporters and editors in their struggle to achieve recognition and status within these large institutions and to provide accurate coverage of events and attitudes within the African American community.

After becoming editorial page editor for the *New York Daily News* in 1991, Cose published *A Nation of Strangers: Prejudice, Politics, and the Populating of America* (1992). This work provided a historical overview of the role of racism in the formulation of American immigration policy. Beginning his account with the impact of the 1790 Naturalization Law, which reserved naturalization to "free white" immigrants, Cose argued that the issue of race had explicitly or implicitly influenced every attempt to reform American immigration law or practices.

In 1993, after being named a contributing editor of *Newsweek* magazine, Cose published *The Rage of a Privileged Class*. The book considered many aspects of prejudice that have affected and even infuriated successful middle-class blacks: the assumption that all blacks are criminals to be feared, the belief that blacks cannot be good managers and thus are promoted to comply with AFFIRMATIVE ACTION guidelines rather than on the basis of merit, and the insulting attitude of white clerks and receptionists who ignore or casually snub black clients and customers.

At the same time, Cose examined the resentment that exists within the black community between the impoverished underclass and those who have attained success. He also explored the issue of discrimination by blacks against other blacks based on the lightness or darkness of an individual's complexion. Although providing discussion of the grievances expressed by white men who believe they have been harmed by affirmative action, Cose expressed ambivalence about whether such programs could continue to be effective in aiding blacks to overcome prejudice in the workplace.

In his 1995 book *A Man's World: How Real Is Male Privilege—and How High Is Its Price?*, Cose tried to refute the contemporary mindset that envisioned the world as composed primarily of perpetrators and victims, of bad boys and good girls. He analyzed statistical claims that had been advanced by feminists and demonstrated that many of their conclusions were not supportable by statistical evidence. According to Cose, most men were simply struggling to get by; only certain men of a specific color, class, and rank could truly be considered to wield patriarchal power over others. *See also:* Columnists; Immigration and ethnic origins of African Americans; Print journalism.

**Costigan-Wagner bill:** Proposed antilynching legislation. The Costigan-Wagner bill was introduced into Congress in 1935, one of several similar bills in the years between WORLD WAR I and the 1940's. The powerful white southern lobby prevented passage of all of them. This bill was abandoned in 1938.
*See also:* Dyer antilynching bill; Lynching.

**Cotten, Elizabeth** (January, 1893, Chapel Hill, North Carolina—June 29, 1987, Syracuse, New York): Folksinger, songwriter, and guitarist. Elizabeth "Libba" Cotten was a strong influence on the folk-song movement and BLUES revivals of the early 1960's. Several of her songs became standards; her lilting, two-finger guitar-picking technique was also influential.

Libba Cotten was raised and lived most of her life in rural North Carolina, where she taught herself to play the guitar. Because she was left-handed, she played in an unusual backwards and upside-down manner. She wrote her most famous song, "Freight Train," which eventually became a folk classic, at the age of twelve. Cotten stopped playing the guitar when she began to support herself through work as a domestic, which she did for more than forty years. She might never have played professionally had she not moved to Washington, D.C.

There she worked as a maid for the family of ethnomusicologist Charles Seeger. She entertained and taught Seeger's three children, Pete, Peggy, and Mike. In 1958 Mike Seeger recorded Cotten for Folkways Records, sparking a performing and recording career that continued for the rest of her life. She appeared at many folk and blues festivals, inspiring younger performers to copy her warm, light guitar style. She was honored with the 1972 National Folk Association's Burl Ives Award for her contributions to American folk music. Libba Cotten won a Grammy Award for her

last album, *Elizabeth Cotten Live!* It was recorded in 1985, when she was well into her eighties.

*—Jim Baird*

*See also:* Music.

**Cotton Club:** New York City nightclub. The Cotton Club flourished in the 1920's, declined in the 1930's, and finally closed in 1940, after moving from its original HARLEM, New York, location in 1936. Owned (after 1922) and tightly controlled by bootleggers, its floor shows, called "Cotton Club Parades," were performed to capacity audiences. Although the performers, such as the bands of Duke ELLINGTON, Cab CALLOWAY, and Jimmie LUNCEFORD, were black, no African Americans were admitted as club guests. Important performers included dancer Bill ROBINSON, comedian Dusty Fletcher, and singer Ethel WATERS. Francis Ford Coppola's 1984 film, *The Cotton Club*, attempted to capture the flavor of the era as well as the important contributions of the performers to their culture.

**Council on African Affairs:** Nongovernmental group committed to ending colonialism in AFRICA. The council was founded by Paul ROBESON and Max Yergan in the late 1930's. By the mid-1940's, it was considered to be the most important organization in the United States dealing with Africa and working for liberation of African countries. The group was largely financed in its early years by Frederick V. Field, a member of the wealthy family associated with the Chicago department store bearing the family name.

In 1944 a conference of the council drafted a program for Africa's liberation and advancement at the end of WORLD WAR II. The program called for concrete help for the people of Africa, dissemination of accurate information about Africa and promotion of awareness of the condition of people there, influence by the council on government policies to promote liberation, and prevention of American loans and armaments from being used to crush freedom struggles in Africa. The council expressed disappointment at the proposals for trusteeship over territories that were made at the United Nations conference held in April and May of 1945. Specifically, those proposals did not put limits on the length of time territories would be under supervision and did not insist that the Allied Powers put territories on the path to independence or self-government.

By the mid-1940's, the FEDERAL BUREAU OF INVESTIGATION had branded the Council on African Affairs a communist organization. The council saw the Soviet Union as promoting liberation of the countries of Africa, a goal the council also supported. The council also was named on a list of subversive organizations released by Attorney General Tom Clark in 1947. A faction within the council led by Yergan came to believe that the group should declare nonpartisanship. Robeson opposed such a declaration as playing into the hands of anticommunists. Yergan then deliberately obstructed the policy committee, prompting its chairman, W. E. B. DU BOIS, to resign his position in protest. Yergan was discredited and accused of trying to keep the council's political, social, and financial affairs in his own hands. He was suspended as executive director on May 26, 1948, and was expelled from the council in September. The split in policy caused several members to stop attending meetings and six, out of a total of less than one hundred, to resign, including Adam Clayton POWELL, Jr.

The Council on African Affairs sponsored a cross-country speaking and concert tour by Robeson in September of 1949. In 1950 Robeson's passport was declared invalid on the grounds that his travel abroad would be contrary to the best interests of the United States. The council planned a concert rally in protest, but Madison Square Garden refused to rent its facilities to the group.

Robeson and the council continued in the early 1950's to support rebels in South Africa who resisted segregation and discrimination, as well as those in Kenya who were imprisoned for insisting on the return of their land to them. Several members of the council, Robeson among them, were called to testify before the House Committee on Un-American Activities. In June of 1955, the council disbanded, stating that continuing government harassment, including refusal to grant Robeson a new passport, made further work impossible.

*See also:* Africa and African American activism; Pan-Africanism.

Lena Horne and Paul Robeson reviewing plans for a Council on African Affairs rally staged at New York City's Madison Square Garden in May, 1946. *(AP/Wide World Photos)*

**Counter Intelligence Program:** Also known as COINTELPRO, government surveillance program established by the FEDERAL BUREAU OF INVESTIGATION (FBI) in 1956. The program was formally ended in 1976, following public disclosures and congressional investigations.

The first COINTELPRO effort was launched against the COMMUNIST PARTY, U.S.A. Later programs covered a variety of organizations, primarily on the political Left, including the Socialist Workers' Party (SWP), the National Lawyers Guild (NLG), the American Indian Movement (AIM), and many anti-VIETNAM WAR organizations. The SOUTHERN CHRISTIAN LEADERSHIP CONFERENCE (SCLC), the STUDENT NONVIOLENT COORDINATING COMMITTEE (SNCC), and the BLACK PANTHER PARTY (BPP) were among the many African American organizations that were targeted by COINTELPRO.

The purpose of this program, according to one U.S. Circuit Court of Appeals, was to "expose, disrupt, misdirect, discredit, or otherwise neutralize the activities" of organizations deemed subversive by the FBI "including those involved in legitimate, nonviolent activities." During the period from 1956 to 1974, the FBI kept files on the activities of approximately 500,000 Americans. It proposed 3,247 specific COINTELPRO operations during that time with 2,370 being carried out. The program included the previously established Security Index, which contained the names of people who were to be summarily arrested and detained in the event of a national emergency. Among the thousands of names on the list were those of writers such as Norman Mailer and public officials such as Democratic senator Paul Douglas of Illinois. During the 1960's, the names of Martin Luther KING, Jr., and about fifteen hundred other African Americans were included on the list.

The types of illegal activities conducted by the FBI under the program included break-ins, bugging, wiretapping, mail-tampering, character defamation, and using paid informants or undercover agents to infiltrate organizations. Sometimes these informants assumed the role of agents provocateurs, trying to instigate the engagement of individuals or organizations in illegal activities. The information gained from such operations sometimes was shared with the media or public officials who used this information for their own purposes. The FBI went to great lengths to conceal these operations. COINTELPRO documents were marked "do not file" and were not assigned an FBI sequential filing system serial number. Therefore, official FBI files did not contain any COINTELPRO documents or have any missing serial numbers.

The COINTELPRO operations were revealed to the public in the 1970's as a result of Watergate findings, congressional hearings, and information obtained under Freedom of Information Act (FOIA) requests. In 1975 members of the U.S. Congress established two bipartisan committees—the Church Committee (Senate) and the Pike Committee (House)—to investigate the intelligence agencies. Based on the findings of these committees, Attorney General Edward H. Levi issued guidelines to limit the agencies' covert activities. Under the administration of President Ronald Reagan, however, these standards were relaxed, and domestic security investigations again proliferated. Fifty-two of the FBI's fifty-nine regional offices were involved in domestic security investigations during the 1980's. In addition to maintaining surveillance on African American organizations such as the Southern Christian Leadership Conference, the FBI investigated the Committee in Solidarity with the People of El Salvador (CISPES), the sanctuary movement, the Maryknoll Sisters, the American Federation of Teachers (AFT), the United Auto Workers (UAW), and various antinuclear groups.

## Origins

Even though COINTELPRO programs did not officially begin until the 1950's, the FBI had been involved in domestic surveillance since its creation in 1909. During the 1920's, for example, the FBI kept files on approximately two hundred thousand Americans, many of whom were associated with the labor movement. In 1936 President Franklin D. Roosevelt authorized the bureau to investigate subversive organizations. Under that authority, the FBI proceeded to engage in surveillance against organizations such as the Socialist Workers' Party, Communist Party, American Civil Liberties Union (ACLU), American Friends Service Committee (AFSC), Screen Actors Guild (SAG), and NATIONAL ASSOCIATION FOR THE ADVANCEMENT OF COLORED PEOPLE (NAACP). It also conducted security investigations of many writers and artists, including prominent African Americans such as Paul ROBESON and James BALDWIN.

## "Racial Matters"

Throughout the history of domestic surveillance in the United States, the African American community has been subjected to many such operations. Much of the information gathered was retained in FBI files under the heading "Racial Matters." As early as 1919, the FBI launched domestic surveillance programs that targeted African Americans. The bureau recruited blacks as informants in various black associations, lodges, and churches. It was especially interested in individuals who called for social equality and equal rights. It infiltrated a wide range of African American organizations, from the moderate NAACP to the nationalist UNIVERSAL NEGRO IMPROVEMENT ASSOCIATION (UNIA), led by Marcus GARVEY. The most ambitious program of surveillance and disruption was waged against UNIA and Garvey. After years of effort, the FBI secured an indictment against Garvey on a charge of mail fraud, resulting in his conviction and deportation. During this period, the FBI also launched a major investigation of the black press. It conducted surveillance of black writers and editors such as Chandler OWEN, A. Philip RANDOLPH, and W. E. B. DU BOIS.

Powerful FBI director J. Edgar Hoover became particularly concerned with black activism in the 1930's, especially any connections between African Americans and the Communist Party. The party's active role in the legal defense of the SCOTTSBORO Nine (or the "Scottsboro boys"), nine black Alabama teenagers sentenced to death for the alleged rape of two white women, led Hoover to increase surveillance of the black community. By the early 1940's, Hoover was preparing weekly reports for government officials on trends within the black community. He equated advocacy of equal rights with radicalism, so civil rights organizations were regularly monitored.

In 1942 the FBI launched a nationwide investigation of "foreign-inspired" agitation in "colored" communities. In addition to recruiting paid informants, tapping telephones, and bugging offices, the bureau specifically targeted black-owned newspapers. Among the groups investigated were the National Negro Congress, the NAACP, the Southern Conference for Human Welfare, the organizers planning a protest march on Washington (1941-1943), the Woodlawn AFRICAN METHODIST EPISCOPAL CHURCH of Chicago, and the National Urban League. When the Truman-appointed President's Committee on Civil Rights summoned Hoover to testify before it in 1947, Hoover attempted to intimidate the committee by gathering information from FBI files on most of the committee members.

As the CIVIL RIGHTS movement developed in the South during the 1950's, the FBI tried to remain on the sidelines. It did not conduct preliminary investigations of alleged civil rights violations unless specifically directed to by the attorney general. Nevertheless, the bureau's interest in monitoring the black community and conducting domestic surveillance operations continued. By the 1960's, this interest would intensify into harassment of civil right activists and initiation of official COINTELPRO operations.

### The FBI and Martin Luther King, Jr

Hoover's hostility toward the Civil Rights movement became focused on Martin Luther King, Jr., after the MARCH ON WASHINGTON in August of 1963. King had criticized the FBI for not doing more to protect the CIVIL RIGHTS of black citizens. FBI internal memorandums began labeling King as "the most dangerous and effective Negro leader in the country." According to a memo dated February of 1962, Hoover stated that "King is no good." The FBI launched a full-scale campaign to discredit King. It bugged the offices of King's organization, the Southern Christian Leadership Conference; investigated his bank and charge accounts; installed electronic surveillance devices in King's Atlanta apartment; sent a forged letter in King's name to SCLC contributors warning them that the IRS was about to investigate the organization; fostered discord between King and NAACP director Roy Wilkins; and recruited members of the SCLC staff to serve as informants.

Dozens of counterintelligence operations were carried out against King. The political and personal information obtained was then disseminated to the White House, members of Congress, the media, other government and public organizations, and even King's wife, Coretta Scott King. In the private sector, the information was used to try to discredit King with foundations, university administrators, and labor leaders. After King received the Nobel Peace Prize in 1964, the FBI flooded the White House, government agencies, and U.S. embassies across Europe with negative information about King's character. Later that year,

Hoover labeled King "the most notorious liar in the country."

The outrageous culmination of the campaign against King was a smear campaign and a note to King recommending that he commit suicide. The FBI prepared a tape of King's alleged adultery. It sent edited copies of the tape to King along with the suicide note. The FBI also offered edited transcripts to a variety of newspapers and other media, to civil rights leaders, and to public officials. Hoover's ultimate goal was to replace King with a civil rights leader whose views were more acceptable to the FBI.

While the counterintelligence campaign against King received the most attention during this time, the FBI conducted similar operations against many other individuals who were active in the Civil Rights movement. In 1967 the FBI instituted an officially designated COINTELPRO program directed at the African American community.

### COINTELPRO-BLACKPRO

Following several years of major urban riots in ghetto areas, and with black nationalist groups growing in strength, the federal government instituted a new two-track surveillance system to gather information within the African American community. The FBI set up a new COINTELPRO that targeted both black nationalist leaders and civil rights leaders under a "black hate group" label. Simultaneously, the Justice Department instituted a series of community surveillance programs directed at the broader African American community.

The community surveillance program started in 1966, when the Justice Department assigned a few law students to organize government data, including some FBI material, about developments in the black community. By late 1967, Attorney General Ramsey Clark authorized a much broader program and established an Interdivisional Intelligence Unit

(IDIU) to gather a wider spectrum of such information. The IDIU relied on FBI intelligence reports to compile a master index, on a city-by-city basis, of individuals and organizations active in African American communities. The FBI was ordered to use maximum available resources to collect information, including developing or expanding the use of informants in black organizations.

In conjunction with the community surveillance program, the FBI started the TOPLEV (Top Level) Informant Program, later known as BLACKPRO. The purpose of this program was to infiltrate militant black organizations and to identify community activists who might become leaders and/or "agitators." The FBI placed informants not only within black nationalist groups but also in more conventional civil rights organizations such as the Southern Christian Leadership Conference and the Poor People's Campaign of 1968.

In 1967 the FBI set up an even more pervasive program of informants known as the "Ghetto Listening Post" or the "Ghetto Informant Program." The bureau recruited more than three thousand individuals—employees and owners of taverns, liquor stores, drugstores, barbershops, pawnshops, and other businesses as well as janitors, veterans, taxi drivers, salespersons, and bill collectors—to pass on information to local FBI agents. This information then was processed into reports at a rate of more than thirty-five hundred per month. On average, the bureau had between five and ten thousand active cases on racial matters during this period.

This information was used for many purposes, including selecting groups and individuals as targets for operations under the COINTELPRO-Black Hate Group/Black Nationalist program. The most prominent groups targeted were the NATION OF ISLAM, the Student Nonviolent Coordinating Committee, the Revolutionary Action Movement

(RAM), and the Black Panther Party. The full scope of the program, however, was much broader. It included hundreds of organizations, few of which posed any danger and many of which did not actually support black nationalist goals.

The program's objectives, in the words of the directive that established it, were "to expose, disrupt, misdirect, discredit, or otherwise neutralize the activities of black nationalist, hate-type organizations and groupings, their leadership, spokesmen, membership, and supporters." The operational goals included preventing groups from forming coalitions, attracting support, gaining respectability, or developing charismatic leaders.

The FBI planned and carried out numerous operations to meet these goals. For example, it disrupted RAM by arranging for the Philadelphia police to arrest RAM members on every conceivable minor charge until they could no longer make bail. In a technique known as a "bad-jacket" or "snitch-jacket," false information was disseminated about SNCC leader Stokely CARMICHAEL. The bureau tried to undermine his leadership in the black community by circulating false information that he was a CIA agent. The bureau also conducted an operation to prevent the Republic of New Africa (RNA) from purchasing land in Mississippi.

### The FBI and the Black Panthers

The most systematic illegal activities were carried out against the Black Panther Party (BPP), which by 1968 was perceived by Hoover as the "the greatest threat to the internal security of the country."

Hoover decided that the Panthers had to be destroyed. Consequently, the campaign against the BPP was unique in its disregard for legal rights and even human life. By 1969 all forty-two chapters of the BPP were under surveillance. The bureau tried to create distrust both among members of the BPP and between it and other organizations. This activity was carried on even though FBI officials acknowledged that it could lead to injuries or death.

In OAKLAND, CALIFORNIA, the FBI bugged BPP members' homes and offices and tried to break up Panthers' marriages with letters to Panthers' wives. Bureau operatives also carried out dozens of other operations, including the disruption of the Panthers' breakfast-for-children program and harassment of Panther attorney Charles Garry. In Chicago, the FBI office used counterfeit letters, false information, and other tactics to prevent an alliance between the BPP and the Blackstone Rangers, a Chicago street gang. The most notorious operation in Chicago concluded in the shooting of BPP leader Fred HAMPTON by Chicago police. After the killing, the FBI withheld information from the grand jury about its role in the killing. Full information about the FBI's role did not become available until nearly a decade later.

Fred Hampton, perhaps the Counter Intelligence Program's most famous victim, speaking to a college group in the late 1960's. (© Roy Lewis Archives)

Similar operations were directed against the BPP around the country until the party was effectively destroyed as an organization.

As information about these COINTELPRO operations became public, criticism grew. The National Conference of Black Lawyers and other groups petitioned the United Nations, charging the FBI with human rights violations. Amnesty International found that the FBI had interfered with the judicial process through selective enforcement of the law. Perhaps the final report of the Senate's Church Committee best summarizes the character of the COINTELPRO programs:

> The chief investigative branch of the Federal Government, which was charged by law with investigating crimes and preventing criminal conduct, itself engaged in lawless tactics and responded to deep-seated social problems by fomenting violence and unrest.

—*Carl Swidorski*

Suggested Readings:

Blackstock, Nelson. *COINTELPRO: The FBI's Secret War on Political Freedom*. New York: Vintage, 1975.

Churchill, Ward, and Jim Vander Wall. *The COINTELPRO Papers: Documents from the FBI's Secret Wars Against Domestic Dissent*. Boston: South End Press, 1990.

Donner, Frank J. *The Age of Surveillance: The Aims and Methods of America's Political Intelligence System*. New York: Alfred A. Knopf, 1980.

Garrow, David J. *The FBI and Martin Luther King, Jr.: From "SOLO" to Memphis*. New York: W. W. Norton, 1981.

Mitgang, Herbert. *Dangerous Dossiers: Exposing the Secret War Against America's Greatest Authors*. New York: Donald I. Fine, 1988.

O'Reilly, Kenneth. *Racial Matters: The FBI's Secret File on Black America, 1960-1972*. New York: Free Press, 1989.

Theoharis, Athan. *The Boss: J. Edgar Hoover and the Great American Inquisition*. Philadelphia: Temple University Press, 1988.

Washburn, Patrick S. *A Question of Sedition: The Federal Government's Investigation of the Black Press During World War II*. New York: Oxford University Press, 1986.

Welch, Neil J., and David W. Marston. *Inside Hoover's FBI*. Garden City, N.Y.: Doubleday, 1984.

**Cowboys:** Thousands of black cowboys worked in the Great Plains and farther west in the mid- to late nineteenth century. More than five thousand African American cowboys played significant roles in developing the cattle industry. They became cowboys, despite the danger and hardship of the work, because their salaries could equal those of whites and because there was relatively little prejudice on a job that required teamwork to control large herds of cattle.

One of the most famous cowboys was Nat LOVE, born a slave in TENNESSEE in 1854. He was hired as a cowpuncher to drive cows from TEXAS to the railroad in Dodge City, KANSAS. In 1876 he was nicknamed "Deadwood Dick" after winning several roping and shooting

During his rodeo days, Bill Pickett invented the technique of "bulldogging": twisting a steer's head by its horns and pulling it to the ground. *(Arkent Archive)*

contests in Deadwood, SOUTH DAKOTA. He became known as the champion roper of the western cattle country.

During the 1920's and 1930's, Charlie Glass was top foreman of the Lazy Y Cross Ranch in western COLORADO and eastern UTAH. He became involved in the cattlemen-sheepmen wars and killed a Basque shepherd in 1921. Acquitted of the murder charge, he later died under peculiar circumstances.

Rodeo, a Spanish word meaning "roundup," began when cowboys, meeting on cattle drives, began to challenge each other to competitions. They participated in contests in taming horses, roping, and riding, often betting their earnings on the outcome. In 1888 Prescott, ARIZONA, held the first

Riders in the twenty-third annual Black Cowboys Parade in Oakland, California, in October, 1997. *(AP/Wide World Photos)*

649

commercial rodeo, offering prize money and charging admission. Bill PICKETT, the first black rodeo star, invented "bulldogging," an event in which a cowboy wrestles a steer to the ground. To accomplish this feat, Pickett imitated the cattle dogs' technique of biting the steer on the lip to control the steer. HOUSTON, TEXAS, hosts a yearly Bill Pickett Invitational Rodeo in honor of the man who became the first African American admitted to the National Cowboy Hall of Fame.

Many cities, such as Houston and DALLAS, hold annual rodeos, hoping to attract stars such as Myrtis Dightman and Charlie Sampson, two of the nation's top-rated bull riders. In 1982 Sampson became the first black world champion, riding in 148 rodeos and earning $91,402.

*See also:* Frontier society; Frontier marshals and sheriffs; Frontier wars.

**Cox, Ida** (Ida Prather; February 25, 1896, Toccoa, Georgia—November 10, 1967, Knoxville, Tennessee): BLUES singer. Cox sang in the AFRICAN METHODIST EPISCOPAL CHURCH before running away from home at age fourteen to perform as a "pickaninny" in a MINSTREL show. Within a year she was singing "torch songs" and blues. By 1922 Cox was an established soloist for the THEATRE OWNERS BOOKING ASSOCIATION (TOBA), the major group responsible for booking black performers on the VAUDEVILLE circuit.

By the mid-1920's, Cox was at the peak of her career, making some of her best recordings and continuing her touring engagements. She made more than seventy records for Paramount during the 1920's, while recording for other companies under the pseudonyms Julia Powers, Velma Bradley, and Kate Lewis. In 1929 TOBA chose her *Raisin' Cain Revue* to open at the APOLLO THEATER in HARLEM.

With a singing voice that lacked the vibrato of other famous blues singers, Cox could con-

Ida Cox during the mid-1930's. *(Archive Photos/Frank Driggs Collection)*

vey sadness and mourning or sauciness and daring to her audiences through her emotional intensity and her unusual rhythm patterns. Her songs ranged from traditional blues to the newer, more arrogant style popular in big-city vaudeville. She carved a niche for herself with somber blues songs, including "Death Letter Blues," "Black Crepe Blues," "Coffin Blues," and "Graveyard Bound Blues."

Although the GREAT DEPRESSION and shifting musical tastes of the 1930's caused a decline in the popularity of the blues and of vaudeville shows, Cox continued to tour the South and Midwest. In 1939 she was spotlighted in a Carnegie Hall concert managed by John Hammond, a scout for Columbia records.

As a young performer, Cox married a trumpeter who died in WORLD WAR I. She later married Eugene Williams, with whom she had a daughter. Her third husband, Jesse Crump, played piano for her and later served as her agent. She and Crump separated in the 1930's. After a stroke in 1944, Cox retired to Knoxville, Tennessee, and became active in her church. At the urging of Hammond, she came out of retirement in 1961 and made several recordings with such musicians as Coleman HAWKINS and Roy ELDRIDGE.

**Craft, Ellen, and William Craft** (Ellen Smith Craft: Clinton, Georgia, 1826—Charleston, South Carolina, 1891; William Craft: Georgia, 1824—Charleston, South Carolina, 1900): SLAVE RUNAWAYS noted for their ingenious and daring escape.

Ellen Craft, the enslaved daughter of a GEORGIA plantation owner, grew up in Milledgeville, Georgia, where she had been sold because of her light skin and resemblance to her owner. She became a seamstress. She also fell in love with a young enslaved carpenter, William Craft. They married, and, because they did not want their children born in SLAVERY, they also decided to escape to PHILADELPHIA. As skilled, and therefore somewhat privileged, slaves, they had some sense of geography, money earned by hiring themselves out, and knowledge of white southerners' behavior. Still, they could not read or write, Philadelphia was hundreds of miles away, their masters would certainly come after valuable skilled slaves, and blacks not accompanied by whites needed proof of their freedom or master's approval to be traveling alone.

With her light skin, Ellen pretended to be a young white man traveling with his slave. Since she could not read or write and had no facial hair, she claimed to suffer from severe rheumatism, and she kept her right hand in a sling and face wrapped in a poultice. During the trip, she talked freely with other passengers. In a disguised voice she berated abolitionists and lazy slaves. She was so convincing that a fellow traveler vouched for them when she could not produce proof that she owned William. After arriving safely in Philadelphia, they went to BOSTON to give speeches for the ABOLITIONIST MOVEMENT concerning their escape. When they learned that their masters were searching for them, they fled the country for England. After the CIVIL WAR, they returned to Georgia, where they started an industrial arts school.

—*Rita Smith-Wade-El*

**Creole:** Term used to designate different groups of people at different moments in history. The French word *créole* was adapted from the Spanish *criollo*, a widely used term for native peoples of the tropics in the WEST INDIES or Central or South America.

From the sixteenth to eighteenth centuries, "Creole" referred to children born in the Americas of Spanish, and then French, parents. In some areas the term then expanded to include any inhabitants of LOUISIANA or the Caribbean who were not native to the region, including people of both European and African descent. In Louisiana in the 1700's, "Creole" came to mean people of mixed race

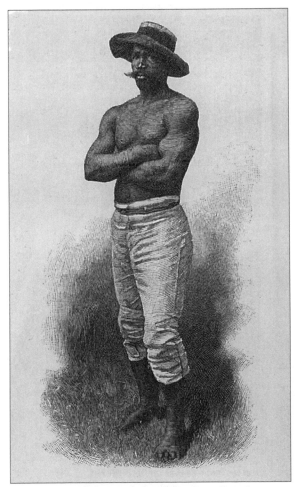

Nineteenth-century engraving of a Creole man. *(James L. Shaffer)*

descended from European colonists and slaves with whom they had sexual relations.

In the 1800's, after the United States purchased the Louisiana Territory, European-descended residents of Louisiana began calling themselves Creoles in order to distinguish themselves from the English-descended Americans moving into the area. They even passed a law that only they could be called Creole—legally excluding not only slaves but also the free blacks who had previously generally been included within the category.

After the CIVIL WAR, Louisiana people of mixed European (primarily French) and African ancestry—both upper-class free blacks and former slaves—once again began referring to themselves as Creoles, sometimes as Creole Negroes or "Creoles of color." "Creole" also came to be used to describe styles of music and cooking that blend European and African traditions.

*See also:* Central America.

**Crichlow, Ernest** (b. 1914, New York, New York): Painter and illustrator. Crichlow studied at New York University and worked as an artist for the Works Progress Administration in the 1930's. His early paintings portray the joys and fears of childhood, adolescence, and motherhood. Crichlow's realistic illustrations of African American youngsters for such children's books as Jerrold and Lorraine Beim's *Two Is a Team* (1945) helped establish African American youth as positive, nonstereotyped characters in general children's literature.
*See also:* Children's literature; Painters and illustrators; Visual arts.

**Crim, Alonzo** (October 1, 1928, Chicago, Illinois—May 3, 2000, Atlanta, Georgia): Educator and educational administrator. After service in the Navy at the end of WORLD WAR II, Crim attended Roosevelt College in CHICAGO,

graduating in 1950. He did postgraduate work at Chicago Teachers College. After nine years as a teacher in the Chicago public schools, Crim moved into administration, serving as a principal in elementary and high schools and in other senior positions. He also continued his own education, acquiring a master's degree from the University of Chicago and a doctorate in education from Harvard University.

In 1970 Crim became head of the Compton Unified School District in Southern CALIFORNIA. He won recognition for his ability to deal effectively with a diverse student population in a school system undergoing racial and ethnic change. In 1973 he left Compton for ATLANTA, GEORGIA, where he became the first African American superintendent of the city's public schools. Crim went to Atlanta as part of a controversial compromise between local black leaders and the public school system. As part of the agreement, demands for large-scale BUSING as a means to achieve integration were dropped in return for the appointment of a

Alonzo Crim in 1983. *(AP/Wide World Photos)*

black superintendent and a thorough integration of the system's faculty and administrative structure. More than half of the city's schools were left all-black, and less than 3 percent of students were bused for integration purposes.

The NATIONAL ASSOCIATION FOR THE ADVANCEMENT OF COLORED PEOPLE (NAACP) condemned the agreement as insufficient, but local African American leaders believed that black administrative leadership would serve the community's interests better than would busing on a massive scale. It fell to Crim to implement the agreement, and he did so efficiently. Although the compromise did not prevent WHITE FLIGHT from making the school system's pupil population overwhelmingly African American, the transition from white to black control was relatively smooth. Among Crim's later achievements was the reorganization of the school system's structure through the introduction of middle schools. He also proved adept at building bridges to Atlanta's business leaders during his fifteen years as superintendent.

Crim received many awards as an educator and as a leader in human relations, and his achievements were recognized with a number of honorary degrees. He retired from his superintendent position in 1988 to take a position as professor of educational administration at Georgia State University. In May, 2000, Crim died at the age of seventy-one from injuries suffered in an automobile accident.

See also: Education; Segregation and integration.

**Crime and the criminal justice system:** The relationships among African American communities, crime, and the criminal justice system are complex. Among the aspects of these relationships are blacks as perpetrators of crime, blacks as victims of crime, the criminal justice system's treatment of blacks, and the number of blacks who work in the justice system.

In raw numbers, whites commit many more violent and nonviolent crimes than blacks do each year in the United States. However, statistically, blacks commit a higher proportion of crimes (at least the types of crimes that are most carefully reported and tracked) in relation to the size of the African American population. (On the other hand, there are also crimes that are disproportionately committed by whites.)

Among African Americans there is considerable fear of crime and frustration with the justice system's inability to keep it under control. These feelings led in the 1980's and 1990's to increasingly conservative attitudes among blacks toward the criminal justice system's treatment of criminals; for example, increasing numbers of African Americans were in favor of the death penalty and mandatory sentencing of violent repeat offenders.

On the other hand, many blacks also maintained attitudes ranging from skepticism to distrust toward the criminal justice system as being biased against blacks, and ample statistical evidence supports charges of racial bias or "differential justice." One part of the reason that a disproportionate number of blacks are arrested is that many police officers stop blacks for questioning more often than they stop whites. Moreover, once under the supervision of the justice system, blacks tend to receive harsher treatment than whites convicted of similar crimes.

One part of the picture that is often overlooked is the fact that blacks are more likely than whites to be the victims of crime—both violent crime and property crime—as most crimes by blacks are perpetrated against other blacks.

### Blacks as Crime Victims
Blacks are much more likely than whites to be victimized by crime, especially violent crimes such as HOMICIDE, robbery, and aggravated assault. A 1997 report by the U.S. Bureau of

Justice Statistics found that black households are nearly three times more likely than white ones to fear crime in their neighborhoods. In many black neighborhoods, especially in the central areas of large cities, the fear is justified. The FEDERAL BUREAU OF INVESTIGATION (FBI), in its annual Uniform Crime Reports (UCR), considers the following as violent crimes: robbery, aggravated assault, forcible rape, murder, and nonnegligent manslaughter. For all

### Violent Crime Victimizations per 1,000 Persons

| Year | White | Black |
|------|-------|-------|
| 1973 | 20.0 | 37.3 |
| 1974 | 20.9 | 37.3 |
| 1975 | 19.1 | 36.7 |
| 1976 | 18.8 | 38.2 |
| 1977 | 19.4 | 34.4 |
| 1978 | 18.8 | 33.2 |
| 1979 | 19.6 | 33.2 |
| 1980 | 18.7 | 34.0 |
| 1981 | 19.7 | 40.4 |
| 1982 | 19.0 | 36.9 |
| 1983 | 16.3 | 33.1 |
| 1984 | 17.1 | 32.7 |
| 1985 | 15.6 | 28.9 |
| 1986 | 15.6 | 25.2 |
| 1987 | 15.0 | 33.8 |
| 1988 | 16.0 | 31.4 |
| 1989 | 16.1 | 29.5 |
| 1990 | 15.4 | 31.8 |
| 1991 | 16.2 | 31.3 |
| 1992 | 16.9 | 33.0 |
| 1993 | 17.8 | 34.3 |
| 1994 | 17.1 | 33.5 |
| 1995 | 13.5 | 26.4 |
| 1996 | 13.3 | 26.3 |
| 1997 | 12.9 | 20.7 |
| 1998 | 11.6 | 19.2 |

Source: U.S. Bureau of Justice Statistics.
Note: Data are for "serious violent crime" victimization, which includes homicide, rape, robbery, and aggravated assault. Data are for persons age 12 and older. Rape, robbery, and assault data are from the National Crime Victimization Survey (NCVS); homicide data are collected by the FBI's Uniform Crime Reports (UCR) from reports from law enforcement agencies. Homicide rates for 1998 are estimated, based on 1998 preliminary data.

these crimes except rape, blacks were more likely than whites to be victims in the 1990's. The victimization rates for rape were not significantly different between African Americans and whites.

For most Americans the chances of being the victim of a serious crime diminished in the 1990's, but this was not the case for black urban residents. In 1997, for example, blacks were the victims of robbery at a rate about double that of whites. The most frequent victims of serious violent crimes are unemployed people, young people, central city residents, less-educated persons, and poor people. African Americans are statistically overrepresented in these categories.

POVERTY is strongly correlated with crime victimization. Members of households with annual incomes less than $15,000 are robbed, raped, beaten, and killed more often than members of higher-income households. Blacks are disproportionately poor; as many as one-third of all African American households live below the official poverty line (compared with one-tenth of white Americans). Poor persons do not have the political, social, and economic resources that their middle-class suburban counterparts have to combat crime. Many more black Americans than white Americans live in neighborhoods that have abandoned buildings, liquor stores, unlit and unsupervised parks, and other magnets of criminal activity.

Blacks represent about 13 percent of the population of the United States; however, they represented 49 percent of the country's murder victims in 1997. Blacks were seven times more likely than whites to be murdered. The difference for young men was even greater: A young black man was eleven times more likely to be murdered than a young white man. When blacks are murdered, they are most often murdered by blacks. From 1976 to 1997, 94 percent of black victims were killed by blacks; 85 percent of white victims were killed by whites.

Black youth, especially young men, experience violent crime at rates significantly higher than the rates for other age or racial groups. The National Crime Victimization Survey (NCVS) collects data on nonfatal violent crimes against persons age twelve or older, both reported and not reported to the police.

While black men between the ages of sixteen and twenty-four represent roughly 1 percent of the population age twelve or older, they experience about 5 percent of all violent victimizations. African American youths are more likely than white youths to be victims of crimes involving weapons, especially guns. When young black men, sixteen to twenty-four, are victimized, they are 1.5 times as likely as white men to be victimized by an armed assailant. When black male teenagers, sixteen to nineteen, are victimized, they are four times more likely than teenage whites to be victimized by someone with a handgun.

African American households are also more likely than white households to be victims of property crimes. Black households have 50 percent higher rates of household burglary than do white households. In addition, black households experienced motor vehicle theft at rates twice that of whites.

These statistics help explain why African Americans consistently report greater levels of fear of crime and criminals than do whites and members of other racial groups. A survey conducted by the Joint Center for Political and Economic Studies found that African

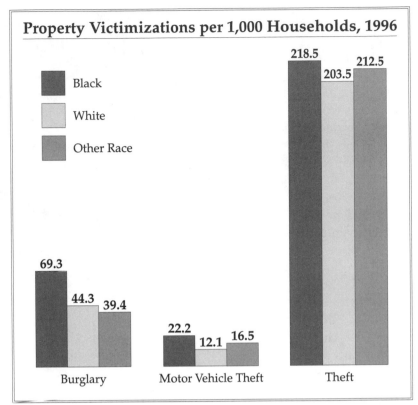

Source: U.S. Bureau of Justice Statistics, *Criminal Victimization 1996*, 1997.
Note: Figures represent crime reports by victims.

Americans are more likely than the general public (26 percent versus 16 percent) to say that they or someone close to them was a recent victim of violent crime. Fifty-two percent of blacks, compared with 31 percent of members of other races, fear walking alone even when they are within three blocks of their home.

The anger and frustration created by criminal victimization is reflected in increasingly conservative attitudes among blacks regarding crime and punishment. For example, by the late 1990's, most African Americans favored life prison terms for three-time violent offenders. Changing attitudes concerning capital punishment also reflect this frustration. In 1974 about 40 percent of blacks favored capital punishment. Many blacks opposed it in part because they believed that white JUDGES and juries would not impose it fairly;

indeed, a disproportionate number of death row inmates are black. However, by 1996, a poll conducted by the National Opinion Research Center at the University of Chicago found that 57 percent of the blacks surveyed supported the death penalty.

## Blacks as Criminals

There are criminals in every racial group. Whites, for example, are more likely than blacks to be serial murderers, domestic terrorists, violent vigilantes, professional robbers, drunk drivers, and producers and purchasers of child pornography. Whites are also involved more often than blacks in corporate crimes, computer crimes, insider trading, violation of civil rights, sex offenses other than rape and prostitution, and environmental crime. Despite the heavy involvement of whites in these types of crime, many Americans associate criminal behavior with blacks. There are a number of reasons for this situation.

One is simply historic patterns of racial stereotyping in the United States; the fact that crimes and criminal trials involving African Americans tend to be well publicized in the media is both an effect and a further cause of this stereotyping. Another is that police are more likely to stop and question or search people in low-income areas heavily populated by blacks; blacks are more often viewed by LAW ENFORCEMENT as suspicious and are therefore more likely to be detained. An overriding issue is the fact that American society tends to define "real crime" as street crime, particularly violent crime, and blacks are disproportionately arrested and convicted of violent

Acclaimed as an exceptionally realistic depiction of judicial procedures, the 1962 film *To Kill a Mockingbird* is about a white lawyer (Gregory Peck, front left) assigned to defend a black man (Brock Peters, front right) falsely accused of rape in a southern town during the 1930's. *(Museum of Modern Art, Film Stills Archive)*

crime. Violent crime receives far more media attention than nonviolent crime in television and newspaper coverage, and fictionalized violent crime in films and television frequently portrays blacks as criminals.

In 1997 the UCR reported 10,516,707 arrests in the United States. Whites made up 67.1 percent of the arrestees and blacks 30.4 percent. Other races accounted for the remainder. The percentage of African American arrests was significantly higher than the percentage of the U.S. population that is African American. In other words, blacks were overrepresented in all arrest categories except for driving under the influence and violation of liquor laws. It should be noted that most of the criminal categories in which whites dominate and blacks are underrepresented are not reported in the UCR.

About 56 percent of the murder suspects arrested in 1997 were African Americans. (Most of their victims were also black.) Blacks represented 40.1 percent of the arrests for violent crimes and 32.4 percent of the arrests for property crimes. African Americans accounted for roughly 40 percent of all persons arrested for automobile theft and 30 percent of the burglary arrestees in 1997. Additionally, blacks were overrepresented as arrestees for forcible rape (39.7 percent of all arrests), aggravated assault (36.6 percent), larceny-theft (32.4 percent), and arson (24.9 percent). Blacks were also overrepresented as arrestees for drug abuse violations (36.8 percent of all arrests), prostitution and commercial vice (40.4 percent), gambling (67.1 percent), disorderly conduct (35.9 percent), vandalism (24.7 percent), and suspicion of illegal activity (33.9 percent).

### Criminal Justice System

Statistically, blacks are overrepresented as prison and jail inmates and underrepresented as attorneys, judges, police chiefs, and prison and jail officials. In 1999 about 1.2 million Americans were in federal and state prisons and almost another 600,000 in the nation's jails. Black men, representing about 6 percent of the U.S. population, represent just over 50 percent of the country's incarcerated population. Indeed, African American men are seven

times more likely to be incarcerated than white men.

In 1998 the U.S. Department of Justice published a special report entitled *Lifetime Likelihood of Going to State or Federal Prison*. Using standard demographic life-table techniques—which assume that recent incarceration rates remain unchanged—the report estimated that white men in the United States have a one in twenty-three chance of going to prison, whereas black men have a greater than one in four chance of serving time in prison. In other words, just over 4 percent of white men will enter prison at some time but more than 28 percent of black men will be incarcerated at some time. There are more black men in federal and state prisons than in all American colleges and universities. Blacks, Hispanics, Asians, and Native Americans collectively represent two-thirds of all incarcerated Americans, even though white Americans constitute about 75 percent of the population.

The Sentencing Project, a group of activists and researchers who examine the characteristics of the prison population searching for trends, released a report in 1990. It stated that one in four young black men was in prison, in

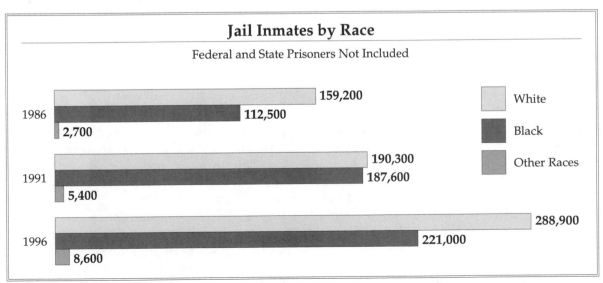

**Jail Inmates by Race**

Federal and State Prisoners Not Included

1986
White 159,200
Black 112,500
Other Races 2,700

1991
White 190,300
Black 187,600
Other Races 5,400

1996
White 288,900
Black 221,000
Other Races 8,600

*Source:* U.S. Bureau of Justice Statistics.
*Note:* Figures rounded to nearest hundred.

jail, or on parole or probation. This statistic shocked the nation. Conservatives argued that this appalling statistic was the result of too much welfare, too many single-parent households, the proliferation of gangs and crack, role-modeling by deviant and criminalistic adults, and a general dearth of values. Liberals countered that blacks were victimized by institutional racism, systemic economic discrimination, and a criminal justice system that treats them more severely than other Americans. In 1995 and 1999 the Sentencing Project released new reports which claimed that on any given day, one in three black men in their twenties was under the control of the criminal justice system.

Not all these persons were incarcerated. At the beginning of 1997 just over a third of probationers (765,700) and nearly half of parolees (297,000) nationwide were black. Nonetheless, the report that so many young black men, and increasing numbers of black women, were being supervised by the criminal justice system in one way or another led to a national debate.

While liberals and conservatives debated why so many blacks were being arrested, the Sentencing Project's second major conclusion was being ignored. The project reported that the increase in black men being arrested was not because more black men were engaging in violent crimes—the violent crime rate, though high, had stabilized. Instead, the Sentencing Project found, black men are going to jail more because of a significant increase in arrests for nonviolent drug offenses, especially arrests involving crack.

The Sentencing Project study claimed that blacks are arrested for drug offenses markedly out of proportion to black drug use. While blacks accounted for about 13 percent of drug users, the study said, they accounted for 35 percent of arrests for drug possession, 55 percent of convictions, and 74 percent of prison sentences. Federal sentencing guidelines impose a five-year minimum sentence if a defendant is convicted of selling five grams of crack; the sale of an equal amount of powder cocaine receives a one-year sentence. Crack defendants are often black, whereas powder cocaine defendants tend to be white. Crack users are more likely than powder cocaine users to be arrested, found guilty, denied probation, incarcerated, and denied parole. This situation explains some of the racial imbalance in the nation's prisons.

*Black Law Enforcement Personnel*
There was some progress in the hiring of African American police officers in the 1980's and 1990's. The U.S. Department of Justice reported that as of June, 1993, blacks accounted for about 11.3 percent of all sworn officers, as compared with 10.5 percent in 1990 and only 9.3 percent in 1987. Most of these officers are in entry-level positions rather than supervisory positions. Moreover, many small towns and suburban areas continued to have all-white police departments and prosecutorial and judicial staffs. On the other hand, blacks have served as police chiefs in a number of large cities, including New York, Los Angeles, Chicago, Houston, Miami, Detroit, and Atlanta. In 1996 blacks constituted 2 percent of judges, 4 percent of lawyers, 11 percent of police detectives, and 28 percent of prison officers in the United States.

The typical involvement of an African American in the system follows a tragically predictable pattern. A young black man is arrested in a mostly black area by a police officer for committing a crime, most likely a nonviolent drug offense. He is represented by a public defender who does not know him, and prosecuted by a white deputy prosecutor, who argues before a white judge. He is sentenced to a facility where all the administrators and most of the guards are white. He is incarcerated with a population that is mostly black and brown.

## Racial Disparities

Many law-abiding blacks see themselves caught between violent young criminals and a criminal justice system that regularly deals more harshly with blacks than whites. As noted earlier, African Americans are arrested more often than white Americans for most violent crimes. Most researchers agree that this is partly in response to higher crime rates. In other words, blacks do commit more violent crimes and are justifiably arrested for committing those crimes. However, violent criminals do not account for the bulk of the incarcerated black population: Most were convicted of nonviolent felonies relating to drug possession. Some researchers and community activists contend that racially biased policies contribute to the high arrest and punishment rates of blacks for such crimes.

Racial disparity, sometimes called differential justice, in the criminal justice system is reflected in a variety of ways, ranging from the probability that an individual will be stopped by police officers to the extremely serious issue of implementation of the death penalty.

Seventy-two percent of drivers pulled over for routine traffic stops in the mid-1990's were black, although African American motorists represented barely a fraction of that number, according to statistics from the U.S. Justice Department and the U.S. House Judiciary Committee. These black motorists are often the victims of "racial profiling," which occurs when police officers, without probable cause, stop and interrogate blacks and Hispanics because they fit a so-called criminal profile. The MARYLAND State Police were suspected of racial profiling in the late 1990's and were ordered by a

In 1999 racial "profiling" by police became a controversial issue. Here, two young African Americans who were stopped by New York State police and shot show their scars at a September, 1999, news conference called to focus public attention on profiling. *(AP/Wide World Photos)*

court to examine their records of highway stops. Their own records showed that 73 percent of the drivers who were stopped and searched on Interstate 95 between Baltimore and the Delaware state line were black. The American Civil Liberties Union (ACLU) conducted a study that estimated that only 14 percent of the drivers on that section of highway were African Americans.

In FLORIDA the *Orlando Sentinel* studied more than three thousand traffic stops on the Florida Turnpike between January, 1996, and April, 1997. The newspaper claimed that black drivers on the turnpike were 6.5 times more likely to be stopped and searched than were white drivers. By the late 1990's lawsuits were pending in RHODE ISLAND, Maryland, ILLINOIS, and NEW JERSEY by black motorists who claimed that they were stopped by police because of their race. Representative John Conyers, Jr., a Democrat from Michigan, sponsored a bill whose aim was to discourage racial profiling as the primary reason for police making traffic stops and searching vehicles. Conyers, an African American, said that "very few of us have been stopped by police and not

King Downing of the People's Organization for Progress at a July, 1999, news conference, where his organization of one of several civil rights groups denounced the racial profiling practices of New Jersey state police. *(AP/Wide World Photos)*

believed that the purpose was simple racial harassment."

Sociologists have demonstrated that police, irrespective of their race, deal with black youths more harshly than with white youths. A 1991 study reported by the U.S. Sentencing Commission reported that blacks and Hispanics are more likely than whites to receive mandatory minimum sentences in federal courts. The commission claimed that whites have their cases plea bargained more often and thereby receive lighter sentences than do blacks. A variety of statistics have indicated that blacks are accused of crimes, arrested, denied bail (or given higher bail), forced to rely on public defenders, prosecuted, convicted, and denied early parole more than whites. They are also detained in jail longer before trial and given harsher penalties than whites.

Blacks have a greater likelihood of being on death row and of being executed than do whites. In 1997, for example, seventeen states executed seventy-four prisoners. Those executed were all men: forty-five whites, twenty-seven blacks, one Asian, and one American Indian. Blacks therefore represented 36.5 percent of those executed even though they make up 13 percent of the population. At the beginning of 1998, thirty-four states and the federal prison system held 3,335 men and 44 women on death row. There were 1,876 whites, 1,406 blacks, 28 American Indians, 17 Asians, and 8 people of other races awaiting execution. African Americans, then, represented 42.2 percent of those on death row. In Georgia in the 1990's, all forty-six state prosecutors who have the responsibility of deciding whether to seek the death penalty were white; 40 percent of those criminals sentenced to death between 1976 and the late 1990's were black. Of the twelve blacks executed in Georgia between 1983 and 1999, six were found guilty and sentenced in trials in which the prosecutors successfully removed all potential black jurors.

The sociological term "victim discounting" refers to the practice of viewing crimes as less significant if the victim can be seen as somehow less important than most people—for example, if the victim is a member of a minority group. The concept of victim discounting offers another way of looking at disparities in how African Americans fare within the criminal justice system. Much of black crime is intraracial—involving blacks victimizing blacks, sometimes referred to as "black-on-black crime." It appears that when blacks are victimized, society in general and the criminal justice system in particular are not as outraged as when whites are victimized. A telling statistic is that half of all homicide victims in the United States from 1977 to 1992 were black, but 85 percent of prisoners executed for murder were punished for killing whites.

—*David Pilgrim*

*See also:* Black-on-black violence; Convict release system and chain gangs; Gangs; Hate crime; Jury selection; Sentencing Project Report of 1995; Substance abuse; Three-strikes laws.

Suggested Readings:

Baldus, David C., George Woodworth, and Charles A. Pulaska, Jr. *Equal Justice and the Death Penalty.* Boston: Northeastern University Press, 1990.

Bureau of Justice Statistics. *Criminal Victimization in the United States* (National Crime Victimization Survey). Washington, D.C.: U.S. Government Printing Office, published annually.

Federal Bureau of Investigation. *Crime in the United States* (Uniform Crime Reports). Washington, D.C.: U.S. Government Printing Office, published annually.

Mann, Coramae Richey. *Unequal Justice: A Question of Color.* Bloomington: University of Indiana, 1988.

Mauer, Marc, and Tracy Huling. *Young Black Americans and the Criminal Justice System: Five Years Later.* Washington, D.C.: The Sentencing Project, 1995.

Miller, Jerome G. *Search and Destroy.* New York: Cambridge University Press, 1996.

Petersilia, Joan. *Racial Disparities in the Criminal Justice System.* Santa Monica, Calif.: Rand Corporation, 1983.

Reid, Sue Titus. *Crime and Criminology.* Boston: McGraw Hill, 1997.

Walker, Samuel, Cassia Spohn, and Miriam DeLeone. *The Color of Justice: Race, Ethnicity, and Crime in America.* Belmont, Calif.: Wadsworth, 1996.

**Crisis, The:** Magazine. The first and longest-lived African American magazine, *The Crisis* began publication in 1910. The magazine was subtitled *A Record of the Darker Races*, a phrase that suggests the magazine's importance in literary history: *The Crisis* has indeed recorded the voices of significant African Americans since it began publication. *The Crisis* was created and first edited by W. E. B. Du Bois, who also helped found the National Association for the Advancement of Colored People (NAACP). The magazine was established as a publication of the NAACP.

Begun as an outlet for Du Bois's message about black development and white enlightenment, *The Crisis* was viewed as required reading in many African American households during the period of Du Bois's editorship, which lasted from 1910 to 1934. It had a large audience, approximately one hundred thousand readers, by the end of its first decade. In the pages of *The Crisis*, Du Bois revealed the evolution of his thinking from his early commitment to racial justice to his later call for black separatism.

*The Crisis* was an important medium for young African American writers of the Harlem Renaissance, a term used to describe a flowering of African American arts in the 1920's. Many influential African American artists of the time lived in the part of New York City known as Harlem. Among the notable writers who appeared in the pages of *The Crisis* were poets Arna Bontemps, Langston Hughes, and Countée Cullen and novelist-poet Jean Toomer. *The Crisis* later began to emphasize current events over literary works, focusing on issues related to the NAACP, civil rights, and important African Americans. The magazine is a significant record of African American culture and history.

—*Marjorie Smelstor*

*See also:* Black press.

**Crite, Allan Rohan** (b. March 20, 1910, Plainfield, New Jersey): Painter and illustrator. A specialist in liturgical art, Crite completed works for the the chapel at the Massachusetts Institute of Technology. He recorded African

American social events during the 1930's in such drawings as *One of Our Exhibitions and Teas* (1939). Sparseness and precision are the hallmarks of Crite's art, which bears the message that life contains hardship and suffering as well as serenity and beauty.

*See also:* Painters and illustrators, Visual arts.

**Critical race theory:** Critical race theory involves both theory and practice; it is an activity as well as an area of study. The goal of this activity is to combat and eventually eliminate racial oppression. Critical race theorists work toward this goal as part of the broader effort to end all forms of oppression. Many minority scholars have recognized that their experiences differ from the experiences of white scholars. Specifically, many critical race theorists themselves have experienced racism, sexism, or heterosexism in their personal lives and in their professions. Critical race theory helps name, document, and contest oppressive structures and practices. Scholars use a variety of means in practicing critical race theory. One method is to produce research that challenges prevailing "logics of rationality" that are deemed responsible for the continuation of oppression.

### White Supremacy

The prevailing logic of rationality that is most often identified by critical race theory is that of WHITE SUPREMACY. Critical race theorists accept as a central premise the idea that dominant ideas, beliefs, and values in the United States are based on an American historical context that esteems whiteness. This theory highlights the observable effects of white supremacy. For example, critical race theory may focus on the dual wage systems in which people of color are paid less than whites; on segregated living spaces where communities of color are targeted as sites for toxic disposal or polluting industries; on racist HATE SPEECH and how it violates the rights of students of color on university and college campuses; or on inherent racism in the interpretations of laws and court decisions. Critical race theory examines both the effects and the way in which white supremacy in the United States operates to subordinate people of color.

Some scholars of critical race theory have focused on the political, scientific, and religious operations that reproduce white supremacy. According to some of these scholars, these operations function to perpetuate a mythology that reproduces and legitimizes the subordination of ethnic minorities as conditions that are logical and natural.

### Internal Critique

One method used by proponents of critical race theory to combat white supremacy is internal critique. Internal critique is based on the assumption that people can demand change effectively only in ways that reflect the logic of the institutions that they are challenging. Critical race theory maintains that ideological and structural changes of institutions are triggered by crisis, and internal critique is a method that creates a crisis in an institution by turning the logic of the institution inward. Scholars applying critical race theory look for internal contradictions within the institution to challenge the operations of white supremacy.

Many critical race theory scholars have pointed out that white supremacy often includes claims of neutrality, objectivity, color-blindness, and meritocracy. Most critical race theorists reject these claims as inherently political. They express skepticism toward claims of neutrality and objectivity because "race" in those contexts is presented as an ahistorical social characteristic. Furthermore, racial inequality is presented as a pattern of randomly occurring individualized acts. Critical race theory challenges these claims and insists that analysis of racial inequality should be grounded in the historical experiences of people of color. Adherents of this theory attempt to ground all products of white supremacist logic within a historical context to challenge and then force change.

A central theme of critical race scholarship centers on the critical examination of myths, stories, and narratives of dominant groups. Some scholars have explained how myths, stories, and narratives are used to justify racial subordination. Other scholars have also used myths, stories, and narratives to contest the logic used to justify racial subordination. In his study *Black Male Deviance* (1995), sociologist Anthony J. Lemelle uses several methods to analyze and examine the ways white male supremacy is used as a logic to produce and reproduce black men as deviant. One way he does this is by doing a critical analysis of Richard WRIGHT's *Native Son*. By focusing on the character Bigger Thomas, Lemelle brings to the foreground the fate of deviance for black men in a society that reproduces racial subordination. In other words, the production of black male deviance serves as a way to keep "race" as a commonly recognized social divider.

*Law and Racial Minorities*
Kimberlé Williams Crenshaw, a professor of law, was instrumental in developing critical race theory in the area of law. She emphasized the role of racism in constructing black Americans as a subordinated "other." She critiques the legitimating role of legal ideology and legal rights reforms. She argues that legal ideology based on a colorblind stance contributes to the material subordination of blacks. Crenshaw argues that antidiscrimination law has succeeded in eliminating the symbolic manifestations of racial oppression, but has allowed the perpetuation of inequalities in the actual distribution of goods and resources, status, and prestige. According to Crenshaw, the fact that antidiscrimination discourse is ambiguous represents an ongoing ideological

Kimberlé Williams Crenshaw helped develop the critical race theory in the field of law. *(Kimberlé Williams Crenshaw)*

struggle. The occasional winners of this ideological struggle harness the moral, coercive, and consensual power of law.

Crenshaw stresses three crucial aspects of a critical analysis of race in the American legal context:

> First, racism is a central ideological underpinning of American society. Critical scholars who focus on legal consciousness alone thus fail to address one of the most crucial ideological components of the dominant order. . . . Second, the definitional tension in antidiscrimination law, which attempts to distinguish equality as process from equality as result, is more productively characterized as a conflict between the stated *goals* of antidiscrimination law. . . . Finally, the Black community must develop and maintain a distinct political consciousness in order to prevail against the co-opting force of legal reform.

Crenshaw argues that these three aspects of race in the American legal context can contribute to an effort to understand hegemony and the politics of racial reform. Focusing on a critical race analysis of antidiscrimination law, Crenshaw identified the two basic conflicts in anti-discrimination law: The restrictive view that focuses on equality as a process and the expansive view which centers on equality as a result. Supporters of the expansive view of antidiscrimination law interpret the objective as the "eradication of the substantive conditions of black subordination and attempts to enlist the institutional power of the courts to further the national goal of eradicating the effects of racial oppression." In contrast, supporters of the restrictive view of antidiscrimination law are not concerned with social policies that consistently reproduce inequality. Rather, the restrictive view focuses on individualistic "wrongdoing." Crenshaw describes "wrongdoing" as a focus on "isolated actions against individuals rather than as a societal policy against an entire group."

### Racial Colorblindness

Crenshaw uses critical race theory to interrogate the logic of the restrictive view. Her analysis reveals that the restrictive view of antidiscrimination law centers on a belief in colorblindness. Neil Gotanda, professor of law, has argued that the practice of colorblindness is an impossibility. To use colorblindness, people would have to "fail to recognize race in [their] everyday lives." Gotanda takes a critical stance to present an evident argument that the idea of colorblind nonrecognition is an impossible goal:

> Nonrecognition differs from nonperception. Compare color-blind nonrecognition with medical color-blindness. A medically color-blind person is someone who cannot see what others can. It is a partial nonperception of what is "really" there. To be racially color-

blind, on the other hand, is to ignore what one has already noticed. The medically colorblind individual never perceives color in the first place; the racially colorblind individual perceives race and then ignores it. . . . The characteristics of race that are noticed (before being ignored) are situated within an already existing understanding of race. That is, race carries with it a complex social meaning.

Critical race theory enables scholars to challenge ideas, such as colorblindness, that are supposed to eliminate racial inequality. Critical race theorists feel that reforming a racist society is an ongoing struggle. Critiquing ideas that perpetuate racial inequality, such as the belief of race colorblindness, is part of that struggle.

### Dual Consciousness

Robin D. Barnes, a critical race theorist, describes the unique features of dual consciousness that minorities experience:

> Many of us remember when we first *realized* that we were black, and that discovery had a more profound impact than every other thereafter. We do not escape the reality of our experience as members of a racially oppressed group when we enter the legal academy.

The sense of violation that individuals experience as minorities opens their eyes to a reality that is quite different from the reality that white scholars experience. Their frame of reference has forced them to contend with racism, as well as with other oppressive structures, when many of their white colleagues are content with denying the legacy of racism. According to Barnes, this frame of reference created by past and present experiences of racist violation has created within minority individuals a sensitivity "to the fact that any transformation, whether initiated by those seeking to preserve or dismantle the status quo might exact the high price of further suffering and marginalization."

Critical race theory is enhanced by this sensitivity to oppressive struggles. It also operates as part of the struggle continually to remind mainstream scholars that social policy and law are essentially political tools because they are both products and promoters of racism as well as tools of social change. The sensitivity many minority scholars have to racism and the understanding of social policy and law as political tools is most evident in discussions on First Amendment rights. Critical race scholars have called for doctrinal changes from an absolutist First Amendment response to hate speech to one with legal sanctions for racist hate messages.

Critical race theorists opened the debate on the interpretation of First Amendment rights by describing how hate messages have the effect of perpetuating racism. Situating racist hate messages within an American historical context of racial violence and genocide illustrates how hate messages deeply affect minorities. Critical race theory has been significant in reframing political languages to clarify important issues. For example, the political language of "free speech" regarding hate messages can be reframed using critical race theory as the right to victimize versus the right not to be victimized. This process of reframing and contextualizing issues helps decision makers clearly understand the impact their decisions will have.

### Race and Gender

Another crucial area that scholars have examined is the relationship between racial oppression and gender oppression. Anthony Lemelle examined the political sociology of black masculinity. Through a critical analysis of gender, Lemelle argues that black men have been culturally produced as another gender to be possessed by white men. Lemelle ex-amines the structural tropes of the Eurocentric master fantasy to engage the construction of whiteness as a universal value rendering black men as a form of women. By contextualizing the construction of black masculinity into America's historical context of colonization, enslavement, and internal colonialism, Lemelle suggests that racism is a form of sexism:

> The patterned institutional roles relegated black men into a particular brand of masculinity. The idea of the spectacular representation is that black men are not complete men, are not real men, and are therefore unworthy of white desire. What emerges is a type of performance where the black male body doggedly solicits recognition of the real (white) man, who refrains from acknowledging the black male as Man in accordance with the specifications of Eurocentric folkways.

Critical race theory seeks to unveil the many processes of subordination. Its theorists use many methods to describe the various ways the processes of racism and sexism are experienced by people who are subordinated and to describe the experiences of the people who are privileged by those processes. Examining and engaging prevailing "logics of rationality" is one way that this approach attempts to empower people of color to embrace a political consciousness of reform.

—*Lydia Rose*

*See also:* Institutional racism; Intellectuals and scholars; Race, racism, and race relations; Racial discrimination; Racial prejudice.

Suggested Readings:

Brown, Eleanor M. "The Tower of Babel: Bridging the Divide Between Critical Race Theory and 'Mainstream' Civil Rights Scholarship." *The Yale Law Journal* 105, no. 2 (1995): 513.

Crenshaw, Kimberlé W. *Critical Race Theory:*

*The Key Writings That Formed the Movement.* New York: New Press, 1995.

———, ed. "Mapping the Margins: Intersectionality, Identity Politics, and Violence Against Women of Color." *Stanford Law Review* 43 (July, 1991): 1241-1299.

Delgado, Richard, ed. *Critical Race Theory: The Cutting Edge.* Philadelphia: Temple University Press, 1995.

Gotanda, Neil. "A Critique of 'Our Constitution Is Colorblind.'" *Stanford Law Review* 44 (November, 1991): 1-68.

Lemelle, Anthony J. *Black Male Deviance.* Westport, Conn.: Praeger, 1995.

Matsuda, Mari J., ed. *Words That Wound: Critical Race Theory, Assaultive Speech, and the First Amendment.* Boulder, Colo.: Westview Press, 1993.

Monahan, Peter. "'Critical Race Theory' Questions Role of Legal Doctrine in Racial Inequity: Lani Guinier, Ill-Fated Justice Dept. Nominee, Is One of Its More Traditional Adherents." *The Chronicle of Higher Education* 39 (June 23, 1993): A7.

Parker, Laurence, Donna Deyhle, and Sofia A. Villenas, eds. *Race Is—Race Isn't: Critical Race Theory and Qualitative Studies in Education.* Boulder, Colo.: Westview Press, 1999.

**Crockett, George W., Jr.** (August 10, 1909, Jacksonville, Florida—September 7, 1997, Washington, D.C.): U.S. representative from MICHIGAN. Crockett grew up in FLORIDA and attended Morehouse College in ATLANTA, GEORGIA, where he graduated with an A.B. degree in 1931. He studied law at the University of Michigan and earned his J.D. degree in 1934. After graduation, Crockett returned to Jacksonville to begin private practice as an attorney.

In 1939 Crockett moved to Washington, D.C., to take a position as an attorney with the Department of Labor, becoming the first African American lawyer to serve on the department's staff. President Franklin D. Roosevelt appointed Crockett to serve as a hearing examiner with the newly created Fair Employment Practices Commission in 1943. Crockett also served as senior attorney for the Fair Labor Standards Act Administration. In 1944 he moved to DETROIT, MICHIGAN, to work for the International United Auto Workers as founder and director of its fair employment practices department.

Crockett remained active in labor law upon his return to private practice in 1946 and provided legal advice and representation for civil rights organizers and labor unions. He also represented clients who were brought before the House Committee on Un-American Activities and handled cases before the U.S. SUPREME COURT. Crockett became a judge of the Detroit Recorders Court in 1946 and served for twenty years. He was elected as presiding

In 1949 George W. Crockett, Jr. (left) and two other attorneys were found guilty of contempt of court while defending members of the Communist Party in a federal conspiracy trial. *(AP/Wide World Photos)*

judge of the Recorders Court in 1972 and served until 1978. Crockett became a senior partner in the law firm of Goodman, Crockett, Eden, and Robb and served as acting corporation counsel for the city of Detroit in 1980. He also was a visiting judge on the Michigan Court of Appeals.

In 1980 Crockett declared his intention to run for the seat vacated by Congressman Charles DIGGS, who resigned in June of that year after the Supreme Court declined to review his conviction on mail fraud and other charges. Crockett was elected to fill the remainder of Diggs's term and to serve a full term in the next congressional session. He took his seat on November 12, 1980, and was appointed to serve on the House Committee on Foreign Affairs, the House Committee on the Judiciary, and the House Select Committee on Aging.

Crockett's interest in foreign affairs led him to serve as a member of the U.S. congressional delegation to the 1981 International Parliamentary meeting in Havana, CUBA, as well as the Seventh United Nations Congress on Prevention of Crime held in Milan, Italy, in 1984. President Ronald Reagan appointed Crockett to serve as a public delegate in the U.S. delegation to the U.N. General Assembly. Crockett also became chairman of the House Foreign Affairs Subcommittee on Western Hemisphere Affairs. In addition to his work on Latin American affairs, Crockett used his influence on the Foreign Affairs committee to speak out against apartheid in South Africa. When he was defeated in his reelection campaign in 1990, he retired from politics.
*See also:* Congress Members; Politics and government; Strikes and labor law.

**Cromwell, Oliver** (May 24, 1753, Black Horse, New Jersey—January 24, 1853, Columbus, New Jersey): Revolutionary War soldier. Cromwell crossed the Delaware River with George Washington on December 25, 1776. He participated in several major battles in the war and claimed to have seen the last direct casualty of the AMERICAN REVOLUTION at Yorktown, Virginia. After more than six years of service, Cromwell was separated from the military. He bought a farm with his military pension.

**Crop lien system:** Contract system requiring tenant farmers to surrender part of their crops in return for their use of land. The contracts seldom covered family needs such as clothing and food, and often they did not cover farm equipment or other necessities. As a result, tenant farmers made separate agreements in which they secured loans by taking a lien on growing or future crops. The system was most prevalent in the years surrounding the CIVIL WAR.

Impoverished and illiterate black tenant farmers were not able to challenge the authority of lenders, who frequently charged exorbitant rates of interest. To make matters worse, lenders sometimes falsified accounts so as to place tenants at a further disadvantage. High rates of illiteracy and social subordination greatly reduced the chance that unfair practices would be resisted.

The crop lien system was a major form of exploitation of impoverished rural African Americans. POVERTY and lack of opportunities created a situation in which black tenant farmers often were dependent on cash advances to see them through the growing season. If crops failed or if share agreements were harsh, black families wound up in debt for generations.

Although the practice of tenant farming persisted into the late twentieth century, the degree of exploitation of black and other tenant farmers had been reduced or modified. As credit markets developed, farmers most often owed debts not to a plantation store or merchant but to a bank or finance company. Mortgages on property replaced liens on crops. Competition by lenders for business and the increasing literacy and sophistication of farmers greatly reduced the potential for exploitation.

*See also:* Agriculture; Sharecropping; Southern Tenant Farmers' Union.

**Cross, Theodore L.** (b. February 12, 1924, Newton, Massachusetts): Lawyer and author. Cross received the A.B. degree from Amherst College in 1946 and trained in law at Harvard University, from which he graduated in 1950. He was admitted to the bar in NEW YORK and MASSACHUSETTS. Along with holding corporate positions, he lectured at Harvard, Cornell, and the University of Virginia. Cross wrote *Black Capitalism: Strategy for Business in the Ghetto* (1969) and *The Black Power Imperative: Racial Inequality and the Politics of Nonviolence* (1984).

*See also:* Black capitalism; Black Power movement.

**Crouch, Andrae** (b. July 1, 1942, Pacoima, California): GOSPEL singer, composer, and pastor. Writing and singing songs that carry a message of hope, Crouch became recognized as an international music star. Beginning his musical career in his father's Southern California church, Andrae Crouch began playing the piano and writing music at the age of nine. By the early 1960's, he had formed his own group, Andrae Crouch and the Disciples. The group traveled the world and built a reputation for exciting live performances.

Crouch soon became one of the most vital and influential artists in modern music. His songs transcend color, class, and creed with a message of hope, faith, and joyous celebration. By 1999 Crouch had nine Grammy Awards and an Academy Award nomination to his credit. Crouch's recordings extend from

Singer Andrae Crouch at the 1982 Grammy Awards ceremony. *(AP/Wide World Photos)*

such timeless gospel classics as "My Tribute," "The Blood Will Never Lose Its Power," and "This Is Another Day" to film-score contributions to *Free Willy* (1993) and *The Lion King* (1994). To honor his contributions to gospel music, some of the top names in gospel and contemporary Christian music spent two years making an album entitled *Tribute: The Songs of Andrae Crouch* (1996).

Crouch consistently sold out concerts throughout Europe, the Americas, Africa, and the Far East, and his music has been translated into at least twenty-one languages. Crouch had recorded fourteen albums by the late 1990's, many selling more than a million copies. In 1995 he began serving as the pastor of the Christ Memorial Church of God in the LOS ANGELES area.

*—Alvin K. Benson*

*See also:* Gospel music and spirituals.

**Crowdy, William S.** (d. 1908): Clergyman. Crowdy founded the CHURCH OF GOD AND SAINTS OF CHRIST in 1896. He was among the first clergymen to proclaim that African

Americans were descended from the ten lost tribes of Israel. His church, sometimes referred to as the "black Jews," observes the Old Testament calendar.

*See also:* Hebrew Israelites; Spiritual Israel Church and Its Army.

**Crudup, Arthur "Big Boy"** (1896?, Forest, Mississippi—March 28, 1974, Nassawadox, Virginia): Musician. Crudup is considered by many to be the true father of rock and roll. Crudup was a highly regarded BLUES guitarist and a prolific songwriter. His songs have made many other artists both wealthy and popular. His "That's All Right" (1946) was one of eighty sides he recorded for RCA-Victor between 1941 and 1956, and the song later became Elvis Presley's first major hit. Crudup, discouraged by witnessing other performers reap the benefits of his work, left the music world in 1956 but enjoyed a brief period of celebrity status during the blues revival of the 1960's.

*See also:* Rhythm and blues.

**Crummell, Alexander** (March 3, 1819, New York, New York—September 10, 1898, Point Pleasant, New Jersey): Black nationalist leader. A pioneer of PAN-AFRICANIST thought and black nationalism, Alexander Crummell was instrumental in establishing a tradition of African American scholarship. A brilliant classical scholar, Christian mystic, EPISCOPAL priest, and missionary to LIBERIA, he established the precedent of placing scholarship in the service of protest and race advancement. His ideas on leadership, education, race, work, and moral uplift foreshadowed the concepts espoused by such leaders as W. E. B. DU BOIS, Booker T. WASHINGTON, and Marcus GARVEY.

*Early Life*

Crummell was born in NEW YORK CITY to Charity Hicks Crummell, a free African American, and Boston Crummell, a former slave employed as an oysterman. Alexander's father, who claimed to be the son of a Temne prince, was taken from Sierra Leone at age thirteen. According to Crummell, as a child he was inspired by visions of Africa supplied by his father, and he resolved early in life to go there. Reared in a deeply Christian African American community that believed keenly in mental and moral improvement, Crummell was educated at the African Free School, alumni of which included Henry Highland Garnet and Ira Aldridge, and the Canal Street High School, which was run by Peter Williams and Theodore S. Wright, leading clergymen and abolitionists. In 1835 Crummell, along with Garnet and several others, matriculated at the Noyes Academy in Canaan, NEW HAMPSHIRE, but only after being driven from the town by farmers angered by their abolitionist activities. The following year, Crummell entered the Oneida Institute at Whitesboro, New York, from which he graduated in 1839. Run by abolitionists, Oneida combined manual labor with a classical curriculum and provided Crummell with an excellent education.

Following his mentor, the Reverend Peter Williams, Crummell chose a clerical career in the EPISCOPALIAN church and, in 1839, applied for admission to the General Theological Seminary in New York City, only to be rejected on the basis of race. Determined to gain admission, he petitioned the seminary's trustees but was rejected again. For four years, he studied privately with leading Episcopal clergymen in BOSTON and in Providence, RHODE ISLAND. After unsuccessfully attempting to establish a mission church among African Americans in Providence, Crummell moved in 1844 to PHILADELPHIA, where he was ordained by Bishop Lee of Delaware. Refused full admission to the Philadelphia diocese, he returned to New York. With support from John Jay and other elite Episcopalians, he succeeded in organizing a congregation, but he did not succeed in securing sufficient funds to construct a church.

Known as a scholar, Crummell was frequently requested to work for racial-uplift projects. He also became active in the Negro Convention movement. At the Albany Convention in 1840, he drafted a petition to the New York legislature on lifting restrictions against African Americans' right to vote. In 1847, at the National Colored Convention in Troy, New York, he collaborated with Frederick DOUGLASS on abolitionist strategies and worked with James McCune SMITH on establishing black colleges.

### Work in England and Africa

Bitter about racial discrimination within his church and the poverty of his family and congregation, Crummell took John Jay's advice and traveled to England to seek funds to build a church. He lived there from 1848 to 1853, years he regarded as among the most satisfying of his life. In addition to raising money through lectures, he studied at Queen's College of the University of Cambridge, from which he received a B.A. degree in 1853.

After five years in England, Crummell chose to undertake mission work in Liberia. Never particularly healthy, he sought a warmer climate. Moreover, he believed that Liberia, an African American settler colony, would offer him greater opportunities to serve his race. Dedicated to African "redemption," Crummell became a citizen of the republic and an articulate spokesman for Liberian nationalism. Between 1857 and 1872, he worked as a farmer, businessman, high school principal, college professor, and missionary.

Crummell's church work always came first. Although he established several new churches, he was usually at odds with his missionary colleagues, whom he accused of importing "the malignant and spiteful caste spirit" from the United States. In 1862 together with Edward W. Blyden, another pan-Africanist, he was appointed to the faculty of Liberia College in Monrovia. Frequently recruited to speak at public events, Crummell came to see himself as a public teacher, exhorting love of race and country, moral uplift, and political restraint. In 1861 the Liberian legislature appointed Crummell, Blyden, and J. D. Johnson, a wealthy merchant, to encourage emigration to Liberia among African Americans and to develop U.S. philanthropic support. In these efforts, he worked closely with the AMERICAN COLONIZATION SOCIETY, a white-run organization that promoted emigration. Traveling to the United States to lecture on the responsibility of African Americans to work for African "regeneration," he was opposed by many, including Frederick Douglass, who remarked that Crummell "almost glories in his unmixed negro blood."

Dismissed from Liberia College in 1867 over "caste" differences, Crummell began his own school, modeled after the Oneida Institute. Before construction of the school could begin, however, the country became enmeshed in political turmoil between the mixed-race ruling group and the faction of Crummell and President Edward Roye, who identified with "pure blacks." Roye was deposed and murdered in 1871, and his secretary of state, Crummell's son Sidney, was jailed. Since Crummell had long opposed the Liberian color-caste system and campaigned on behalf of indigenous Africans, his life was also threatened. In ill health, anxious, and rather disillusioned, Crummell left Liberia in 1872, but he continued to advocate the Christianization and civilization of Africa by educated persons of African descent.

### Work in America

In 1873 Crummell and his family settled in WASHINGTON, D.C., where he later founded St. Luke's Church, the object of his pastoral duties until his retirement in 1895. As Crummell was the senior African American priest in the Episcopal Church, his advice and leadership were prized. In 1883 he convened a meeting of clergy and laity to protest the absence of African American bishops in the church; that meeting produced the Conference of Church Workers Among Colored People. A frequent public vindicator of the race, he lectured and wrote as disfranchisement and segregation spread after Reconstruction. His message remained unchanged: Educated and skilled African Americans had to lead the redemption of the race. To help create such committed leadership, he often addressed college audiences and from 1895 to 1897 taught at Howard University. In 1897 he organized the American Negro Academy, a group formed to encourage intellectual excellence and oppose racist propaganda. Its forty members included W. E. B. Du Bois, John W. Cromwell, and Paul Laurence DUNBAR.

Crummell's philosophy and concerns are laid out in several books of sermons and addresses: *The Relations and Duties of Free Colored Men in America to Africa* (1861); *The Future of Africa* (1862); *The Greatness of Christ and Other Sermons* (1882); *The Race-Problem in America* (1889); *Africa and America: Addresses and Discourses by Alex Crummell* (1891); *The Attitude of the American Mind Toward the Negro Intellect* (1898); and *Civilization, the Primal Need of the Race* (1898). His writings synthesize history, philosophy, sociology, and religion, all directed toward elevating Africans and African Americans. Throughout his life, he believed and expressed a pan-African conviction: All persons of African descent were linked by ties of kinship and social experience that transcended class and place. All were victims of a "color caste" that led whites to assume an inherent superiority and—more devastating to Crummell—led blacks to a belief in their own inferiority.

Crummell was molded by the Victorian Christian beliefs of his time, and his concept of race advancement and rejection of racism was rooted in the Christian ideal of brotherhood. He believed that a person's expression of love of God should be through service to others. In his view, one's first responsibility was to one's immediate family, the second to one's race. As Crummell once said, "a race is a family." By temperament a critical man, Crummell at heart was a Christian moralist who judged individuals and nations by their moral character.

Formal portraits of Crummell reveal him, with full gray beard and erect posture, as a proud, reserved man. He was at times ill-tempered, and some considered him an insufferable genius. A man of great energy despite his constant medical complaints, he was a political and religious thinker of consistent excellence and occasional brilliance. He was described by contemporaries as autocratic, and his philosophy was authoritarian and elitist, but not unchanging. Crummell willingly contradicted himself and offered radical measures to preserve traditional values. He reversed his position in support of emigration, but not on the race's responsibility to Africa. His primary concern remained the education of black leaders, whose duty it was to apply intellectual knowledge to solve the problems confronting blacks.

An individual of eloquence and great dignity, Alexander Crummell provided inspiration and intellectual guidance to an influential minority of nineteenth-century leaders in Liberia and the United States. As a result, he played a significant role in setting the terms of discourse and defining the issues affecting African Americans: the relationship of African Americans to Africa; the nature of African civilization; the value of political participation; the educational needs of the race; and the nature and responsibilities of its leaders. Crummell's racial thought and pan-Africanism are the source of many ideas found among later thinkers; Marcus Garvey's race pride, W. E. B. Du Bois's TALENTED TENTH, and the pan-Africanism of many others can be traced to him.

—*Kathleen K. O'Mara*

*See also:* Black nationalism.

Suggested Readings:

Crummell, Alexander. *Civilization and Black Progress: Selected Writings of Alexander Crummell on the South.* Edited by J. R. Oldfield. Charlottesville: University Press of Virginia, 1995.

_____. *Destiny and Race: Selected Writings, 1840-1898.* Edited by Wilson J. Moses. Amherst: University of Massachusetts Press, 1992.

Du Bois, W. E. B. *The Souls of Black Folk: Essays and Sketches.* Chicago: A. C. McClurg, 1903.

Oldfield, J. R. *Alexander Crummell (1819-1898) and the Creation of an African-American Church in Liberia.* Lewiston, N.Y.: Edwin Mellen Press, 1990.

Moses, Wilson J. *Alexander Crummell: A Study of Civilization and Discontent.* New York: Oxford University Press, 1989.

Rigsby, Gregory U. *Alexander Crummell: Pioneer in Nineteenth Century Pan-African Thought.* New York: Greenwood Press. 1987.

Scruggs, Otey M. "We the Children of Africa in This Land: Alexander Crummell." In *Africa and the Afro-American Experience: Eight Essays.* Edited by Lorraine A. Williams. Washington, D.C.: Howard University Press, 1977.

**Crumpler, Rebecca Lee** (1858-?): Physician. Crumpler may have been the first African American woman to practice as a physician in the United States. Another woman, Rebecca J. COLE, is given that honor in some accounts. Crumpler, however, was the first African American woman to earn a medical degree, which she earned at the New England Female Medical College.

*See also:* Medicine.

**Cruz, Emilio** (b. March 15, 1938, New York, New York): Artist and poet. Cruz studied at the Art Institute of Chicago and the Art Students League (1955). His paintings, such as *Silver Umbrella*, reflect imagination and fantasy. He was the winner of fellowships from the Cintas Foundation (1965-1966) and the Walter Gutman Foundation (1962), was awarded a grant from the National Endowment for the Arts (1970-1971), and won a John Hay Whitney Fellowship (1964-1965).

*See also:* Painters and illustrators; Visual arts.

**Cuba:** The largest island in the WEST INDIES, Cuba is home to more than 11 million people. Estimates of the island's Afro-Cuban population vary, but Afro-Cubans probably account for two-fifths to one-half of this total. While the percentage of Afro-Cubans in the island's overall population is smller than comparable figures for Jamaica and HAITI, the number of people of African ancestry in Cuba is nevertheless approximately 5 million, which is about twice the total population of JAMAICA and not far below that of Haiti.

The first Africans arrived in Cuba in 1517 as slaves of Spanish settlers, but SLAVERY's most rapid expansion on the island did not take place until after 1790. The slave uprising and consequent destruction of the sugar industry in Haiti in the 1790's gave planters in Cuba the opportunity to produce this popular commodity using African slave labor. Between 1791 and 1830, the Spanish imported half a million African slaves. Working conditions in the cane fields were harsh during the harvest season, with its tropical heat and humidity.

Africans in Cuba resisted slavery in several ways. Runaway slaves formed communities called *mambises* in isolated mountainous regions or swamplands. Open rebellions such as the uprising in Matanzas province in 1843 posed a threat to the plantation owners. The Matanzas uprising was followed by a brutal

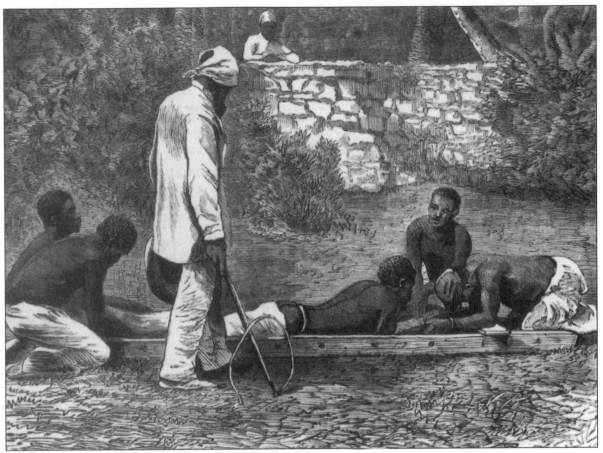

This illustration of Cuban slaves being whipped accompanied an 1868 article in *Harper's Weekly* calling for Cuban independence from Spain. *(Library of Congress)*

repression in which several hundred slaves were killed as colonial officials and planters used bloodhounds to track down the rebels. Cuba's late nineteenth-century revolts against Spanish rule included a strong movement for the abolition of slavery. The Spanish government responded with a gradual end to slavery (1870-1886), but this action and the end of Spanish rule in 1898 did not mean the end to discrimination against Afro-Cubans.

Communist leader Fidel Castro's revolution of 1959 owed much to Afro-Cubans such as Juan Almeida, who fought alongside Castro from defeat at Moncada in 1953 to triumph in the Sierra Maestra in the late 1950's. The revolutionary state sought to end poverty and racial discrimination, but it achieved only

partial success in both areas. These socioeconomic problems continued to plague Afro-Cubans.

Nevertheless, the role of Africans in Cuban culture has been especially prominent. Perhaps the most widely recognized influence is in folk and popular music. The rumba evolved from local street songs to win worldwide audiences in the 1920's. Individual Afro-Cuban musicians earned fame in various genres. Jazz percussionist Chano Pozo, for example, collaborated with the legendary North American trumpeter Dizzy GILLESPIE. Afro-Cubans also excelled in professional baseball, led by Orestes "Minnie" Minoso, a speedy outfielder and prolific hitter for the Chicago White Sox and Cleveland Indians in the 1950's. SAN-

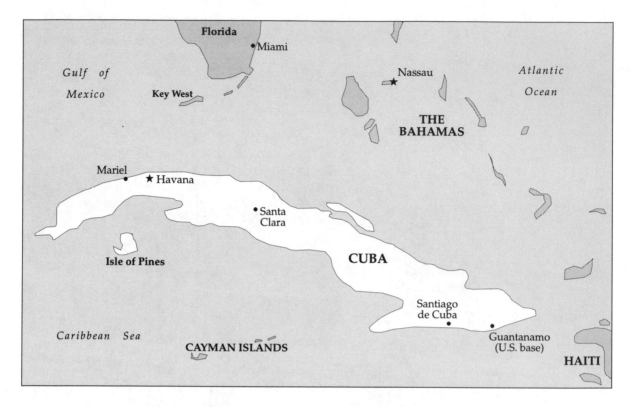

TERÍA, a religious movement with African roots, spread from rural Cuba to the cities, becoming an important factor in national life in the 1990s.

Although much of Cuba's history since the late 1950's was dominated by Castro's revolutionary struggles, Afro-Cubans can point to a longer record of struggle—first against slavery in the colonial era and then against discrimination and poverty.

*—John A. Britton*

*See also:* Jamaica and Jamaican Americans; Puerto Rico.

Suggested Readings:

Daniel, Yvonne. *Rumba: Dance and Social Change in Contemporary Cuba.* Bloomington: Indiana University Press, 1995.

Helg, Aline. *Our Rightful Share: The Afro-Cuban Struggle for Equality, 1886-1912.* Chapel Hill: University of North Carolina Press, 1995.

Oppenheimer, Andres. *Castro's Final Hour.* New York: Simon and Schuster, 1992.

**Cuffe, Paul** (January 17, 1759, Cuttyhunk Island, Massachusetts—September 9, 1817, Westport, Massachusetts): Businessman and colonizer. A wealthy merchant sailor and philanthropist in colonial America, Cuffe was a pioneer pan-African activist. Known for his leadership in the settlement of African Americans in West Africa, he played a primary role in initiating the African American emigration and missionary movements to Africa.

*Early Life*

Cuffe's life was shaped by the sea, a rough frontier in the sailing-ship era. The seventh of ten children born to Cuffe Slocum, a former slave, and Ruth Moses, a Wampanoag Indian, he grew up among the Native Americans of Cuttyhunk and Martha's Vineyard in MASSACHUSETTS until his father bought a farm in Westport. Self-taught—even at maturity he was only semiliterate—Cuffe spent his youth in hard work. When Cuffe was thirteen, his father died, bequeathing the family farm and the care of Cuffe's mother and three young sisters to Paul and his eldest brother, John.

Dissatisfied with farming, Cuffe at sixteen became a sailor, apprenticing on whaling and commercial vessels plying the Atlantic, the Caribbean, and the Gulf of Mexico. In 1779 he and his brother David went into business for themselves and, with a small ship, traded along the Massachusetts-Rhode Island coast. After an attack by buccaneers, David Cuffe returned to farming, but Paul continued trading, investing his profits in a larger ship.

Cuffe married Alice Pequit, of his mother's Wampanoag tribe, in 1783. His real success came after the AMERICAN REVOLUTION. His codfishing in an eighteen-ton ketch earned subsidies under federal acts of 1792 and 1794. He engaged in whaling off Newfoundland and carried lumber, animals, and foodstuffs between New Bedford and Nantucket. His vessels were found off St. Georges Banks; Wilmington, Delaware; Baltimore, Maryland; the Caribbean; and the Baltic Sea. Sailing with a crew of African Americans and Native Americans, Cuffe confronted racism and physical threats with modesty, firmness, and integrity.

A pioneer in the struggle for minority rights, as early as 1778 Paul, along with his brother John, refused to pay county property and poll taxes because Massachusetts blacks were not allowed to vote. Arrested in 1780, they paid the taxes but joined with other Massachusetts African Americans to petition the state, county, and local governments to grant relief from the payment of taxes. The request was rejected, but a court decision in 1783 granted Massachusetts blacks the right to vote.

*Merchant Mariner and Humanitarian*
By age thirty, Cuffe was on his way to amassing great wealth. Every few years he built bigger trading vessels. He began with ten- and fifteen-ton schooners. In the late 1780's, Cuffe's flagship became the twenty-five-ton schooner *Sun Fish*; it was followed by the forty-ton schooner *Mary*, which in turn was followed in 1795 by *Ranger*, a sixty-nine-ton schooner. By 1800 he had built the 162-ton brig *Hero*, pur-

Contemporary silhouette of Paul Cuffe. *(New Bedford Whaling Museum)*

chased a $3,500 farm on the East Branch of the Westport River where his six daughters and two sons were reared, and established a school on his farm for a community unwilling to build one itself.

As his enterprises expanded, so did Cuffe's contacts with the business elite of southeastern New England. The sponsorship of leading Quakers and Quaker doctrines aided his success. Cuffe's closest associate was William Rotch, Jr., a scion of New Bedford's richest whaling-banking-manufacturing family, who encouraged and counseled Cuffe and entered into joint enterprises with him. Moses Brown and other members of his important Providence, RHODE ISLAND, family were also influential Cuffe supporters. Quaker businessmen dominated the region, and the Society of Friends' involvement in abolitionist activities drew Cuffe into its orbit. Quakers captained his vessels and shared his beliefs that the spiritual and material worlds were intertwined and that industry and thrift were characteristics of a true Christian. In 1808 Cuffe formally joined the Westport Society of Friends, an unusual event, as local Quaker meetings generally refused to admit African Americans. His wealth did not protect him, however, from virulent RACIAL discrimination in travel and accommodations.

### Supporter of the Colonization Movement

Cuffe's effort to colonize Sierra Leone and Christianize Africans created his international reputation. The origin of his concern for the "redemption" of Africa is unclear; perhaps joining the Quakers was part of a deep religious experience that made him feel a religious duty to convert Africans. Enslaved African Americans, he felt at the time, were ultimately better off than Africans, because many slaves were converts to Christianity. Christianity and Westernization, Cuffe believed, would free Africans from dependence on slave-trade profits, and African American immigrants would be the agents of change.

Cuffe made two voyages to Sierra Leone, a colony of New World Africans established by abolitionists in 1787. His first voyage (1810-1812) was exploratory and was broken by a nine-week stay in England. That visit incurred much press attention and secured the admiration of William Wilberforce and other prominent British abolitionists. In 1812 Cuffe and Quaker friends galvanized support and won audiences with Secretary of the Treasury Albert Gallatin and President James Madison to regain Sierra Leone cargo taken from Cuffe's ship *Traveller* that had been seized for violating laws against trade with Great Britain during wartime.

The visit to England secured for Cuffe support from English Quakers and the African Institution, an emigration and antislavery philanthropy. His stay in Sierra Leone fired his imagination and laid the basis in personal contacts for what he hoped would be a long-term commercial and missionary endeavor in Sierra Leone. Cuffe made friends with John Kizell, an African American settler and leading shipper and merchant based at Sierra Leone's Sherbro Island. To facilitate trade between Africa and America, Cuffe purchased a house in Freetown, Sierra Leone, and encouraged the formation of an African trading society. He was present at the first meeting of the Friendly Society of Sierra Leone, a cooperative African settler trading society. He intended to visit Sierra Leone annually, bringing with him skilled immigrants and needed goods and exporting African produce. The War of 1812, however, intervened and interrupted his plans; Americans were prohibited from doing business with the British, which included the British colony of Sierra Leone.

Cuffe's second trip was thus delayed until December, 1815. After peace was declared, his ship *Traveller* left for Sierra Leone with thirty-eight settlers (eighteen adults and twenty children), the nucleus of a "model" community.

Arriving in Freetown in February, 1816, the emigrants met with a cool reception from British authorities, who were displeased with the possibility of an African American exodus and who imposed heavy import duties on Cuffe's cargo. Since he paid for the settlers' expenses, he lost more than four thousand dollars on the venture; his first trip had entailed a thirty-five-hundred-dollar loss. Yet Cuffe returned home convinced that settlement in Sierra Leone and southern Africa was a viable solution to the oppression and enslavement of African Americans. Realizing that not all American blacks would want to emigrate, Cuffe also proposed an African American settlement along the western fringes of the Louisiana Purchase.

*Plans for Mass Emigration*

By 1816 Cuffe's program for African redemption had turned into a mass-emigration plan for African Americans. The plight of blacks in the United States assumed priority over his notion of saving Africa. Racial tension was growing, as reports of purported slave plots increased southern slaveholders' fears. Some humanitarians argued that slaveholders could be persuaded to emancipate their slaves if the emigration of the freed slaves were assured. In reality, most slaveowners viewed the "peculiar institution" as a permanent one. Moreover, only a handful of African Americans favored emigration as an alternative to ending discrimination and poverty and winning equality. Before Cuffe's death in 1817, though, a few African American leaders such as Philadelphian James FORTEN lent their support to plans for African colonization.

The final impetus to Cuffe's endorsement of large-scale African American emigration came from white supporters of a COLONIZATION MOVEMENT, especially Samuel J. Mills and Robert Finley, two clergymen eager to promote colonization of freedmen as a means of solving the race problem. They sought support and information from Cuffe, who, because of his experience in Africa, was regarded as America's most knowledgeable Africanist. Cuffe agreed to cooperate with Mills and Finley, but he fell ill before their organization, the AMERICAN COLONIZATION SOCIETY, began work. He died on September 9, 1817, after several months of illness.

—*Kathleen K. O'Mara*

*See also:* Fishermen and whalers; Native American and African American relations.

Suggested Readings:

Harris, Sheldon H. *Paul Cuffe: Black American and the African Return.* New York: Simon & Schuster, 1972.

Redkey, Edwin S. *Black Exodus: Black Nationalist and Back to Africa Movements, 1890-1910.* New Haven, Conn.: Yale University Press, 1969.

Staudenraus, P. J. *The African Colonization Movement, 1816-1865.* New York: Columbia University Press, 1961.

Thomas, Lamont D. *Paul Cuffe: Black Entrepreneur and Pan-Africanist.* Champaign: University of Illinois Press, 1988.

_____. *Rise to Be a People: A Biography of Paul Cuffe.* Urbana: University of Illinois Press, 1986.

Wiggins, Rosalind C., ed. *Captain Paul Cuffe's Logs and Letters, 1808-1817: A Black Quaker's "Voice from Within the Veil."* Washington, D.C.: Howard University Press, 1996.

**Cullen, Countée** (May 30, 1903, New York, New York—January 9, 1946, New York, New York): Poet. Cullen was reared by his maternal grandmother until he was thirteen years old, when he was adopted by the Reverend Frederick A. Cullen, pastor of the Salem AFRICAN METHODIST EPISCOPAL CHURCH OF HARLEM, New York. The Reverend Cullen provided middle-class opportunities for Countée. After graduation from DeWitt Clinton High School, he attended New York University, where he made Phi Delta Kappa, an elite honor society, and graduated at the top of his class. He earned a master's degree at Harvard University.

Cullen reached the height of his poetic expression early, writing many of his best poems while he was still in college. His first book of poems, *Color*, was published in 1925, the same year he graduated from New York University. Publication of *Color* gave Cullen sudden recognition as an important poet of the HARLEM RENAISSANCE. He received the first prize for literature awarded by the William Harmon Foundation for this book. In 1927 Cullen produced two more volumes of verse and an anthology of verse written by black poets: *Copper Sun*, *The Ballad of the Brown Girl: An Old Ballad Retold*, and *Caroling Dusk*, respectively.

In 1928 Cullen won a Guggenheim Fellowship and decided to travel to Paris to study. Before leaving the United States, he married W. E. B. DU BOIS's daughter, Nina Yolande Du Bois, but the marriage ended within two years, while Cullen remained in Paris. When Cullen returned to New York City, he started his public school teaching career, which lasted until the year of his death. In 1940 he remarried and moved to Tuckahoe, New York.

Cullen combined teaching with editing and writing, serving as editor of *Opportunity* for a short period and writing two more volumes of poems, a children's book, a satirical novel, and a musical play. Before he died, he gathered some of his best poems together upon request; they were published posthumously under the title *On These I Stand: An Anthology of the Best Poems of Countée Cullen* (1947).

Cullen admired the classical style of John Keats and refused to experiment with jazz forms or free verse. Although he said that he approached racial themes in his writings with reluctance, some of his best poems are based on the dilemma of his being black in America. In "Yet Do I Marvel," Cullen's best-known poem, he poignantly posed the paradox of his life: "Yet do I marvel at this curious thing: / To make a poet black and bid him sing!"

**Culture of poverty theory:** Theory asserting that the poor, particularly minorities, have a culture that is different from that of the nonpoor. The social scientists and policy makers who subscribe to the theory often argue that this culture is in part responsible for POVERTY.

The theory was first popularized by anthropologist Oscar Lewis in his study of the Puerto Rican poor, *La Vida: A Puerto Rican Family in the Culture of Poverty* (1966). This theory postulates that poor people lack an orientation toward the future, cannot delay gratification, tend to be untrusting and unstable in relationships, are more likely to be depressed, and cannot commit to any job or institution or relationship for very long. According to this theory, the poor lack the internal controls and discipline characteristic of the middle class. Therefore, they are incapable of attaining middle-class employment, and even if they did, they would be incapable of capitalizing on such an opportunity.

This theory has generated enormous debate and criticism. Many conservative urban and poverty theorists, such as Edward Banfield and Charles Murray, adopted it to explain the persistence of late twentieth-century urban poverty and to argue that government antipoverty programs cannot overcome the culture of poverty and may even reinforce it by promoting welfare dependency and family breakdown by making the government the chief provider for poor women and children.

Opponents of the theory contend that poverty is caused by economic insecurity and inequity—made worse by racism in the case of minorities. From this viewpoint, the poor are victims of forces beyond their control, and the culture of poverty theorists are blaming victims for their condition. Other scholars have contended that poverty is caused by economic and racial oppression and that the debilitating effects cause the poor to create dysfunctional cultures. Certainly character and culture do not account for all poverty, because many people with middle-class values and mores have been thrown into poverty. Still, poor communities do exhibit the kinds of problems described by the culture-of-poverty theorists. Government antipoverty policies of the 1980's and 1990's and the politics that supported such policies reflected the views of the culture-of-poverty theorists.

*See also:* Employment and unemployment; War on Poverty.

*Cumming v. Richmond County Board of Education:* U.S. SUPREME COURT decision in 1899 regarding equality of education. The Supreme Court unanimously refused to grant relief to African Americans in Richmond County, GEORGIA, in the form of forcing local authorities to allocate county education funds more equally. Therefore, throughout the South, unequal education continued to flourish. African American children continued for decades to attend small, short-term, underfunded schools while white schools received enough funding for longer terms, better facilities, and more educational supplies.

*See also: Plessy v. Ferguson.*

**Cunard, Nancy** (March 10, 1896, Neville Holt, Leicestershire, England—March 17, 1965, Paris, France): Poet, publisher, and patron of the arts. A student and collector of African art and African American LITERATURE enthusiast, Cunard conceived, edited, and published *Negro* (1934), the first comprehensive anthology of literature by African and African American writers, artists, and political and cultural figures.

The daughter of Sir Bache Cunard—who was a grandson of Samuel Cunard, founder of the Cunard steamship line—and Maud Burke, an American socialite, Cunard rebelled against social expectations and showed more interest in associating with artists than with debutantes. After the dissolution of a brief marriage, Cunard moved to Paris in 1920 and made her home there among poets, painters, and novelists. She met and developed a friendship with Henry Crowder, an African American musician whom Cunard persuaded to collaborate with her in her purchase and installation of a printing press. It formed the basis of Hours Press, which published works by Samuel Beckett and Ezra Pound, among others.

From her increasing fascination with African American art and culture rose Cunard's conception of *Negro*, which includes writings by notable figures such as Langston HUGHES, Zora Neale HURSTON, W. E. B. DU BOIS, Arna BONTEMPS, and Cunard herself. (She wrote memorably about the SCOTTSBORO CASES, in which nine young black men were arrested

Nancy Cunard in 1927. *(Library of Congress)*

and falsely accused of raping two white women in Scottsboro, Alabama.) Throughout her life, she remained a controversial figure because of her association and friendships with Africans and African Americans, and she remained a champion of their artistic and intellectual contributions.

—*Holly L. Norton*

**Curtis, Austin Maurice, Sr.** (January 15, 1868, Raleigh, North Carolina—1939, Washington, D.C.): Surgeon and hospital administrator. Curtis earned a medical degree from Northwestern University in 1891, and in 1896 he was the first African American to be appointed as a surgeon at the Cook County Hospital in CHICAGO, ILLINOIS. He later served as chief administrative officer at Freedmen's Hospital in Washington, D.C., and as professor of surgery in HOWARD UNIVERSITY's medical college.
*See also:* Medicine.

Austin Maurice Curtis, Sr. *(National Library of Medicine)*

# D

**Dailey, Ulysses Grant** (August 3, 1885, Donaldsonville, Louisiana—April 22, 1961, Chicago, Illinois): Surgeon. Dailey began his career as surgical assistant to Daniel Hale WILLIAMS, the founder of Provident Hospital. After founding his own hospital in Chicago, Dailey made significant advances in anatomy and surgery. He extended his influence on the medical field by serving as associate editor of the NATIONAL MEDICAL ASSOCIATION's journal.

**Dallas, Texas:** The eighth-largest city in the United States and home to the country's sixth-largest African American community. Dallas's black residents number more than 20 percent of the city's population of about one million. Dallas County's black population exceeds 400,000. Dallas's South and East Sides together represent the largest contiguous settlement of African Americans.

Dallas's black history began with the settlement of a trading post on the west bank of TEXAS's Trinity River in 1837 near the current downtown business district. Historical records state that a slave named Smith moved to Dallas with the Gilbert family from Tennessee that year. Allen Huitt, a slave and a blacksmith by trade, is believed to have been the first African American in Dallas County. He was brought to Farmers Branch by John Huitt in 1843. There he worked and farmed near present-day Carrolton. Over the years, many settlers and travelers came to depend on him to make tools they needed and fixed wagons. It is recorded that by 1846 there were forty-five slaves in Dallas County and no freemen of African descent.

Records of the 1860's show about 1,000 people of African American heritage. By 1873, thirty years after Allen Huitt's arrival, 1,200 of the city's 7,000 residents were African American. By the beginning of the twentieth century, black people represented 10 percent of the population of 42,000.

Enormous changes occurred during the first quarter of the twentieth century. While agriculture still played an important part in American society, many people started moving to the cities, where jobs were available in the labor market. As Dallas continued to grow in population, agrarian African Americans migrated to the city and found employment. By the mid-twentieth century the Dallas population had reached almost 500,000 and the African American total was approaching 100,000.

As Dallas grew, its African American community was faced with a highly segregated city. Segregation was a part of a southern culture that had intensified after the end of the CIVIL WAR in 1865 and the RECONSTRUCTION era. In the late 1950's and early 1960's, race issues occasionally surfaced in the city regarding housing and educational separation. African American community leaders wanted an end to segregation and demanded the integration of schools and housing.

In March, 1960, the powerful Dallas Citizens Council, consisting of 250 heads of companies that employed or controlled nearly all the city's workforce, formed what was known as the Biracial Committee, a fourteen-member group. The committee and the city maintained a commitment to peaceful desegregation. Seventeen months after talks started, the commercial businesses of Dallas removed the restrictions that had been placed on African Americans. In the fall semester of 1961, school desegregation began with first-graders.

In 1971 Al Lipscomb became the first African American to run for MAYOR of Dallas. It was a landmark, if symbolic, gesture. Lipscomb had very little chance of winning, and he did not. In 1995, however, Ron Kirk did become the first black mayor of Dallas. Voter turnout among minorities was 25 percent, nearly double the usual figure.

*—Earl R. Andresen*
*See also:* Segregation and integration.

**Dance:** Although the image of the African American as a natural dancer with innate rhythm is an enduring stereotype in America, blacks have not had the same access to dance as a career as have whites. By the 1920's, black dancers had become familiar on the stage as they performed tap, soft-shoe, and jazz routines. These styles of dance were considered acceptable for blacks, as such dances tended to reinforce the image of the black with natural rhythm who required little or no training. Not all people of color, however, were content to limit themselves to certain styles of dance. In fact, some clearly resented the image of what was acceptable for them as dancers. The desire of blacks to enter the larger world of dance in some respects parallels the struggles of African Americans to gain entry to and recognition in other areas of American life.

*Early Dance Artists*
Some of the first blacks to challenge prevailing stereotypes and appear in concert dance were Hemsley Winfield, Edna Guy, Charles Williams, Charlotte Moton Kennedy, and Wilson Williams.

Born in Yonkers, New York, in 1907, Winfield, like other black artists of the 1920's, was inspired by the HARLEM RENAISSANCE, a cultural movement that sought to rid black literature and art of the "docile Negro" image by emphasizing literature and art forms based on the experiences of blacks in the West Indies and America. Accordingly, Winfield organized the Negro Art Theatre in HARLEM, which later became the Negro Art Theatre Dance Group. This troupe gave its first concert—billed as the first black dance performance in America—on April 29, 1931. Two years later, Winfield directed the ballet for the Metropolitan Opera Company's production of *The Emperor Jones*. Backed by his own dancers, he danced the part of the witch doctor, thus becoming the first African American to dance at the Met.

When members of Winfield's troupe performed their first concert, they were assisted by Edna Guy, another early African American pioneer in the field of concert dance. Guy had studied with Ruth St. Denis and is credited with introducing the dance spiritual, which became part of the repertoire of many modern-dance groups. Guy had become interested in black themes and had begun dancing to them after listening to the singing of Paul ROBESON.

Although Harlem in the 1920's and 1930's was the most likely place to find a successful black dance company, the Creative Dance Group, composed of students at the HAMPTON INSTITUTE in Hampton, Virginia, was performing at schools throughout the country. Formed in 1925 by Charles H. Williams, director of the college's physical education program, and Charlotte Moton Kennedy, the group's dances were based on a variety of African and African American themes.

Another pioneer black dance group was the sixteen-member Negro Dance Company. Founded in New York City by Wilson Williams, this troupe was intended to eliminate the minstrel stereotype of the black dancer. In its first performance in 1943, the group performed two dances by Wilson Williams—*Prodigal Son* and *Spring Ritual*. In addition, well-known dancer Anna Sokolow choreographed and danced *Breaking the Ice*.

*Dance and Anthropology*
Katherine DUNHAM and Pearl PRIMUS are credited with paving the road to the acceptance of black dancers as concert artists before

the modern CIVIL RIGHTS era. Dancer and scholar Dunham received a Rosenwald Fellowship, which allowed her to study anthropology and dance in the WEST INDIES. As a result of an eighteen-month stay in the islands, Dunham not only completed a master's thesis in anthropology but also became immersed in dances that she would later incorporate into her repertoire.

In 1940 Dunham and a company of nine dancers presented their first concert—*Tropics and Le Jazz Hot*. Subtitled *From Haiti to Harlem*, this revue earned many favorable reviews. Later that year, Dunham's dancers appeared in the all-black Broadway mu-

Katherine Dunham (right front) with the Katherine Dunham Dancers in 1946. *(Library of Congress)*

sical *Cabin in the Sky*. Afterward, Dunham danced for and choreographed dances for several motion pictures.

As a choreographer and teacher, too, Dunham experienced success. In 1945 she opened the Dunham School of Dance in New York City. She choreographed the Metropolitan Opera's new production of *Aida* for their 1963-1964 season. Dunham also developed cultural programs, including dance instruction, for the disadvantaged. She received numerous awards, including the Samuel H. Scripps American Dance Festival Award in 1986.

Like Dunham, TRINIDAD-born Pearl Primus trained as an anthropologist and a dancer. In 1944 she made her Broadway debut at the Belasco Theatre. Her performance included dances based on African and Haitian themes—*African Ceremonial*, *Strange Fruit*, and *The Negro Speaks of Rivers*. Primus received very favorable reviews, and at least one critic hailed her performance as historic. Primus not only sought

to acquaint audiences with black themes from the Caribbean and the United States but also introduced "dances of protest." These compositions, which she choreographed, were intended to call attention to the injustices, such as lynchings, experienced by African Americans.

### Alvin Ailey, Jr.'s Dance Success

As Americans became more familiar with the sufferings and injustices meted out to blacks during the early years of the civil rights era, many also became aware of the literary and artistic contributions of African Americans. Alvin AILEY took the African American experience via dance to more people than any other performer. Since the founding of his American Dance Theatre in 1958, his dancers have appeared throughout the world before more than fifteen million people.

Ailey's childhood memories of the church and the dance hall provided inspiration for

*(continued on page 688)*

## Notable Dancers

**Ailey, Alvin, Jr.** *See main text entry.*

**Allen, Debbie.** *See main text entry.*

**Atkins, Cholly.** *See main text entry.*

**Bates, Peg Leg.** *See main text entry.*

**Briggs, Bunny** (b. Feb. 26, 1922, New York, N.Y.): Briggs adapted the "paddle and roll" technique to such pantomime routines as pretending to have a backache and imitating a galloping horse. Throughout the 1930's and 1940's, he tap danced at clubs. In the 1960's, Briggs danced with Duke ELLINGTON's band. In 1989 he opened in the Broadway musical *Black and Blue.* He also appeared in occasional films.

**Bubbles, John.** *See main text entry.*

**Burge, Gregg** (b. c. 1960, Merrick, Long Island, N.Y.): As a child, he danced in television commercials and on *The Electric Company.* At seventeen, he played the Scarecrow in the Broadway production of *The Wiz.* He made his film debut in *A Chorus Line* in 1985. Burge also opened a dance studio in his hometown.

**Coles, Honi.** *See main text entry.*

**Collins, Janet** (b. Mar. 2, 1917, New Orleans, La.): The cousin of choreographer Carmen De Lavallade, Collins was the first African American to perform on the Metropolitan Opera Company's stage, in *La Giocanda* in 1951. An enthusiastic teacher as well as performer and student of dance, she studied with Carmelita Maracci, Lester Horton, and Mia Slavenska.

AP/Wide World Photos

**Dove, Ulysses** (Jan. 17, 1947, Jonesville, S.C.—June 11, 1996, New York, N.Y.): After seeing Dove perform with Merce Cunningham's company, Alvin AILEY invited Dove to join his company. Dove began working as a freelance choreographer in 1983. His works have been performed by dance companies throughout the world, including the American Ballet Theater and the Royal Swedish Ballet. His last ballet, *Twilight,* was premiered by the New York City Ballet in 1996, shortly before his death from complications related to ACQUIRED IMMUNODEFICIENCY SYNDROME (AIDS).

**Dunham, Katherine.** *See main text entry.*

**Glover, Savion** (b. c. 1974, Newark, N.J.): A natural tap dancer, Glover began dancing at the age of four. In 1984 he wowed Broadway audiences in *The Tap Dance Kid.* Six years later he returned to Broadway in *Black and Blue.* In 1991 he played Jelly Roll MORTON as a young man in the smash Broadway hit *Jelly's Last Jam.* Glover won a 1996 Tony Award as best choreographer for his work in the hit Broadway show *Bring in 'da Noise, Bring in 'da Funk.*

**Green, Charles "Chuck"** (1919?, near Atlanta, Ga.—Mar. 7, 1997, Oakland, Calif.). Green's gentlemanly dance style won him acclaim in the 1940's as a member of the comedy tap duo of Chuck and Chuckles. Green dedicated his later years to sharing his tap dancing talents with a new generation of dancers and fans. In the 1990's, he demonstrated different tap dancing styles in dancer Honi COLES's *Masters of Tap* instructional program.

**Guy, Jasmine** (b. Mar. 10, 1964, Boston, Mass.): Guy trained as a dancer at the Alvin Ailey Dance Center in New York City. Her career progressed to performances with the Atlanta Junior Ballet Company and then to theater, where she also incorporated her vocal talents in the plays *The Wiz, Bubbling Brown Sugar, Beehive,* and *Leader of the Pack.* She also appeared in such

NBC Photo

films as *School Daze* (1988) and *Harlem Nights* (1989). Her television movie roles include appearances in *A Killer Among Us* and *Stompin' at the Savoy.* She is probably best known for the character she played on the television series *A Different World.*

**Hines Brothers** Dance team of Maurice and Gregory HINES, who performed in nightclubs and theaters across the United States, displaying their tap-dancing talents to audiences for much of their childhood. Gregory (b. 1946), and Maurice (b. 1944), toured the United States and Europe first as the Hines Kids from 1949 to 1955 and as the Hines Brothers from 1955 to 1963. Joined by their father, they were billed as Hines, Hines, and Dad from 1963 to 1973. The brothers starred as a family dance act in the film *The Cotton Club* (1984).

**Hinkson, Mary** (b. 1930, Philadelphia, Pa.): Affiliated with Martha Graham and her company for many years, Hinkson is best remembered for her role in *Circe*, created for her in 1963. She has performed as a guest artist with numerous companies and has taught at the Graham School, the Juilliard School of Music, and the DANCE THEATER OF HARLEM.

**Holder, Geoffrey** (b. Aug. 1, 1930, Port-of-Spain, Trinidad): At the age of twelve, Holder made his stage debut in his brother Roscoe Holder's *Dance o' Trinidad*. He formed his own dance company in 1950. In 1954, Holder made his Broadway debut in *House of Flowers*. He was a solo dancer with the Metropolitan Opera from 1956 to 1957. From 1956 to 1960, he performed in concerts with the Geoffrey Holder Dance Company in New York City. He choreographed and designed *Three Songs for One* (1964). He again took multiple roles as director, designer, and choreographer for the musical *Timbuktu* in 1978.

**Jackson, "Baby" Laurence** (1921, Baltimore, Md.—1974, New York, N.Y.): As a master of close-to-the-floor tap virtuosity, Jackson was one of the few tap dance stars of the 1930's who managed to adapt his routines to striking changes in American popular music. Especially active from the 1930's through the 1950's, Jackson is considered to be one of the most original dancers of the JAZZ, swing, and BEBOP eras.

**Jamison, Judith** (b. May 10, 1943, Philadelphia, Pa.): Jamison began her artistic career when she joined the Alvin Ailey Dance Theater in New York City in 1965. She was the company's principal dancer until 1980, when she left to form her own company. In 1989 she returned to become artistic director of the Alvin Ailey Dance Theater. Her role in the Ailey-choreographed dance *Cry* is perhaps her best known—a fifteen-minute solo performance that is an ode to the sufferings of black women. Jamison published her autobiography, *Dancing Spirit*, in 1993.

**Johnson, Louis** (b. Mar. 19, 1933, Stateville, N.C.): Founder and director of the Louis Johnson Dance Theater, Johnson has choreographed performances for the Cincinnati Ballet, the Alvin Ailey Dance Company, the Dance Theater of Harlem, and the Metropolitan Opera Theater Ballet, and for such films as *Damn Yankees* (1958) and *The Wiz* (1978). He received a Tony Award nomination in 1970 for his choreography of *Purlie*.

**Johnson, Virginia Alma Fairfax** (b. Jan. 25, 1950, Washington, D.C.): Johnson began her career as a principal dancer for Dance Theater of Harlem in 1971 and kept that position for more than twenty years. She has been a guest artist for numerous major ballet companies and performed at the White House for Jimmy Carter and Ronald Reagan. Her numerous honors include a 1991 *Dance Magazine* award.

**Lane, William Henry.** *See main text entry.*

**Lemon, Ralph** (b. 1952?, Minneapolis, Minn.): Lemon did not learn to dance until he was in college. Uncomfortable with how other people wanted him to dance, he created his own dance routines. In 1985 he formed the Ralph Lemon Company, based in New York City, to perform his dance compositions. The company toured extensively in the U.S. and internationally from 1985 to 1995. In 1996 Lemon restructured his company from a group of seven dancers to an assorted group of collaborators and performers.

**LeTang, Henry** (b. 1915?, New York, N.Y.): Founder and director of the Henry LeTang School of Dance, LeTang had a long history as a teacher as well as performer of dance. His tap-dance students included Lena HORNE, Billie HOLIDAY, Lola Falana, Debbie ALLEN, and Harry BELAFONTE. He contributed numbers to Broadway musicals including *The Wiz* in 1975 and *Bubbling Brown Sugar* in 1976. He choreographed *Eubie!* in 1978 and received both a Tony nomination and a Drama Critics Award.

**Long, Avon** (June 18, 1910, Baltimore, Md.—Feb. 15, 1984, New York, N.Y.): Long's career spanned more than fifty years. He danced at the COTTON CLUB in 1931 and made his debut on the black VAUDEVILLE

*(continued)*

circuit in 1934. His performance as Sportin' Life in the 1942 revival of *Porgy and Bess* won him widespread acclaim. His career was revived in the early 1970's, when he was cast in the films *The Sting* (1973) and *Harry and Tonto* (1974). Later stage credits include *Don't Play Us Cheap* (1972), for which he received a Tony nomination, and *Bubbling' Brown Sugar* in 1975.

AP/Wide World Photos

**Miller, Bebe** (Beryl Adele Miller; b. Sept. 20, 1950, Brooklyn, N.Y.): Miller established her own modern dance company in New York City in 1984. After 1978 she became active as a choreographer. Her works suggest content, atmosphere, and feelings, especially in personal solos such as *Spending Time Doing Things* (performed to a version of Duke Ellington's song "In My Solitude") and *Rain* (1989). Her group works include *Trapped in Queens* (1984), *The Hendrix Project* (1991), and *Hidden Boy: Incidents from a Stressed Memory* (1991).

**Millinder, Lucius Venable "Lucky"** (Aug. 8, 1900, Anniston, Ala.—Sept. 28, 1966, New York, N.Y.): A dancer, jazz composer, and bandleader, Millinder performed under the stage name Lucius Venable. He became the leader of his own jazz band in 1931 on the R.K.O. circuit. In 1933 he became the leader of the Mills Blue Rhythm Band. He formed the Lucky Millinder Orchestra, featuring vocalist Sister Rosetta THARPE, in 1940. The band played regularly at the Savoy Ballroom and in the early years included such talented young jazz musicians as Dizzy GILLESPIE, Freddie Webster, and Eddie "Lockjaw" Davis.

**Mitchell, Arthur** (b. Mar. 27, 1934, New York, N.Y.): Known to many as the "Pied Piper of Dance," Mitchell was the first black principal dancer in a major company, making his debut with the New York City Ballet in 1955. Mitchell founded the Dance Theater of Harlem in 1969. In 1988, he realized a longtime dream and took the company to the Soviet Union, where it met with full houses and standing ovations. In 1992, he took the company to newly democratic South Africa to perform and to give lectures and demonstrations.

**Nicholas Brothers** (Fayard Nicholas, b. Oct. 20, 1914, Mobile, Ala.; Harold Nicholas, 1924, New York, N.Y.—July 3, 2000, New York, N.Y.): In 1931, the Nicholas Brothers made their professional debut tapping on "The Horn and Hardart Children's Hour," a RADIO program. The duo soon started performing at the Cotton Club where their routine combining tap and acrobatics, performed with sophistication and elegance, gained them immense popularity. They performed in numerous films throughout their career and during the latter part of their career, the brothers were sought as consultants for shows and films featuring tap dance. They have received numerous awards including a 1995 *Dance Magazine* award.

**Nugent, Pete** (b. 1910?): Best known as the leader of Pete, Peaches, and Duke, Nugent built a career on a classic tap style that set the standard for many dance acts during the 1930's. As an individual dancer, Nugent made full use of the stage and was famous for stylish body motion. As a choreographer, he is credited with the remarkable teamwork of Pete, Peaches, and Duke, as well as for the continuity of the solos. The dance trio broke up in 1937. Years later, Nugent starred in Duke Ellington's short-lived musical *Jump for Joy* (1941). In 1944, he was hired to dance with Billy ECKSTINE's bebop band.

**Primus, Pearl.** *See main text entry.*

**Ray, Gene Anthony** (b. May 24, 1962, New York, N.Y.): Actor and dancer. Best known for his role as Leroy on the long-running television series *Fame* from 1982 to 1987, Ray also appeared on the television shows *Livewire* (in 1984) and *Hollywood Squares* (in 1987).

**Rector, Eddie** (late 1890's, Orange, N.J.—1962, New York, N.Y.): Considered to be the greatest soloist among soft shoe dancers and the forerunner of the sleek "class-act" style, Rector was in his heyday during the 1920's. He excelled in the waltz clog and invented a much-copied traveling-time step known as the bambalina, but he is especially noted for bringing full body motion and elegance to tap dancing. His hallmark was a graceful sand dance, a soft shoe variation performed on sand that has been sprinkled onstage to give a swishing sound to the steps. He performed in numerous revues and shows throughout his dance career.

**Richardson, Desmond** (b. Sumter, N.C.): Richardson joined the Alvin Ailey Dance Company in 1987 and remained with the company for six years. He has worked with many of the dance world's leading talents including Judith Jamison and Ulysses Dove. He joined the American Ballet Theatre as a principal dancer in 1996. In 1999 he received acclaim for his performance in the Broadway musical *Fosse*. He went on to codirect a new dance company, Complexions.

**Robinson, Bill "Bojangles."** *See main text entry.*

**Sims, Howard "Sandman"** (b. 1918): Sims improvised his way from one-footed rattles to comical galumphing, making a unique contribution to tap with his sand dancing. Through the 1950's and 1960's, "Sandman" Sims was a fixture at the APOLLO THEATER, headlining with his dancing, working Amateur Night from the box, or mentoring backstage. Many accomplished dancers came under his tutelage, including Ben Vereen and Gregory Hines. Sims's credits include guest appearances on such television programs as *The Cosby Show*, video documentaries such as *No Maps on My Taps* (1979) and *Tappin': The Making of Tap* (1989), and the feature film *Tap* (1989).

**Slyde, Jimmy** (b. Atlanta, Ga.): Slyde started studying tap when he was about twelve years old. A teacher influenced him to incorporate sliding into his dancing and sliding became his trademark. He joined Jimmy "Sir Slide" Mitchell to form the Slyde Brothers, performing in nightclubs, burlesque houses, and theaters throughout the United States. Slyde was most active in the 1940's, starting work while a teenager, and the 1950's.

**Step Brothers:** A top tap act from the 1920's through the mid-1960's, the Step Brothers won distinction with acrobatics and flash. The Step Brothers were not actually brothers; they were members of a group that often changed. Known for their diversity and durability, they incorporated singing, comedy, and the latest dance trends—from flips, splits, and dance acrobatics to boogie-woogie and jitterbug-style tap—into routines. They were the first African American performers to appear on many stages that previously had been the exclusive terrain of white entertainers.

**Vereen, Ben** (b. Oct. 10, 1946, Miami, Fla.): Singer, dancer, and actor. Vereen is best known for his work on television, particularly his Emmy-nominated performance as Chicken George in *Roots* (1977). In 1984 he appeared in both the dramatic miniseries *Ellis Island* and the made-for-television film biography *The Jesse Owens Story*. Ever versatile, Vereen also hosted *Zoobilee Zoo*, a syndicated children's program. In April of 1993, he joined the cast of the Broadway musical *Jelly's Last Jam*—a move that revived his theatrical career.

AP/Wide World Photos

**Washington, Lula** (b. c. 1951): Dancer and choreographer. Washington is artistic director of the Los Angeles Contemporary Dance Theater, which performs modern dance. It is part of the Lula Washington Contemporary Dance Foundation, which also operates the Children's Jazz Dance Ensemble. Washington founded her company in 1980, created and ran the Rainbow Outta This World Dance Festival in 1981, danced in the opening ceremonies of the Olympic Games in 1984, and choreographed the 1989 film *The Little Mermaid*. Into the late 1990's Washington continued to dance and choreograph pieces.

**Whitman Sisters.** *See main text entry.*

**Winfield, Hemsley** (1907, Yonkers, N.Y.—1934): As the founder of the New Negro Art Theatre Dance Group, Winfield brought tribal African dance forms and African American themes to the stage in a serious dance format. He made history as a pioneer of black concert dance. Winfield began his career as an actor in the Broadway plays *Lulu Belle* (1926) and *Harlem* (1929). The highlight of Winfield's career was the New York Metropolitan Opera's 1933 presentation of *The Emperor Jones*. Winfield became the first African American to appear at the Metropolitan Opera. His company took the place of the Metropolitan Opera's *corps de ballet*.

some of his earliest dance compositions. Both his *Blues Suite*, which critics praised, and his *Revelations*, which became synonymous with his name, were based on the artist's experiences in a small Texas town. These experiences were shared by many other African Americans, and Ailey's creativity made the dance world aware of two major themes in the molding of many black lives.

Ailey received numerous awards for his work as a dancer and choreographer. One of the most prestigious was his being named one of the five outstanding American artists to be honored by the Kennedy Center for the Performing Arts in 1988. When President Ronald Reagan presented the award to Ailey, he noted that the artist had transfigured the dance world.

### Blacks in Ballet

Although African Americans have become fixtures, even trendsetters, in the world of

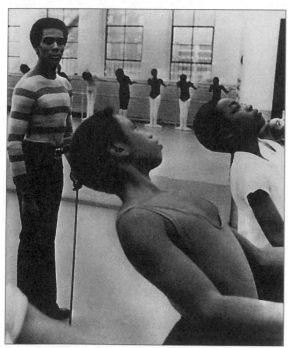

Arthur Mitchell (left) directing an exercise session at the Dance Theater of Harlem. *(AP/Wide World Photos)*

modern dance, black dancers have found fewer opportunities in classical ballet. The small number of African Americans in the field has been attributed, in large part, to stereotypical images of the successful ballerina as white. Some African Americans, however, have challenged the notion that they are "not suited" for classical ballet.

From 1951 to 1954, Janet Collins was the *premiere danseuse* of the Metropolitan Opera Ballet. Although she danced the role of the Ethiopian in the opera *Aida* at the Met, she was not limited to roles that called for people of color. She also danced a gypsy in *Carmen* and was the leading dancer in "Dance of the Hours" in *La Gioconda*.

In the 1970's Arthur MITCHELL became the most successful African American in classical ballet. He was a graduate of the New York High School of the Performing Arts and a recipient of a scholarship at the School of the American Ballet, yet his entry into classical ballet was not easy. His opportunities were limited by his color, although he was a member of the prestigious New York City Ballet. One of his most famous roles, in the *pas de deux* from *Agon*, was created especially for him. He was frequently partnered with white ballerinas, but his performances with them were restricted as late as the 1960's.

In what has been described as a reaction to the assassination of Martin Luther King, Jr., Mitchell organized a school called the DANCE THEATER OF HARLEM in 1969. He envisioned the school as an institution that would promote interest in classical ballet among young blacks and offer courses in modern and ethnic dance. Mitchell wanted to interest youngsters in the dance as a career, but more important, he wanted to prove that a black ballet school and a black classical ballet company could be successful.

The Dance Theatre of Harlem made its official debut in 1971 at the Guggenheim Museum in New York City. Three of Mitchell's works,

*Rhythemtron*, *Tones*, and *Fete Noire*, were premiered. Like the American Dance Theatre, Mitchell's Dance Theatre of Harlem appeared before audiences throughout the world. One of the company's most triumphant performances occurred at the Kirov Theater in Moscow in 1988. Soviet ballet fans appeared awestruck, while the members of the troupe had the satisfaction of knowing that they had "arrived" in the land that had perfected the classical ballet.

Members of the Los Angeles cast of *Bring in 'da Noise, Bring in 'da Funk* in 1998. *(AP/Wide World Photos)*

*Developments in the 1990's*

In 1997 the *New York Times* conducted a survey among ten of the leading ballet companies in the United States. The results of the survey divulged that of 495 members, only 23 or 4.6 percent were African American. The survey also listed only two classically oriented African American dance companies—The Dance Theater of Harlem and Ballethnic. In the ensuing years, a few ballet companies have made attempts to interest African American youth in ballet. In 1997 one of the leading ballet companies in the nation—the New York City Ballet—included work by noted black choreographers John Alleyne and Ulysses Dove and also included four African American dancers.

In the late 1990's several well-established, as well as younger dancers and choreographers continued to contribute to the world of African American dance. In addition to her numerous acting, dancing, and choreography projects, Debbie Allen has choreographed the dance programs of several Oscar programs. Savion Glover brought new recognition to the field of tap dancing. After starring in two hit Broadway plays, *Black and Blue* and *Jelly's Last Jam*, Glover went on to star in his biggest hit, the critically acclaimed *Bring in 'da Noise, Bring in 'da Funk*. The Broadway hit developed by Glover and George Wolfe presented the chronology of black America in tap dance form and won four 1996 Tony Awards, including one for Glover as best choreographer.

—*Betty L. Plummer*
—*Updated by Andrea E. Miller*

See also: African music and dance; American Negro Ballet.

Suggested Readings:

Emery, Lynne F. *Black Dance: From 1617 to Today*. 2d rev. ed. Princeton, N.J.: Princeton Book Company, 1988.

Gottschild, Brenda D. *Digging the Africanist Presence in American Performance: Dance and Other Contexts*. Westport, Conn.: Greenwood Press, 1996.

Haskins, James. *Black Dance in America: A History Through Its People*. New York: Thomas Y. Crowell, 1990.

Kraus, Richard, Sarah Chapman Hilsendager, and Brenda Dixon. "Black Dance in America." In *History of the Dance in Art and Education*. Englewood Cliffs, N.J.: Prentice-Hall, 1991.

Long, Richard A. *The Black Tradition in American Dance.* New York: Rizzoli, 1989.

Malone, Jacqui. *Steppin' on the Blues: The Visible Rhythms of African American Dance.* Urbana: University of Illinois Press, 1996.

Shook, Karel. *Elements of Classical Ballet Technique as Practiced in the School of the Dance Theatre of Harlem.* New York: Dance Horizons, 1977.

Small, Linda. "Black Dancers, Black Travelers." *Dance Magazine* (October, 1979): 78.

**Dance Theater of Harlem:** DANCE company and school founded by Arthur MITCHELL, a New York City Ballet dancer, in 1969. It provided young African Americans with the chance to learn classical ballet and to perform with the theater's affiliated performing company. In 1974 the company had its first major New York City season. It soon became one of the United States' premier ballet companies. The company toured extensively and internationally and won many major awards and honors.

**Dandridge, Dorothy** (November 9, 1924, Cleveland, Ohio—September 8, 1965, Los Angeles, California): Actor and singer. Dorothy Dandridge was the first black actor to be presented to the American public as a sex symbol as well as an actor.

*Early Performing Career*
Dandridge was born in Cleveland, Ohio, to Cyril and Ruby Dandridge. Cyril Dandridge left his wife and oldest daughter, Vivian, just before Dorothy was born. Ruby Dandridge discovered quickly that her children were talented performers. Under her instruction, the shy, introverted Dorothy and the outgoing Vivian became known as the Wonder Kids and began performing in cities across the South. Hoping for better opportunities for her family,

Ruby Dandridge moved her family to Hollywood, California. During the GREAT DEPRESSION, the Wonder Kids worked hard to help supplement the income their mother earned working as a maid and in restaurants. Memories of those lean times would remain with Dorothy. Throughout her career, no matter how much money she made, she was always conscious of each dollar she spent.

A comedian and actor in her own right, Ruby Dandridge carved her own niche in Hollywood. During the course of her career, she appeared on radio programs including *Beulah*, *The Judy Canova Show*, and the AMOS 'N' ANDY radio and television programs. She also appeared in such films as *My Wild Irish Rose* (1947) and *Cabin in the Sky* (1943).

In 1934 the Wonder Kids added Etta Jones to the group and became the Dandridge Sisters. The group won amateur contests and during the early 1940's had bit parts in a few films. As a result of these small successes, the Dandridge Sisters toured the country with several bands and earned an opportunity to perform at the COTTON CLUB in HARLEM, New York, with such well-known performers as Cab CALLOWAY and Duke ELLINGTON. During this engagement, fourteen-year-old Dorothy met the man who would be her first husband, Harold Nicholas, half of the famous Nicholas Brothers dance team.

Dandridge and Nicholas were married four years later. While Dorothy was inexperienced and uninformed, Nicholas was worldly and impatient, and the marriage immediately began to crumble. Within days, Nicholas began seeing other women. Dandridge, who had stopped performing, became pregnant within three months. At the end of her first year of marriage, she gave birth to a daughter. Her baby was born mentally disabled, and she could not handle the challenge of raising it. This tragedy and the disillusion of her marriage left Dandridge believing herself to be a failure as a wife, lover, and mother.

Determined to be successful in some aspect of her life, she plunged headlong into training herself as an actor and performer, perfecting her vocal style. She worked tirelessly with a daily exercise program and acting classes to prepare herself for what seemed inevitable, the failing of her marriage. After five years of marriage, Dandridge and Nicholas were divorced, and Dorothy found herself in financial trouble. She needed money to take care of her daughter and keep a roof over her head.

### Cultivating a New Image

In the late 1940's, Dandridge began working with composer Phil Moore. Moore's instinct and talent helped to cultivate such great performers as Lena HORNE and, later, Diahann CARROLL. Dandridge became Moore's protégé. He helped her define her vocal and performing style, choosing her music, hairstyles, wardrobe, and makeup, ensuring that Dandridge looked the part of the glamorous, sophisticated performer she was trying to be. Their professional relationship became intimate.

Moore introduced Dandridge to Earl Mills, a man who would become her agent and lifelong friend. Mills got Dandridge singing engagements around LOS ANGELES, but in the beginning, the money she earned barely paid expenses. When she did have money left over, Dandridge poured it into her wardrobe and costumes for her stage show. Having the right look on stage was very important to Dandridge's success.

The bashful Dandridge would sometimes experience a loss of breath, chest spasms, leg cramps, and a tingling sensation in her hands and feet before a performance. Moore helped her through these anxiety attacks by joking and talking to her on stage, helping her to relax during the performance. Dandridge learned to control her stage anxieties and was on her way to becoming one of the hottest nightclub performers in the country. Her collaboration with Moore also resulted in two songs that would remain a part of her repertoire throughout her career, "Talk Sweet to Me" and "Blow Out the Candle."

### Success

Dandridge attained true success when she opened at La Vie en Rose, a nightclub in NEW YORK CITY. The engagement was originally supposed to last two weeks, but because of her tremendous appeal and success at the club, Dandridge stayed on for sixteen weeks. During her engagement at La Vie en Rose, *Look* magazine ran an extensive spread on her, introducing her to millions of its readers. As she performed in clubs throughout the country, she received write-ups in several prominent magazines, including *Quick* and *Esquire*, and was featured on the cover of *Life* magazine.

While in New York, Dandridge met the young, handsome Harry BELAFONTE, who would later become world-famous as a singer and performer. Dandridge and Belafonte were

Dorothy Dandridge as Bess, with Sammy Davis, Jr., as Sporting Life, in the film *Porgy and Bess* (1958). (*AP/Wide World Photos*)

destined to become professionally and personally involved. Professional rivalry would cause the two to end their personal relationship, but they remained friends. Dandridge continued performing around the country. Her success was putting a wedge between herself and her mentor, Moore. He felt that Dandridge was allowing her heightened success to go to her head. Moore believed that he was indispensable to her career; Dandridge proved he was not.

As her fame began to grow, Dandridge found herself pursued by rich and powerful men, most of whom were white. She had a string of unsuccessful romances with several men, including actor Peter Lawford and producer Otto Preminger. She found that these men would go out with her because of her beauty and sensuous style but would not marry her because of her color.

Dorothy Dandridge and Harry Belafonte in *Carmen Jones*; Dandridge's performance in this film earned for her the first nomination for a best-acting Academy Award ever given to an African American. *(Museum of Modern Art, Film Stills Archive)*

### Film Career

In the early 1950's, Dandridge's FILM career began blossom. She played an African princess in the 1951 picture *Tarzan's Peril*. In the film, Dandridge's character is kidnapped by an enemy tribe and is tied between two stakes. The twisting, turning, and screaming that Dandridge did during the scene marked the first time that a black woman was presented to white moviegoers as an erotic fantasy.

Her next picture, *The Harlem Globetrotters* (1951), cast Dandridge as a loving wife to a husband tempted to go wrong. *Bright Road* (1953) featured an all-black cast, including Harry Belafonte; Dandridge received high praise for her portrayal of a sensitive schoolteacher. EBONY and *Life* magazines covered the film with stories built on Dandridge and her impending elevation to a place among Hollywood's top female stars.

Then came the chance of a lifetime. Dandridge learned that Otto Preminger was about to produce a film adaptation of the Billy Rose stage hit *Carmen Jones*. She knew the role was meant for her. When Dandridge met with Preminger to audition for the part of Carmen, she was her usual sophisticated, glamorous self. Preminger did not believe that she was capable of being Carmen because she was so sophisticated. Dandridge, however, was determined. She convinced Preminger to let her read for the part again the next day.

Dandridge wasted no time. She vowed to return to Preminger's office as Carmen. She put on heavy makeup, a wig, a low-cut blouse worn off the shoulder, and a provocative skirt. When she walked into his office the next day, Preminger is said to have shouted, "My God, it's Carmen!" Dandridge got the role.

*Carmen Jones* was the most successful all-black film of its time. This modern adaptation of Georges Bizet's opera *Carmen* tells the story of a black factory worker, Carmen, who lures Joe, played by Harry Belafonte, away from his sweetheart and then dumps him for a famous prizefighter. In the end, Carmen is the victim of her own beauty, passions, and manipulation.

The 1954 smash made Dandridge a star of the first magnitude. She won rave reviews for her portrayal of the devious, insecure, and confused Carmen. She received an Academy Award nomination as best actor, the first time that a black actor was nominated for a best-acting award in a leading role. The media gave Dandridge unprecedented coverage for a black performer. Almost every publication ran feature stories about her. She was formally invited by the French government to the Cannes Film Festival for a special screening of *Carmen Jones*.

### Later Career

After her success in *Carmen Jones*, Dandridge's career and personal life began to falter. There were limited opportunities for black women in Hollywood, and three years passed before she made another film.

In 1957 Dandridge costarred with Belafonte and James Mason in *Island in the Sun*. The film caused great controversy at a time when the lines that defined the racial climate of America were well established. Dandridge became the first black woman on the American screen to be held in the arms of a white man. Some movie houses in the South boycotted the film, and southern lawmakers attempted to pass a law that would impose a five-thousand-dollar fine on any theater showing the film. Regardless, *Island in the Sun* grossed $8 million.

Over the next few years, Dandridge made several more films, including *The Decks Ran Red* in 1958, *Tamango* in 1959, and 1960's *Malaga*. None of these films was a commercial success. In 1959, too, Dandridge played Bess in Preminger's film version of *Porgy and Bess*; it was her last major success. As in *Carmen*

*Jones*, she played a sultry, sassy, woman; Bess leaves her man for a seemingly more exciting life but finds tragedy instead.

Dandridge married her second husband, restaurateur Jack Dennison, that year, and soon found herself pouring money into his ill-fated business ventures. Dennison was draining her and giving nothing in return. Dandridge returned to nightclub singing to hold the creditors back. Her life was falling apart; she began having severe bouts of depression, and her doctor prescribed antidepressant pills. Her money ran out, and her marriage failed. Dandridge sold her home and filed for bankruptcy after divorcing Dennison in 1962. She unsuccessfully attempted a comeback in the early 1960's. She died of an overdose of antidepressants in September, 1965.

—*Gwen Sparks*

Suggested Readings:

Bogle, Donald. *Brown Sugar: Eighty Years of America's Black Female Superstars*. New York: Harmony Books, 1980.

_____. *Dorothy Dandridge: A Biography*. New York: Amistad Press, 1997.

Dandridge, Dorothy, and Earl Conrad. *Everything and Nothing: The Dorothy Dandridge Tragedy*. New York: Abelard-Schuman, 1970.

Mills, Earl. *Dorothy Dandridge*. Los Angeles: Holloway House, 1970.

Steinem, Gloria. "Women in the Dark: Of Sex Goddesses, Abuse, and Dreams." *Ms.* (January/February, 1991): 35-37.

**Darden, Christopher A.** (b. April 7, 1956, Richmond, California): Attorney. After graduating from San Jose State University in 1977, Darden received his J.D. degree from the University of California's Hastings College of Law in San Francisco in 1980. As a deputy district attorney with the Major Crimes Division of the Los Angeles County district attorney's office, Darden became involved in a number

Christopher A. Darden at the O. J. Simpson trial in 1995.
(AP/Wide World Photos)

of high profile court cases. After completing work on the Reginald Denny beating case, he served as an assistant prosecutor on the O. J. SIMPSON murder trial. During the trial, Darden clashed often with African American defense attorney Johnnie COCHRAN, prompting Judge Lance Ito at one point to cite Darden for contempt of court. Although Darden's handling of the case was commended, the media attention given to his behavior and that of the other attorneys prompted renewed discussion concerning the role of television in the courtroom.

In December of 1995, Darden announced his plans to take a leave of absence from the district attorney's office in order to teach classes full-time at Southwestern University of Law, where he had been serving as an adjunct professor. After signing a lucrative book deal with ReganBooks, a division of HarperCollins, Darden published *In Contempt* (1996). This book about the Simpson trial reached the top of *The New York Times Book Review*'s best-seller list.

*See also:* Legal professions.

**Dash, Julie** (b. 1952, New York, New York): FILM director. Dash's films explore subjec-

tive and historical dimensions of black women's experience. Her short works include *Four Women* (1978), which uses a Nina SIMONE song as its focus, *Diary of An African Nun* (1976), based on an Alice WALKER short story, and *Illusions* (1982), which depicts a light-skinned Hollywood executive passing for white in the 1940's. *Illusions* was named the BLACK FILMMAKER FOUNDATION's best black film of the decade. Dash's critically acclaimed first feature, *Daughters of the Dust* (1991), lyrically depicts the lives of GULLAH women of the early twentieth-century Sea Islands off the coast of SOUTH CAROLINA. It was the first feature film directed by an African American woman to be released nationally in the United States. Dash also directed the 1999 film *Funny Valentines*.

**Davis, Angela** (b. January 26, 1944, Birmingham, Alabama): Activist and educator. Angela Yvonne Davis came to national prominence during the late 1960's and early 1970's, when she was involved in two legal cases affecting her political and CIVIL RIGHTS as an American citizen. Underlying both of these cases were her COMMUNIST PARTY affiliation and the fear on the part of public officials that that affiliation generated.

*Youth and Education*
Davis matured in a family committed to social change. She grew up in a segregated BIRMINGHAM, ALABAMA, neighborhood known locally as Dynamite Hill because it was the site of frequent bombings of black homes. These occurrences, coupled with her parents' involvement with the NATIONAL ASSOCIATION FOR THE ADVANCEMENT OF COLORED PEOPLE (NAACP), the Southern Negro Youth Congress, and the SCOTTSBORO CASES, were the inspiration for her later activism. As a youngster, she received a scholarship that allowed

her to attend Elizabeth Irwin High School, a progressive private institution in NEW YORK CITY. While attending high school, Davis lived with the Melish family, who were long acknowledged for their radical politics. Davis was thus exposed to socialist thought at home and at school, and attendance at Communist Party youth meetings rounded out her early progressive activities.

Upon her graduation, Davis was awarded a full scholarship to Brandeis University in Waltham, MASSACHUSETTS, where she majored in French literature. Her experience at Brandeis proved to be a turning point in her intellectual development. Spending her third year of college studying at the Sorbonne in Paris, Davis witnessed the discrimination and brutality directed against Algerians in France. These events sharpened her awareness of the political plight of diasporan Africans. Returning to Brandeis in her senior year, she experienced the awakening of her black feminist consciousness when she heard MALCOLM X speak at Brandeis. Intellectually, she matured under the tutelage of Herbert Marcuse, the celebrated Marxist philosopher, who influenced her decision to do graduate studies at Frankfurt University. Graduating from Brandeis magna cum laude in 1965, Davis shifted her interest from French literature to contemporary philosophy and pursued graduate studies in Frankfurt.

In Europe, Davis's political activities included attending the World Youth Festival in Helsinki and participating in anti-VIETNAM WAR demonstrations. After two years of study at the Institute for Social Research at the University of Frankfurt in Germany, Davis returned to the United States.

*Activism*

Davis earned her master's degree in philosophy in one year at the University of California at San Diego, simultaneously becoming a doctoral candidate in the same field. Her political activism, nurtured by the Civil Rights movement, intensified. She joined the STUDENT NONVIOLENT COORDINATING COMMITTEE (SNCC) and the BLACK PANTHER PARTY and became the leader of the Che Lumumba group, an all-black arm of the American Communist Party, which she had joined in 1968.

In 1969 Davis was hired as an assistant professor of philosophy at the University of California at Los Angeles, where she was completing work on her doctoral dissertation. Governor Ronald Reagan of California, citing a state law that prohibited Communist Party members from teaching at state universities, fired Davis. Davis took her case to court. The California courts upheld Davis's appeal and declared the law unconstitutional, and Davis was reinstated.

Davis's political involvement with the Black Panther Party soon made her aware of the plight of black prison inmates. Most par-

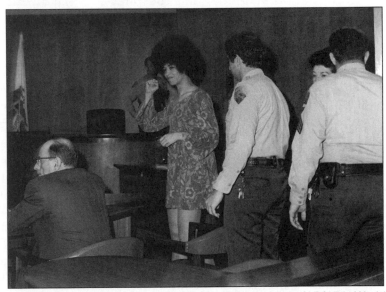

Angela Davis reporting to a California court in late 1969. *(AP/Wide World Photos)*

ticularly, she spoke out on behalf of the SOLEDAD BROTHERS, three inmates at a prison in Soledad, California, who had been charged with killing a prison guard. She became personally involved with their leader, George JACKSON. Her political activism again came to the attention of the California officials. She was fired a second time in 1970, this time for speeches she had given in support of the Soledad Brothers that had allegedly interfered with her effectiveness as a teacher. A faculty committee, however, held that she had not compromised her faculty position.

### The Soledad Brothers

In that same year, 1970, Davis was catapulted to national prominence. In August, Jonathan Jackson, George Jackson's brother, sought to negotiate the Soledad Brothers' release by seizing hostages during a trial at the Marin County, California, courthouse. In the subsequent courtroom shootout, Jonathan Jackson and a judge were both killed. Since guns that Davis had purchased were used by Jackson in the courtroom shootout, Davis was seen as Jackson's coconspirator, and she was charged with murder, kidnapping, and conspiracy. Fleeing California, Davis became a fugitive; the FEDERAL BUREAU OF INVESTIGATION (FBI) placed her on its most-wanted list. Captured two months later, she emerged as a political symbol to the international community. Immediately, there was a response on her behalf from political activists. Under the umbrella of the National United Committee to Free Angela Davis, civil rights and leftist activists mobilized for her defense.

In 1972 the case went to trial, and Davis was acquitted of all charges. She made an international and national tour to thank her supporters. Within the year, her defense committee was renamed the National Alliance Against Racist and Political Repression, with Davis serving as one of the founders and cochair. The alliance undertook to bring politically re-

Angela Davis in 1989. *(AP/Wide World Photos)*

lated criminal cases, the majority involving black and Latino defendants, to the attention of the public. The alliance grew to more than twenty chapters throughout the United States.

### Later Academic Career

Davis continued to pursue her career as an educator. In addition to teaching on the faculties of San Francisco State University and the University of California at Santa Cruz (UCSC), she continued her volunteer work teaching black female inmates in California prisons and correctional facilities. Also remaining active in the Communist Party, she was the party's vice presidential candidate in the 1980 and 1984 elections. In 1991 she was appointed professor of the history of consciousness interdisciplinary graduate program at UCSC. Her areas of concentration include the fields of cultural studies, African American studies, and black feminist theory.

In 1995 Davis was appointed to the University of California Presidential Chair at UCSC. Among the highest academic honors awarded within the University of California system, the chair was created in 1991 to encourage new interdisciplinary programs at each of the campuses within the system. Davis's appointment was approved by the administration at UCSC after her proposal was selected by a campus review committee. Her appointment, immediately controversial, was the subject of a protest movement led by William Leonard, a Republican state senator from Upland who demanded that her appointment be rescinded.

University of California president Jack Peltason refused to accede to Leonard's demands, and a host of other University of California officials and faculty members came to Davis's defense. Under pressure as the result of misrepresentations in the press, officials at UCSC issued a statement to clarify the terms of the three-year appointment. The statement also noted that, "far from encouraging division among ethnic and racial groups, [Davis is] internationally known for her effort to build bridges across them and to overcome racial, ethnic, and national antagonism."

The endowment afforded Davis the opportunity to pursue several longtime interests, one being the study of the criminalization and incarceration of women in the United States. Each year of her appointment, Davis spent one academic quarter teaching a graduate seminar at UCSC and acted as a consultant to the university's Department of Black Studies to develop a graduate program. Davis also outlined plans to develop lower-division undergraduate courses to examine the intersection of race, class, gender, and sexuality in minority cultures.

Davis's books include *If They Come in the Morning: Voices of Resistance* (1971), *Angela Davis: An Autobiography* (1974), *Women, Race, and Class* (1981), *Blues Legacies and Black Feminism* (1998), and a collection edited by Joy James entitled *The Angela Davis Reader* (1998).

—Gayle T. Tate
—Updated by Shirley G. Kennedy

Suggested Readings:

Aptheker, Bettina. *The Morning Breaks: The Trial of Angela Davis*. 2d ed. Ithaca, N.Y.: Cornell University Press, 1999.

Davis, Angela. *Angela Davis: An Autobiography*. New York: Random House, 1974.

_____. *The Angela Y. Davis Reader*. Edited by Joy James. Cambridge, Mass.: Blackwell, 1998.

_____. *If They Come in the Morning: Voices of Resistance*. New York: Third Press, 1971.

Gidding, Paula. *When and Where I Enter: The Impact of Black Women on Race and Sex in America*. New York: Bantam Books, 1984.

Marable, Manning. *How Capitalism Underdeveloped Black America*. Boston: South End Press, 1983.

**Davis, Arthur Paul** (b. November 21, 1904, Hampton, Virginia): Educator and literary critic. Davis wrote *From the Dark Tower: Afro-American Writers, 1900-1960* (1974) and coedited, with Sterling Allen Brown and Ulysses Lee, *The Negro Caravan* (1941), an anthology. Davis received his B.A., M.A., and Ph.D. from Columbia University. He taught at North Carolina College for Negroes (later called North Carolina Central) from 1927 to 1928, at Virginia Union University from 1929 to 1944, and then at HOWARD UNIVERSITY.

*See also:* Literature.

**Davis, Benjamin O., Jr.** (b. December 18, 1912, Washington, D.C.): MILITARY officer. Davis became the first African American Air Force general on October 27, 1954. He was only the second African American general in the armed forces, following his father, Benjamin O. DAVIS, Sr. He was also the first African American to command an air base on U.S. soil when he took command of Godman Field in Kentucky on June 21, 1945. President Lyndon Johnson promoted him to the rank of lieuten-

Benjamin O. Davis, Jr., the first African American general in the U.S. Air Force. *(U.S. Air Force)*

ant general on April 16, 1965. He was the first African American to reach that rank in any of the U.S. armed forces branches.

Davis was educated at TUSKEGEE INSTITUTE, the Western Reserve University, the University of Chicago, and the U.S. Military Academy at West Point. When he enrolled at West Point in 1932, he was the only African American in attendance. He graduated in 1936, ranking thirty-fifth in a class of 276. He joined the Army Air Corps in 1941, becoming one of the TUSKEGEE AIRMEN. Previously, African Americans had not been allowed in aviation training programs. At Tuskegee, a group of African American officers was trained.

Davis became commander of the NINETY-NINTH PURSUIT SQUADRON, the first black Air Corps unit. He rose to commander of the 332d Fighter Group, another all-black unit. The 332d Fighter Group won a series of commendations for its actions in WORLD WAR II. Davis himself flew sixty missions while commander of the group.

In 1965 Davis was named chief of staff of U.S. forces in Korea and chief of staff of the U.S. commission in Korea.

**Davis, Benjamin O., Sr.** (July 1, 1877, Washington, D.C.—November 26, 1970, North Chicago, Illinois): MILITARY officer. Davis became the first African American to reach the rank of general in the regular army when President Franklin D. Roosevelt promoted him to brigadier general on October 16, 1940. Davis had begun military service in 1898, during the SPANISH-AMERICAN WAR. He later served in the all-black Ninth Cavalry. He served in several wars before retiring from military service in 1948.

Davis won many awards during his military career, including the Distinguished Service Medal, the Bronze Star, the French Croix de Guerre with Palm, and the grade of Commander of the Order of the Star of Africa from

Brigadier General Benjamin O. Davis, Sr., in 1942. *(AP/Wide World Photos)*

the Liberian government. He taught military science at Wilberforce University and TUSKEGEE INSTITUTE, and to the Ohio National Guard. He also served as military attaché to Liberia. He was instrumental in implementing the desegregation of armed forces facilities in Europe. *See also:* Ninth Cavalry and Tenth Cavalry.

**Davis, Charles Twitchell** (April 29, 1918—March 25, 1981): Scholar. Davis wrote extensively about African American prose, drama, and poetry, as well as building a considerable personal following for his counsel and teaching. Born into a family that listed the remarkable slave-born William Roscoe Davis as its patriarch, he went from the Hampton, VIRGINIA, schools of his boyhood to Dartmouth College, where he was elected Phi Beta Kappa and received his B.A. in 1939. After obtaining an M.A. in early twentieth-century African American rhetoric from the University of Chicago in 1942, he enlisted in the Army and rose to the rank of captain. Five years after his 1946 discharge, he earned a Ph.D. in American drama from New York University, where he taught through 1955.

Davis became Princeton University's first black professor (1955-1961), then moved to Pennsylvania State University (1961-1970), doing a Fulbright year in Turin, Italy (1966-1967). He was appointed to the University of Iowa to chair the newly created Afro-American studies program (1970-1972). In 1972 he took up residence at Yale University, where he served until his death as both professor of English and chair of Afro-American studies. He also, in 1973, became master of Calhoun College (named for one of slavery's best-known proponents).

Davis's critical writing covered a wide range. His first published article, "Prose Literature of Racial Defence: A Preface to the Harlem Renaissance" (1942), led to a litany of lively essays on African American figures, including Robert HAYDEN (1973), Jean TOOMER (1974), Richard WRIGHT (1979), Ralph ELLISON (1979), and Paul Laurence DUNBAR (1980). These have been collected posthumously under the editorship of his former student Henry Louis GATES, Jr., as *Black Is the Color of the Cosmos: Essays on Afro-American Literature and Culture, 1942-1981* (1982). Together with his editions of Walt Whitman (1955) and E. A. Robinson (1960), his *Richard Wright: A Primary Bibliography* (1982, with Michel Fabre), and his considerable body of journal contributions and reviews, Davis's scholarship amounts to a legacy of genuine distinction.
*See also:* Harlem Renaissance; Intellectuals and scholars; Literature.

**Davis, Frances Reed Elliott** (1882, Knoxville, Tennessee—May 2, 1965, Michigan): Nurse and educator. The illegitimate daughter of a plantation heiress and a black farm worker, Davis was orphaned at the age of six and spent much of her early life in a series of foster homes. Nevertheless, she eventually graduated from Knoxville College and taught history for a few years before pursuing a career in nursing. She received her medical training at the Freedmen's Hospital School of Nursing and graduated in 1913. After working for nearly a year as a private-duty nurse, Davis accepted employment at Provident Hospital in BALTIMORE, MARYLAND. While working in Baltimore, she became interested in joining the American Red Cross Nursing Service. After completing additional nursing studies at Columbia University, Davis in 1918 became the first African American woman to serve with the American Red Cross Nursing Service.
*See also:* Freedmen's Bureau; Health care professionals.

**Davis, Henrietta Vinton** (1860, Baltimore, Maryland—November 23, 1941, Washington, D.C.): Political organizer. Best known for her connections with Marcus GARVEY's UNIVERSAL NEGRO IMPROVEMENT ASSOCIATION (UNIA)., Davis had an earlier career as an actor and dramatic reader.

The daughter of Musician Mansfield Vinton Davis, she was born in Baltimore, MARYLAND, and educated in nearly WASHINGTON, D.C. She started teaching school in Maryland when she was only fifteen and briefly worked for Louisiana's board of education. After returning to Washington, she got a job as a copyist in the federal government's Office of the Recorder of Deeds, where she worked under Frederick DOUGLASS in the early 1880's.

During that period she studied dramatics. In April, 1883, she made her debut on the stage in a one-person show in which she did readings from Paul Laurence DUNBAR, Mark Twain, and William Shakespeare; she was introduced by Douglass. Afterward, she conducted a brief but successful tour of eastern cities, resigning her government post in 1883 to concentrate on her dramatic career. She married Thomas T. Symmons, who managed her career. In 1893 she established her own dramatic company in CHICAGO, ILLINOIS, and produced plays by African American dramatists.

In 1912 Davis accompanied contralto Nonie Bailey Hardy on a tour of Jamaica, where she organized a black American benevolent society. The following year she and Hardy toured Central America before returning to the United States. While doing fundraising work for a girls' school in Jamaica in 1919, Davis met Garvey. After accepting his invitation to speak in HARLEM, she gave up her theatrical career to work for the UNIA and stayed with the organization until her death twenty-two years later.

Quickly absorbed into the UNIA's top leadership, Davis participated in many of the organization's most important events. Such was her importance to the UNIA that Garvey himself called her the "greatest woman of the Negro race today" and made her a lady commander of the Sublime Order of the Nile.

Davis believed in the UNIA's goal of African American emigration to Africa and in black pride. Her eloquent speeches, enhanced by her dramatic training, helped spread her nationalist philosophy. In 1923-1924 she was a member of a UNIA group sent by Garvey to LIBERIA to negotiate a land-settlement agreement with that nation's government.

After Garvey went to federal prison on mail-fraud charges in connection with the UNIA's Black Star shipping line in 1925, Davis's personal loyalty to him waned, and she focused her attention on the UNIA's New York division. Nevertheless, when the organization split between pro- and anti-Garvey wings in 1929, Davis became secretary general of the loyalist "UNIA (August 1929) of the World" faction. At the same time, she also remained affiliated with the rival "UNIA, Inc., of New York" and served as its first assistant president general. However, with Garvey deported and permanently removed from the United States, both organizations faded into near obscurity by the time of Vinton's death in 1941.

—*Updated by Christopher E. Kent*
See also: Bruce, John E.

**Davis, Miles** (May 26, 1926, Alton, Illinois—September 28, 1991, Santa Monica, California): Jazz trumpeter, fluegelhornist, and composer. Known by many as the "Picasso of jazz," Davis both created and profoundly influenced the style of JAZZ for four decades.

Miles Dewey Davis was a genius of transformation. He was relentless in his pursuit of staying with his times, and he was often ahead of them. He had a talent for surrounding himself with the most appropriate musicians for arriving at the particular sound he was seeking. Many times during his career, he received criticism for employing white musicians, but his primary concern was the sound of his music, not its color. Regardless of his musical environment, Davis's unique and personal sound on the trumpet and fluegelhorn can be recognized by jazz fans in an instant.

### Early Years

Miles Dewey Davis III was born to well-established members of the African American middle-class community of East St. Louis, ILLINOIS, where his family moved shortly after his birth. His father, Miles Dewey Davis II, was a prominent businessman and dentist, and his mother, Cleota Henry Davis, was an organ teacher's daughter and an amateur pianist.

Davis began to study the trumpet formally around the age of ten. The two most influential teachers during his time in East St. Louis were Elwood Buchanan, who was partially responsible for Davis's vibratoless sound, and a German trumpeter named Gustav, who played with the St. Louis Symphony Orchestra. Davis began playing professionally at the age of sixteen, with a group called Eddie Randle's Blue Devils. He was also playing at jam sessions around St. Louis, Missouri, across the Mississippi River from East St. Louis, and learning from the great touring jazz players of the day, such as Lester YOUNG, Clark Terry, Sonny STITT, and Fats NAVARRO. Perhaps the moment that inspired Davis to leave St. Louis for New York was his brief stint with Billy ECKSTINE's big band. Charlie "Bird" PARKER, John Birks "Dizzy" GILLESPIE, and Art BLAKEY were all members of the band at this time. After having the opportunity to play with musicians of this caliber, Davis moved to New York in the fall of 1944.

Davis went to New York ostensibly to study at the Juilliard School of Music, but it was obvious to him that the real opportunity to learn to play BEBOP would be found in the

Miles Davis performing with the Miles Davis Quintet. *(Jan Persson/ Sony Music)*

clubs of Harlem and on 52nd Street. He quickly found Dizzy Gillespie and Charlie Parker and began playing in the jam sessions of New York City, sharpening his skills. Within a year, he was playing regularly with Parker and had recorded his first album as a member of Parker's quintet. His partnership with Parker continued for a number of years, ending in 1948 when Davis realized that it was time for him to pursue a new path.

### The 1950's

When Davis had met Canadian composer/ arranger Gil Evans in 1948, they decided to work on a project together. Known as *Birth of the Cool* (1950), that project marked the first of Davis's transformations: The instrumentation had changed from a typical bebop setting (two or three wind instruments with piano, bass, and drums) to a group that included a French horn and a tuba. The music itself was different in that it was more relaxed in pace than most bebop. Davis and Evans would record several more albums together; *Sketches of Spain* (1959) and *Porgy and Bess* (1958) are two of their best-known collaborations.

In the 1950's Davis frequently performed and recorded with a quintet composed of John COLTRANE on tenor saxophone, Red Garland on piano, Paul Chambers on bass, and drummer Philly Joe Jones. His recorded work with this lineup, *Round About Midnight* (1955) and *Milestones* (1958), with alto saxophonist Julian "Cannonball" ADDERLEY, are great albums in their own right, but the single album for which Davis is best known was still to come. *Kind of Blue* (1959) featured Davis on trumpet, Coltrane on tenor saxophone, Adderley on alto saxophone, Bill Evans and Wynton Kelly on piano, Paul Chambers on bass, and Jimmy Cobb on the drums. All but one song on the album were recorded on the first take. Decades after its recording, *Kind of Blue* remains a seminal jazz work. It has sold almost two million copies, an extremely rare feat for a jazz album.

### The 1960's and 1970's

True to his innovative spirit, Davis formed another group a few years after the release of *Kind of Blue*. The new quintet comprised Wayne SHORTER on tenor saxophone, Herbie HANCOCK on piano, Ron Carter on bass, and Tony Williams on drums. This quintet was heavily influenced by the currents of "free jazz." The group was known for its controlled chaos, pushing the limits of a song's harmony and rhythm yet always managing to stay within the form of the song. This quintet stayed together for five years, recording albums such as *Seven Steps to Heaven* (1963) and *E.S.P.* (1965) before Davis decided it was time to change again.

Davis realized that the music of the times in the late 1960's was rock and roll, played on electric instruments. His albums *In a Silent Way* (1969), *Bitches Brew* (1969), *Live-Evil* (1971), and *On the Corner* (1972) all feature electric guitars (such as the work of John McLaughlin) and electric keyboards (organ and piano), and they pay homage to musical sources as diverse as James BROWN and the rock band the Grateful Dead. (Davis was particularly impressed by Jimi HENDRIX's music, and the two hoped to record together, a plan that never reached fruition because of Hendrix's death in 1970.) This phase of Davis's career pioneered the style of music that became known as "fusion," a blending of jazz and rock elements that was continued independently by such Davis players as Hancock, Williams, McLaughlin, Shorter, Josef Zawinul (who founded Weather Report), and Chick Corea. Thirty years of performing and intense musical energy had taken a heavy toll on Davis, and in 1975 he stopped performing for five years.

### Davis's Return

When Davis returned to music, he had yet another opportunity to change his style. Synthesizers and the growing phenomenon of rap music played a part in his new style. He began touring again with new groups, picking young musicians who could play well within the spirit of the times. Among Davis's 1980's albums are *The Man with the Horn* (1981) and *Tutu* (1986). In the early 1980's, Davis also began to explore painting as a means of artistic expression. He adopted this art form with considerable success, and his paintings have been featured in many exhibitions.

Davis continued playing and touring for more than a decade after his sabbatical, constantly changing the sound of his music, constantly searching for new sounds. By the 1990's, his health was worsening—Davis had had many health problems through the years—and he died on October 28, 1991, of pneumonia, respiratory failure, and a stroke, two months after his last performance, at the Montreaux Jazz Festival in Switzerland.

—*Alexander DuBois Jordan*

Suggested Readings:

Chambers, Jack. *Milestones 1: The Music and Times of Miles Davis to 1960*. New York: Beech Tree Books, 1983.

_____. *Milestones 2: The Music and Times of Miles Davis Since 1960*. New York: Beech Tree Books, 1985.

Crisp, George. *Miles Davis*. New York: Franklin Watts, 1997.

Davis, Miles, with Quincy Troupe. *Miles: The Autobiography*. New York: Simon & Schuster, 1989.

Nisenson, Eric. *'Round About Midnight: A Portrait of Miles Davis*. New York: Dial Press, 1982.

Williams, Richard. *The Man in the Green Shirt: Miles Davis*. New York: Henry Holt, 1993.

**Davis, Ossie** (b. December 18, 1917, Cogdell, Georgia): Actor, director, and playwright. Ossie Davis's roles span the range of those in the dramatic arena, having worked on stage, screen, and television as a writer, actor, director, and producer. His primary interest and his most enduring successes were as a playwright; he has been described as one of the most gifted men in the modern American THEATER. In addition, he was long active as a lecturer on college campuses, as a social activist for black causes, and as a community and church leader.

*Background*

Ossie Davis was the first of five children born to Kince Charles Davis and Laura Cooper Davis. Because his father was a railroad construction foreman, an unusual position for a southern black at that time, the Davis family moved around to a number of small, rural towns until they finally settled in Waycross, GEORGIA, where Ossie grew up. It was while he was attending Central High in Waycross that he first developed a love for the theater, even writing and producing his first play. Davis later said that he was compelled to write because of the treatment that he saw his father receive at the hands of white bigots. Davis's gift for comedy, revealed in later life, undoubtedly was shaped by his father's ability to soften the harsh realities of racial prejudice with humor; Davis once recalled, "Some of the sweetest memories I have are of my father telling us stories. It gave us a chance to laugh at the world." Davis's social conscience was also revealed at a young age when, in 1935, he and a friend attempted to enlist in the Ethiopian army in order to fight the invading Italian army under the command of Benito Mussolini.

After his graduation from high school in 1935, having received a National Youth Administration Scholarship, Davis hitchhiked to WASHINGTON, D.C., where he lived with a relative and pursued his education at HOWARD UNIVERSITY. At Howard, he fell under the influence of Professor Alain Locke, a philosopher and drama critic who encouraged Davis in his desire for a career in the theater. Locke also advised him to learn about the theater by going to New York and working with Off-Broadway groups after he finished college.

Too impatient to wait, Davis headed for NEW YORK CITY after his junior year with thirty dollars in his pocket and a recommendation from Locke to Rose McClendon, who operated a small theater group in HARLEM. Davis's early years in New York were a struggle, but he learned theater while working with the Rose McClendon Players. Sometimes he swept floors, sometimes he built and painted sets, and sometimes he acted in plays, including *Joy Exceeding Glory* in 1941. He also had to perform a variety of odd jobs around town as a way of making ends meet, and sometimes he had to resort to sleeping on park benches and taking meals at a church mission.

In 1942 Davis was inducted into the U.S. Army, where he served as a surgical technician and, while stationed in LIBERIA, wrote and directed his play *Goldbrickers of 1944*. In 1945 Davis returned to Georgia, where he was soon contacted by Richard Campbell, the director of the Rose McClendon Players, who told Davis to come to New York to try out for the lead role in a new play by Robert Ardrey entitled *Jeb*. While the play itself was not a success, running for only nine performances, Davis received his first recognition from the critics. He also met Ruby Dee, another performer in the play. After Davis and Dee toured with the national company of *Anna Lucasta*, they were married on December 9, 1948. The couple had two daughters, Nora, born in 1950, and LaVerne, born in 1956, and a son, Guy, born in 1952.

### Theater Career

During the 1950's, Davis's acting career developed before his writing. After appearing in *The Leading Lady* (1948) and *The Smile of the World* (1949), he began to be warmly received by the critics in such roles as Jacques the servant in *The Wisteria Trees*, Joshua Logan's adaptation of Anton Chekhov's *The Cherry Orchard*. This play, which originally opened on March 29, 1950, was revived in 1955 with Davis again playing Jacques. Another role that brought Davis acclaim was the part of Gabriel in a revival of Marc Connelly's *Green Pastures* in 1951. In 1951 Davis also appeared as Jo in George S. Kaufman's *The Royal Family* and as Al Clinton in *Remains to Be Seen*.

Davis continued to expand his theatrical career when in 1954 and 1955 he worked as stage manager for Howard Da Silva's Off-Broadway production of *The World of Sholem Aleichem*, based on the stories of the Yiddish author. Davis says that he identified with the characters, that the Yiddish "people were my people," because they too were a downtrodden minority. After appearing as a lieutenant in *No Time for Sergeants* in 1956, he played Cicero in the long-running *Jamaica*, starring Lena Horne, which opened on October 13, 1957, and ran for 555 performances. In 1959 Davis again played opposite his wife, Ruby Dee, when he took over from Sidney POITIER in the role of Walter Younger in *A Raisin in the Sun*, which ran until June 25, 1960.

### Film and Television

Davis's FILM career also flourished during the 1950's and 1960's. He first appeared in film in *No Way Out* in 1950 and continued appearing in films such as *Fourteen Hours* (1951), *The Joe Louis Story* (1953), *The Cardinal* (1963), and *The Scalphunters* (1968).

Davis's television acting career also prospered during this time. One of the most memorable moments of his career came in 1955, when he appeared as Brutus Jones in a television production of Eugene O'Neill's *The Emperor Jones*. Numerous television appearances followed, including a role as narrator of the nine-part series *History of the Negro People* in 1965. For his depiction of a handyman who helps a retarded boy in *Teacher, Teacher*, on the Hallmark Hall of Fame in 1969, he was nominated for an Emmy Award. From 1990 to 1994, Davis had a recurring role as Burt Reynolds's character's restaurateur friend on the TELEVISION SERIES *Evening Shade*.

### Playwriting

While successful as an actor, Ossie Davis had always had a strong desire to write about the black experience. His first important work was a one-act play called *Alice in Wonder*, first staged in 1952; it was expanded into a full-length work in 1953 and renamed *The Big Deal*. Set in Harlem, the play deals with a black singer who holds a position with a public-relations firm; in order to keep his job, he must testify against another black, who is also a political activist. The real issue of the play, however, involves the singer's wife, who, when she realizes that her husband has compromised his principles and thus their relationship, must decide whether to stay with a man whom she no longer respects. In the original production, the part of the wife was played by Ruby Dee. Loften Mitchell said that the play "roared the truth about the Negro's plight in America," while another critic complained that it was more like a "tract" than a play; regardless, it drew attention to Davis as an emerging black playwright.

### Purlie Victorious

The most successful of Davis's works is the play *Purlie Victorious*, which opened on September 28, 1961, with Davis playing the part of Purlie, Dee playing Lutiebelle, and Godfrey Cambridge as Gitlow. The play ran for 261 performances and has been widely anthologized and recognized as an important black play. The play tells the story of Purlie Victorious Judson, an itinerant black preacher who has returned home, accompanied by his girlfriend Lutiebelle, to South Georgia after years of absence. Purlie intends to acquire Big Bethel, an old barn and former church, in order to preach to integrated audiences. His main obstacle is old Captain Cotchipee, a white landowner who keeps his black workers in virtual enslavement and who holds a five-hundred-dollar inheritance that is owed to Purlie. After much comic confusion, Purlie gains ownership of Big Bethel, receives the captain's son, Charlie, into his congregation, witnesses Cotchipee dropping dead—"the first man in all the world to drop dead standing up"—and, in a stirring epilogue, preaches the captain's eulogy in Big Bethel.

In 1963 the film version, with Davis again as Purlie, was released as *Gone Are the Days*. In 1970 the play was adapted into a musical called *Purlie* by Davis and others and presented on Broadway as, according to one critic, "by far the most successful and richest of all black musicals." It also enjoyed a highly successful run and was nominated for a Tony Award as best musical.

Other plays by Davis include *Mr. Aldridge, Sir* (1968), written for the Ira Aldridge Society, and *Escape to Freedom: A Play About Young Frederick Douglass* (1976). Examples of his other works are the screenplay *Cotton Comes to Harlem* (1969) and the television script *Schoolteacher* (1963). In 1992 he published *Just Like Martin*, a work of historical fiction for young readers. A memoir written jointly by Davis and Ruby Dee, *With Ossie and Ruby: In This Life Together*, was published in 1998.

—Tony J. Stafford

Ossie Davis (right) in a 1961 production of *Purlie Victorious*, with, left to right, Godfrey Cambridge, Ruby Dee, and Helen Martin. *(AP/Wide World Photos)*

Suggested Readings:

Abramson, Doris. *Negro Playwrights in the American Theatre 1925-1959*. New York: Columbia University Press, 1969.

Davis, Ossie, and Ruby Dee. *With Ossie and Ruby: In This Life Together*. New York: William Morrow, 1998.

Funke, Lewis. *The Curtain Rises: The Story of Ossie Davis*. New York: Grosset & Dunlap, 1971.

Haskins, James. *The Black Theatre in America*. New York: Thomas Y. Crowell, 1982.

Norment, Lynn. "Three Great Love Stories." *Ebony* (February, 1988): 150-152.

Wishengrad, Susan. "The Two Worlds of Ossie Davis and Ruby Dee." *Good Housekeeping* 192 (April, 1981): 2.

**Davis, Preston Augustus** (b. c. 1925, Norfolk, Virginia): Management consultant and political appointee. Davis attended West Virginia State College and graduated with a bachelor of science degree in business administration in 1949. He served in the Army between 1943 and 1970, achieving the rank of lieutenant colonel. During his MILITARY service, Davis was awarded the Purple Heart, the Bronze Star, and the Army Meritorious Service Award in addition to other commendations. Davis earned his master of science degree in executive management from the Command and General Staff College in 1965.

After leaving the Army, Davis worked at Morgan State University as vice president of development from 1970 to 1971. He left the school to take a position as senior management analyst with the Department of Agriculture in 1971 and served as an analyst until 1978. Davis earned his master of social work degree from George Washington University in 1974. He was appointed as director of Small Business Affairs at the Department of Agriculture in 1979 by President Jimmy Carter. In 1989 he founded Davis and Davis Consultant Associates, a management consulting firm. He was executive manager of international children's programs for Kiwanis International in Washington, D.C., from 1990 to 1992, before becoming a management consultant for Kiwanis in 1992. Davis wrote various classified articles on military topics, including "Firepower Chinese Communist Army" and "Signatures of Soviet Nuclear Missile Systems."

**Davis, Sammy, Jr.** (December 8, 1925, Harlem, New York—May 16, 1990, Beverly Hills, California): Singer, dancer, and actor. Born in HAR-LEM, Sammy Davis, Jr., was the son of VAUDEVILLE troupers Elvera Sanchez Davis and Sammy Davis, Sr. When Sammy, Jr., was born, his parents were at the peaks of their careers. A lead dancer in his adopted uncle Will Mastin's touring *Holiday in Dixieland*, his father was a "high-stepper," while his mother danced as the lead chorus girl.

Because his parents were continuously traveling with the road show, Davis and his sister Ramona (two years younger) were reared by their grandmother, Rosa B. "Mama" Davis. By the time he was three, his mother and father were divorced, and father Sam took custody of Sammy, Jr. Soon the young child was traveling with the Mastin Troupe and appearing on stage, first as a "cute" human prop, later as a full-fledged entertainer. In 1933 he appeared in his first motion picture, *Rufus Jones for President*, a two-reel talkie for Vitaphone-Warner filmed at the Warner studios in Brooklyn. Davis starred in the title role in the comedy; he played a boy who fell asleep in his mother's lap and dreamed that he was president of the United States. Soon thereafter, he had a role in *Season's Greetings*, another Vitaphone-Warner vehicle that starred Lita Grey.

Although the popularity of vaudeville declined in proportion to the FILM industry's rise, Davis continued the road circuit until the 1940's, eventually becoming his troupe's headliner. Along the way, he met and became good friends with other young performers who would one day be stars, including Frank Sinatra, who was singing with Tommy Dorsey's band and who would help Davis's career in the decades to come.

In 1943 the U.S. Army drafted Davis. While stationed at Fort Francis E. Warren in Cheyenne, WYOMING, he was befriended by an African American sergeant who gave him remedial reading lessons and the rudiments of a high-school education. The Wyoming experience was not all positive, however; Davis also encountered deep, inbred racism for the first time, and he spent much of his time in basic training engaging in bare-knuckles fighting with belligerent whites. Once basic training was behind him, he was transferred to a special services outfit and toured various military installations, performing a new version of his old vaudeville act.

### Rise to Prominence

After the war, Davis resumed his vaudeville and nightclub circuit. He performed in New York, Chicago, and Los Angeles and in a host of smaller cities. Through his friend Jesse Price, a drummer, he began his recording career in 1946, when he cut records for Capitol for fifty dollars a side. *Metronome* chose his "The Way You Look Tonight" as the record of the year, and it named Davis the "most outstanding new personality" of the year. Probably more important, after the war Davis was frequently coming into contact with other rising stars. In 1947 and 1948, he toured with another new star, Mickey Rooney. For a time, he was on the bill (headlined by Sinatra) at Manhattan's Capitol Theatre; he played at Slapsie Maxie's in Los ANGELES and next won a featured bill with Bob Hope, who was giving police benefit shows. Davis met Jack Benny, who got him and his trio a booking at Hollywood's fashionable Ciro's. Next, Eddie Cantor gave Davis a spot on *The Colgate Comedy Hour* television program. Soon Davis's small troupe became a summer replacement for one of NBC's regular shows. Then it was off to the Copacabana in New York.

By 1954 Davis was obviously a rising star with great potential. Decca Records signed him to a contract; soon, thousands were hearing the new star's songs and comedy routines. Yet in the midst of success, tragedy struck. In November, 1954, as he drove from Las Vegas back to Hollywood, he had a serious automobile accident that took his left eye and almost

Sammy Davis, Jr., in 1984. *(Arkent Archive)*

took his life. Davis turned the negative into a positive, however: During his hospital stay, he experienced a spiritual renewal. The son of a Roman Catholic mother and a Baptist father, he had never been personally religious, but during his confinement he converted to Judaism.

### A National Star

While Davis was hospitalized, his star continued to rise; his fans realized that they had almost lost one of their idols. Therefore, Davis was in great demand once he could perform again. After appearing in such cities as Philadelphia, Chicago, and Los Angeles, he opened on Broadway on March 22, 1956, starring in *Mr. Wonderful*, a musical comedy about a young African American entertainer who used talent and will to overcome racial odds on the way to becoming a star; the show ran for 383 performances.

By the end of the 1950's, Davis was appearing regularly on television variety shows such as Ed Sullivan's *The Toast of the Town* and had serious acting roles in such television anthology series as *The Dick Powell Theatre* and *General Electric Theater*. In the 1960's successes continued; television, movies, record albums—everything Davis touched turned to gold. He had feature or starring roles in such films as *The Benny Goodman Story* (1956); *Anna Lucasta* (1958); *Porgy and Bess* (1959), in which he played the role of Sportin' Life; *Pepe* (1960); *Convicts Four* (1962); and a host of others.

In the 1960's, Davis also became a member of the so-called Rat Pack, a loose-knit group of hard-living performers led by Sinatra and including such Hollywood stalwarts as Dean Martin, Peter Lawford, Joey Bishop, Tony Curtis, and Henry Silva. Davis costarred in sundry films with others in the "pack," including *Ocean's Eleven* (1960), *Sergeants Three* (1962), *Robin and the Seven Hoods* (1964), and *Salt and Pepper* (1968).

In the mid-1960's, Davis made a triumphant return to the stage when Clifford Odets's play *Golden Boy*, as revised by producer Hillard Elkins, opened on Broadway with Davis in the leading role. The play ran for 568 performances. Davis's depiction of a young African American boxer trying to break out of a poverty-ridden slum drew a rave review from Howard Taubman of *The New York Times*; later, *Cue* magazine tabbed Davis as entertainer of the year.

Through the 1960's, Davis continued to appear on television in both variety shows and serious dramas. By the late 1960's, however, his Rat Pack life—fast living, heavy smoking, and hard drinking—was taking its toll; he developed liver and kidney problems. Finally hospitalized in February of 1974, he came away something of a new man; he modified the habits that had injured his health. By the end of the year he was back onstage, doing a review, *Sammy on Broadway*. After that run, he again turned to performing in Las Vegas clubs.

*Honors*

For his career accomplishments, Davis received several awards. EBONY magazine in 1979 gave him its first lifetime achievement award. In 1986 he received an honorary degree from Howard University. Much earlier, in 1965, the NATIONAL ASSOCIATION FOR THE ADVANCEMENT OF COLORED PEOPLE (NAACP) had given him the coveted Spingarn Medal in recognition of his service in the cause of civil rights; among other actions, Davis had performed in many benefits to raise money for the movement. Additionally, he received honors from various Jewish organizations in recognition of his work in helping bring about a rapport between JEWISH AMERICANS AND AFRICAN AMERICANS—indeed, Davis became an international symbol in that regard.

Although Davis became less active in the 1980's, in 1988 he made a national tour with Frank Sinatra, Dean Martin, and Liza Minnelli. The five-foot, six-inch Davis burned so much energy on stage that his weight always held at approximately 130 pounds. Davis was featured in the 1989 film *Tap* (1989). Costarring Gregory HINES, the film was a salute to all the "hoofers" who had entertained so many for so long.

Davis's hobbies included golf and photography. His personal life had its highs and lows. He was married three times, first to Loray White (1959-1960), a dancer, then to May Britt (1960-1968), a Swedish actor, and finally to Altovise Gore (from 1970 until his death). With Britt he had a daughter, Tracey; additionally, Davis adopted Britt's children, Mark and Jeff.

Davis died in 1990 of throat cancer. Fellow entertainers Milton Berle, George Burns, LITTLE RICHARD, Bill COSBY, and Sidney POITIER were among the many who praised the man and his career, as was the Reverend Jesse JACKSON. All the lights on the Las Vegas Strip were turned off for ten minutes to honor his memory.

—*James Smallwood*

Suggested Readings:

Bennett, Lerone. "Sammy Davis, Jr., 1925-1990: The Legacy of the World's Greatest Entertainer." *Ebony* (July, 1990): 118-120.

Branch, Taylor. *Parting The Waters: America in The King Years, 1954-1963.* New York: Simon & Schuster, 1988.

_____. *Pillar of Fire: America in the King Years, 1963-1965.* New York: Simon & Schuster, 1998.

Davis, Sammy, Jane Boyar, and Burt Boyar. *Yes I Can: The Story of Sammy Davis, Jr.* New York: Farrar, Straus, & Giroux, 1965.

Davis, Tracey, and Delores A. Barclay. *Sammy Davis Jr., My Father.* Los Angeles: General Publishng Group, 1996.

Tirro, Frank. *Jazz: A History.* New York: W. W. Norton, 1977.

**Dawson, William Levi** (April 26, 1886, Albany, Georgia—November 9, 1970, Chicago, Illinois): Congressman. Dawson represented the First Congressional District of ILLINOIS from 1943 until his death. He was the first African American to chair a major congressional committee, the Government Operations Committee. He was also the first African American vice president of the Democratic National Committee.

A graduate of Northwestern University Law School, Dawson ran unsuccessfully for Congress as a Republican in 1928 and 1929. He went on to manage Judge John Lyle's CHICAGO mayoral campaign. This activity put Dawson into the Chicago political machine, enabling him to win election as an alderman in 1935. Dawson became disenchanted with the Republican Party and switched to the DEMOCRATIC PARTY. He was elected as a Demo-cratic committeeman in 1940. After his election to the House of Representatives, Dawson became a strong supporter of racial integration of the U.S. armed forces and repeal of poll taxes.

Dawson built an African American political organization in Chicago, and as leader of this machine he dealt with white organizers across the city to obtain concessions. Dawson expanded his political base from the relatively small Second Ward in Chicago. By 1949 he controlled the whole South Side of Chicago. This broad base of support was responsible for his election to the U.S. Congress. Dawson's political organization started to break down during Mayor Richard J. Daley's administration, even though Dawson supported Daley in 1944. Daley began appointing African Americans to boards and commissions, but the appointees were not affiliated with Dawson.

Dawson campaigned vigorously for Harry S Truman's presidential bid in 1948. As part of his recognition of Dawson's help and of African American support in general, Truman invited African Americans in record numbers to his inaugural ball. Dawson was active in pur-

William Levi Dawson was the first African American member of Congress to chair a major committee. *(Library of Congress)*

suing civil rights, but he was also a traditional party member. He supported fair employment practices in Congress and urged the government to pursue full employment. He voted against bills that would affect minorities adversely or would harm the poor or disadvantaged.

**Deacons for Defense and Justice:** Civil rights organization. Organized in July, 1964, ostensibly to protect and defend CIVIL RIGHTS activists from white terrorism in the South, the Deacons for Defense and Justice also protected black communities and defused potentially volatile interracial situations. The Deacons were organized in Jonesboro, LOUISIANA.

The main event that led to the group's founding was a twenty-five-car KU KLUX KLAN (KKK) parade, accompanied by police escort, that drove through the town's black community. The parade disseminated leaflets intended to intimidate community residents and keep them from participating in civil rights activity. Black community residents realized that the coupling of the KKK and law officials meant that they had to empower themselves to end the widespread church burnings, bombings, killings, and physical intimidation during the Civil Rights movement. The Deacons, armed with a variety of weaponry, patrolled the black community and effected a gradual decline in white terrorist activities, particularly cross burnings and physical intimidation.

By 1965 the Deacons were organizing cadres throughout Louisiana, MISSISSIPPI, and ALABAMA, with additional plans to establish the organization in every southern state. Chapters in Jonesboro and Bogalusa, both in Louisiana, remained the organization's strongest. As its retaliation against harassment from whites became known, the organization drew broad-based support, particularly in the

Deep South but also from northern black militants. By June of 1965, Ernest Thomas of Jonesboro, serving as both vice president and full-time organizer, stated that the Deacons had approximately fifty chapters. Spokespersons for the Deacons, including the president, Percy Lee Bradford of Jonesboro declined to comment on membership figures, but others estimated the group's size as between five thousand and fifteen thousand members. Such northern groups as the Friends of the Deacons provided financial support to the organization through massive rallies.

Civil rights groups which were active in Jonesboro and Bogalusa, particularly the CONGRESS OF RACIAL EQUALITY (CORE), were on friendly terms with the Deacons and did not see a conflict with the Deacons' armed self-defense strategy. Although Martin Luther KING, Jr., was reluctant to work with the Deacons, Richard Haley, the southern director of CORE, noted an increase in the safety of his activists when the Deacons protected their activities. Haley believed that the theory of nonviolence, because it assumed the innate goodness of people and depended on public opinion, suffered from a delayed reaction time of both conscience and public awareness. In the meantime, activists who were in constant danger increased their safety by having the Deacons defending their lives. As the Civil Rights movement waned in the late 1960's and the BLACK POWER MOVEMENT moved the center of struggle to northern cities, the Deacons lost their influence.

**Dearfield, Colorado:** Agricultural colony settled in the early twentieth century by African Americans. Dearfield's founder was Oliver T. Jackson, who was born in Ohio in 1862 and went to COLORADO in 1887. Although Jackson believed that racism was less prevalent and less overt on the frontier than in the older states of the East, European Americans in the

West nevertheless generally assumed that blacks were their inferiors. Consequently, when Jackson opened a restaurant, he had difficulty hiring whites, most of whom thought that working for an African American was demeaning. Likewise, black farmers in the West often found themselves unable to employ their white neighbors to help harvest crops.

Eventually, Jackson decided that the easiest way for blacks to prosper in the West was to create segregated cooperative communities, a popular theory in the late nineteenth and early twentieth centuries. In 1910 Jackson claimed 320 acres of public land in Weld County on the high plains of northeastern Colorado and began creating Dearfield.

Like other all-black communities in the West, Dearfield was a town surrounded by farms. Jackson welcomed settlers who wanted to operate businesses as well as those who wanted to engage in agriculture. Thus, the urban and rural components of the colony would complement each other. Among the problems the colonists had in becoming established at Dearfield was a lack of funds with which to purchase farm animals, supplies, and equipment. Some of the settlers were so poor that Jackson had to lend them their homestead filing fees.

What the Dearfield settlers lacked financially, however, they made up through hard work. The farmers raised hogs, cattle, and poultry while growing hay, melons, and a variety of vegetables (potatoes, squash, beans, beets, cabbage, and pumpkins) and grains (corn, barley, and oats). Their town boasted a cement block factory, a blacksmith's forge, a boardinghouse, a store, and a church. The colonists fished in the nearby Platte River and hunted game animals on the surrounding prairie to supplement their diets. They worked together to build houses and collect fuel in the form of buffalo chips, driftwood from the river, and sagebrush. Outside capital came to the community through the sale of ex-cess farm products that were shipped to Denver via a nearby railroad.

For several years, Dearfield grew and prospered. By 1926 nearly seven hundred people lived there; the future appeared promising. The GREAT DEPRESSION of the late 1920's and the drought of the 1930's, however, ruined Dearfield. With farm prices falling and irrigation too expensive for the colonists to put into use, some black settlers began leaving for Colorado cities and others left for California farms. The settlers sold their small farmhouses for as little as five dollars or simply abandoned them.

Despite these setbacks, Jackson continued to operate a small convenience store and service station on the highway that brought a few travelers through the once-thriving community. After his death in the late 1940's, his niece inherited his estate. Jenny Jackson lived in Dearfield as the settlement's only resident until she died in 1973.

*See also:* Black towns; Boley, Oklahoma; Frontier Society; Langston, Oklahoma.

Suggested Readings:

Gard, Carolyn J. "Dearfield." *Cobblestone* (February, 1999): 30-33.

Waddell, Karen. "Dearfield . . . A Dream Deferred." *Colorado Heritage* no. 2 (1988): 2-12.

Wayne, George H. "Negro Migration and Colonization in Colorado—1870-1930." *Journal of the West* 15 (January, 1976): 102-120.

**DeCarava, Roy** (b. 1919, New York, New York): Photographer. DeCarava studied painting at Cooper Union, the HARLEM Art Center, and the George Washington CARVER Art School. He began using photography to capture ideas for paintings. A Guggenheim Fellowship allowed him to work with poet Langston HUGHES to create a photodocumentary journal of Harlem titled *The Sweet Flypaper of Life*

Photographer Roy DeCarava in 1991. *(AP/Wide World Photos)*

(1955). DeCarava's work can be found in many important collections throughout the United States.

*See also:* Photographers.

**De facto segregation:** Separation of racial or other groups that occurs even though there may be no law or rule establishing it. SEGREGATION in schools may occur, for example, because racial groups live in different geographic areas rather than because of laws requiring schools to be segregated. In 1973 the U.S. SUPREME COURT ruled that schools that were de facto segregated as a result of housing patterns must be desegregated. By the late 1990's, the courts were releasing schools from this obligation. *See also:* Busing; De jure segregation.

**De jure segregation:** Separation of racial or other groups that occurs through laws and regulations. Laws restricting home ownership to certain racial groups or establishing certain schools as exclusive to members of a particular group, for example, would cause de jure segregation. *See also:* De facto segregation.

**Delaney, Beauford** (1901, Knoxville, Tennessee—1979, Vincennes, France): Painter. A self-taught artist famous for expressionist paintings and abstractions with lavish applications of paint, Delaney launched his career in Boston, Massachusetts, as a portrait painter. He studied with Thomas Hart Benton, Don Freeman, and John Sloan. His subjects included writer Henry Miller and opera singer Marian ANDERSON. Delaney's first one-man show was held at the Artist's Gallery in New York City in 1948. He lived for many years in Paris, where he received widespread professional recognition, then rare for black artists in the United States. He was the brother of painter Joseph Delaney. *See also:* Painters and illustrators; Visual arts.

The sign at the left on this Jim Crow-era Florida store provides evidence of de jure segregation. *(National Archives)*

**Delany, Martin Robison** (May 6, 1812, Charles Town, Virginia [later West Virginia]— January 24, 1885, Wilberforce, near Xenia, Ohio): CIVIL RIGHTS activist and emigrationist. Martin Delany was the youngest of seven children born to Samuel and Patti Delany. Martin's father was a slave; his mother was free, having been born after her parents had attained their freedom. Young Delany thus became a free black: Under VIRGINIA law, children inherited the status of their mother. Delany's paternal grandfather was an African chief who had been captured in a war and sold to slave traders who brought him to America. Delany's maternal grandfather was also reputed to have been a prince prior to his capture and enslavement.

*Youth and Education*

Though legally free, Delany was not immune from racism. He witnessed the hardship and travail of his forebears. As he matured, he noticed fundamental differences in society's treatment of blacks. His most telling experience occurred when he accompanied his white playmates to school and was prevented from entering the classroom. Undeterred, he spent the next few days behind the classroom window, eavesdropping on the lessons. His chance finally came when he acquired a copy of a reading and spelling primer from an itinerant trader. Since it was an offense in Virginia for blacks to be educated, the family kept the book a secret and held nocturnal study sessions. Soon, every family member had gained literacy. Rumors spread that the Delanys had violated the law, and prosecution seemed imminent, so on September 22, 1822, Patti escaped with the children to Chambersburg, PENNSYLVANIA. Samuel joined them several years later after he obtained his freedom.

Young Delany began school in Chambersburg, where, despite a relatively permissive atmosphere, racism persisted. Chambersburg, moreover, had no provisions for black education beyond the primary school level. Determined to advance further, Delany proceeded to Pittsburgh, Pennsylvania, in July, 1831. When he made the move, he was nineteen, and he had matured physically. Delany was of medium height, compact, and strongly built, with broad shoulders. Everything about him, especially his sharp and piercing eyes, suggested energy and determination. His dark features made him a prime target for discrimination, but he projected his features as a mark of distinction.

*Activist and Abolitionist*

In Pittsburgh, Delany committed himself to fighting the enemies of his race. He came in contact with blacks from diverse backgrounds who shared a commitment to the black struggle. Almost all were economically self-made men who cherished the values of thrift, industry, education, and temperance and who extolled the practice of "moral suasion"—the effort to end SLAVERY by demonstrating its immorality.

Delany attended an AFRICAN METHODIST EPISCOPAL CHURCH school. His ideological mentors were Lewis WOODSON and William Whipper, two of the leading advocates of moral suasion. After high school, Delany apprenticed himself to a Dr. McDowell, a leading Pittsburgh physician, to train as a medical assistant specializing in "bleeding, cupping, and leeching."

In 1843 Delany married Kate Richards, the daughter of a prosperous Pittsburgh businessman. The couple had eleven children, seven of whom survived. The year 1843 also marked the first publication of Delany's Pittsburgh newspaper, the *Mystery*. The paper ran for four years, during which it attacked slavery and racism and advised blacks on methods of self-betterment.

In 1847 Delany gave up his paper and moved to New York City at the invitation of Frederick DOUGLASS, who had asked him to serve as coeditor of the *North Star*. Delany used the pages of the new paper to condemn slavery and toured black communities all over the country, organizing antislavery meetings and lectures and urging blacks to cultivate moral suasionist values.

Delany left the *North Star* in 1849; the next year, 1850, Congress passed the FUGITIVE SLAVE LAW, which, among other provisions, strengthened slavery by facilitating the apprehension of escaped slaves. Though directed at fugitives, the law also threatened free blacks with enslavement. Delany initially tried to resist the law, but he soon gave up when he became convinced of the futility of resistance. In the fall of 1850, he entered Harvard Medical School to study medicine, but a protest by white students forced his withdrawal after

As a surgeon serving in the Fifty-fourth Massachusetts Colored Infantry during the Civil War, Martin R. Delany was the first African American to receive a commission in the U.S. Army. *(Archive Photos)*

one semester. Despite this setback, Delany became a leading physician in Pittsburgh.

### Emigrationist

Disillusioned with the realities of black life in the United States, Delany embraced the idea of black emigration. The publication of his *The Condition, Elevation, Emigration, and Destiny of the Colored People of the United States, Politically Considered* (1852) formally launched the emigrationist movement. In his book, Delany described blacks as an oppressed "nation within a nation" that had no hope of advancement except through emigration, and he recommended Central and South America and the WEST INDIES as possible relocation sites. He reiterated his separatist conviction two years later at a national convention in Cleveland, where he delivered a paper entitled "Political Destiny of the Colored Race on the American Continent." The convention appointed him president of a national board of commissioners set up to advance emigration.

In 1856 Delany moved to Chatham, Canada West, where he continued his emigrationist plans while building a medical practice. Early in 1859, the American board of commissioners authorized him to undertake an exploratory visit to Africa. The trip took him through West and Central Africa. In Abeokuta, Nigeria, he persuaded the local Yoruba rulers to provide land to him for the resettlement of black Americans. On his way back from Africa, he stopped in London to address the International Statistical Congress and to raise funds for black emigration. His presence at the convention infuriated the American delegates, who walked out in protest.

### Civil War Activism

Delany returned to the United States in December, 1860, at which time Abraham Lincoln had just been elected president and the nation had moved to the brink of the CIVIL WAR. His mind set on emigrating, Delany ignored the gathering storm and published his *Official Report of the Niger Valley Exploring Party* (1861). Shortly thereafter, however, he abandoned his commitment to emigration and became a Civil War activist. He urged blacks to join the Union forces and contribute to the destruction of slavery. He became an outspoken critic of the government's policy of excluding blacks from the military, and he met with President Lincoln, who eventually approved black enlistment and made the emancipation of slaves in the CONFEDERACY a war strategy. Lincoln commissioned Delany as the first black combat major in the Union army, and he was assigned duties under General Rufus Saxton in South Carolina. Delany assisted in recruiting former slaves to join several black Union regiments, but the war ended before his combat ability was tested.

*Postwar Activism*

Delany was reassigned as a subassistant commissioner of the FREEDMEN'S BUREAU and posted to Hilton Head, South Carolina, at the beginning of the RECONSTRUCTION era. He served as a bureau agent from 1865 to 1868, during which time he struggled to secure land for newly freed slaves. Convinced that freedom was meaningless without a solid economic foundation, he advised blacks on how best to solidify their freedom through the acquisition and efficient management of land.

After the collapse of the bureau in 1868, Delany joined the REPUBLICAN PARTY and became active in SOUTH CAROLINA politics. Though a Republican, he opposed the radical policies of the Andrew Johnson administration and the RADICAL REPUBLICANS, which he insisted undermined the prospect of black elevation. He suggested that the Democrats had changed and would accommodate the realities of post-Civil War America if the Republicans abandoned their radical policies. His pleas for moderation ignored, in 1874 Delany joined the Conservative Independent Republican Movement in a bid to wrest control of the Republican Party from the radicals. Though the movement failed to unseat the radicals, Delany intensified his opposition and, in 1876, joined and campaigned for Democrats who pledged to pursue a liberal course.

The Democrats for whom Delany campaigned failed to keep their campaign pledges, and an upsurge of racism regenerated emigrationist consciousness. Disappointed and disillusioned, Delany joined the exodus movement of the late 1870's. In 1879 he published his *Principia of Ethnology: The Origins of Races and Color, with an Archaeological Compendium of Ethiopian and Egyptian Civilization*, a work that sought to refute notions of black inferiority and attempted to trace the origins of civilization to black Africa. Late in 1884, Delany fell ill and returned to Wilberforce, Ohio, where his family had settled. He died on January 24, 1885.

—*Tunde Adeleke*

*See also:* Abolitionist movement.

Suggested Readings:

Griffith, Cyril E. *The American Dream: Martin R. Delany and the Emergence of Pan-African Thought*. University Park: Pennsylvania State University Press, 1975.

Hill, Daniel G. *The Freedom-Seekers: Blacks in Early Canada*. Agincourt, Canada: The Book Society of Canada, 1981.

Levine, Robert S. *Martin Delany, Frederick Douglass, and the Politics of Representative Identity*. Chapel Hill: University of North Carolina Press, 1997.

Rollin, Frank A. *Life and Public Services of Martin R. Delany*. Reprint. New York: Arno Press, 1969.

Sterling, Dorothy. *The Making of an Afro-American: Martin Robison Delany, 1812-1885*. Garden City, N.Y.: Doubleday, 1971.

Ullman, Victor. *Martin R. Delany: The Beginnings of Black Nationalism*. Boston: Beacon Press, 1971.

**Delany, Samuel R.** (b. April 1, 1942, New York, New York): Writer. The first African American to excel as a writer of SCIENCE FICTION, Samuel Ray Delany, Jr., won numerous awards and became one of the most respected authors in the genre.

While still in his twenties, Delany published many acclaimed novels and short stories. After this early success, he produced more controversial works, often written in a difficult, highly literary style and featuring explicit sexual material. He also became a noted critic of science fiction.

Although Delany was born and raised in New York City's economically depressed HARLEM, he was educated in private schools in wealthier areas of the city primarily inhabited by whites. This early exposure to two sharply contrasting cultures contributed to his ability to create a wide variety of futuristic societies populated by characters of many different races and backgrounds.

At the age of nineteen, Delany had his first novel, *The Jewels of Aptor* (1962), accepted for publication. A trilogy of novels later collected as *The Fall of the Towers* (1970) was published from 1963 to 1965, followed by *The Ballad of Beta-2* (1965), *Empire Star* (1966), *Babel-17* (1966), *The Einstein Intersection* (1967), and *Nova* (1968). These early novels were colorful adventures set in the far future, often dealing with mythology and linguistics.

Delany's first published short story was "Aye, and Gomorrah. . . ." (1967). A tale of space travelers who have been transformed into sexless beings and of the persons who are sexually attracted to them, it was an early example of the controversial themes Delany would deal with in later works. This story, *Babel-17*, *The Einstein Intersection*, and the novella "Time Considered as a Helix of Semi-Precious Stones" (1969) all won the Nebula Award.

A new phase began in Delany's career with the publication of *Dhalgren* in 1975. A long, complex, experimental novel dealing with a nameless protagonist wandering through a city nearly destroyed by an unexplained disaster, *Dhalgren* was as controversial for its literary style as for its explicit scenes of sex and violence. Praised by some critics, it was rejected by others as meaningless. Delany's next novel, *Triton* (1976), returned to a more traditional style and a more conventional futuristic setting but continued to deal with sexual, social, psychological, and political themes. *Stars in My Pocket Like Grains of Sand* (1984) was a similar work set in a vast galactic civilization in the far future.

Delany has also published several volumes of literary analysis, and in 1985 he won the Pilgrim Award for science fiction criticism. His fiction took a new direction in 1979 with the publication of the first volume in the Neveryon series, in which he brought the same literary sophistication to fantasy that he did to science fiction.

*—Rose Secrest*

*See also:* Literature.

Suggested Readings:

McEvoy, Seth. *Samuel R. Delany*. New York: Frederick Ungar, 1984.

Weedman, Jane Branham. *Reader's Guide to Samuel R. Delany*. West Linn, Oreg.: Starmont, 1979.

**De Large, Robert Carlos** (March 15, 1842, Aiken, South Carolina—February 14, 1874, Charleston, South Carolina): U.S. representative from SOUTH CAROLINA during RECONSTRUCTION. De Large was born into SLAVERY but acquired a sparse education by attending Woods High School in Charleston. He was employed as a farmer and a tailor before working as an agent for the FREEDMEN'S BUREAU and an organizer of the South Carolina Republican Party.

After serving as a delegate to the state constitutional convention in 1868, De Large was elected to the state House of Representatives and in 1870 was appointed land commissioner. He was then elected to the U.S. House of Representatives from South Carolina's Second District and took office in 1871 amid controversy over his narrow margin of victory. He was appointed to serve on the House Committee on Manufactures. In poor health and needing time to prepare a defense in response to a congressional investigation of his election, De Large took a leave of absence from Congress in April of 1872.

Later that year, he decided not to run for reelection. In January of 1873, the House Committee on Elections was unable to determine a clear winner in the 1870 election and so declared the seat to be vacant. De Large retired to Columbia, South Carolina, and then returned to Charleston after being appointed city magistrate in 1873. He died of tuberculosis the following year.
*See also:* Congress members; Politics and government.

Carmen De Lavallade in 1977. *(AP/Wide World Photos)*

Robert Carlos De Large, one of several African American congressmen from South Carolina during Reconstruction. *(Library of Congress)*

**De Lavallade, Carmen** (b. March 6, 1931, Los Angeles, California): Dancer and choreographer. The cousin of dancer and choreographer Janet Collins and wife of dancer and choreographer Geoffrey Holder, De Lavallade danced with Lester Horton and then with Alvin AILEY from 1950 to 1954. She was premiere danseuse at the Metropolitan Opera Company from 1955 to 1956 and appeared with Josephine BAKER and her company in 1964. De Lavallade appeared in numerous films and television shows and received the *Dance Magazine* Award in 1966 and 1967 as well as a Monarch Award in 1982. She was choreographer and performer-in-residence at the Yale School of Drama for more than a dozen years.
*See also:* Dance.

**Delaware:** One of the original thirteen colonies, Delaware had an African American population of about 140,000 people in 1997—a figure representing nearly a fifth of the state's total population. Among all the states, Dela-

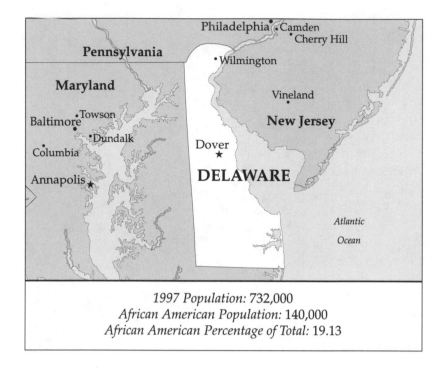

1997 Population: 732,000
African American Population: 140,000
African American Percentage of Total: 19.13

by Richard ALLEN, who founded the AFRICAN METHODIST EPISCOPAL CHURCH. During RECONSTRUCTION, AME Church minister Theophilus Gould Steward attacked segregation and advocated equal educational opportunities for African Americans in Delaware.

In 1901 Thomas Postles became the first African American to be elected to a Delaware public office when he became a member of the Wilmington City Council. In 1947 William J. Winchester was the first African American to be elected to the Delaware General Assembly. In the 1990's a black conservative Republican, Margaret Rose Henry, was elected a Delaware state senator.

In 1954 a Delaware court case concerning school desegregation, *Gebbart v. Belton*, was among five similar cases that were combined by the U.S. SUPREME COURT as BROWN V. BOARD OF EDUCATION. The city of Wilmington officially began desegregation that same year. However, because schools did not become desegregated in actuality, in the 1970's a federal court ordered that a large-scale BUSING effort be instituted to encompass Wilmington and ten suburban school districts. The busing program led to a court challenge, and when the Supreme Court ruled on the case in *Delaware State Board v. Evans* (1980), it ruled that the program should stand.

—*Rose Secrest*

ware ranked ninth in the percentage of African American residents.

In 1639 Swedish settlers first brought African Americans to Delaware. The Swedish settlement of Fort Christina, which had been founded only a year before, was the destination of the slave ship *Black Anthony* from the West Indies. By 1700 African Americans composed about 5 percent of the population. Slaveowners and slaves began to immigrate into Delaware in sizable numbers during the eighteenth century, swelling the number of slaves to 25 percent of the population. By 1790 there were eighty-nine hundred slaves in the state.

The efforts of an ABOLITIONST MOVEMENT led by Quakers and METHODISTS resulted in many voluntary manumissions in the 1800's that freed 75 percent of Delaware's slaves. By 1860 there were only eighteen hundred slaves. African Americans were drawn to the Methodist Church that was behind these efforts, but racial slights within the church led Peter Spencer to found the African Union Church in Delaware in 1813. He was followed in 1816

**Dellums, Ronald V.** (b. November 24, 1935, Oakland, California): U.S. CONGRESS MEMBER from California. Ronald Dellums began representing California's Seventh Congressional District in 1971, and he served in Congress until 1998. Even though Dellums's home district was predominantly white, he was able to demonstrate a special sensitivity to the needs of its black citizens. Because of the power he wielded for many years as the chairman of the House Committee on the District of Columbia, Dellums was called "the mayor of the mayor" of WASHINGTON, D.C.

### Early Life

After graduating from prep schools on the west side of OAKLAND, CALIFORNIA, Dellums attended Oakland City College and received a bachelor's degree from San Francisco State College in 1960. He also received a master's degree in social work from the University of California at Berkeley in 1962.

From 1962 to 1968, Dellums pursued a career as a psychiatric social worker, working for the California Department of Mental Hygiene (1962-1964) as program director of the Bayview Community Center (1964-1965), as associate director and director of the Hunter's Point Youth Opportunities Center (1964-1966), as planning consultant to the Bay Area Social Planning Council (1966-1967), and as director of the Concentrated Employment Program of the San Francisco Economic Opportunity Council (1967-1968). By the end of the decade, Dellums decided that he could better meet the needs of the people in his district by entering politics.

### Early Political Career

In 1970 Dellums was elected to the U.S. Congress as a representative from the Berkeley-Oakland area and began his rise into the power orbit of the DEMOCRATIC PARTY even though he was clearly no champion of the status quo. Even before he was sworn in, Dellums addressed the World Conference on Vietnam, Laos, and Cambodia in Stockholm, including representatives of the Khmer Rouge and the

South Vietnamese National Liberation Front. In 1971 he addressed a massive May Day protest in the District of Columbia against the VIETNAM WAR. At the time, Dellums was a vocal champion of such radical groups as the BLACK PANTHER PARTY.

In 1973 Dellums became the first legislator to introduce legislation calling for comprehensive economic sanctions against South Africa. In the 1970's, he also became a member of the CONGRESSIONAL BLACK CAUCUS. Even though he dissented from the caucus's support of President Jimmy Carter's boycott of the 1980 Olympics, Dellums eventually became chairman of the group because of the integrity he displayed. After becoming one of the original cosponsors of the Nuclear Freeze Resolution in 1979, he was appointed by House Speaker Thomas P. (Tip) O'Neill as a member of a U.S. congressional delegation to Moscow, where he and the other delegates discussed a pending arms-limitation treaty.

California congressman Ronald V. Dellums. *(Library of Congress)*

In 1979 Dellums was also elected chair of the House Committee on the District of Columbia, becoming the first member of the House class of 1970 to be elected chair of a full House committee. As chairman, he held considerable power over the management of the nation's capital. To avoid usurping the authority of the district's elected mayor, however, he always tried to restrict congressional involvement in the city's affairs.

## Later Career

In the 1980's, Dellums campaigned to reduce the power of the MILITARY. In 1980 he was elected chairman of the House Armed Services subcommittee, thereby becoming the first African American placed in charge of a defense-oriented body on Capitol Hill. As senior member of the House Armed Services Committee in 1982, he became the first member of Congress to introduce and debate on the House floor an alternative military budget based on the policies of conventional arms reduction and a rejection of the doctrine of nuclear superiority. Dellums was also the first to introduce legislation to terminate all funding for the MX Pershing II and Midgetman missile programs. By the mid-1980's, Dellums had become the principal leader in the effort to control military spending.

Dellums's political career was interrupted in 1982. Robert Yesh, who had been a supervisor in the House Democratic cloakroom, told police that he had sold cocaine to Dellums and one of his aides, John Apperson. In August, 1983, however, the U.S. Justice Department closed its investigation without bringing a single criminal charge. In November, the House Ethics Committee conducted an investigation of its own and found the evidence insufficient to bring charges against Dellums or his aide. Many political observers interpreted the attack on Dellums as an attempt to steer him into softening his opposition to the defense budget.

Once Dellums's name had been cleared, he attacked the REAGAN ADMINISTRATION's reliance on military intervention rather than diplomacy when the United States invaded the small Caribbean island of Grenada. In November, 1983, he was one of four House members sent on a four-day fact-finding mission to Grenada to determine whether the U.S. invasion had truly been necessary to protect some six hundred American medical students on the island. Even though House Speaker O'Neill concluded after hearing the congressmen's report that the sending of American troops to Grenada was justified, Dellums and Representative Louis STOKES of Ohio told newsmen later that they thought the medical students had never been in any real danger.

Because Dellums's 1973 comprehensive sanctions legislation to bring economic pressure against South Africa had not yet been acted upon by Congress, Dellums persevered in the 1980's in his campaign against the white apartheid regime. Following a demonstration against apartheid on Washington's Embassy Row in December, 1984, Dellums and fourteen other protesters were arrested for refusing to leave the South African embassy. In July, 1986, Dellums sponsored a bill to support a sweeping trade embargo requiring the withdrawal of all U.S. businesses and investments from South Africa. The bill also called for a ban on South African aircraft entering the United States.

In spite of President Ronald Reagan's veto, Dellums's bill was approved by the House and passed by the Senate in a modified form. The next year, Dellums introduced another version of his 1973 legislative initiative; that bill also applied to the situation in Namibia and the role of U.S. allies who continued to trade with the apartheid regime there. The House overwhelmingly passed the bill in 1988, but the Senate failed to act on it. Dellums also used his chairmanship of the Congressional Black Caucus to make South Africa sanctions a priority in the 101st Congress.

Although South Africa was Dellums's highest priority in the late 1980's, he did not abandon entirely his mission to curb military spending. He was a leading opponent of the Strategic Defense Initiative (SDI) program since its first proposal in 1984. In addition, he consistently voted against any military aid to El Salvador, Guatemala, or the Nicaraguan contras. In 1987 House Speaker Jim Wright appointed Dellums a member of the U.S. delegation to the North Atlantic Assembly, where he participated in programs designed to enhance the security of the North Atlantic community. Dellums also lectured throughout the United States and Europe on the need for verifiable arms control and reduction.

*Controversy*

Despite Dellums's liberal voting record, he was designated for membership to the House Intelligence Committee, primarily because of the way he had protected highly classified information as chairman of the key House Subcommittee on Research and Development. Staunch conservatives such as William F. Buckley, Jr., and Oliver North openly expressed their opposition to Dellums's appointment. They pointed to his entering into the Congressional Record in 1972 a five-hundred-page classified government report on Vietnam, thereby destroying the report's secrecy. They also cited a statement made by Dellums to the effect that every intelligence committee should be dismantled. Nevertheless, Dellums's appointment was confirmed on October 6, 1991. On January 27, 1993, House Democrats voted 198 to 10 to make Dellums chairman of the House Armed Services Committee. He was the first African American to serve in this post.

Dellums emerged as one of the most powerful black leaders in Congress in the 1980's and 1990's. As a result of his chairmanship of the Congressional Black Caucus and the House Committee on the District of Columbia, Del-lums became an effective force within the white establishment on Capitol Hill. He derived much of his power from the fact that he not only represented his white constituents in California but also strengthened the efforts of black lawmakers to address the legislative concerns of black citizens everywhere. In 1997, after serving in Congress for twenty-seven years, Dellums announced his decision to retire early in 1998 rather than run for reelection.

—*Alan Brown*

*See also:* Politics and government.

Suggested Readings:

Booker, Simeon. "Four Blacks Hold Key Committee Posts in House of Representatives." *Jet* (January 8, 1981): 8-9.

Golphin, Vincent F. A. "Congressman Dellums Takes the Less-Traveled Road." *National Catholic Reporter* (September 6, 1985): 6-7.

Muravchik, Joshua. "Dellums' Dilemma." *New Republic* (March 11, 1991): 14-16.

Nichols, John. "Exit Left: Ron Dellums Leads the Liberals Out of Congress." *The Progressive* (February, 1998): 30-32.

Ragsdale, Bruce A., and Joel D. Treese. *Black Americans in Congress, 1870-1989.* Washington, D.C.: U.S. Government Printing Office, 1990.

Randolph, Laura B. "Top of Capitol Hill: Majority Whip and Five Black Committee Chairmen Are at Summit of Congressional Power." *Ebony* (December, 1989): 144-147.

"Rep. Ron Dellums Winds Up a Stellar Twenty-seven Years on Capitol Hill." *Jet* (December 8, 1997): 4-5.

"Ronald V. Dellums." *Current Biography* 54 (September, 1993): 14-17.

**Demby, William** (b. December 25, 1922, Pittsburgh, Pennsylvania): Novelist and educator. As the son of William and Gertrude Hendricks Demby, young William Demby grew up in the

WEST VIRGINIA coal-mining town of Clarksburg, where his father worked for the Standard Oil Company. Demby attended West Virginia State College before being drafted into the U.S. Army during World War II. He served in Italy as a correspondent for *Stars and Stripes*. When he returned to the United States, Demby became a student at FISK UNIVERSITY and completed his bachelor's degree in 1947. He returned to Italy to study art history at the University of Rome. During the next two decades, Demby lived in Rome, was married to an Italian woman, and began writing screenplays for film and television. He also worked on translating film scripts into English for Italian film director Roberto Rossellini.

While living in Italy, Demby published his first novel, *Beetlecreek* (1950). The novel drew heavily on memories of his boyhood in West Virginia. In the novel, an idealistic young African American boy leaves Pittsburgh to live with his aunt and uncle in the stagnant, economically depressed Southern town of Beetlecreek. There, the young boy befriends a white recluse who lives in the town's black neighborhood. Although they struggle to transcend the narrow prejudices of Beetlecreek, the boy, his uncle, and the white loner see their hope and lives ruined by the destructive racist influences of their environment.

Demby's second novel, *The Catacombs* (1965), abandoned the realistic style of *Beetlecreek* for an impressionistic, cinematic style that cut from one scene to the next, between real and imagined images. Set in Rome from the spring of 1962 to the spring of 1964, the novel has a grim mood and intersperses depressing news items from papers of the time between stream of consciousness passages and realistic scenes. Demby explores the interrelationship between an expatriate black novelist and the black actor (involved in an affair with an Italian count) about whom he is writing a novel. At the conclusion of the novel, the love affair has ended, the actor disappears into the Catacombs, and the novelist decides to return to the United States.

Demby's third novel, *Love Story Black* (1978), revolves around the relationship between a black professor of English and an aging, once-famous black singer whose life story he is writing. While Demby gleefully satirizes the professor's relations with the academic world and with his militant students, he also celebrates the bond that grows between the professor and the nearly ninety-year-old singer who teaches him about love.

Demby himself returned to the United States and accepted a position as professor of English at the City University of New York's College of Staten Island from 1969 to 1989. Although his novels won critical acclaim, they were less successful commercially. He enjoyed renewed attention after Northeastern University Press reissued *The Catacombs* in 1991 as part of its Northeastern Library of Black Literature, including the novel among other classic works of African American LITERATURE.

**Democratic Party:** By maintaining an unwavering allegiance to the Democratic Party, African Americans emerged in the 1930's as one of the most unified constituencies in American politics. Prior to the 1930's, the few African Americans who could vote tended to vote Republican. The REPUBLICAN PARTY was seen as the party of Abraham Lincoln, emancipation from SLAVERY, and the short-lived African American gains of the RECONSTRUCTION era. The Democratic Party had a strong stigma attached to it, since historically many party leaders were southern segregationists. Democratic president Franklin D. Roosevelt (who took office in 1933) and his New Deal programs changed the situation dramatically.

*The New Deal*
With the emergence of a more liberal ideological consensus during the 1930's, largely attrib-

utable to the GREAT DEPRESSION, a productive and loyal political relationship developed between African Americans and the Democratic Party. Roosevelt created an array of federal programs and agencies, nicknamed the New Deal, to fight the widespread unemployment and desperation created by the Depression.

White House meetings, job initiatives, and the efforts of first lady Eleanor Roosevelt all created a favorable impression in the black community that helped inspire and invigorate CIVIL RIGHTS activists. African American voters consequently shifted their allegiance from the party of Lincoln and endorsed the president's more proactive federal stance on equality and racial injustice. Although the administration did not directly challenge the segregationist position of several southern Democrats—the president needed southern votes in order to pass New Deal legislation—his stance on racial issues had a significant effect on American politics.

Northern migration in the early twentieth century had produced vibrant African American urban communities, and Roosevelt eagerly courted their vote. He appointed several prominent civil rights activists to administrative positions in the federal government, he conducted meetings with leading black professionals, and he selected William HASTIE to become the first black federal judge. The president championed the career of Mary McLeod BETHUNE as a leading director in the National Youth Administration (NYA). Roosevelt often consulted with a group dubbed the "black cabinet" or "black brain trust," and in 1937 the NYA held a three-day conference on the Problems of the Negro and the Negro Youth. This conference was designed to produce government programs for the African American community, and even some of Roosevelt's staunchest critics admitted that the president's policies represented a meaningful turning point in American politics.

Roosevelt also benefited from the work of his wife, Eleanor. She consistently used her leverage as first lady to push the Democratic Party further to the left on race issues, and she persuaded numerous congressmen to ease discrimination practices in New Deal programs. She angered southerners by pushing for antilynching legislation, and her attacks on segregation restrictions earned her the title "nigger-lover Eleanor" among some white racists. In 1939 she resigned from the Daughters of the American Revolution when the organization blocked a concert by renowned black contralto Marian ANDERSON at its Constitution Hall. Eleanor Roosevelt exposed this incident in her newspaper column and later arranged for Anderson to perform outdoors before the Lincoln Memorial for an audience of thousands. These acts, albeit largely symbolic in nature, seemed to signify the dawning of a new era in race relations in the United States.

The gradual improvement in living conditions after the mid-1930's also increased the Democratic Party's popularity among African Americans. The National Youth Administration aided black secondary schools and universities. The Public Works Administration (PWA) devised a quota system to curtail discrimination against black workers, and it allowed hundreds of African Americans to penetrate the barriers of the white-dominated southern construction industry. Life expectancy increased from forty-eight to fifty-three years, and more than a million African Americans benefited from government-sponsored literacy programs. Although Roosevelt refused to adopt an aggressive stance toward antilynching legislation, he pressured southern states on the matter, and lynchings dropped from twenty-eight in 1933 to two in 1939.

Because of the overall sense of optimism generated by several New Deal programs, voters eagerly joined the Democratic Party's coalition. Incumbent Republican president Herbert Hoover had received 70 percent of the African American vote in 1932, but by 1940 Roosevelt had secured 68 percent. As a result, African Americans would play an increasingly visible role in Democratic Party politics for the remainder of the twentieth century.

### World War II

WORLD WAR II accelerated African Americans' quest for full racial equality. The U.S. SUPREME COURT eliminated a number of legal barriers that hindered black participation in politics and blocked black enrollment in colleges and universities. In 1944 the Supreme Court decision in *Smith v. Wainwright* outlawed the all-white primary in the South. Subsequent rulings held that segregation of law schools and state colleges, even if supposedly "SEPARATE BUT EQUAL" facilities existed for black and white students, was not legal.

The GI Bill of Rights freed black veterans from poll tax requirements, and economic opportunities in the North prompted many workers to relocate in major cities such as Detroit, Chicago, and Cleveland. A more aggressive class of religious leaders and newspaper editors, moreover, demanded a return on their electoral investment: They pressured the Democratic Party to introduce more vigorous and confrontational civil rights legislation that would dismantle the voting restrictions and segregationist practices that had historically oppressed African Americans.

### The 1948 Election

President Harry S Truman, who took office in 1945 after Roosevelt's death, maintained that the Democratic Party's chances for victory in 1948 depended on a large turnout among its African American constituency. He formed the President's Committee on Civil Rights. The committee produced a report that called for an end to all voting obstacles in the South, desegregation of the armed forces and inter-state transportation, greater government employment, and more assertive and proactive protection for blacks from the Justice Department.

The report generated a revolt among southern Democrats that threatened Truman's election campaign in 1948. Although Truman attempted to downplay the importance of the committee's report to appease southern Democrats, African American leaders forced the president's hand. Truman's Cold War rhetoric and criticisms of the Soviet Union's destruction of democracy in its satellite system left the president vulnerable to criticism from blacks for his lackluster stance on civil rights at home.

Comparing the African American experience in the South with living conditions in Soviet-controlled Eastern Europe, the NATIONAL Association for the Advancement of Colored People (NAACP) asked the United Nations to intervene in American domestic affairs in order to protect an oppressed minority. Labor leader A. Philip RANDOLPH, who had orchestrated the successful March on Washington movement that forced Roosevelt to abolish discrimination in war production during World War II, suggested that all blacks should evade the draft until segregation was eliminated in the armed forces.

Other black radicals, such as Paul ROBESON, Charles HOUSTON, and W. E. B. DU BOIS, offered their support to Truman's opponent for the Democratic nomination, Henry Wallace. In addition, the Republican candidate, Thomas Dewey, included a plank in the party platform calling for desegregation of the military.

These pressures moved Truman to unveil two executive orders. One act established fair employment practices in federal hiring, outlawing racial discrimination in the federal workplace. The second began a process that would ultimately result in the desegregation of the military during the KOREAN WAR. Truman also called a special session of Congress and endorsed Minnesota Senator Hubert

Humphrey's liberal civil rights platform. Southern Democrats were appalled. They bolted from the party, formed an independent Dixiecrat Party, and ran Senator Strom Thurmond of South Carolina for president.

Truman's actions produced considerable success for the Democratic Party. He received 69 percent of the African American vote in northern cities, and black support helped him carry the key states of California, Illinois, and Ohio. Southern politicians would continue to fight to protect segregation, but the electoral strength of the African American community strongly influenced the Democratic Party and created a powerful force that would eventually dismantle Jim Crow segregation following the Supreme Court's BROWN V. BOARD OF EDUCATION decision in 1954.

### Legislation and Voter Registration

The Democratic Party attempted to satisfy both sides of its coalition by proceeding slowly on civil rights during the 1950's, but events such as a school desegregation crisis in Little Rock, Arkansas, lunch-counter protests in North Carolina, and murder in Mississippi catapulted civil rights into the national spotlight. On August 28, 1963, Martin Luther KING, Jr., delivered his "I Have a Dream" speech before an enthusiastic crowd of more than 250,000 in Washington, D.C. Yet young black radicals were already criticizing King for dragging his feet and for avoiding confrontational initiatives.

King's MARCH ON WASHINGTON persuaded President John F. Kennedy that the Democratic Party had to rebuild its bridges to the black community. He drafted civil rights legislation, but he was assassinated in 1963 before Congress had acted on the measure. Lyndon B. Johnson became president upon Kennedy's death, and he pushed Congress to pass the landmark Civil Rights Act of 1964. Yet the right to vote freely and without intimidation was still a crucial issue for African Americans, and a growing number of radicals argued that voting rights could be obtained only through violence.

Since MISSISSIPPI still maintained the most brutal system of Jim Crow segregation in the South, young activists decided to launch a voter registration campaign throughout the state in 1964. This project, Freedom Summer, was organized by Bob MOSES and others to challenge the stranglehold that white Democrats held over the party machinery in Mississippi. Moses and the STUDENT NONVIOLENT COORDINATING COMMITTEE (SNCC) invited white college students from some of the most prestigious institutions in the country to come to Mississippi and help in the drive. Moses believed that if whites were exposed to the same violence that blacks were, the situation would generate greater national support for African American voting rights. One black and two white activists were subsequently murdered; the FEDERAL BUREAU OF INVESTIGATION (FBI) conducted an investigation and made several arrests. However, the Justice Department refused to provide protection against the beatings, shootings, and firebombings that voting rights organizers encountered on a daily basis.

### Mississippi Freedom Democratic Party

Freedom Summer created a viable alternative to white-run southern politics and led to the emergence of the MISSISSIPPI FREEDOM DEMOCRATIC PARTY (MFDP). Buoyed by the voter registration drive, activist African American Democrats argued that they had been excluded from the process of selecting delegates for the 1964 Democratic National Convention. As a result, they demanded that they be recognized as the legitimate representatives from Mississippi. They provided startling testimony to support their case. Fannie Lou HAMMER recalled how local police departments curtailed voter registration drives and tolerated acts of intimidation. Before a national television audience, she asked how such things could occur if America was truly the land of the free.

Johnson attempted to enact a compromise: He granted the MFDP two at-large seats. However, the convention recognized only state regulars who had already promised their forty-four votes for Johnson's nomination. Martin Luther King, Jr., and prominent leaders from the NAACP maintained that the compromise represented a notable accomplishment, and subsequently, over 90 percent of all African Americans voted Democratic. After the election, Johnson successfully lobbied for the passage of the VOTING RIGHTS ACT OF 1965. The MFDP experience angered young radicals, however, and pushed them away from King's nonviolent tactics and toward the black power positions advocated by groups such as the BLACK PANTHER PARTY and leaders such as MALCOLM X.

At the 1968 Democratic National Convention, Georgia state legislator Julian Bond (center)—seen here touring Brooklyn after the convention—led a successful challenge against the delegation of Georgia governor Lester Maddox. *(AP/Wide World Photos)*

*Continued Loyalty*

The Democratic Party's commitment to the welfare state—that is, to a system in which the government assumes much responsibility for the social well-being of its citizens—cemented its relationship with the African American community. In addition, more blacks attained positions of power in the party. Representative Barbara JORDAN of Houston emerged as one of the most prominent members of the House Judiciary Committee during the Watergate hearings, and in 1976 she delivered the keynote address at the national convention. Harold WASHINGTON became the first black mayor of Chicago in 1983. In 1989, with the aid of more than 90 percent of the black vote, David DINKINS was elected mayor of New York City. Jesse JACKSON was unsuccessful in his bid for the Democratic presidential nomination in 1988; nevertheless, most blacks were increasingly satisfied with the Democrats' devotion to social legislation and racial advancement. Furthermore, the CONGRESSIONAL BLACK Caucus possessed an increasing amount of clout in the 1990's. The caucus influenced crime bills that led to a greater examination of effects of race in death-penalty cases.

African American voters were important to the Democratic Party's electoral success. For example, in 1976 former Georgia governor Jimmy Carter won the presidency by a narrow margin, but he received over 90 percent of the black vote. His margin of victory was only 1.7 million, but approximately 5.2 million blacks voted Democratic.

Some African American leaders have questioned black voters' steadfast loyalty to the Democratic Party. POVERTY, crime, and poor EDUCATION still affect a disproportionate number of blacks, and federal programs have failed to obliterate discrimination or the racial class system. More blacks are becoming disillusioned with white Democrats; a 1986 survey indicated that 53 percent desired more black candidates. Jesse Jackson's presidential bid in 1988 was primarily an attempt to create more leverage for the black community in the nominating process.

—*Robert D. Ubriaco, Jr.*

*See also:* Clinton administration; Mayors; Politics and government.

The faces on these children in a Toronto kindergarten class reflect the growing racial and ethnic diversity in North America. *(Dick Hemingway)*

Suggested Readings:

Dionne, E. J. *They Only Look Dead.* New York: Simon & Schuster, 1996.

Franklin, John Hope, and August Meier, eds. *Black Leaders of the Twentieth Century.* Urbana: University of Illinois Press, 1982.

Lawson, Steven F. *Running for Freedom.* New York: McGraw-Hill, 1991.

McAdam, Doug. *Freedom Summer.* New York: Oxford University Press, 1988.

Sitkoff, Harvard. *A New Deal for Blacks.* New York: Oxford University Press, 1978.

Weiss, Nancy J. *Farewell to the Party of Lincoln.* Princeton: Princeton University Press, 1983.

**Demography:** The statistical study of human populations. The question of how many African Americans there are in the United States is more than a question of numbers: It is also an issue with serious political implications. For example, the number of representatives that an area or state can elect to the U.S. House of Representatives is based on the number of people living in its electoral districts. Moreover, population size also often affects the allocation of government funds. Therefore, if the number of African Americans is underestimated, areas in which African Americans are concentrated may be deprived of both fair political power and resources.

*Census Issues*

Since 1790 the U.S. Census Bureau has attempted to count all the people in the United States every ten years. At various intervals between the ten-year counts, it takes samples on specific subjects.

When the 1990 Census of Population and Housing was first completed, many African American leaders—and many demographers—believed that African Americans had been undercounted. For this reason, the Census Bureau later decided to revise its 1990 figures. The question of whether an actual "head count" or a number obtained through the process of statistical sampling would yield more accurate population figures continued to be a controversial one throughout the twentieth century.

A second controversy involved the definition of "race." Many census officials and political leaders advocated adding a "multiracial" category to the 2000 census, arguing that increasing numbers of Americans could not easily identify themselves simply as "black," "white," or "Asian." Others objected to the multiracial category, however, believing that it would undercut the political influence of African Americans by removing many people with African ancestry from the "black" category.

Ultimately, the Census Bureau decided to allow people to select more than one racial category in the 2000 census. This approach was also controversial, because some black leaders believed that it might lessen their ability to present their group as a unified bloc. Nevertheless, evidence indicated that allowing people to identify themselves with more than one race would probably not greatly affect African American demographics. In a test survey conducted by the Census Bureau in 1996, only

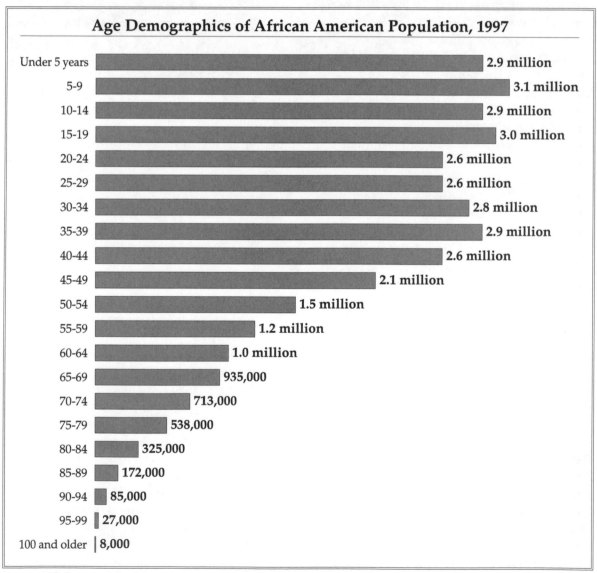

**Age Demographics of African American Population, 1997**

|  |  |
|---|---|
| Under 5 years | 2.9 million |
| 5-9 | 3.1 million |
| 10-14 | 2.9 million |
| 15-19 | 3.0 million |
| 20-24 | 2.6 million |
| 25-29 | 2.6 million |
| 30-34 | 2.8 million |
| 35-39 | 2.9 million |
| 40-44 | 2.6 million |
| 45-49 | 2.1 million |
| 50-54 | 1.5 million |
| 55-59 | 1.2 million |
| 60-64 | 1.0 million |
| 65-69 | 935,000 |
| 70-74 | 713,000 |
| 75-79 | 538,000 |
| 80-84 | 325,000 |
| 85-89 | 172,000 |
| 90-94 | 85,000 |
| 95-99 | 27,000 |
| 100 and older | 8,000 |

*Source:* U.S. Bureau of the Census.

about 1 percent of respondents identified themselves as biracial or multiracial.

### Population Increase

African Americans were at their highest point as a proportion of the American population in 1790, at the time of the first U.S. Census, when they made up about 19.3 percent of the population, or about one out of every five people in the United States. Although their numbers have continued to grow throughout American history, they declined as a proportion of the American population throughout the nineteenth and early twentieth centuries, largely because there was massive immigration from Europe during this period and virtually no immigration from AFRICA. Shortly after WORLD WAR II, however, African Americans began to increase as a proportion of the population by about one-half of a percentage point every ten years.

This increase as a proportion of the population is primarily attributable to the fact that African Americans tend to have somewhat larger families than the majority and to the fact that more African Americans have been of child-bearing age. There is still relatively little immigration of persons of African ancestry into the United States. In 1990, for example, only 363,819 people in the country—fewer than 2 percent of all foreign-born people in the United States—had been born on the continent of Africa.

### Geographical Distribution

Until WORLD WAR I, African American communities were concentrated mostly in the former slave states of the South. In 1910 nearly 90 percent of the nation's black residents still lived in that region. During the war, however, the demand for industrial labor in northern cities could no longer be satisfied by immigration from Europe, and northern industries began to recruit African Americans. African Americans, in turn, were seeking better lives

than those offered by the rigidly segregated South. The movement of African Americans from the South to the Northeast and to CALIFORNIA—a movement known as the GREAT MIGRATION—continued through most of the twentieth century. It was stimulated by rural unemployment resulting from falling crop prices and mechanization of farming, as well as by southern violence and discrimination. This mass movement resulted in the URBANIZATION of millions of African Americans.

By 1970 the Great Migration had ended. After that year the regional distribution of the African American population became comparatively stable. A majority of the group (almost 55 percent by 1997) continued to live in the South. A slight increase in the percentage of the black population located in the South during the 1990's indicated that the Great Migration had not only ended but even begun to reverse. The end of the Jim Crow system of segregation, increasing economic opportunities in the South, and the very fact that large black populations could be found in the South all contributed to the growing attractiveness of this region for many African Americans.

In the 1990's, more than one of every five Virginians and more than one of every five residents of NORTH CAROLINA were African American. More than one of every four people in ALABAMA, GEORGIA, and MARYLAND were African American. About one of every three people in LOUISIANA and SOUTH CAROLINA was African American. MISSISSIPPI was the most African American of all states, with an African American population of more than 36 percent. The majority of people living in WASHINGTON, D.C., were African American.

Because some states have much larger populations than others, the states with the highest African American percentages are not always the states with the largest African American populations. For example, in 1997 Mississippi was 36.4 percent African Ameri-

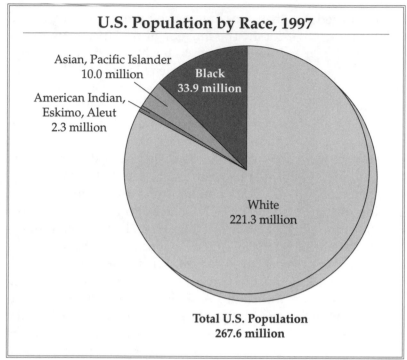

### U.S. Population by Race, 1997

Asian, Pacific Islander
10.0 million

Black
33.9 million

American Indian,
Eskimo, Aleut
2.3 million

White
221.3 million

**Total U.S. Population
267.6 million**

*Source:* U.S. Bureau of the Census.

*Cities and Suburbs*

Not only did African Americans tend to be concentrated in particular areas of the United States at the end of the twentieth century, but also they were much more likely to dwell in central areas of large cities than were other Americans. According to Census Bureau estimates, a clear majority of African Americans (54.5 percent) lived in the central parts of cities in March, 1998, while only 22.0 percent of white non-Hispanic Americans lived in central urban areas. This situation was a drastic change from that at the beginning of the twentieth century, when African Americans lived primarily in rural areas.

The American countryside has been losing population for a long time. While African Americans have become an overwhelmingly urban population, white Americans have become suburban. In 1998 more than half (53.8 percent) of white Americans lived in metropolitan areas outside central cities. This situation represents a trend toward increasing racial segregation in places of residence, discussed by Douglas Massey and Nancy Denton in their book *American Apartheid: Segregation and the Making of the Underclass* (1993).

*Age and Family Characteristics*

African Americans in 1998 were younger than white Americans, and they had larger, younger families—both characteristics that predict continued population growth of the black population. The median age of African Americans in March, 1998, was 29.0 years, compared with 37.2 for whites. One-third of all African

can, but only 2.9 percent of all African Americans lived in Mississippi. In the 1990's, the largest number of African Americans lived in heavily populated NEW YORK STATE.

New York was only about 18 percent African American in 1997, yet almost one of every ten African Americans in the United States lived in the state. Similarly, the large state of TEXAS contained just under 7 percent of all the African Americans in the nation even though the percentage of Texans who were African American was slightly under the percentage of all Americans who were of African ancestry.

Of the nearly 19 percent of African Americans who lived in the Northeast, about half lived in New York. The vast majority of the African Americans who lived in the West lived in California. Other nonsouthern states that contained fairly large proportions of the total African American population were ILLINOIS, MICHIGAN, NEW JERSEY, OHIO, and PENNSYLVANIA.

Americans were under eighteen years of age, whereas fewer than one-fourth of all white Americans were under eighteen. At the other end of the age range, only 7.8 percent of African Americans were sixty-five or older, compared with nearly 14 percent of the majority racial group. More than two-thirds of African American families contained children under eighteen years of age, compared with just under half of white American families. The census estimated an average of 3.4 persons per family in African American families and an average of 3.1 persons per family in white American families.

African American families also tended to differ from the majority in family structure. There has been a trend toward single-parent, female-headed families within the group. The reasons for this trend are a matter of considerable debate; some social scientists have argued that it is a result of economic pressures and high rates of joblessness among men. The fact that SINGLE-PARENT HOUSEHOLDS headed by women are somewhat more common in central city areas, where the majority of African Americans now reside and where economic pressures are especially intense, supports this view.

*The Middle Class*

The years following the Civil Rights movement saw the growth of a large African American middle class. A good study of this phenomenon, Bart Landry's *New Black Middle Class* (1987), found that in 1960, on the eve of the Civil Rights movement, only 13.4 percent of working African Americans could be found in middle-class jobs. By 1981, however, the proportion of African Americans in the middle class had almost tripled, to 37.8 percent. Although Landry's work was done before the 1990 census, his calculations indicated that this middle class would reach 48.6 percent by 1990 and 56.4 percent by 2000, suggesting that the United States would enter the twenty-first century with the majority of African Ameri-

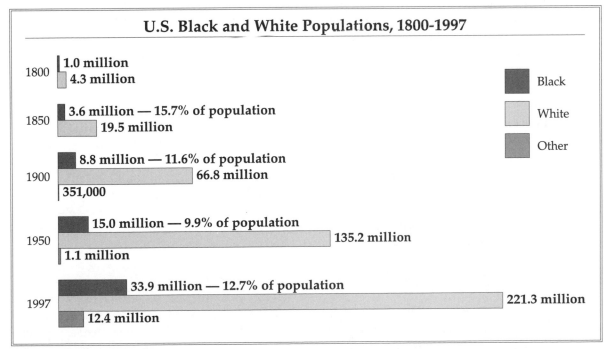

**U.S. Black and White Populations, 1800-1997**

1800
1.0 million
4.3 million

1850
3.6 million — 15.7% of population
19.5 million

1900
8.8 million — 11.6% of population
66.8 million
351,000

1950
15.0 million — 9.9% of population
135.2 million
1.1 million

1997
33.9 million — 12.7% of population
221.3 million
12.4 million

■ Black
▢ White
■ Other

*Source:* U.S. Bureau of the Census.
*Note:* "Other" includes American Indian, Asian, and Pacific Islander.

cans in the middle class. One of the problems with determining how many African Americans were middle class by the end of the twentieth century was that there are different definitions of middle-class status.

A number of researchers have pointed out that government employment is particularly important to the black middle class. In 1998 one out of every five employed African Americans worked for federal, state, or local governments. Middle-class African Americans, therefore, (as well as the poor) were particularly vulnerable to cutbacks in government spending.

### Income and Employment

While many achieved great economic advances, the African American population continued to be at a disadvantage, relative to other Americans, in income and employment as the United States entered the last decade of the twentieth century. The term "median income" refers to the income that is in the middle of all incomes received: Half of all incomes are above that level, and half are below it. The median income for African American families in 1998 was $28,602, compared with $49,640 for white families. If one looks at incomes for each individual, rather than for households, the difference between the two racial groups was even greater.

The unemployment rate of African American civilians was more than twice that of the majority population: It was 9.6 percent for the former, compared with only 4.0 percent for the latter. If one looks at the percentage of African Americans in managerial and professional occupations—the types of jobs that are generally the best-paying and have the greatest social status—one sees that only 16.7 percent of African Americans are in these jobs, compared with 31.2 percent of white Americans.

It would be a mistake to characterize the U.S. population of African ancestry as uniformly at the bottom of American society. As noted, there is a large and growing black mid-

dle class. Despite this trend, however, African Americans continue to struggle against serious disadvantages. POVERTY is one of the greatest of these disadvantages, and it is a disadvantage that is especially great for the youngest people.

### Poverty

During the late 1990's, the numbers and percentages of African Americans living in poverty dropped substantially. From 1996 to 1997, the number of poor African Americans went from 9.7 million to 9.1 million. In 1996 28.4 percent of African Americans were poor. One year later, this percentage was 26.5 percent. Although these figures indicate that black economic difficulties were lessening, the United States was still far from racial equality: Only 8.6 percent of white Americans lived in poverty. In other words, fewer than one of every ten whites lived below the poverty level, while more than one of every four African Americans lived in poverty. Among young people, rates of poverty were much greater. In 1998 11.2 percent of white children and 37.2 percent of black children were poor.

Those who lived in single-parent households were most likely to be poor. In 1996 43.7 percent of black, single-parent, female-headed families were poor. One year later, 39.8 percent of these families were poor; this percentage remained constant through the first half of 1998. Young people were particularly vulnerable to poverty, especially if they lived in single-parent families. More than half (55.3 percent) of single-parent, female-headed African American families with children under eighteen lived in poverty in March of 1998, according to U.S. Census estimates.

### Predictions of Future Trends

In absolute numbers, the African American population may be expected to continue to grow. However, from a late-1990's perspective, it appeared that it would increase only slightly from its late twentieth-century levels as a proportion of the total U.S. population. According to late-1990's projections, by 2020 there will be roughly 45 million African Americans, making up about 14.0 percent of the U.S. population. Ten years later, in 2050, there will probably be about 55 million African Americans—about 14.9 percent of the population.

The white population, by comparison, was expected to drop to 79.0 percent by 2020 and to 76.1 percent by 2040. Much of the growth in the U.S. population as a whole was expected to be attributable to the growth of the Hispanic population and the growth of various "nonwhite" groups.

Increased SUBURBANIZATION of African Americans was expected to result from a continuing expansion of the African American middle class. On the other hand, even as more African Americans join the middle class, it appeared as though unemployment and poverty would pose even greater threats for nonmiddle-class African Americans. Therefore, African Americans could find themselves divided into two groups, the privileged and the underprivileged, with a diminishing working class between.

—*Carl L. Bankston III*

*See also:* Census of the United States; Employment and unemployment; Immigration and ethnic origins of African Americans; Income distribution; Redistricting.

Suggested Readings:

Landry, Bart. *The New Black Middle Class.* Berkeley: University of California Press, 1987.

Massey, Douglas S., and Nancy A. Denton. *American Apartheid: Segregation and the Making of the Underclass.* Cambridge, Mass.: Harvard University Press, 1993.

Patillo-McCoy, Mary. *Black Picket Fences: Privilege and Peril Among the Black Middle Class.* Chicago: University of Chicago Press, 1999.

Smith, Jessie Carnie, and Carrell Peterson Horton, comps. *Historical Statistics of Black America.* 2 vols. New York: Gale, 1995.

U.S. Bureau of the Census. *Characteristics of the Black Population, 1990 Census of Population.* Washington, D.C.: U.S. Government Printing Office, 1994.

Wilson, William Julius. *When Work Disappears: The World of the New Urban Poor.* New York: Knopf, 1996.

**DePriest, Oscar** (1871, Florence, Alabama— May 12, 1951, Chicago, Illinois): ILLINOIS politician. DePriest became, in 1928, the first African American elected to the U.S. Congress in the twentieth century. DePriest took accounting classes after settling in CHICAGO in 1889, and his subsequent interest in business provided him with exposure to Chicago's growing political machine. DePriest, who earned a fortune in real estate, achieved his first political victory with his election as Cook County commissioner in 1904. This, coupled with an African American migration from the South into Chicago, put DePriest in a unique position to become a successful politician. He

Oscar DePriest, the first African American elected to Congress in the twentieth century. *(Library of Congress)*

could deliver the African American vote as a bloc. In 1908 he was an alternate delegate to the Republican National Convention, and in 1915 he became Chicago's first African American alderman. His next political position was as a congressman.

DePriest's membership in the REPUBLICAN PARTY eventually became a handicap for him in his support for African American causes in Congress. By the 1930's it was the DEMOCRATIC PARTY that supported and implemented programs that were espousing and advancing (in very small steps) political and civil rights for African Americans and all minorities in the United States. DePriest's association with the Republican Party was partially responsible for his loss to Arthur Wergs MITCHELL, the first African American Democrat elected to serve in Congress, in 1934.

DePriest continued to be an influential political figure in Chicago following his defeat. He finished his political career as an alderman in the Third Ward of Chicago (1943-1947). DePriest's contribution to African American politics goes beyond his political career in Congress. He was the forerunner of the numerous big-city African American MAYORS, city councilmen, and other local politicians in the post-1965 era. He recognized that African Americans could use their right to vote as a tool to win concessions from politicians and ultimately to elect politicians.

The concentration of African Americans in one area of Chicago created a bloc of political power that DePriest could use. Depression politics and the rise of the Democratic Party, however, signaled the end of DePriest's power, as the Democratic mayor turned over the African American ward to William DAWSON.
*See also:* Congress members; Politics and government.

**Dessalines, Jean-Jacques** (c. 1758, West Africa—October 17, 1806, Jacmel, Haiti): Military and political leader. Dessalines was a shrewd military leader who led HAITI to independence and became its first ruler.

Being an illiterate plantation slave, Dessalines adopted the surname of his master. In the early 1790's, he joined the struggles in Haiti against both French rule and the mulatto elite, becoming one of TOUSSAINT L'OUVERTURE's chief lieutenants. Eventually, Dessalines led Haiti to independence, making Haiti the first free nation in Latin America.

When the French mounted an attempt to reconquer Haiti in 1802, Dessalines fought desperately to hold on by strategically burning towns and executing any Frenchmen whom he captured. Eventually, however, L'Ouverture, Dessalines, and the other Haitian leaders surrendered upon being granted a promise of amnesty. Later in 1802, the French broke their agreement and arrested L'Ouverture. Dessalines then inherited the black leadership of the colony and worked out an alliance with the mulatto leader Alexandre Petion. In October 1802, Dessalines and Petion led a revolt against the French. After many months of brutal, vicious fighting, the forces under Dessalines and Petion finally drove the French from Haiti.

On January 1, 1804, Dessalines announced the independence of Haiti, and his generals named him governor-general. Later in 1804, Dessalines proclaimed himself Emperor Jacques I. Ruling as a dictator, Dessalines nationalized all property held by Europeans and forced the black lower class to either work as field hands or enter the military. Despite his attempts, Dessalines was unable to restore order and prosperity in Haiti, and rebellion ensued. He was assassinated on October 17, 1806, in a revolt led by Petion.

*—Alvin K. Benson*

**Detective fiction:** Black writers have been writing detective fiction since the beginning of the twentieth century. From the first, they transformed the usual conventions of detective fiction to their own ends, altering the concept of the detective persona, infusing their novels with black vernacular creations, and using the popular culture form to examine issues of race, class, and gender. Authors such as Pauline HOPKINS, John E. BRUCE, Rudolph FISHER, Chester HIMES, Ishmael REED, Clarence Major, and Walter MOSLEY have written detective novels that contain one or more black detectives. These authors have established a tradition of black detective fiction that demonstrates the ways in which African Americans have transformed a predominantly Eurocentric popular art form.

*Genesis of Detective Fiction*

Detective fiction is a relatively young literary field. Edgar Allan Poe is credited with having created the first detective hero in such stories as "The Murders in the Rue Morgue" (1841) and "The Purloined Letter" (1844). His brilliant amateur detective Dupin was the first model for what has proved to be an extremely popular genre type. Poe also established many of the conventions of the detective novel, including a story narrated by a close associate of the detective, a bumbling police force, an eccentric detective, the locked-room mystery, and the idea of clues leading to the discovery of the criminal. Even though the detective formula was invented in the 1840's, however, there were few literary detectives until the widespread success of Arthur Conan Doyle's Sherlock Holmes stories late in the nineteenth century. In the United States in the 1920's, Dashiell Hammett and Raymond Chandler created a new variation of the detective story featuring a hardboiled hero who narrates his story in the first person.

Evidence from black periodical literature indicates that African Americans were quick to pick up on the popular art form. In the late eighteenth and early nineteenth centuries, the works of African Americans were generally not published by white-owned and edited magazines and newspapers. Alternative black-owned publications were formed, such as the *Colored American*, published in Washington, D.C.; the *Colored American Magazine*, from Boston; and *McGirt's Weekly*, based in Philadelphia. From the beginning, these periodicals were popular culture compendiums of poetry, fiction, and essays written by African Americans for black audiences. The writers for these publications showed a fascination with sensational mystery and detective-story formats. African Americans, though, also used detective conventions for a purpose other than entertainment. Black writers used detective conventions to dramatize African American political and social concerns.

*First Black Detective Novels*

The two earliest known black detective novels are Pauline Hopkins's *Hagar's Daughter* (1901-1902), published in the *Colored American Magazine*, and John E. Bruce's *The Black Sleuth* (1908-1909), published in *McGirt's Weekly*. Much of the periodical literature published for African Americans is lost or lying in libraries uncollated. Therefore, there may be undiscovered earlier examples of black detective novels.

Both these novels contain black detectives who immediately break the pattern of the isolated, eccentric detective of both the classical and hardboiled varieties. In these two early black novels, the detectives work together in a team to solve crimes, and their families are important aspects of their identities. *Hagar's Daughter* features two black detectives, the primary one a servant girl named Venus Johnson who becomes a detective and solves the mystery of Hagar's missing daughter. These two novels also establish the tradition of black detective novels in other important ways through their inclusion of black vernacular, references to folk religion, and the presentation of "double consciousness"—the awareness of many African Americans of the possession of two distinct cultural identities. Although the novels contain sensational elements, they are written primarily as social critiques of the color line in pre- and post-Civil War southern society.

Pauline Hopkins was an editor of the *Colored American Magazine* as well as a prolific author and social activist; in *Hagar's Daughter*, her primary metaphor for the evil of slave society and racial prejudice is the phenomenon of PASSING, both consciously and unconsciously. *The Black Sleuth* stresses the importance of black pride and centers its black detective firmly in an African tradition of kinship. These two early novels also make affirmative African American cultural statements by stressing the positive aspects of African American vernacular creations such as blues and spirituals, specific foods, and community religious practices that often refer back to an African origin. Finally, the detectives in these novels use the double-conscious awareness of their blackness in positive ways to solve the mystery.

*Harlem Themes and Settings*
In 1932 Rudolph Fisher, a HARLEM RENAISSANCE writer, published his detective novel *The Conjure Man Dies: A Mystery Tale of Dark Harlem*. In that novel, Perry Dart, the only black detective on the New York police force, joins with a black doctor named Archer to solve the case of the murdered conjure man, Frimbo. All the novel's action takes place in HARLEM, and all the book's characters are black. Frimbo is depicted as a black African with a degree from Harvard University as well as a spiritual connection to generations of black hoodoo priests. *The Conjure Man Dies* combines elements of the classical locked-room mystery with Harlem Renaissance themes. In some ways, Frimbo represents the "new Negro," a black man proud of his Afrocentric heritage as well as his African American

can cultural achievements. Once again, black vernaculars such as language use, music, and, particularly, Afrocentric religious practices are presented as positive talents of the black American.

Chester Himes also used the detective novel to criticize racist practices and to examine class issues and BLACK-ON-BLACK VIOLENCE in Harlem. He wrote a series of detective novels concerning the two black detectives Coffin Ed Johnson and Grave Digger Jones: *For Love of Imabelle* (1957), *The Crazy Kill* (1959), *The Real Cool Killers* (1959), *All Shot Up* (1960), *The Big Gold Dream* (1960), *Cotton Comes to Harlem* (1965), *The Heat's On* (1966), and *Blind Man with a Pistol* (1969). Himes restructures the traditional hardboiled detective narrative by introducing a simultaneous time frame while creating a mythical landscape of Harlem that is both satirical and absurd. In some ways, Harlem itself becomes as important as plot and character are in these novels.

Through the use of black vernacular, Himes creates a rich cityscape illustrating the complexities of African American culture. The novels also follow a progression from first to last, as the plots become more complex and the two detectives become less effective. One of the primary assumptions of detective fiction is that the detective can solve the crime; however, in the final novel of the series, *Blind Man with a Pistol*, crimes multiply into chaos as a back-to-Africa group, a black Jesus movement, and a black brotherhood parade battle in the Harlem streets. No crime is ever solved, and Coffin Ed and Grave Digger are reduced to shooting rats in an abandoned building, defeated by the web of corruption that has influenced their white superiors to withhold evidence. Until this book, African American detective novels had remained faithful to the detective convention of the restoration of moral order. Himes's vision became increasingly apocalyptic as black-on-black violence accelerated and as armed black revolution seemed to many the only way to attain freedom.

*Works of the 1970's*
Ishmael Reed's *Mumbo Jumbo* (1972) and *The Last Days of Louisiana Red* (1974) and Clarence Major's *Reflex and Bone Structure* (1975) continue the experimentation with the detective form initiated by Himes. *Mumbo Jumbo* introduces the detective Papa LaBas, who, as an astral detective, represents Reed's "Neo-Hoodoo" aesthetic. Neo-Hoodoo is a positive African American worldview supported by African American creations in the areas of vernaculars, double-consciousness, and religion. *Mumbo Jumbo* mixes time frames and references to other popular culture forms into a new hybrid detective novel that revises history with an Afrocentric emphasis. Reed uses the detective-novel format to satirize white mainstream racist practices and to critique class divisions within the black world.

*Reflex and Bone Structure* is a metaphysical detective novel in which the formula of detective fiction is totally subverted. The narrator of the story and the reader are forced to become detectives in trying to solve the case. Because there is a crime, detectives, and an investigation, certain rudiments of the detective-novel genre are satisfied. The investigation stalls, however, and the unsolved crime stands as a metaphor for the rest of the novel, in which nothing gets resolved. Chronological time frame and developed characterization dissolve into surreal episodes that infuse language with poetic power, creating a new perspective on detective fiction. The reader is forced to interact with the text in such a way as to question the nature of fiction and reality.

*Continuing Influence*
Finally, African American detective fiction established a tradition that continues to influ-

Walter Mosley, author of the Easy Rawlins detective stories. *(© Roy Lewis Archives)*

ence other black writers. Richard WRIGHT had an extensive collection of detective magazines and material in his library. With *Devil in a Blue Dress* (1990), Walter Mosley began a series of novels that feature Easy Rawlins, a black detective in postwar Los Angeles. *Devil in a Blue Dress* and *A Red Death* (1991) share characteristic hardboiled techniques in their first-person narration and their black urban Los Angeles milieu. African American vernaculars are once again stressed, and Easy's blackness is an integral aspect of his worldview. Mosley continued the Rawlins series with later titles including *Black Betty* (1994), *A Little Yellow Dog* (1996), and *Gone Fishin'* (1997).

From Hopkins to Mosley, African American detective fiction constitutes a significant literary tradition that demonstrates African American ability to transform European-derived forms into distinct black creations.

*—Stephen F. Soitos*
*See also:* Literature; Science fiction; Slang and street language.

Suggested Readings:

Bailey, Frankie Y. *Out of the Wood-pile: Black Characters in Crime and Detective Fiction*. New York: Greenwood Press, 1991.

Berger, Roger A. "'The Black Dick': Race, Sexuality, and Discourse in the L.A. Novels of Walter Mosley." *African American Review* 31 (Summer, 1997): 281-294.

Cochran, David. "So Much Nonsense Must Make Sense: The Black Vision of Chester Himes." *The Midwest Quarterly* 38 (Autumn, 1996): 11-30.

Crooks, Robert. "From the Far Side of the Urban Frontier: The Detective Fiction of Chester Himes and Walter Mosley." *College Literature* 22 (October, 1995): 68-90.

Himes, Chester B. *Conversations with Chester Himes*. Edited by Michael Fabre and Robert E. Skinner. Jackson: University Press of Mississippi, 1995.

Mason, Theodore O., Jr. "Walter Mosley's Easy Rawlins: The Detective and Afro-American Fiction." *Kenyon Review* 14 (1992): 173-83.

Muller, Gilbert H. "The Greatest Show on Earth: The Detective Fiction." In *Chester Himes*. Boston: Twayne, 1989.

Skinner, Robert E. *Two Guns from Harlem: The Detective Fiction of Chester Himes*. Bowling Green, Ohio: Bowling Green State University Popular Press, 1989.

Tillery, Carolyn. "The Fiction of Black Crime: It's No Mystery." *American Visions* 12 (April/May 1997): 18-21.

"Walter Mosley." *Current Biography* 55 (September, 1994): 40-43.

In March, 1963, Martin Luther King, Jr. (center front with dark tie) led a freedom march in Detroit, joined by Mayor Jerome Cavanaugh (two persons to the right of King). *(AP/Wide World Photos)*

**Detroit, Michigan:** Largest city in MICHIGAN, seventh largest city in the United States (1990 census), and home to the country's third largest African American community. The 777,000 African Americans in Detroit account for 75 percent of the city's population. In the city's early history, African Americans were a distinct minority. In 1850 persons of African descent accounted for approx2imately 3 percent of the city's population of twenty thousand. There was, however, an active antislavery movement in the black community, and the city served as abolitionist Henry Bibb's home base.

After the CIVIL WAR, black Detroit grew slowly and along lines largely separate from the white population. Detroit was characterized by much DE FACTO SEGREGATION, and its African American community was confined largely to the city's east side.

After 1910 Detroit changed rapidly as a result of the combined effects of its burgeoning automobile industry and the GREAT MIGRATION of southern blacks to the North. The outbreak of WORLD WAR I created a need for labor, and Detroit became a popular destination for southern blacks, especially those from Georgia and Alabama. Between 1910 and 1930, the African American population increased from 5,700 to 120,000. WORLD WAR II had an even more dramatic effect. By 1960 African Americans represented almost 30 percent of the city's population.

The city's black newcomers encountered considerable de facto segregation and discrimination, and racial tensions flared periodically. In 1943 Detroit experienced a serious race riot in which twenty-five African Americans and nine white people died. In 1967 large areas of the city were devastated by what was the country's worst race riot to that time. Forty-three people were killed, five thousand were injured, and hundreds of millions of dollars worth of property was destroyed.

All was not strife, however, as Detroit witnessed the rise of a black community of national influence. The NATION OF ISLAM was started in Detroit in the 1930's. In the 1960's, the city had a particularly important influence on popular music in the United States as Mo-TOWN emerged as a major recording label.

By 1970 Detroit had a black majority, and the city elected Coleman YOUNG as its first African American mayor in 1973. Transition to black political control proved easier than in some cities, though it was complicated by problems in the American automobile industry. The creation of the Renaissance Center and other redevelopment projects in the 1970's was seen as evidence of biracial cooperation.

However, during his twenty-year tenure as mayor, Young antagonized leaders in the white suburbs around the city, and his rhetoric seemed to heighten racial polarization. The city suffered a significant amount of WHITE FLIGHT, and its tax-revenue base shrank. By the late 1980's the city had become infamous for urban decay and crime, including an extremely high homicide rate.

Dennis ARCHER was elected mayor in 1993, running against a Young-approved opponent. Archer managed to improve the city's situation in basic ways such as filling potholes in the streets, improving trash collection, and making its bus system more effective. In 1994 an impoverished 18-square-mile area near downtown was designated a federal empowerment zone, making Detroit the recipient of $100 million of funding for the area over a ten-year period.

Archer generated controversy of a different sort than his predecessor had. He sought to work with business leaders and to build partnerships with suburban leaders. Such tactics cost him support from the city's African Americans, many of whom began to see him as unsympathetic to their own needs. Re-elected in 1997, he survived a recall effort early in 1999. Meanwhile, in the late 1990's, controversial plans were put into action to overhaul Detroit's troubled public schools, and some economic relief was expected to occur when three new gambling casino projects opened. Nonetheless, the city was facing an extremely difficult struggle on the road to economic and social health.

*See also:* Detroit riots.

**Detroit riots:** Two major disturbances in DE-TROIT, MICHIGAN, one in 1943 and the other in 1967. The 1943 riot was the most destructive to occur during WORLD WAR II. Interracial tensions were heightened by equal employment opportunity rulings and housing project discrimination. Equal employment rulings and promotions of black workers created resentment among white workers and resulted in unauthorized walkouts at automobile plants in the city.

In 1942, the year before the riot, the city's Sojourner Truth housing project was the target of a white mob attack. Potential black tenants had been excluded from the project, and their

Detroit police scuffle with a man during the 1943 disturbance. *(AP/Wide World Photos)*

attempt to integrate it was met with white violence and a lack of police support. In June, 1943, a fight in a Belle Isle amusement park erupted into rioting. Police responded by using aggressive enforcement measures against black rioters but treated white participants lightly. As a result, twenty-five of the thirty-four people killed in the riot were black, including seventeen killed by police.

The Detroit riot of 1967 was symbolic of black protest against economic subordination and political invisibility. One in a series of major collective disturbances that erupted in the 1960's, the Detroit riot resulted in more than forty deaths, five thousand injuries, and an estimated $250 million in property loss. The precipitating incident for the riot was an after-hours police raid on a black speakeasy on July 23. As the shakedown progressed, a crowd of African Americans formed. Police failed to contain it. Rioters set garbage on fire and threw rocks and firebombs. The disturbance spread, and massive looting began. Before the rioters were brought under control, federal troops had to be brought in. Toward the end of the rioting, snipers retaliated against police, the National Guard, and federal troops.
*See also:* Race riots.

Before National Guard troops reached Detroit in July, 1967, looters pillaged businesses. *(AP/Wide World Photos)*

**Dett, R. Nathaniel** (October 11, 1882, Drummondsville, Ontario, Canada—October 2, 1943, Battle Creek, Michigan): Composer, conductor, and educator. One of the first African American composers to win recognition in the concert hall, Dett was also a distinguished teacher and administrator.

Although born in Canada, Robert Nathaniel Dett achieved prominence in the musical society of the United States. As a composer and teacher associ-

R. Nathaniel Dett. *(Library of Congress)*

ated for many years with Virginia's HAMPTON INSTITUTE, he tirelessly championed the cause of African American music. Dett grew up in a musically gifted family, and he first heard African American spirituals from his maternal grandmother. Dett himself played the piano from the age of three.

Dett graduated from the Oberlin Conservatory in 1908, becoming the first African American to earn its bachelor of music degree. Further studies took him to Columbia and Harvard Universities and to the Eastman School, where he earned a master of music degree in 1932. He also studied with famed music teacher and composer Nadia Boulanger in France. Dett's career as an educator culminated in his years at the Hampton Institute (1913-1932), where he created its School of Music and the Hampton Institute Choir. Dett toured Europe with the Institute Choir in 1930.

Familiar with spirituals since his youth, Dett was inspired to use them in his works after hearing a piece by Czech composer Antonin Dvorak based on folk tunes. Dett's com-

positions include several dozen choral works, two collections of arranged spirituals, and eight piano suites. His most popular composition has proved to be the lively piece "Juba Dance" from the 1913 suite *In the Bottoms*.

—*Grove Koger*

**Dialect poetry:** A colloquial style of poetry that includes elements of BLACK ENGLISH. Written by such poets as Paul Laurence DUNBAR and James D. CORROTHERS and later taken in new directions by Langston HUGHES, Gwendolyn BROOKS, Lucille Clifton, and others, this type of poetry has been said to have originated at least partly in Negro spirituals. Twentieth century African American poetry that incorporates dialect and SLANG also sometimes includes elements of BLUES and JAZZ.

Dunbar was the first African American in the nineteenth century to become widely famous for writing poetry. He wrote both dialect poetry and poetry in Standard English; the white reading public and white critics favored his dialect poetry. Although Dunbar, the most popular African American writer of his day, was born in 1872, his dialect poetry shows the influence of slave narratives that arose from the oral tradition. In "An Ante-Bellum Sermon," the speaker of the poem expresses gratitude to God, "de gracious Mastah Dat has gin us liberty."

One of his well-known poems, "When Malindy Sings," compares Malindy's beautiful singing with the deficient singing of "Miss Lucy": Lucy's singing "ain't got de tu'ns and twistin's/ Fu' to make it sweet and light," whereas Malindy sings better than "Robins, la'ks, an' all dem things." Dunbar himself was somewhat frustrated that audiences preferred his dialect poetry to his poetry in Standard English. In the poem "The Poet" he refers to dialect poetry as "a jingle in a broken tongue."

Nineteenth century dialect poetry became

controversial in the twentieth century. James Weldon JOHNSON, for example, denounced it in a 1922 essay. Scholars and CIVIL RIGHTS activists disdained it as representing African American speech in an inaccurate, even cartoonish way and portraying black life and speech in ways that conformed to white stereotypes. Indeed, in the nineteenth and early twentieth centuries, dialect poetry developed its own set of conventions that did not realistically echo rural black speech. It was written by both white and black writers (Joel Chandler Harris, the creator of Uncle Remus, was one well-known white writer of dialect poetry.) Dialect poetry tended to be either lighthearted and humorous or, conversely, filled with pathos. It often portrayed rural or plantation African Americans who lived simple, even childlike lives.

By the 1990's, however, a broader understanding of the role of dialect poetry had emerged. Scholars acknowledged its place in literary and cultural history while remaining aware of its negative aspects. Some critics noted that writing in dialect fell into the African American tradition, born of necessity, of wearing psychological masks in order to get along in a white-dominated culture. In his standard-diction poem "We Wear the Mask," Dunbar explores the issues of masking and identity. At the time he wrote it, African Americans had greater access to education but still felt pressured to mold themselves to the dominant society's expectations—to wear a mask—in order to succeed.

Many twentieth century African American poets continue the tradition of using nonstandard elements in their work. They use slang and dialect to depict a wide variety of life situations far different from the stereotypical portrayals of early dialect poetry. Born four years before Dunbar died, Langston Hughes perpetuated the use of dialect, but he added a twentieth-century sensibility, drawing on HARLEM street slang and the rhythms of jazz and blues music. In "Mother to Son," Hughes uses dialect to suggest the hardships faced by a lower-middle-class woman for whom "life ain't been no crystal stair." Characteristic of the determination that the speakers of Hughes's poems show, she tells her son, "Don't you set down on the steps/ 'Cause you finds it's kinder hard," and reminds him, "I'se still going, honey, I'se still climbin'."

Gwendolyn Brooks's work portrays the experiences of African Americans in an urban setting that has become increasingly violent and threatening. In "We Real Cool," she uses a syncopated jazz rhythm to describe a group of pool players. In the short final line of the poem, "We die soon," Brooks provides social

In 1975 the U.S. Postal Service honored Paul Laurence Dunbar's dialect poetry with a postage stamp. *(Arkent Archive)*

commentary on the self-destructiveness they demonstrate.

In "come home from the movies," Lucille Clifton encourages "black girls and boys" to be more socially conscious, to "take off some flowers and plant them," "pick up some papers and read them," and "stop making some babies and raise them." Her poetry characterizes an increased sense of urgency in a time when, rather than feeling empowered, many African Americans still feel disfranchised. In using the vernacular of the audience to whom the poem is addressed, she seeks to motivate those people to lead more productive, fulfilling lives.

The popularity of dialect poetry continues in spoken performances such as *for colored girls who have considered suicide/ when the rainbow is enuf* (1976) by Ntozake SHANGE. The resurgence in the popularity of poetry readings in the 1980's and 1990's was partially attributable to the rediscovery of the oral tradition to which dialect poetry pays tribute.

—*Holly L. Norton*

See also: African languages and American English; Literature; Slang and street language; Songwriters and composers.

Suggested Readings:

Gates, Henry Louis, Jr., and Nellie Y. McKay, eds. *The Norton Anthology of African American Literature*. New York: W. W. Norton, 1997.

Harper, Michael S., and Anthony Walton, eds. *Every Shut Eye Ain't Asleep: An Anthology of Poetry by African Americans Since 1945*. New York: Little, Brown, 1994.

Sherman, Joan R., ed. *African-American Poetry of the Nineteenth Century: An Anthology*. Urbana: University of Illinois Press, 1992.

**Diaspora, African:** Dispersal of people of African descent around the world. A diaspora is the distribution of members of any group of people far removed from their original homeland. The concept of the African diaspora gained popularity in the 1960's, a time when a multitude of newly independent nations emerged from former European colonies in AFRICA.

There are three major aspects to the African diaspora concept. The first is the physical global dispersal of Africans, which resulted largely, but not exclusively, from the transatlantic SLAVE TRADE. The second concerns settlement outside Africa, with a resultant blending, over time, of African ethnicity with the culture of the new land. The third is identification with the African homeland, expressed in either psychological or physical return. Since the 1960's, scholars have attempted the complex task of mapping diaspora migration pattern and analyzing the cultural adaptations of former Africans to their adopted environments.

*Diaspora to Eurasia*

In ancient times, African merchants ventured throughout the Middle East and beyond into the Indian subcontinent. Often small settlements were established. With the rise of the Roman Empire, following the defeat of Carthage in the third century B.C.E., SLAVERY became a major social institution. Africans began to be used as "exotic" slaves, serving as household staff and entertainers. As ISLAM rapidly expanded in the eighth century, tens of thousands of Africans were captured and used as household slaves, soldiers, sailors, bodyguards, and clerks. Free Africans traveled to Islam's holy cities of Mecca and Medina. Some settled in these cities or in other major cities such as Cairo, Damascus, and Baghdad. Africans also followed the spread of Islamic dominance to northern India. Islam encouraged the education of slaves, their treatment as family members, and MANUMISSION (the releasing of a slave from bondage). The use of slaves for plantation labor was not common.

Islamic control of Spain, Portugal, and Sicily brought Africans to Europe. Frederick II, the thirteenth century Holy Roman Emperor who was born in Sicily, employed Ethiopians in his army. Africans were also brought into southeastern Europe by the Ottoman Turks, who ruled from their capital of Constantinople (later Istanbul) in the fifteenth century. The Turks freely used Africans as soldiers, bureaucrats, and eunuchs who guarded the sultan's harem. By 1450 Africans were being used as slaves in Portugal and Spain. Thousands also became laborers, servants, and court pages in England, France, and Holland. However, it was with the discovery of the New World that the major saga of the African diaspora began. By 1800 at least ten million Africans had been forcibly transported to the Americas.

### Diaspora to the Americas

Particularly in the eighteenth century, Africans far surpassed any other single group entering the Americas. About 47 percent were destined for the Caribbean, where disease, debilitating labor, and brutal treatment resulted in high mortality rates. Because Caribbean planters found it to be cheaper to replace slaves than to breed them, the Caribbean received continuous shipments of newly enslaved Africans. By this process, traditional African culture was continually revitalized. Africans quickly became the majority population on the plantation islands. Another 38 percent of Africans taken as slaves were sent to Brazil (which did not abolish slavery until 1888), 6 percent were transported to Spanish America, and nearly 5 percent were sent to North America. Most slaves were transported from centers on the Guinea Coast of West Africa, Congo, and Upper Angola. Africans from diverse ethnic and tribal backgrounds were brought together for the transatlantic crossing. Slaves from different areas were mixed again at their country of destination in order to reduce possibilities for revolt.

### Continuities and Adaptations

In their alien and hostile new environments, slaves were forbidden to practice their native religions or to speak their native languages. Moreover, their owners made no real attempts to assimilate Africans into European culture. The end result was that the slaves created a synthesis of African and Western traditions.

While the transplanted Africans adopted Western languages, they also maintained a rich variety of cultural expressions, symbols, and pronunciations held over from their native languages. Diverse African languages melded, producing new ways of communicating about common experiences. In a wide variety of CREOLE languages, and in the GULLAH and pidgin English spoken on the islands off the SOUTH CAROLINA and GEORGIA coasts, a significant amount of Africanisms survived. Traditional African proverbs and folk tales were also handed down by storytellers from one generation to the next.

Skills in AGRICULTURE honed in the Old World were applied in the New. Traditional communal cooperation in planting and harvesting was also maintained. Since many slave communities grew their own foods, traditional African foods, herbs, and spices were duplicated or approximated. African cooking styles were a significant influence in many regions of the Americas. Skills in woodcarving and blacksmithing were also brought from Africa to be handed down from generation to generation across the Atlantic.

### Transformations in Religion, Art, and Music

In the area of RELIGION, African beliefs and practices were absorbed into Christian traditions. African spirit possession and sacred dance were incorporated into the shouting, shaking, and clapping of African American BAPTISTS and PENTECOSTALISM, and they may have influenced the emotionally charged practices of white Evangelical denominations. African ROMAN CATHOLICS in the Americas transposed African gods into Catholic saints and thereby continued familiar practices of festive processions of statues and masks. In addition, religious imagery rich in mountains, rivers, animals, and plants allowed the continuation of animistic beliefs in powerful spiritual forces in nature. Purer forms of African religions were maintained as well, and they can be seen in VOODOO in HAITI and Macumba in Brazil. Voodoo and Macumba contain more severe forms of initiation than Christian baptism as well as greater emphasis on divination and rites involving animal sacrifice.

Rhythmic MUSIC and song, always integral parts of African religious celebration, became vital parts of African American Christianity. Gospel and spiritual singing helped give rise to the blues. Rhythmic pulses and beats emanating from Africa continued to evolve in diverse locales, and they helped form the bases of such musical genres as jazz, blues, BEBOP, rock and roll, pop, and RAP in the United States, bomba in Puerto Rico, and REGGAE and calypso in the Caribbean. Indeed, modern forms of music and the expressionistic dance movements that often accompany music such as the samba and tango are among the major contributions of the African diaspora to world culture.

The African diaspora has also noticeably influenced the VISUAL ARTS. African masks, carvings, and geometrical designs, as well as the African emphasis on capturing three dimensionality along with the inner spiritual essence of the artistic subject, contributed in significant ways to the growth of modern and contemporary art.

### The African Homeland

The concept of the African diaspora also involves a consciousness of Africa as a homeland, an awareness often expressed by psychological identification with Africa and African cultures. The CIVIL RIGHTS era and the turbulent 1960's brought this consciousness of African heritage to the forefront, catapulting black pride and black power to the forefront of African American LITERATURE, art, and FASHION. It also led to concerted political action. By the 1970's an awareness among African Americans of historical and cultural connectedness with Africa had become the norm rather than the exception.

Consciousness of the African homeland has also taken the form of physical return to Africa. This development began in the early nineteenth century with the British establishment of Sierra Leone. After the United States outlawed the slave trade in 1807, Sierra Leone became a base for the return of slaves. Sierra Leone also became a place to which free blacks from British colonies could return. The founding of LIBERIA in 1821 by the AMERICAN COLONIZATION SOCIETY established a center in Africa where free African Americans, along with Africans captured and freed from the now illegal slave trade, could settle.

As African American educational institutions and organized denominational churches expanded after the abolition of slavery, major actions were taken to "bring the light" of Christianity and Western education to Africa. Missions, schools, and medical facilities staffed by African Americans were established in various parts of Africa.

Ideas of black connectedness were articulated by intellectuals such as Alexander CRUMMELL, Edward Wilmot Blyden, and W. E. B. DU BOIS. Ultimately the work of Du Bois and others led to the first Pan-African Congress, which was held in London in 1900. Pan-African consciousness was also catalyzed by Marcus GARVEY, a Jamaican immigrant to the United States who established a "back to Africa" movement in HARLEM in 1917. Garvey's UNIVERSAL NEGRO IMPROVEMENT ASSOCIATION (UNIA) owned its own steamship line, the BLACK STAR LINE, and newspaper, THE NEGRO WORLD, which spread the message of pride in African heritage.

### The Continuing Diaspora

Patterns of migration and settlement are in a continual state of flux. In Europe, for example, the two world wars resulted in tens of thousands of former African troops becoming permanent residents of France, England, and the Netherlands. Liberal immigration policies following decolonization resulted in the migration of many more Africans to Europe and Great Britain in the 1960's and early 1970's until stricter immigration policies were enacted in the mid-1970's.

In the United States during the first half of the twentieth century, a massive migration took place from the rural South to the industrial cities of the North. During the second half of the century, people from Caribbean islands such as PUERTO RICO, Jamaica, CUBA, and Haiti immigrated to major Eastern cities. Also, large numbers of African students began to study abroad, and many remained abroad after completing their studies. They were joined by African professionals escaping from political turmoil and harsh economic conditions in their native lands. Hence many African states suffered a "brain drain" caused by the loss of talented and educated people. Unusual, even singular, events have taken place as well, such as Israel's airlifting of nearly fifteen thousand black Jews from Ethiopia (the Falasha) between 1983 and 1985 to rescue them from famine.

—*Irwin Halfond*

*See also:* African cultural transformations; African languages and American English; African music and dance; Colonization movement; Folklore; Foodways; Jamaica and Jamaican Americans; Liberia; Pan-Africanism.

Suggested Readings:

Azevedo, Mario, ed. *African Studies: A Survey of Africa and the African Diaspora*. Durham, N.C.: Carolina Academic Press, 1997.

Conniff, Michael L., and Thomas Davis. *Africans in the Americas: A History of the Black - Diaspora*. New York: St. Martin's Press, 1994.

Harris, Joseph E. *Global Dimensions of the African Diaspora*. 2d ed. Washington, D.C.: Howard University Press, 1993.

Harris, Joseph E., et al. *The African Diaspora*. Edited by Alusine Jalloh and Stephen E. Maizlish. Arlington: Texas A&M University Press, 1996.

Holloway, Joseph. *Africanisms in American Culture*. Bloomington: Indiana University Press, 1990.

Raboteau, Albert J. *Slave Religion: The Invisible Institution in the Antebellum South*. New York: Oxford University Press, 1978.

Segal, Ronald. *The Black Diaspora*. New York: Farrar, Straus and Giroux, 1995.

Thompson, Vincent B. *The Making of the African Diaspora in the Americas 1441-1900*. New York: Longman, 1987.

Walters, Ronald W. *Pan Africanism in the African Diaspora: An Analysis of Modern Afro-Centric Political Movements*. Detroit: Wayne State University Press, 1993.

Zahan, Dominique. *The Religion, Spirituality, and Thought of Traditional Africa*. Chicago: The University of Chicago Press, 1978.

**Diddley, Bo** (Ellas McDaniel; b. December 30, 1928, McComb, Mississippi): RHYTHM-AND-BLUES guitarist, songwriter, and singer. Bo Diddley's influence on other musicians and on popular music as a whole extended well beyond his own individual career. His unique "chunk-a chunk-chunk" guitar rhythms, sometimes simply called the "Bo Diddley beat," was an influence on the shaping of rock and roll; as Diddley himself once said, "I was a rock-and-roll artist before rock and roll existed."

Diddley was born Ellas Bates but was adopted by the McDaniel family early in his life, and he grew up with the name Ellas McDaniel. In 1934 the McDaniel family moved to CHICAGO, ILLINOIS. Diddley studied violin there, from 1934 to 1946, with Professor O. W.

Frederick at Ebenezer Baptist Church. He attended Foster Vocational High School and began to teach himself guitar, harmonica, and trombone. By the early 1940's, he was active as a trombonist with the Baptist Congress Band and had also formed his own band.

In the late 1940's, his experiences included a stint as a semiprofessional boxer and some performances with a washboard trio. In 1951 he began to perform as a singer and guitarist in Chicago clubs, achieving moderate success. In 1955 he signed a recording contract with Chess Records. He adopted the name Bo Diddley, by which he was called as a youth. The name is a folk expression identifying an individual as being mischievous or a bully. The single was "Bo Diddley," backed with "I'm a Man," in 1955.

In the mid- and late 1950's, Diddley toured with the Alan Freed show, appeared on Ed Sullivan's television program, and performed on the circuit of black clubs. In 1960 he established ARC Music Publishers. He continued to perform on college campuses throughout the 1960's. He appeared in the film *The Big T.N.T. Show* (1966) and in a short biographical film, *The Legend of Bo Diddley* (1966). He made frequent appearances on the rock-and-roll revival circuit for the next several decades, while continuing to record.

Diddley's reputation relies upon the mesmerizing rhythm generated by his guitar, but he also proved himself a fine singer and writer. His musical inheritance includes both the Mississippi Delta and Chicago traditions, making him a unique contributor to rock and roll. One of his important contributions to music is his sense of humor, which has functioned as a subtle form of social criticism, especially in the 1950's culture of conformity. "Road Runner," "I'm a Man," "Who Do You Love," "Mona," and "Hey Bo Diddley" became rock-and-roll standards and have been recorded often by other artists. His early experimentation with guitar feedback helped pave the way for artists such as Jimi HENDRIX and helped to establish Diddley as a unique performer.

Diddley toured and performed into the 1990's, and a new generation gained some familiarity with him through the "Bo knows" Nike commercials he did with Bo Jackson. The album *This Should Not Be* was released in 1993; the title song refers to the problem of homelessness. Bo Diddley was inducted into the Rock and Roll Hall of Fame in 1987 and was given a Rhythm and Blues Foundation lifetime achievement award in 1996.

*See also:* Blues; Rhythm and blues.

**Diggs, Charles C., Jr.** (December 2, 1922, Detroit, Michigan—August 24, 1998, Washington, D.C.): U.S. CONGRESS MEMBER from MICHIGAN. Charles Coles Diggs served in the U.S. House of Representatives for thirteen terms. His twenty-five years of service were distinguished by his tireless campaigning for CIVIL

Michigan congressman Charles C. Diggs, Jr. *(Library of Congress)*

RIGHTS, but his congressional career ended in scandal.

## Early Life

The only child of Charles, Sr., and Mayne Diggs, Diggs attended school in DETROIT's public school system. After graduating from Miller High School in 1940, Diggs went to the University of Michigan, where he won the school's oratorical championship in 1941. In 1942 Diggs transferred to FISK UNIVERSITY. He was forced to suspend his education in 1943, when he was drafted into the U.S. Army Air Corps. Before being honorably discharged in 1945, he achieved the rank of second lieutenant and had become the youngest administrative officer at Tuskegee Army Air Field.

Diggs resumed his education at Wayne State University School of Mortuary Science. After graduating in 1946 he earned his law degree from the Detroit College of Law. After graduating, he founded the House of Diggs, a collection of four funeral homes in Detroit and its suburbs. The business, which used the slogan, "If you ain't buried with Diggs, you ain't lived," was an instant success.

## Early Political Career

Diggs first entered POLITICS in 1951, when he was elected to the Michigan State Senate. While serving as the youngest member, he headed Governor C. Memmen Williams's human relations program. At a time when few blacks exercised any kind of political power, Diggs was viewed as an inspiring example by Detroit's blacks.

In 1954 Diggs became the first black congressman from the state of Michigan. When he arrived in Washington, D.C., he was accompanied by a trainload of supporters from Michigan's Thirteenth District. Once he took his seat in Congress, he immediately made the problems of southern blacks his first priority. In 1963 he asked President John F. Kennedy to send federal troops and National Guard units to MISSISSIPPI to protect black citizens who were attempting to exercise their constitutional right to vote. Two years later, Diggs was the leader of a congressional fact-finding group dispatched to Selma, ALABAMA. In 1966 he reported the complaints of black soldiers to Secretary of Defense Robert McNamara. Because of his efforts on behalf of civil rights, Diggs earned the nickname "the Mississippi congressman at large."

By 1970 Diggs had become the most popular and the most effective black member of the House of Representatives. He owed much of his political savvy to the advice he had received from such notable black politicians as Chicago's William DAWSON and HARLEM's Adam Clayton POWELL, Jr. Diggs, though, was able to do what these other politicians could not: form an organization of black members of Congress, the CONGRESSIONAL BLACK CAUCUS. Diggs himself was the first chairman. The Congressional Black Caucus became the only independent civil rights entity in the United States with members elected by African Americans themselves.

## Later Career

Having labored extensively for the rights of blacks in the United States, Diggs then tried to narrow the gap between black Americans and black Africans. His African initiative began in 1971, when he resigned from the U.S. delegation to the United Nations to protest the policies of the NIXON ADMINISTRATION dealing with African nations. Throughout the 1970's, Diggs presided over hearings as chairman of the House Foreign Affairs African Subcommittee. He also traveled to every nation on the African continent to champion the rights of black Africans. As a result of his verbal attacks against segregation, Diggs was eventually barred from South Africa altogether.

During the 1970's, Diggs struggled to bring home rule to the District of Columbia. He also piloted through Congress legislation establishing the University of the District of Columbia, the largest black-oriented institution of higher learning in the country.

## Scandal

Despite appeals on his behalf by former United Nations ambassador Andrew YOUNG and Coretta Scott KING, Diggs was convicted in 1978 of twenty-nine counts of defrauding the federal government of more than $60,000 in an elaborate payback scheme involving mail fraud. He was also accused of making false statements in connection with his use of his congressional payroll. While he was trying to fight his conviction during the next two years, Diggs gave up his chairmanship of the House District of Columbia Committee and the Foreign Affairs African Subcommittee. After being censured publicly in the House, Diggs announced that he would retire from Congress in January, 1981. In his final act as a member of Congress, Diggs endorsed seventy-year-old Judge George W. CROCKETT, Jr., as his successor. In June, 1980, Diggs's two-year fight to clear his name ended when the U.S. Supreme Court rejected his appeal without comment. After agreeing to repay the government $40,000 in $500-a-month installments, Diggs served a half-year term in federal prison.

## Life After Politics

Diggs experienced some difficulty returning to normal life after serving his prison sentence. In January, 1981, the Maryland Board of Funeral Directors and Embalmers refused to grant him an apprentice funeral director's license. A year later, Diggs lost his Michigan mortician's license when the Michigan State Board of Mortuary Science ruled that Diggs lacked the "good moral character" that it deemed necessary to be an undertaker.

Until Diggs was granted the right to open funeral homes in 1983, he served as a consultant without pay on foreign policy to the Congressional Black Caucus. From March, 1982, to August, 1983, Diggs criticized the REAGAN ADMINISTRATION for moving from a "hands-off" relationship with South Africa to a renewal of technical and military contacts. He was disappointed by the Congressional Black Caucus's inability to influence the president's policies.

After 1983 Diggs resumed his career as a mortician, this time in Prince Georges County, Maryland. During this time, he also married his fourth wife, Darlene Expose. Diggs attempted to make a political comeback in 1990; he admitted that, after leaving Congress, he had harbored a desire to return. Arguing that blacks were underrepresented in several areas of the state, Diggs entered the race for the Maryland House of Delegates for one four-year term as the first step toward a return to Congress. After losing the election, he once again returned to his mortuary business.

During twenty-five years in Congress, Charles Diggs became one of the first black leaders to penetrate the Democratic power orbit in the House of Representatives. Not only did he found the Congressional Black Caucus, but he also became dean of the Michigan Democratic delegation. Scandals aside, he will be remembered for his campaigns to bring independence to the countries of Africa and for his work in bringing home rule to the District of Columbia. In 1998, Diggs suffered a stroke and died at age seventy-five.

—*Alan Brown*

Suggested Readings:

Booker, Simeon. "Washington Notebook." *Ebony* (October, 1980): 25.

"Diggs Begins Comeback in Maryland State Race." *Jet* (April 30, 1990): 18.

Fox, J. A. "Do or Die for Diggs." *Black Enterprise* (June, 1980): 55.

"Hundreds Pay Tribute to Late Rep. Charles Diggs' Civil Rights Record at Maryland Ceremony." *Jet* (September 21, 1998): 18.

Leerhsen, Charles. "When the House Is No Longer a Home." *Newsweek* (January 18, 1982): 21.

Ragsdale, Bruce A., and Joel D. Treese. *Black Americans in Congress, 1870-1989*. Washington, D.C.: U.S. Government Printing Office, 1990.

**Dinkins, David** (b. July 10, 1927, Trenton, New Jersey): NEW YORK politician. David Dinkins was the oldest of two children born to Sally and William H. Dinkins. When David was six years old, his parents were divorced, and David and his sister Joyce lived briefly with their mother in HARLEM. The two children soon moved in with their father, who had remarried and who still lived in Trenton. Stepmother Lottie (Hartgell) Dinkins was a high school English teacher who encouraged both children to excel in their studies. As he grew up, David worked at odd jobs and ran a newspaper route.

### Education and Military Service

After he graduated from an all-black Trenton junior high school, Dinkins attended Trenton High School, a predominantly white school where African Americans were everyday reminded of their second-class citizenship; black students were even barred from the school's swimming pool. Always a hard worker, an organizer, and a politician, Dinkins grabbed his first bit of political success when he narrowly defeated a white student for election as president of his homeroom class.

After his high school graduation in 1945, Dinkins volunteered for the Marine Corps but was rejected because the Marine Corps had already filled its quota of blacks. Soon drafted by the Army, he was allowed to transfer to the Marines. He spent most of his thirteen-month tour at Camp Lejeune, North Carolina, where, among other assignments, he served as a colonel's chauffeur. In North Carolina, Dinkins was again confronted with racism. Years later, he remembered that he was once denied one of two empty seats on a bus; he had to stand in the back of the vehicle because the bus driver said that the empty seats were reserved for whites.

### College Education and Activism

After he was mustered out of the Marines in 1946, Dinkins used the G.I. Bill to attend HOWARD UNIVERSITY in Washington, D.C., where he received his B.A. degree in mathematics. As he progressed through his undergraduate courses, Dinkins also worked in Trenton, first operating a jackhammer for the Main Line Railroad and then working in an insulation factory. Facing continuing racial discrimination, Dinkins became an activist, filing complaints against the factory with the newly created New Jersey civil rights commission. Soon, his employer had to desegregate factory restrooms. Using the same method, Dinkins later forced a local tavern to open its doors to African Americans.

After graduating from college in 1950, Dinkins received a mathematics scholarship to attend Rutgers University to work on an advanced degree; after one semester, however, he dropped out of school and became an insurance salesman. Three years later, he entered Brooklyn Law School, where he took his J.D. degree in 1956. The same year that he enrolled in law school, he married Joyce Borrows, whose father was a state assemblyman from Harlem; the couple later had two children, David, Jr., and Donna. While still in school, Dinkins began working as a clerk in Borrows's liquor store in Harlem, often running errands for local politicians.

### Dinkins's Public Career

From 1956 to 1975, Dinkins practiced law in NEW YORK CITY. He developed a steady practice handling cases involving real estate, banking, and probates. He soon joined the Carver Democratic Club, hoping to meet potential clients. The club's leader, J. Raymond Jones, soon became Dinkins's mentor. For a time, Dinkins served as a loyal foot soldier for the local Democrats and gained a political reward in 1965, when he was elected to the New York State Assembly. Almost immediately, he began a new campaign for racial justice. For example, he fought a program to give state subsidies to volunteer firemen because minorities were not given a fair chance to serve. He also joined picket lines against the Young Women's Christian Association (YWCA) because it would not recognize its employees' union. In 1967, though, Dinkins's district disappeared in a reapportionment maneuver. He then devoted more time to his private law practice and became a district leader for the Carver Club, work he would perform for more than two decades. In 1970 he became counsel to the New York City Board of Elections and two years later was named to the board itself. He later became the first African American president of the board.

In 1973 Dinkins campaigned on behalf of Abraham Beame, whom voters chose as mayor of New York City. Beame soon named Dinkins deputy mayor for planning, but the mayor withdrew his support after a routine background check revealed that Dinkins had not paid any local, state, or federal income taxes in four years. He explained that he was so busy handling other people's business that he had forgotten to take care of his own. Although he quickly paid the taxes, interest, and penalties, Dinkins was banished from New York's political arena for two years.

Mayor Beame then named Dinkins as the New York City clerk, a post he held until 1985; as clerk, Dinkins gave service that helped him to rehabilitate his political reputation. Noted in his later career for his caution, Dinkins nevertheless attracted the national spotlight in 1984, when he boldly supported Jesse JACKSON's bid for the presidency; most African American politicians were supporting Democratic nominee Walter F. Mondale. The next year, Dinkins attracted even more attention when he condemned Louis FARRAKHAN, the leader of the NATION OF ISLAM, ostensibly because of Farrakhan's anti-Semitic views. In turn, when Farrakhan spoke to a crowd of twenty-five thousand at Madison Square Garden, he condemned Dinkins, calling him a "traitor."

Although Dinkins was assigned special police protection for a time, his political career was not harmed by his bold positions. In 1985 he won election as the president of the Borough of Manhattan, a post he held until 1989. Upon assuming his new position, Dinkins quickly established himself as a friend of the poor, the homeless, and the victims of ACQUIRED IMMUNODEFICIENCY SYNDROM (AIDS). For example, he used his seat on New York City's board of estimate to halt construction of luxury apartments to be subsidized by the city until developers added 132 low-income units. On another occasion, when some conservative leaders argued that money earmarked for

David Dinkins, New York City's first African American mayor. *(James Hamilton)*

shelters for the homeless should be used to build prisons, Dinkins publicly lambasted the idea, calling it "ludicrous" and "unconscionable." In 1987 he cast the tie-breaking vote that allowed New York mayor Ed Koch to subsidize the building of eleven shelters for the homeless and to subsidize the creation of one thousand low-income apartments.

### Mayoral Campaign

In 1989 Dinkins mounted a campaign to unseat Mayor Koch, a fellow Democrat. Dinkins spoke out on issues such as drug abuse, crime, housing, and education. He promised to begin a school-improvement program and lobbied developers to build more units of low- and moderate-cost housing. Dinkins won the Democratic nomination for the mayor's seat by defeating Koch in September, 1989. He then faced the former U.S. attorney for the Southern District of New York, Rudolph Giuliani. Giuliani depicted himself as a "mob-busting" crime fighter.

Dinkins, solidly backed by the black community, managed a narrow victory. As mayor, he tried to draw diverse elements of the city's population together, and he spoke eloquently about a "gorgeous mosaic" of race and religious faith. As a practical matter, however, he had to cope with a budget crisis. He ordered some city agencies to cut services and postponed new hiring in certain departments, including the police department. Still, he advocated reforms as money became available and pressed for a war on drugs and crime, for the creation of homeless shelters and low-cost housing, and for improvements in health care, especially care for children.

Many voters had hoped that Dinkins could help heal the city's racial and ethnic polarizations, but many were disappointed. In the troubled economy of the time, the unemployment and crime rates rose, and health and education services stagnated or declined. The black middle class was enjoying some stability, but it was increasingly relocating to the suburbs.

To many New Yorkers, one event seemed to typify the difficulties experienced by Dinkins. In the racially mixed Crown Heights section of Brooklyn in August of 1991, a Hasidic Jewish motorist accidentally killed a seven-year-old black youth. Tensions between Crown Heights' mostly immigrant black population and Hasidic Jews had been simmering for some time. In retaliation for the death, a black youth murdered a visiting Hasidic rabbinical student from Australia. Racial and religious violence flared over the next few days, and the Dinkins administration's handling of the aftermath was criticized. In 1993 Dinkins lost his reelection bid to Giuliani, whom he had defeated four years before.

### Awards and Recognition

Dinkins won wide recognition over the years. He received the Distinguished Service Award from the Federation of Negro Civil Service Organizations and the Pioneer of Excellence Award from the World Institute of Black Communications. The National Association of Negro Businessmen and Professional Women's Clubs once named him man of the year, as did the Correction Guards Association. He also was active in the NATIONAL ASSOCIATION FOR THE ADVANCEMENT OF COLORED PEOPLE (NAACP), the NATIONAL URBAN LEAGUE, the Greater New York Black-Jewish Coalition, the Council of Black Elected Democrats, and the National Conference of Black Lawyers.

—*James Smallwood*

*See also:* Mayors; Politics and government.

Suggested Readings:

Baer, Donald. "Dealing with Souls on Fire." *U.S. News and World Report* (May 28, 1990): 33-34.

Brenner, Marie. "Being There." *Vanity Fair* (January, 1991): 86-96.

Finch, Peter. "David Dinkins: How's He

Doin'?" *Business Week* (June 18, 1990): 182-186.

Hatchett, David. "David Dinkins: Life After Politics." Interview. *The Crisis*, November/December, 1994, 26-28.

Poinsett, Alex. "The Changing Color of U.S. Politics." *Ebony* (August, 1991): 30-35.

Powledge, Fred. *Free at Last? The Civil Rights Movement and the People Who Made It.* Boston: Little, Brown, 1991.

Randolph, Laura B. "Inside Gracie Mansion with New York's First Black Mayor." *Ebony* (September, 1990): 54-58.

Clinton E. Knox, who served as U.S. ambassador to Dahomey and Haiti during the 1960's. *(AP/Wide World Photos)*

**Diplomats:** In general, African Americans did not participate in official U.S. diplomacy before the twentieth century, except regarding relations with the small Caribbean island nation of HAITI. Ebenezer Bassett and John LANGSTON both served long tenures as U.S. ministers to Haiti. However, the most famous African American to take the post was Frederick DOUGLASS, appointed in 1889. Douglass worked in Haiti from the fall of that year until the summer of 1891. He helped settle debts owed to American and European businessmen, and he unsuccessfully pursued rights for the United States to lease a naval base in Haiti.

In the nineteenth century, most African Americans who were government ministers were granted their posts as a reward for their loyalty to the REPUBLICAN PARTY. In 1906, however, three African Americans entered State Department service after passing civil service exams. The most notable was writer and composer James Weldon JOHNSON. Johnson represented the United States in Venezuela and sent a number of insightful telegrams to the State Department. He noted, for example, how aware South Americans were regarding discrimination against African Americans in the southern United States.

African Americans continued to play only a small role in U.S. diplomacy, because of on-going prejudice, until after WORLD WAR II. The situation began to change in 1945 when Ralph BUNCHE, arguably the greatest of all African American diplomats, participated in the formation of the United Nations. Bunche also began mediating disputes between Arabs and Jews after the formation of Israel in 1948, and he helped achieve a truce in 1949. As a result he received the Nobel Peace Prize in 1950.

The next milestone was passed in 1961, when Clifton WHARTON, SR. became ambassador to Norway; he was the first African American ambassador to a European country. Nonetheless, the State Department hired hardly any African Americans for full-time jobs. Of about 3,700 officers in the U.S. Foreign Service in 1961, only seventeen were black. In the 1960's the State Department began to recruit African Americans in order to redress the imbalance. Some progress was made, and several individuals, such as Ulrich Haynes, made noteworthy contributions to U.S. diplomacy.

In 1976 newly elected president Jimmy Carter appointed ANDREW YOUNG as the U.S. permanent representative to the United Nations (U.N.). In general, Young wanted U.S. foreign policy to seek racial justice rather than to focus nearly exclusively on its attempt to stop the spread of communism. Young put an African American stamp on some major foreign policy issues, most notably in helping to bring peace and independence to Zimbabwe. His successor at the United Nations, Donald MCHENRY, was also African American. McHenry also focused on African issues, especially problems in Namibia. A third African American, Edward Perkins, who had also been the first black U.S. ambassador to South Africa (beginning in 1986), served as ambassador to the United Nations from 1992 to 1993. In 1997 President Bill Clinton appointed Jesse JACKSON as special U.S. envoy to Africa. Continuing participation by African Americans at the highest levels of U.S. diplomacy in the 1990's reflected the dramatic rise in black political power that started in the 1960's.

—*Andy DeRoche*

Suggested Readings:

Jones, Bartlett C. *Flawed Triumphs: Andy Young at the United Nations*. Lanham, Md.: University Press of America, 1996.

Krenn, Michael. *Black Diplomacy: African Americans and the State Department, 1945-1969*. New York: M. E. Sharpe, 1998.

**Disfranchisement:** Depriving a person of civil rights, particularly the right to vote—which is sometimes called the "franchise." African American men in the South obtained the right to vote during RECONSTRUCTION, the period when the southern states were reunited with the Union after the CIVIL WAR. The Republican-dominated Congress of the time believed that most southern whites were disloyal to the United States; consequently, Congress doubted that southern whites could be trusted to bring the states together again. Many members of Congress, on the other hand, considered African Americans in the South to be ardent citizens who would support the Union. Congress thus passed a series of laws beginning in 1867 to grant African Americans suffrage, the right to vote in political elections. Able to participate in elections, African American VOTERS elected many blacks to Congress and to state assemblies during Reconstruction. Beginning in 1877, however, when southern whites regained control, blacks were again disfranchised.

*Historical Overview*

Leaders of the Confederate states were unrepentant after the Civil War; so were most southern whites. Congress verified southern sentiment when it assigned a committee to study the South and report on its attitude toward the Union. President Andrew Johnson conducted his own investigation and assigned Carl Schurz to tour the South. The Congressional Joint Committee on Reconstruction and Schurz arrived at similar conclusions: They found that many whites did not accept defeat as a permanent condition but instead hoped that the South would rise again to later challenge the Union. They also reported that the South treated African Americans and white Union supporters dismally. Beginning in 1865, the former Confederate states adopted the BLACK CODES, a body of laws that reduced blacks to a state of near-slavery. The states also elected high-ranking leaders of the defeated CONFEDERACY—including its former president, Jefferson Davis—to positions in the federal government. The congressional committee and Schurz recommended that the United States disfranchise the rebels and grant suffrage only to Union loyalists.

Congress initiated Reconstruction in March, 1867, when it adopted the Reconstruction Acts, which divided the South into five military districts. Congress declared the southern states to be conquered provinces having no legal governments. Congress then appointed military governors in each district and authorized them to register to vote all qualified men regardless of their race. Congress also instructed the governors to disfranchise high-ranking officials of the Confederacy and any whites who refused to take an oath of loyalty. Large numbers of African Americans registered to vote, and they constituted majorities in Alabama, Florida, Louisiana, Mississippi, and South Carolina. Beginning in 1868, former slaves in the South elected blacks to Congress, state assemblies, and state judicial and administrative posts. Reconstruction was not a peaceful period in American history, however; only the presence of armed federal troops in the South made such changes possible.

The Republican-dominated Congress, however, was not genuinely supportive of African Americans. Many whites wanted only to reunite the nation; once that was accomplished, they began to back away from the policies of Reconstruction. For example, beginning in 1869, whites disfranchised by federal law could petition the government to have their suffrage disability removed. In 1871 Congress repealed a law requiring southerners to pledge unconditional loyalty to the Union as a condition of participation in elections. One year later, Congress adopted the Amnesty Act, which legally forgave most southern whites for their past loyalty to the Confederacy. Reconstruction ended in 1877; after agreeing to a compromise with southern whites to ensure his election, President Rutherford B. Hayes withdrew federal troops from the South. After the troops left, white southerners embarked on a reign of terror to remove blacks from office and disfranchise black voters.

### White Terror

Southern whites resorted to a number of tactics to achieve the disfranchisement of African Americans. Some whites organized into extralegal societies such as the Ku Klux Klan, the White Brotherhood, the Pale Faces, and the Knights of the White Camelia to terrorize blacks into submission. Armed with guns and swords, these societies used violence to drive African Americans from political office and from the polls. They burned down schools, homes, and churches; in a one-year period in 1865-1866, white groups murdered more than five thousand African Americans. Many whites considered such actions a badge of honor; they had the approval of ministers and political leaders, many of whom were themselves members of terrorist groups.

### Political Devices

Violence was only one technique used to disfranchise African Americans. White southerners established polling places far from African American communities and placed roadblocks along the way to discourage African Americans from trying to reach the polls. Often, too, African Americans would go to a precinct expecting to vote only to discover that the polling place had been moved without warning. Literacy tests, in which a black would be asked to read and interpret the Constitution or to answer impossible questions as a condition to vote, were also used to exclude blacks. Ironically, some of the whites who administered literacy tests were themselves illiterate. The GRANDFATHER CLAUSE also disfranchised blacks. Under this scheme, only citizens whose grandfathers had voted before 1865 were eligible to participate in state elections. Obviously, this pretext disqualified African American voters in the states where it was used.

State legislatures also participated in the movement to disfranchise African Americans. State officers, for example, adopted the technique of GERRYMANDERING, dividing large African American communities into small districts in order to dilute potential black political power. Legislators also adopted poll taxes, requiring voters to pay a cash amount to qualify to vote. Like literacy tests, poll taxes were not applied uniformly; indigent whites were rarely disqualified by these laws. Some states adopted the "eight-box" law, which required voters to place each ballot into a specific box designating the office a candidate was seeking; voters who could not read often placed their ballots in the wrong boxes, and such misplaced votes could be legally discarded. Such tactics effectively rendered African Americans, who were largely poor and uneducated, powerless in the southern states.

### Federal Courts

The American judiciary also participated in the movement to disfranchise African Americans. The U.S. SUPREME COURT reviewed a number of cases that seriously impaired civil rights legislation. Congress adopted the Enforcement Act of 1870 in order to protect African Americans from hostile white groups such as the Ku Klux Klan. The statute made it a crime for two or more persons to assemble in order to deny another person certain rights. Whites nevertheless ignored the statute, organized, and drove blacks from polling places.

William Garner, an African American resident of Kentucky, was driven from a precinct in his community. Garner, with encouragement from sympathetic white lawyers, sued to protect his rights. The case went to the Supreme Court in *United States v. Reese* (1875), in which Garner argued that Kentucky citizens had violated his civil rights under the provisions of the Enforcement Act of 1870. The Supreme Court disagreed, explaining that Congress had exceeded its powers when it had adopted the statute. The Court concluded that the Constitution did not authorize Congress to restrain private citizens in such a fashion. Such a power, the Court concluded, belonged exclusively to the states.

The Supreme Court maintained the same point of view in *United States v. Cruikshank*

(1876). The Cruikshank case originated in Louisiana, where whites had murdered Levi Nelson and Alexander Tillman, African Americans who had attempted to participate in a local election. Prosecutors brought charges, claiming that the men had violated the Enforcement Act. In its decision, the Court weakened the FIFTEENTH AMENDMENT, which had been passed by Congress to give blacks the vote, by declaring that the amendment did not in fact confer the right to vote but instead merely declared that a state could not use its authority to deny suffrage on account of race. As long as the state did not use its power to abridge suffrage rights, therefore, African Americans would not benefit from federal protection. The Court used the same reasoning when it struck down the Civil Rights Act of 1875.

### Sharecropping and Migration

Having effectively disfranchised African Americans, southern whites devised labor schemes that made blacks virtual slaves. SHARECROPPING emerged as the most extensive labor system in the South. In the sharecropping system, a family—usually African American—agreed to work land owned by another, usually white. In theory, both parties to the arrangement were to share the harvest at the end of the planting season; however, sharecropping became a quagmire for blacks. Largely because of the machinations of white landowners, African Americans often fell deeply in debt. Indigent African Americans who obtained supplies or loans often found that, after harvest, they owed most of their profits to the landholders. Sharecropping became a trap keeping African Americans in poverty.

Because of their oppressed status in the South, African Americans early began to consider alternatives, and a number migrated to the West soon after Reconstruction. Benjamin "Pap" Singleton and Henry Adams led hundreds to Kansas. Ida B. WELLS also encouraged African Americans to go west in 1892, after whites in Memphis, Tennessee, lynched three African American merchants. More than two thousand black residents left the city. Continuing disfranchisement and violence against African Americans eventually caused the massive black exodus from the South of the early 1900's that became known as the GREAT MIGRATION.

—*Stephen Middleton*

*See also:* Black towns; Voting Rights Act of 1965

Suggested Readings:

Berry, Mary F. *Black Resistance/White Law: A History of Constitutional Racism in America.* New York: Appleton-Century-Crofts, 1971.

Blaustein, Albert P. *Desegregation and the Law: The Meaning and Effect of the School Segregation Cases.* New Brunswick, N.J.: Rutgers University Press, 1957.

Eastland, Terry, and William J. Bennett. *Counting by Race: Equality from the Founding Fathers to Bakke and Weber.* New York: Basic Books, 1979.

Greenberg, Jack. *Desegregation.* Eugene: University of Oregon Press, 1979.

_____. *Race Relations and American Law.* New York: Columbia University Press, 1959.

Kelly, Alfred H., Winfred A. Harbison, and Herman Belz. *The American Constitution: Its Origins and Development.* New York: W. W. Norton, 1983.

Miller, Loren. *The Petitioners: The Story of the Supreme Court of the United States and the Negro.* New York: Pantheon Books, 1966.

Nieman, Donald G., ed. *African Americans and Southern Politics from Redemption to Disfranchisement.* New York: Garland, 1994.

Smith, John D., ed. *Disfranchisement Proposals and the Ku Klux Klan.* New York: Garland, 1993.

Warren, Robert P. *Segregation: The Inner Conflict in the South.* New York: Columbia University Press, 1956.

**Dissing:** Derived from vernacular Black English, a term for disrespectful behavior. To "dis" someone generally involves a public refusal to give attention or show respect for that person in front of witnesses. The root of the word is taken from the prefix "dis-" as found in words such as disregard, dismiss, discount, and discredit. By using the "dis-" prefix as an individual word, the vernacular is compacted, making the meaning of the one term stronger by taking on the combined meaning of all such terms.

*See also:* Slang and street language.

**Dixiecrats:** Political party. The Dixiecrats organized for the 1948 U.S. presidential election. Also called States' Rights Democrats, they were a conservative splinter group of the DEMOCRATIC PARTY organized by southerners who were opposed to the civil rights program of the Democrats; the Democratic presidential nominee was Harry S Truman. The Dixiecrats met in BIRMINGHAM, ALABAMA, on July 17 and nominated Governor Strom Thurmond of South Carolina and Governor Fielding Wright of Mississippi as candidates for president and vice president. The Dixiecrat platform opposed federal regulations in general as a violation of states' rights. The Dixiecrats carried South Carolina, Mississippi, Louisiana, and Alabama, earning thirty-nine electoral votes. More than one million people voted for the Dixiecrat ticket.

**Dixie Hummingbirds:** GOSPEL and SOUL singing group. Baritone James Davis formed the group in Greenville, SOUTH CAROLINA, in 1928. An early member of the group was bass William Bobo, who remained with the group until his death in 1976. Lead singer Ira Tucker joined the group at about the same time as Bobo, in 1939. The two were encouraged to join after the Dixie Hummingbirds beat their

The Dixie Hummingbirds during the mid-1950's. *(Frank Driggs/Archive Photos)*

two groups in a singing competition. Tenor Beechie Thompson and Paul Owens were other early members of the group. James Walker, who eventually became backup lead singer, replaced Owens in the early 1950's when Owens left to join the Nightingales. Several other singers performed with the group during the 1950's. The Dixie Hummingbirds basically remained a vocal quartet but added guitarist Howard Carroll in the early 1950's.

The group first recorded in 1939, on the Decca label. It performed extensively beginning in the 1940's, following a move to PHILADELPHIA, PENNSYLVANIA. It toured the Northeast and broadcast regularly on radio. In 1945 the group began recording for the Apollo and Gotham labels. By the 1970's, the Dixie Hummingbirds were considered to be one of the world's greatest gospel quartets. In 1973 the group did backup music for Paul Simon and

recorded a version of his hit "Loves Me Like a Rock." The Hummingbirds' version won a Grammy Award as best soul gospel performance of the year.

In 1989 the group's fiftieth year in the music business was celebrated by a nationwide tour and several television appearances. EBONY and several other magazines featured the Dixie Hummingbirds on their covers.

**Dixieland jazz:** Marching style of early JAZZ that emerged in New Orleans, Louisiana, around 1900; the terms Dixieland jazz and New Orleans jazz are often used interchangeably. The music was popularized by New Orleans musicians such as Joe "King" OLIVER, Louis ARMSTRONG, Kid ORY, Freddie Keppard, and Sidney BECHET. Dixieland combos usually had between five and eight members, and the cornet and clarinet were the main melody instruments. Trombone was also featured; bands also had drums and sometimes a pianist or tuba player. The musicians took turns playing solos.

Recordings made by a white Dixieland group, the Original Dixieland Jazz Band, in 1917 are generally considered the first known jazz recordings. Kid Ory's group was recorded in the early 1920's. Although Dixieland was originally an African American form, eventually the term "Dixieland jazz" became largely associated with white jazz-revival groups. The style, with its fast tempos and joyous moods, remains popular and can be heard in clubs throughout the United States and on records.

**Dixon, Julian C.** (b. August 8, 1934, Washington, D.C.): CONGRESS MEMBER from CALIFORNIA; the first African American congressman to chair an appropriations subcommittee. After attending college and law school in California, Dixon began his career in POLITICS there, serving in the state assembly from 1972 to 1978. He went on to become an influential congressman. After his election as Democratic representative from the Twenty-eighth Congressional District of California in 1978, he became the chair of a member of several congressional groups and committees. He was chairman of the House Committee on Standards of Official Conduct, a member of the Appropriations Subcommittee on Foreign Operations, and chairman of the Appropriations Subcommittee on the District of Columbia. Dixon was also chairman of the CONGRESSIONAL BLACK CAUCUS (1983-1984), chairman of the 1984 Democratic National Convention Rules Committee, and an original cosponsor of the Equal Rights Amendment.

While in the California State Assembly, Dixon was chairman of the California Assembly Democratic Caucus. In the California State Assembly and in the House of Representatives, he promoted civil and political rights for minorities and women. He consistently voted for and supported legislation designed to improve these areas of society. Dixon kept in touch with individuals and situations within the African American community and sought recognition for their significant contributions. For example, he wrote resolutions passed by the House that called for Benjamin MAYS, an African American educator, university administrator, and CIVIL RIGHTS activist, to receive the Presidential Medal of Freedom, and for the declaration of September, 1983, as SICKLE-CELL ANEMIA Awareness Month. Dixon served in Congress through the 1980's and 1990's.

**Dixon, Willie** (July 1, 1915, Vicksburg, Mississippi—January 29, 1992, Los Angeles, California): BLUES bassist, singer, and songwriter. Dixon's mother, who had a habit of turning most things she would say into rhymes, provided her son with an early interest in lyric writing. The piano style of Eurreal "Little Brother" Montgomery influenced young Dixon musically. In his youth, Dixon worked at an array of menial jobs, rode the rails as a fireman, and spent time in a Mississippi prison farm, where he was first exposed to the sounds of the blues. In the early 1930's, he joined a gospel quartet in Vicksburg led by his musical mentor, Theo Phelps, and called the Union Jubilee Singers.

Although he already considered himself a songwriter, Dixon left for Chicago in 1936 to pursue a boxing career. There he won the 1938 heavyweight Golden Gloves title and had the opportunity to spar with world champion Joe Louis. Dixon's boxing career came to an abrupt halt after a dispute with his management which led to a six-month suspension.

In 1939 Dixon and guitarist Leonard "Baby Doo" Caston

Representative Julian C. Dixon during a press conference in 1989. *(AP/Wide World Photos)* formed the Five Breezes, a group that recorded for Bluebird until Dixon was imprisoned for refusing induction into the Army as a conscientious objector. After a year of prison and trials, Dixon was released and reunited with Caston, and they formed the Big Three Trio with guitarist Ollie Crawford. It was upon meeting Leonard and Phil Chess, Polish emigrés with aspirations to open a record label, that Dixon's career skyrocketed.

In addition to being the in-house bassist for Chess Records, Dixon became the label's most prolific songwriter. In 1954 two well-known blues artists recorded songs written by Dixon—HOWLIN' WOLF recorded "Evil" and Muddy WATERS recorded "I'm Your Hoochie Coochie Man"—and both were successful.

With songs that have become classic blues tracks, including "Hoochie Coochie Man," "My Babe," and his first number-one hit, the oft-pirated "You Need Love" (1955), Dixon laid the foundation for the British blues explosion of the 1960's; the Rolling Stones and Cream, among many other British and American bands, recorded versions of Dixon songs; The Doors recorded his "Back Door Man" on their 1967 debut album.

Other artists frequently reaped the benefits of Dixon's work, because Dixon sold his songs. A 1977 settlement finally won him an increase in his publishing royalties and the return of the copyrights on his songs. With this victory, Dixon wrested control over his own work from the large and powerful recording conglomerates, something that few African American artists had been able to accomplish. He also sued the British band Led Zeppelin in 1985 over their song "Whole Lotta Love," which was a very close reworking of Dixon's (uncredited) "You Need Love"; the case was settled in 1987.

In 1989 Dixon published his autobiography, *I Am the Blues: The Willie Dixon Story*. It chronicles his survival as a bluesman and as an African American in a forbidding environment. He also founded the Blues Heaven Foundation, designed to teach young people about the blues and provide schools with recordings and instruments. Dixon was inducted into the Blues Foundation Hall of Fame in 1980, won a Grammy Award for *Hidden Charms* in 1988, and was inducted into the Rock and Roll Hall of Fame in 1994.

**Dodds, Johnny** (April 12, 1892, New Orleans, Louisiana—August 8, 1940, Chicago, Illinois): JAZZ clarinetist and alto saxophonist. Dodds, sometimes called "Toilet" by his fellow musicians for his deep blues style, rose to prominence playing with bandleader Kid ORY's outfits during the years 1911 through 1917. His youngest brother, Warren "Baby" Dodds, was a renowned and influential drummer in early jazz.

After taking up the clarinet at age seventeen, Dodds performed in several New Orleans and New Orleans-style bands, including Billy and Mary Mack's Merrymakers, legendary trumpeter King OLIVER's band, and Louis ARMSTRONG's Hot Fives and Sevens. Never a very conspicuous performer, Dodds is regarded by historians as a link between the more formalized styles of the turn-of-the-century players and the increasingly popular improvisational styles of Armstrong and fellow clarinetists Sidney BECHET and Jimmy NOONE. Dodds's most enduring attribute was the steadiness and conciseness with which he often afforded the featured performers the opportunity to improvise while he anchored the melodies.

After years on the New Orleans scene, Dodds left for CHICAGO, ILLINOIS, in 1928. He formed a small club act with his brother and released what is arguably his best side, "Bull Fiddle Blues," with Baby Dodds on washboard and bassist Bill Johnson on pizzicato bass, the first bass of its kind ever recorded. Soon, however, Dodds was to fall on hard times. He spent most of the 1930's driving a taxi.

In 1938 Dodds made his only trip to NEW YORK CITY, where he recorded for Decca Records. He experienced little critical success. Suffering from decaying teeth, Dodds returned to Chicago and focused his energies on supervising an apartment community at 39th Street and Madison. He was fitted with false teeth in 1939, making it possible for him to return to the stage.

**Dodge Revolutionary Union Movement:** Revolutionary group formed at the Dodge automobile plant in DETROIT, MICHIGAN, in the late 1960's. The Dodge Revolutionary Union Movement (DRUM) had its origins in the BLACK POWER MOVEMENT of the late 1960's, the urban rebellions in Detroit in 1967, and the wildcat strikes organized by African American workers at the Detroit Dodge main plant of the Chrysler Corporation in May, 1968. All of these events were symptomatic of the frustration of urban blacks at their meager economic opportunities and at being left out of the civil rights protests, which were confined mainly to southern states. In some instances, the growing radical ethos permeating Detroit's black working class included a rejection of Martin Luther KING, Jr.'s philosophy of nonviolent resistance in favor of MALCOLM X's revolutionary black nationalism. Workers were also influenced by the Socialist Worker's Party and the COMMUNIST PARTY, as well as by the FREEDOM NOW PARTY, an all-black political party in Michigan. DRUM formed to transform wildcat strikes into an organized effort with specific goals and grievances.

DRUM alleged that the United Auto Workers (UAW) was a racist union. It demanded increased black representation in the UAW as well as in the Dodge corporation. Although the union and the corporation were slow to respond to these demands, DRUM's influence became increasingly widespread and led to similar organizations in other auto plants. CADRUM (at General Motors's Cadillac plant), FRUM (the Ford Revolutionary Union Movement), and GRUM (the larger GM auto caucus) were some of the auto plant caucuses that grew out of DRUM's influence. Similar organizations were mobilized in the steel and health industries, as well as in other auto plants in California, New Jersey, and Maryland. These organizational caucuses mobilized a broader coalition of students, intellectuals, and workers under an umbrella organization, the League of Revolutionary Black Workers, which had as its goal the socialist transformation of society.

The league founded the *Inner City Voice* in 1967. Most printers refused to print its radical commentary on social and political issues. The *Inner City Voice* eventually was subsumed under the *South End*, a Wayne State University paper that embraced the same principles.

Seeking to radicalize the UAW from within, the League of Revolutionary Black Workers made demands for the recognition of the league as the sole negotiator for black workers with the union and the auto plants, in addition to calling for black upper-echelon officials and the firing of some of the UAW's leadership. The UAW gradually hired moderate blacks into union positions.

By the early 1970's, the League of Revolutionary Black Workers had split into factions. Central to the internal disputes were debates concerning the relative merits of increased plant action versus mass education. By the 1980's, the league adherents, for the most part, had merged into mainstream state and local politics, hoping to achieve social change through those avenues. DRUM, then, served as a political spark for the broader political education and activism of Detroit's African American workers.

*See also:* Organized labor; Strikes and labor law.

**Dolphy, Eric** (June 20, 1928, Los Angeles, California—June 29, 1964, West Berlin, West Germany): Alto saxophonist, bass clarinetist, flutist, and composer. Dolphy made his mark as one of the major instrumental voices in avant-garde JAZZ. He brought to jazz a broad comprehension of musical ideas drawn from the Western classical music heritage, from Asian and African music, and even from the sounds of nature (he was obsessed with bird sounds). His influence on jazz musicians continues to be widespread.

Dolphy's earliest professional stints were in the bands of Roy Porter and Gerald Wilson, but the surfacing of his individuality came with his engagement with a band led by bassist and composer Charles Mingus in 1959. Mingus-led albums such as *Mingus at Antibus* (1976) reveal Dolphy creating vocal sounds on alto saxophone and bass clarinet that resembled an African American preacher "talking in tongues." His improvisations with Mingus reveal Dolphy's ability to improvise creatively with impressive speed.

Also crucial were Dolphy's activities with two other key figures in avant-garde jazz: John COLTRANE and Ornette COLEMAN. Dolphy's understanding of Indian musical modes and African rhythms contributed to the exotic atmospherics of the *Impressions* (1962) and *Africa/Brass* (1961) albums by Coltrane, both major releases during the 1960's on the Impulse label. His bass clarinet playing on Ornette Coleman's *Free Jazz* (1960) offered a clearly distinctive voice in a roaring maelstrom of unconventionally executed sounds.

Dolphy's power as a bandleader and composer is revealed in the nine compact disc boxed set *The Complete Prestige Recordings of Eric Dolphy* (1995) and in *Out to Lunch* (1964). Of particular interest are the recordings Dolphy made with trumpeter Booker Little during a live engagement at the Five Spot, a New York jazz club. These recordings were released by Prestige Records. Dolphy and Little continually challenged one another, and some of Dolphy's most fiery improvising occurred during these sessions. Dolphy's flute playing on "Like Someone in Love" mixes birdlike trills with the breathy phrasing one might associate with a BEBOP-flavored jazz vocalist. The speechlike cadences of his bass clarinet on "Aggression" suggested an instrumental parallel to the angry rhetoric of Black Power activists calling for revolution.

Like many other experimental African American jazz musicians of this period, Dolphy was deeply hurt by barbs from jazz critics who questioned his musical sense and skills. He found highly appreciative audiences in Germany and Scandinavia during an extended tour in Europe, but his triumphs did not last long. He died of a heart attack brought on by complications of diabetes.

Dolphy's impact on the jazz world has been felt on multiple levels. He put a spotlight on the bass clarinet, opening the way for later players such as David Murray. Dolphy's sensitivity to the beauties of non-Western music as sources of inspiration for jazz compositions inspired numerous players looking for new ideas. Further, Dolphy's appreciation of the musicality of bird song sparked interest among musicians using ecological themes.

**Dominican Republic:** Independent WEST INDIES nation occupying the eastern two-thirds of the island of Hispaniola, the second-largest island in the Caribbean Sea. The Dominican Republic's population is 85 to 90 percent black or mulatto and 10 to 15 percent white. The country therefore has the largest African-descended population in the Spanish-speaking Caribbean.

The history of African SLAVERY in the New World started in the Dominican Republic. Beginning in 1502, slaves were kidnapped in West Africa and sold by the Spaniards for labor in gold mines. The country's indigenous

Taino Indian population had been ravaged by the mid-1500's by European-introduced disease and by famine, increasing the Spanish colonists' need for black slave labor.

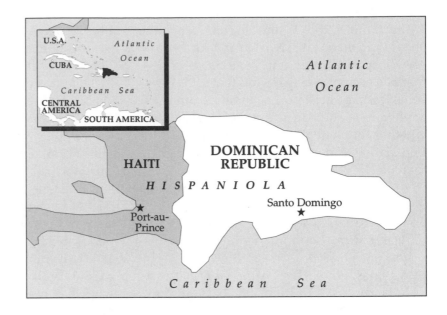

Sugar cane replaced gold as the island's economic mainstay, and slaves provided the necessary labor force. After the sugar economy began to suffer, many whites left in search of mineral wealth discovered in Mexico and other Spanish colonies. As black and mulatto numbers greatly outnumbered whites, some slaves gained freedom. They were not allowed to leave the island, so they stayed and grew in number. Escaped slaves from neighboring Saint Domingue (later HAITI) added to the black population; more Haitians intermingled during the nineteenth century periods of Haitian rule (1802-1803, 1822-1844). After the Dominican Republic's independence in 1844, the government invited West Indian black labor for sugar work. The twentieth century sugar plantations were largely worked by Haitian immigrants under conditions considered by many to be slavelike.

African influence permeates the political, social, cultural, and religious aspects of Dominican culture. The folk religion practiced by many Dominicans is a mix of African-derived traditional religion with Catholic elements. Speech patterns, oral traditions, and specific vocabulary words in Dominican Spanish suggest elements of the slaves' original languages. Dominican music uses European scales, though African influences dominate dance, instruments, and polyrhythms. The diet (plantains, stews) and manner of food preparation is also highly African. African influences penetrate Dominican social organization and interpersonal relations as well as everyday practices highly common in the traditionally more black southern and eastern areas of the country (brightly colored houses, kerchief-wearing by women, carrying objects on the head, and style of body movements).

Despite the overwhelming percentage of African-descended people in the Dominican Republic, the distinct and strong African influence is downplayed. The country's Taino roots receive more attention, although actual Taino influence in Dominican society is very limited. Former dictator Rafael Leónidas Trujillo Molina (leader from 1930 to 1961) officially used the term *indio* to describe mixed-ancestry (black and white) Dominicans, ignoring the majority's African roots. Former president Joaquin Balaguer promoted a similar racial agenda, calling for an end of the "Africanization" of Dominicans in order to "improve" the Dominican people.

As in many countries, Dominican society shows a preference for lighter-skinned individuals, a large percentage of whom are in the upper classes. However, skin color alone does not usually limit social movement; wealth and education seem to be more critical factors. Given the great variation of skin colors, even within families, the Dominican concept of race is less rigid than that in North America. People of African ancestry operate in all classes of Dominican society. It may be said that aside from some leaders' racist propaganda, Dominicans are aware of their Africanness, regardless of whether they actively embrace it, but tend to find national identity as Dominicans rather than blacks.

—*Michelle C. K. McKowen*

Suggested Readings:

*Country Report: Dominican Republic, Haiti, Puerto Rico*. London: Economist Intelligence Unit, 1999.

Moya Pons, Frank. *The Dominican Republic: A National History*. Princeton, N.J.: Markus Wiener Publishers, 1998.

Torres-Sailliant, Silvio. "The Dominican Republic." In *No Longer Invisible*. London: Minority Rights Publications, 1995.

**Domino, Fats** (b. February 26, 1928, New Orleans, Louisiana): Pianist, songwriter, and singer. Antoine "Fats" Domino was the son of a violinist. Self-taught at the piano, Domino began to work in NEW ORLEANS clubs in the early 1940's. He was married in 1945. By the end of the decade, his playing and singing, showing the influence of Louis Jordan, Charles Brown, and Albert AMMONS, took him to Kansas City and the West coast.

After establishing his own group around 1950, Domino recorded for Imperial Records from 1950 to 1963 and became an influential figure in the growth of RHYTHM AND BLUES and the emergence of rock and roll. His appearances in popular teen films of the mid-1950's, including *Shake, Rattle, and Rock* (1956) and *The Girl Can't Help It* (1956), helped to gain for him large audiences of both African American and white listeners. Domino might be classified as one of the first crossover artists. He helped to develop and establish the New Orleans rhythm-and-blues sound and to de-

fine the range of rock-and-roll piano. In doing so, he influenced such performers as Jerry Lee Lewis and Allen Toussaint.

Domino generated a significant number of classic rock-and-roll recordings, including "Ain't That a Shame," (1955), "I'm Walk'n'" (1957), "Blue Monday" (1957), and "Blueberry Hill" (1956). Equally a great singer and a lyrical pianist, he was one of the founders of rock and roll. One measure of the quality and impact of his work is the number of cover versions of his work that have been recorded or performed by other musicians. After the mid-1960's, Domino was active primarily on the rock-and-roll and 1950's revival circuit. His work has been rereleased many times, and more than sixty-five million of his records have been sold.

**Doo-wop:** Musical term derived from the nonsense syllables used by vocal groups of the 1940's and 1950's. Part of the RHYTHM-AND-BLUES genre, doo-wop has its roots in GOSPEL MUSIC harmonies and in black pop vocal groups such as the Mills Brothers and INK SPOTS. Doo-wop groups proliferated in the 1950's, and the vocal device of using nonsense words as a musical backing for lead vocals continued into the 1960's and beyond. Doo-wop songs were often sentimental but were often humorous and good-natured as well, with their background refrains such as "shoop-shoop," "yip-yip-yip," "bomp-a-bomp-bomp," and "dip-de-dip."

Early doo-wop groups include the Orioles, the Penguins, and the El-Dorados; major doo-wop acts include the Platters, the Coasters, the Moonglows, Frankie LYMON and the Teenagers, Italian American group Dion and the Belmonts, and the Marcels. Doo-wop had faded by the "British invasion" of the mid-1960's, but harmonies influenced by doo-wop continued in pop music.

*See also:* Lymon, Frankie, and the Teenagers.

**Dorsey, Thomas A.** (July 1, 1899, Villa Rica, Georgia—January 23, 1993, Chicago, Illinois): GOSPEL MUSIC composer and BLUES musician. Thomas Andrew Dorsey was the first of four children. He was raised in a religious household, and he was a keyboard accompanist for his father, who was a traveling Baptist evangelist. Because of his father's ill health, Dorsey had to help support his family by playing blues piano in saloons and beer halls in AT-LANTA, GEORGIA, as early as 1910. He began composing blues works and adopted "Georgia Tom" as a stage name. He composed some sacred songs, but his reputation as a blues and JAZZ musician spread. In 1916 Dorsey moved to CHICAGO and studied briefly at the Chicago College of Composition and Arranging as he gained a reputation in that city as a blues pianist.

During the early 1920's, Dorsey performed with several jazz groups, including the Whispering Serenaders, and a few of his compositions, such as "Riverside Blues," were recorded by major jazzmen such as Joseph "King" OLIVER. His own group, the Wildcats Jazz Band, accompanied blues singer Ma RAINEY in several of her recordings. He also formed a duo with guitarist TAMPA RED, with whom he composed and recorded "Tight Like That," "Terrible Operation Blues," and other songs.

Although Dorsey was well established as a blues and jazz musician, he continued to cultivate his religious music activity. His song "Someday, Somewhere" was in the landmark collection of the National Baptist Convention, *Gospel Pearls* (1921). Around 1927 he began playing his religious songs in Chicago area churches, accompanying a singer at the keyboard, but the songs were rejected by many ministers because of their stylistic affinity to the blues. In 1931 Dorsey experienced a double personal tragedy when his first wife, Nettie, died in childbirth; the baby also died. This was the occasion when he composed "Take My Hand, Precious Lord," his most celebrated and most frequently heard work.

By the 1930's, Dorsey had abandoned his blues career to devote himself exclusively to composing and promoting gospel music. In 1931 he formed the world's first gospel choir at Ebenezer Baptist Church in Chicago, and he opened the first publishing company devoted to the sale of gospel music. With his colleague, Sallie Martin, he founded the National Convention of Gospel Choirs and Choruses to train gospel choirs and soloists. More than any other individual, Dorsey was responsible for elevating gospel music to professional status. He wrote more than one thousand songs and is even credited with creating the term "gospel song."
*See also:* Gospel music and spirituals.

**Douglas, Aaron** (May 26, 1899, Topeka, Kansas—February 2, 1979, Nashville, Tennessee): Painter and illustrator. Douglas received a B.A. from the University of Kansas (1923), a B.F.A. from the University of Nebraska (1922), and an M.A. from Columbia University Teachers College. He studied with Winold Reiss in NEW YORK CITY (1925-1927) and Othon Friesz in Paris (1931). He received a Rosenwald fellowship and an award from the Barnes Foundation, and he was head of the department of art at FISK UNIVERSITY.

As a painter, illustrator, and muralist, Douglas achieved popular recognition in the 1920's and 1930's, exhibiting throughout the United States. Douglas illustrated James Weldon JOHNSON's *God's Trombones: Seven Negro Sermons in Verse* (1927) and was championed by other HARLEM RENAISSANCE writers and critics. Douglas aptly transformed art deco conventions with African art motifs and African American themes.

Douglas's monumental murals show symbolic figures silhouetted against a series of stylized backgrounds. Murals such as the three he painted for the Hall of Negro Life at the Texas Centennial Exposition (1936) indicate the African roots of his art and his ability to narrate an African American historical perspective. *Aspirations*, a painting from that series, provides a compact narrative in one frame that traces the path from slavery into freedom.

Douglas combined an inspirational vision of African American nobility with proletarian themes. His angular silhouettes offset by jagged intrusions, wavy lines, and pastel circles were a revolutionary step in modern American design. Douglas applied this restless decorative design to African American themes and movement. His murals entitled *Aspects of Negro Life* (1934) are displayed at the SCHOMBURG CENTER FOR RESEARCH IN BLACK CULTURE in the New York Public Library. In them he traces the course of African Americans from Africa through slavery to an enlightened future. The artistic heritage of Africa influenced his paintings of African Americans against a background of geometric cityscapes, suggesting a triumphant urban future. Douglas depicted the dignity, courage, and hope of all African Americans on an epic scale. As a teacher of art at Fisk University for twenty-nine years, Douglas influenced generations of students. His work remains an inspiration for and a celebration of African American cultural identity.
*See also:* Painters and illustrators.

**Douglass, Frederick** (Frederick Augustus Washington Bailey, February, 1817(?), Tuckahoe, Talbot County, Maryland—February 20, 1895, Washington, D.C.): ABOLITIONIST MOVEMENT leader and CIVIL RIGHTS activist. Frederick Douglass was born a slave; by the time of his death, his name was a household word in the United States and was synonymous with the struggle for freedom and individual rights throughout the Western world. Over the course of his life, Douglass was intimately involved in many of the critical incidents and events of nineteenth-century American history. His involvement is the more significant, because through his own eloquence—and in the words and writings of those who opposed him—is preserved a vivid account of those formative years when American society wrestled with the paradox of SLAVERY in a constitutional democracy.

*Struggle and Resistance*
The essential theme of Douglass's life was the struggle to acquire freedom for himself and general improvement in the condition of all African Americans. Consistently, Douglass challenged and confronted those features of American society that functioned to limit individual freedom and opportunity. This course of action was not merely instinctive. Douglass evolved a comprehensive personal philosophy of resistance and actively articulated the need to oppose injustice wherever and however it impinged upon the basic rights of citizenship. This philosophy of resistance was a guideline for living that grew organically from his experiences under slavery and in the struggle to abolish it.

As a youngster, Douglass was taken to BALTIMORE, where he spent a relatively happy period as a houseboy and shipyard laborer. After the death of his master, however, Douglass was moved to the country to work as a field hand. His powerful personality did not fit him well for a life of subservience. In 1834 he was hired out to a local planter to be "broken"; his will to resist was to be destroyed by harsh treatment and mental suffering. A slave had little recourse or protection from cruelty inflicted by a master, such behavior having the force of both law and custom to support it.

*Escape from Slavery*
Douglass came to realize that even the strongest resolve could eventually be overcome by conditions of exhaustive labor, mental stress, and poor nutrition. He determined that his

only hope was to escape completely from the hold of slavery. After an unsuccessful escape attempt in 1834, Douglass was able, through a combination of deception and good fortune, to make his escape from slavery in 1836.

Once Douglass had made good his personal escape, he refused to enjoy his precarious freedom while others still toiled under slavery's yoke. He became a participant in the abolition movement. He first drew attention to himself by the power of his rhetoric and the conviction his words carried, coming as they did from a former slave. In 1845 Douglass published the first narrative of his life under slavery.

The public attention his abolition activities focused on Douglass placed him in danger of recapture and a return to slavery. To avoid this possibility, Douglass fled to England in 1846. While he was in England, a group of his friends purchased his freedom. Douglass returned to the United States in 1847 and founded an abolitionist newspaper, *North Star*.

### The Fight Against Slavery

In 1850 a compromise was devised to settle a multifaceted confrontation between slave states and free states over the conditions under which the new territories stripped from MEXICO during the MEXICAN-AMERICAN WAR would be admitted into the Union. As part of the COMPROMISE OF 1850, Congress adopted a new and more stringent FUGITIVE SLAVE LAW. Under the terms of the compromise, the new law not only expanded the legal responsibilities of all citizens to recapture runaway slaves, under threat of severe penalties for noncompliance, but also pledged the national government to a more active enforcement effort.

John BROWN, an abolitionist who believed that only armed intervention would destroy slavery, laid out for Douglass his plans for an

By all measures, Frederick Douglass was the outstanding African American spokesperson during the nineteenth century. *(Library of Congress)*

assault on the federal arsenal at HARPERS FERRY, Virginia, in 1859. Brown and his followers occupied the arsenal but were surrounded and defeated by federal troops. Eventually, Brown was captured and executed; although Douglass did not join Brown, he was under suspicion as a conspirator in the raid, and he fled the country in 1859 to avoid arrest.

When hostilities between the North and South finally erupted in 1861 into the CIVIL WAR, President Abraham Lincoln's policy toward blacks was one of exclusion from the armed forces. Douglass argued relentlessly that blacks should be allowed to contribute their skill, courage, and blood to the final destruction of slavery. Eventually, the fortunes of war prevailed on Lincoln to reverse his policy, and Douglass worked effectively to recruit blacks for the war effort. Three of his own sons served in the Union forces.

## Life After Emancipation

After the Civil War, Douglass realized that, for African Americans to avoid practical re-enslavement, a great effort would have to be made by the freed slaves. Douglass offered his opinions in many forums on the nature of the problems facing the black population and detailed his prescriptions for their solution. Douglass proclaimed the responsibility of the national government to guarantee and protect the citizenship rights of blacks. He also pleaded the moral responsibility of whites to accept blacks as full-fledged members of American society.

Beyond these general principles, Douglass also had very specific advice for freed blacks. He advised former slaves to become producers of goods and services. He maintained that blacks should be made full citizens and should then actively use the ballot box to protect their freedom. He believed that the former slaves should not remove themselves from the United States under the various colonization plans that gained popularity after the war, and he did not agree that blacks should engage in a wholesale exodus from the postwar South. Douglass believed the final victory over slavery and racial oppression resided in the acquisition by African Americans of financial resources and economic power.

## National Politics

During the RECONSTRUCTION era, Douglass was an active participant in REPUBLICAN PARTY politics. He emerged as the dominant African American leader of his day, serving in positions in national politics never before held by an African American. In 1871 he was appointed to the District of Columbia Governing Council. In 1872 he was selected as a presidential elector from New York. Douglass was appointed as the U.S. marshall for the District of Columbia in 1876 and as the recorder of deeds for the District of Columbia in 1882. In 1889 he served as U.S. minister to HAITI.

Douglass had become the most influential and important black leader in the country. As such, he enjoyed the hard-earned benefits of recognition, fame, and relative material comfort. This prominence, though, was not without its costs and dangers. Douglass had to contend with the hostility of white Americans convinced that blacks were naturally inferior and fitted only for a subordinate place in American society. He also had to contend with whites who were sympathetic to African American problems but who were only comfortable in a paternalistic relationship in which they controlled policies and major decisions. In addition, Douglass bore the constant knowledge that he was a symbol as well as an individual. Every word he uttered, every action he took was judged as a reflection not only on the person but also on the entire race.

Douglass was frequently a groundbreaker in assuming roles and positions never before held by blacks. This not only created difficulties with whites who were unaccustomed to interacting with blacks under nontraditional circumstances but also often created difficulties for Douglass with other blacks who were still trapped in the grip of the racial norms of their day. Douglass's success thus caused him some personal problems in his relationship to black society.

The appointments that Douglass received to high political offices, for example, created problems. Other aspirants to those same offices frequently expressed considerable bitterness at his success. At times, Douglass suffered from the circulation of unjustified rumors that he had personally profited excessively in the name of the black cause. Personal attacks of this kind caused Douglass great distress. In 1882 Douglass married his second wife, Helen Pitts, a white woman. Such a union was repugnant according to the social conventions of the day, and the marriage cost Douglass some support among both whites and blacks.

Douglass died in 1895 after having witnessed and participated in the major events of the nineteenth century that redefined the role of African Americans in American life. His struggle to acquire dignity and equality for himself and his race shaped not only the destiny of African Americans but also the fate of his American generation.

—*Darrell Millner*

Suggested Readings:

Andrews, William L., ed. *Critical Essays on Frederick Douglass.* Boston: G. K. Hall, 1991.

Bontemps, Arna. *Free at Last: The Life of Frederick Douglass.* New York: Dodd, Mead, 1971.

Burke, Ronald K. *Frederick Douglass: Crusading Orator for Human Rights.* New York: Garland, 1996.

Chesebrough, David B. *Frederick Douglass: Oratory from Slavery.* Westport, Conn.: Greenwood Press, 1998.

Diedrich, Maria. *Love Across Color Lines: Ottilie Assing and Frederick Douglass.* New York: Hill & Wang, 1999.

Douglass, Frederick. *Autobiographies.* Edited by Henry Louis Gates. New York: Library of America, 1994.

_____. *Frederick Douglass: The Narrative and Selected Writings.* Edited by Michael Meyer. New York: Vintage, 1984.

Huggins, Nathan I. *Slave and Citizen: The Life of Frederick Douglass.* Boston: Little, Brown, 1980.

Levine, Robert S. *Martin Delany, Frederick Douglass, and the Politics of Representative Identity.* Chapel Hill: University of North Carolina Press, 1997.

McFeely, William S. *Frederick Douglass.* New York: W. W. Norton, 1991.

Quarles, Benjamin. *Frederick Douglass.* Washington, D.C.: Associated Publishers, 1948. Reprint. New York: Atheneum, 1976.

Voss, Frederick. *Majestic in His Wrath: A Pictorial Life of Frederick Douglass.* Washington, D.C.: Smithsonian Institution Press, 1995.

**Dove, Rita** (b. August 28, 1952, Akron, Ohio): Poet, short-story writer, novelist, and educator. Dove has the distinction of serving as the first African American poet laureate of the United States; when she was selected, she was also the youngest poet laureate to that time. In addition, Dove was only the second poet to remain in this ceremonial post, held by the country's leading poets to promote the appreciation of literature, for two years—from 1993 to 1995.

Among her volumes of poetry are *Ten Poems* (1977), *The Only Dark Spot in the Sky* (1980), *The Yellow House on the Corner* (1980), *Mandolin* (1982), *Museum* (1983), *Thomas and Beulah* (1986), *The Other Side of the House* (1988), *Grace Notes* (1989), *Mother Love* (1995), and *On the Bus with Rosa Parks* (1999). In 1987 Dove was awarded the Pulitzer Prize in poetry for *Thomas and Beulah*, an interconnected series of forty-four poems loosely based on the lives of her maternal grandparents, Thomas and Georgianna Hord. This work depicts survival

Rita Dove. *(Fred Viebahn)*

in the lives of ordinary people, "nobodies in the course of history."

Dove's poetry is noted for its color imagery, orality, compressed narrative, objectivity, and themes of history, autobiography, myth, music, adolescence, family, and community. These elements are also evident in her experimentation in other genres. *Fifth Sunday* (1985) is a collection of eight short stories whose subject matter includes adolescents and music. *Through the Ivory Gate* (1992), a novel, is the story of Virginia King, a young black artist who returns to her hometown of Akron, OHIO, and becomes "the Puppet Lady," a visiting artist in the primary schools. As in Dove's poetry, the bits and pieces of the character's life, told through flashback, come together as Virginia grapples with herself, her family, and her painful past.

*The Darker Face of the Earth* (1994, completely revised in 1996), a drama in blank verse, is Dove's retelling of the Oedipus myth. Amalia, a SOUTH CAROLINA plantation's white mistress, gives birth to a black baby who is taken away by the attending physician. Twenty years later, Augustus, a rebellious, "bright-skinned" slave, is acquired by the plantation. Even as the ending moves toward the expected, the drama itself is powerful and insightful.

Dove's love for reading and writing surfaced early. Reared in Akron by educated parents, she wrote her first novel, entitled "Chaos," in third or fourth grade, using the week's spelling lesson as the basis for its chapters. In 1970, ranking among the one hundred top high-school seniors, she was named a Presidential Scholar. In 1973 Dove received her bachelor of arts degree in English, summa cum laude, from Miami University of Ohio. She went on to study at Tübingen University in West Germany on a Fulbright scholarship in 1974. Dove returned to the United States and was accepted into the University of Iowa Writers Workshop, where she received her master of fine arts degree in 1977.

Dove launched her teaching career at Arizona State University, where she taught from 1981 to 1989. In 1989 she received an appointment as Commonwealth Professor of English at the University of Virginia, teaching creative writing. Upon accepting this post, Dove moved to Charlottesville with her husband, novelist Fred Viebahn, and their daughter, Aviva. Refusing the label "black poet," Dove wrote that her poetry is about "humanity . . . which sometimes . . . happens to be black." *See also:* Literature.

**Dozens, the:** Folk game in which contestants attempt to outwit one another through a barrage of insults, usually performed in rhyming verse. It is traceable to a nineteenth-century religious teaching device in which a canto of twelve essential biblical facts was set forth for children to memorize. In a semiliterate world, such mnemonics played an important role in a child's education, and through this method of learning, African American children fashioned a rhyming game of one-upmanship with verbal abuses ranging from an opponent's physical characteristics to his or her mother's sexual activity.

**Dr. Dre** (Andre Young; b. February 18, 1965, Los Angeles, California): RAP producer, composer, vocalist, and entrepreneur. Known as a founding father of West Coast gangsta rap, Dr. Dre grew up in a housing project in Compton, California. He began his musical career as a disc jockey and composer/producer in the dance clubs of Compton. At age seventeen, he joined the funk band World Class Wreckin' Cru and wrote their first successful single, "Surgery" (1982). He left the group in 1984 and began to perform with rap artist ICE CUBE. In 1985 he produced the single "Boys 'N Tha Hood" with rapper Eazy-E. That single sold some ten thousand copies. With the proceeds of that single and the success of the album *Eazy Duz It* (1985), Dr. Dre joined with Ice Cube, Eazy-E, M.C. Ren, Arabian Prince, and fellow Wreckin' Cru member Yella to form N.W.A. (Niggaz with Attitude).

N.W.A.'s 1988 album *Straight Outta Compton* sold more than two million copies and established Compton as the center of the new musical form known as gangsta rap. As producer and composer, Dr. Dre created the heavy bass lines and hard-core beats that characterized the style. Public focus on N.W.A.'s controversial lyrics, which included violent and sexist imagery of gang life on the streets, precluded extensive recognition of Dr. Dre's musical contribution.

Dr. Dre produced two more highly successful albums with N.W.A.—*100 Miles and Runnin'* (1990) and *Efil4zaggin* (1991)—before leaving amid dissension and contract disputes to form his own company with Suge Knight, Death Row Records. He released his solo debut album, *The Chronic*, on the new label in 1993. The album featured music inspired by the 1970's funk of artists such as George Clinton and Bootsy Collins, along with the rap vocals of Dr. Dre's protégé SNOOP DOGG (then Snoop Doggy Dogg). Named after a street term for strong marijuana, the album continued in the urban gangster vein of N.W.A., but with a new melodic tilt—as represented in its hit single "Nuthin' but a 'G' Thang." *The Chronic* was also notable for its verbal attacks on Eazy-E, who subsequently sued Dr. Dre for racketeering in connection with N.W.A. business affairs. The case was dismissed, but the rivalry continued through each artist's solo recordings.

*The Chronic* sold more than three million copies, more than any hard-core rap album before it, reaching number one on *Billboard*'s rhythm and blues chart and number two on the pop chart. Awards for the album included a Grammy Award for best rap solo performance and *The Source* awards for producer, solo artist, and album of the year.

Rapper Dr. Dre in 1992. *(Death Row/Interscope Records, Inc.)*

Dre soon turned more to production, rather than recording as an artist. He produced SNOOP DOGGY DOGG's *Doggy Style* (1993). The next year he won a Grammy Award for best rap solo performance for "Let Me Ride." He also produced the sound-track album for *Above the Rim* and albums by Tupac SHAKUR and others for Death Row Records.

Dr. Dre developed a group approach to production that has been termed "hip-hop orchestra," often drawing on the talents of new and breaking artists in an effort to develop their careers. Dr. Dre's work is featured on releases by The D.O.C. and Michelle as well as Death Row Records artists Snoop Dogg, RBX, Jewell, The Lady of Rage, Dat Nigga Daz, and Kurupt.

In 1996 Dr. Dre sold his interest in Death Row to Knight and started his own company, Aftermath. The first release was a compilation of material produced by Dre called *Dr. Dre Presents . . . The Aftermath* (1996).

Among the most successful 1990's releases on Aftermath was *The Slim Shady LP* (1999) by Eminem, which sold more than two million copies. In 1999 Dre released his own *Dr. Dre 2001*, which featured Snoop Dogg, Korupt, Eminem, and other guest rappers. The album continued Dre's hard-core rap tradition, but its last song, "The Message," was an uncharacteristically reflective song about the death of his younger brother Tyree, killed in a fight in 1998.

**Dreadlocks:** Term for the long hair and beard encouraged by the faith of RASTAFARIANISM and found among the faith's adherents in Africa, the Caribbean, and the United States. The hairstyle features thick, ropelike locks of hair formed by braiding or matting individual strands together. Dreadlocks are intended to symbolize the mane of the standing lion, symbol of Ethiopia—the spiritual home of the Rastafarian sect and the dominion of Jah Ras

MOVE leader Ramona Africa, with her hair styled in dreadlocks in 1995. *(AP/Wide World Photos)*

Tafari (Emperor Haile Selassie I), the Rastafari "God." They also represent the ancient nature of Rastafari culture and its biblical origin. The hairstyle constitutes a covenant between Jah (God) and the Rasta (Rastafarian adherent) confirming strict obedience to the rule of nature. Africa-centered cultural consciousness in the United States led to the wearing of dreadlocks by many non-Rastafarians who identify broadly with Africa and its cultures. *See also:* Hairstyles.

**Dred Scott decision:** Known in U.S. SUPREME COURT documents as *Scott v. Sandford*, or *Dred Scott v. Sandford* (1857), the most devastating proslavery case in U.S. history began in 1834, when Dr. John Emerson of St. Louis, MISSOURI, joined the U.S. Army as a surgeon and was assigned to duty at Rock Island, ILLINOIS. Later, he was transferred to Fort Snelling in the WISCONSIN Territory; in 1838, he returned to Missouri. He was accompanied by Dred Scott, a slave who was his servant. In 1848, after the death of Emerson, Scott, with the help of a sympathetic lawyer, filed a lawsuit against Emerson's widow and her brother, John Sandford, who had been acting as Mrs. Emerson's agent and had in effect become Scott's owner. Since Scott had lived in the state of Illinois and the Wisconsin Territory, where SLAVERY was outlawed, he argued that he was a free man.

Arguments before the U.S. Supreme Court began in 1855. The Court was composed of seven Democrats (five of them from the South) and two Republicans. All were aware that the case was difficult and potentially explosive, and the justices approached it with great reluctance and caution. Two important points were involved: first, was Scott, as a slave, entitled to bring a suit before the courts? Second, was he free as a result of the MISSOURI COMPROMISE, which had prohibited slavery in the territories?

Because of the growing controversy in the country over slavery, it was decided that Chief

Justice Roger B. Taney would write a sweeping decision that would carefully and fully review the entire slavery issue, including the important question of the power of Congress to regulate slavery in the territories. Although all nine justices wrote separate opinions, Taney's majority opinion was the official decision.

The decision was made public on March 6, 1857. It was deliberately delayed until two days after the inauguration of President James Buchanan to avoid embroiling outgoing President Franklin Pierce in the decision during his last few months in office. In a seven-to-two decision, the Court ruled, first, that Scott could not bring suit in a federal court because, free or slave, he was not considered to be a citizen under the law, and no person who was the descendant of slaves was eligible for citizenship. Second, the justices asserted that Scott was not a free man, even though he had lived in a territory closed to slavery. Since he had returned to Missouri, the Court stated, the laws of Illinois no longer applied to him. His residency in the Wisconsin Territory did not make him free either, the Court declared, because the Missouri Compromise, which had allowed Missouri to enter the Union as a slave state in exchange for the prohibition of slavery in the Wisconsin Territory, was unconstitutional.

The effect of this controversial decision was to affirm that slaves were considered as property under the law; their owners were thus protected by the Fifth Amendment to the Constitution, which states that no citizen "shall be deprived of life, liberty, or property without due process of law." A plantation owner's slaves, therefore, were regarded by the federal government in the same way his real estate, his livestock, and the rest of his material pos-

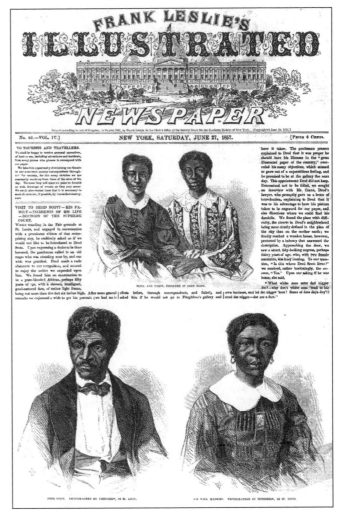

Contemporary newspaper article on Dred Scott. *(Library of Congress)*

sessions were: They were considered to be his personal property, and the fact that they were also human beings was not considered. The Supreme Court interpreted the Constitution as regarding slaves to be mere "chattel property" and held that the words "people" and "citizens," as used in the Declaration of Independence and the Constitution, did not apply to them, Slaves would possess only those rights that individual states chose to grant them. Blacks were thus not only excluded from citizenship but also denied every protection given by the Constitution.

*Legal Criticisms*

The Dred Scott decision has been widely criticized by legal scholars. Many have pointed to the obvious fact that the majority of the justices were southerners. The most widespread criticism of Chief Justice Taney's decision was that most of his comments had little direct bearing upon Dred Scott's actual lawsuit. Taney devoted the majority of his comments to the questions of black citizenship and the territorial question; he wrote only briefly about Scott's contention that residence on free soil had the effect of emancipating a slave.

The citizenship question was considered by the Court to be a moot point: Everyone agreed that both slaves and free blacks were not citizens, and therefore, asserted Taney, they "had no rights which the white man was bound to respect." As for the question of slavery in the territories, the Court's decision seriously threatened the doctrine of "popular sovereignty" championed by Senator Stephen A. Douglas of Missouri, which stated that the question of slavery in the territories should be left up to the settlers themselves. If Congress could not prohibit slavery in a territory, the Court concluded, then neither could a territorial legislature. Until statehood was granted, the right of citizens to own slaves was guaranteed, and could only be excluded where and when state legislatures had voted specifically to abolish it.

The dissenting judges argued that the Constitution did in fact mention African Americans as "persons," and they further pointed out that free blacks were permitted to vote in several states. They also held that, both by common law and in the Constitution, slavery was considered to be purely a state institution.

*Effects of the Decision*

The Dred Scott decision convinced many Americans that the South was engaged in an aggressive attempt to extend slavery. Indeed, southerners hailed the decision as a judicial endorsement of their position on slavery in the territories and announced that they expected the antislavery states to accept it. At the same time, the decision also enhanced the standing of the REPUBLICAN PARTY, which had been established in 1854 as a national antislavery party. Republicans proclaimed that if they secured control of the government, they would change the composition of the Court and have the decision overruled. Taney's ruling also outraged Republicans by implying, in effect, that the Republican Party was organized for an illegal purpose, since slavery was declared a legal institution by the Court. It is certainly arguable that the decision had a critical effect on the emergence of Abraham Lincoln as a national figure and on his election to the presidency in 1860.

The Dred Scott case damaged Taney's reputation; a northern newspaper declared that he would "be held in infamous remembrance"

Writing the Dred Scott decision gave Chief Justice Roger B. Taney a form of notorious immortality. *(Mathew Brady/Collection of the Supreme Court of the United States)*

for his refusal to free Scott. The decision did not, however, seriously weaken the Supreme Court as an institution, even though the Union government during the CIVIL WAR treated the ruling as if it had never been rendered. In June, 1862, Congress abolished slavery in all federal territories; later that same year, Edward Bates, Lincoln's attorney general, issued an official opinion declaring that free blacks born in the United States were to be regarded as citizens. Taney's decision was completely overthrown by the passage of the THIRTEENTH AMENDMENT and the FOURTEENTH AMENDMENT to the Constitution in 1865 and 1868, respectively.

The future of Dred Scott himself did not matter to the country or the courts; the fundamental question that the Supreme Court was seeking to resolve was whether Congress or the local legislatures had the power to outlaw slavery in the territories. Consequently, the verdict made little difference in the lives of those immediately involved in the case. John Sandford died in an insane asylum two weeks after the reading of the decision. Dred Scott was granted his freedom on May 26, 1857, and worked as a porter in a St. Louis hotel. He enjoyed only sixteen months of freedom before succumbing to tuberculosis and dying.

The questions of Dred Scott's freedom and American citizenship were ultimately decided by the Civil War, and there is little doubt that the Scott decision contributed significantly to the growing national crisis over slavery. The tragedy of the Scott case was that the Supreme Court had intervened in what was primarily a political controversy and had come down clearly on the side of the proslavery South. In its ruling, the Court implied that slavery could legally exist anywhere in the country, even in free states. *Dred Scott v. Sandford* stands as the prime historical example of the use (or misuse) of judicial power to subordinate a particular group of people.

—*Raymond Frey*

*See also:* Constitution, U.S.

Suggested Readings:

Ehrlich, Walter. *They Have No Rights: Dred Scott's Struggle for Freedom*. Westport, Conn.: Greenwood Press, 1979.

Fehrenbacher, Don E. *The Dred Scott Case: Its Significance in American Law and Politics*. New York: Oxford University Press, 1978.

_____. *Slavery, Law, and Politics: The Dred Scott Case in Historical Perspective*. New York: Oxford University Press, 1981.

Finkelman, Paul. *Dred Scott v. Sandford: A Brief History with Documents*. Boston: Bedford Books, 1997.

Hall, Kermit L., ed. *Civil Rights in American History: Major Historical Interpretations*. New York: Garland, 1987.

Hyman, Harold M., and William M. Wiecek. *Equal Justice Under the Law: Constitutional Development, 1835-1875*. New York: Harper & Row, 1982.

Kaufman, Kenneth C. *Dred Scott's Advocate: A Biography of Roswell M. Field*. Columbia: University of Missouri Press, 1996.

Sunstein, Cass R. *Constitutional Myth-Making: Lessons from the Dred Scott Case*. Chicago: University of Chicago Press, 1996.

**Drew, Charles R.** (June 3, 1904, Washington, D.C.—April 1, 1950, near Burlington, North Carolina): Surgeon and blood-transfer pioneer. Charles Richard Drew was born into a comfortably middle-class African American family. His mother was a graduate of HOWARD UNIVERSITY; his father was a carpet layer and the only black member and financial secretary of the local branch of his union. Drew and his siblings were exposed to the works of William Shakespeare and taken on trips to museums. The Drew home was filled with warmth and insulated from most of the cold realities of racism.

*Education*

Drew joined similarly privileged African

American young people when he entered Dunbar High School in the fall of 1918. Although segregated, Dunbar was probably one of the best high schools in the nation for the academically gifted. Its faculty was outstanding, and its graduates included many who would gain prominence. At Dunbar, Drew was a popular student and a four-letter athlete, twice winning awards for all-around athletic accomplishment.

In recognition of Drew's athletic abilities, Amherst College in Massachusetts awarded him a partial athletic scholarship. There, he continued to excel in sports, winning several awards, including, in 1925, an honorable mention on one All-American football team as a halfback. By the time of his graduation in 1926, Drew had decided to become a medical doctor; however, he lacked the funds to continue his education immediately.

## Medical School and Residency

Drew became the athletic director and an instructor in biology and chemistry at Morgan State University in BALTIMORE for two years to earn money for medical school. Rejected by Howard University for having earned too few English credits, in 1928 he entered McGill University in Montreal, Canada. At McGill he excelled both in athletics and academics. He won Canadian championships in the high and low hurdles, the high jump, and the broad jump. He also won the Williams Prize for academic excellence and was elected to Alpha Omega Alpha, an honorary fraternity for medical students.

In 1933 Drew received his medical degree from McGill and interned at Royal Victoria Hospital; he completed his residency at Montreal General Hospital in 1935. That year, he became an instructor in pathology at Howard University. During the next three years, Drew worked his way up to a position as instructor in surgery and assistant surgeon at the affiliated Freedmen's Hospital. He impressed his superiors, and in 1938 he was granted a two-year fellowship for advanced training at Columbia University in New York and its affiliate, Presbyterian Hospital.

At Columbia, Drew studied under Dr. John Scudder, who was researching fluid balance during surgery, blood chemistry, and transfusions. During the last year and a half of his fellowship, Drew also filled a vacancy as a surgical resident, honing both his surgical and teaching skills. He still found time to court Minnie Lenore Robbins, whom he married on September 23, 1939.

Drew's dissertation, "Banked Blood," was completed in April, 1940. The use of stored blood for transfusions dated back to 1835, but the practice was not widespread until Russian scientists began to follow it in the 1930's. Drew's dissertation compiled all the existing knowledge on the subject and added the results of his and Scudder's research at Columbia.

## World War II Service

After receiving a doctor of science in medicine degree from Columbia in June, 1940, Drew returned to Howard as an assistant professor of surgery and a surgeon at Freedmen's Hospital. Three months later, WORLD WAR II interrupted Drew's Howard career when he was asked to become medical supervisor of the Blood for Britain program. During a six-month leave of absence from Howard, Drew performed valuable service that would lead to the public's perception that Drew was responsible for developing blood plasma for transfusion.

In 1940 Great Britain was under attack by Germany and desperately needed blood supplies to cope with war casualties. Plasma (blood fluid from which the red corpuscles are removed) was best suited for use in emergency conditions. Plasma could be stored for longer periods of time than whole blood and could be used regardless of a patient's blood type. Several organizations, including the

Blood Transfusion Betterment Association (BTBA) and the American Red Cross, established the Blood for Britain program to supply the British with plasma from American blood donors.

As medical director, Drew made no new contributions in the field of blood-plasma research. What he did do was to synthesize all existing knowledge on the topic and apply it in a practical way to create a workable program for gathering and processing blood supplies. His ideas became the model for national blood-bank programs. To ensure sterility, Drew had mobile units collect blood donations and refrigerate them for processing at one central laboratory. Within a month, Great Britain was receiving sterile plasma in sufficient quantities.

### U.S. Blood-Collection Program

By January, 1941, when the British were able to provide their own blood supplies, the need for a national blood-collection program for the United States was recognized by the BTBA, the National Research Council, the Red Cross, and the armed forces. Drew was asked to stay in New York to help establish such a program.

Racism placed Drew in a peculiar position. The most knowledgeable scientists in the field of blood research knew that all human blood is essentially the same. Yet there was a widespread perception that "black" blood was different from "white" blood. The armed services insisted that only white donors be accepted for any blood to be used by American troops. Drew himself, though an expert in the field and the medical supervisor of the program, therefore could not be a donor.

In March, 1941, Drew resigned his position to return to Howard University. Some people

Blood-typing pioneer Charles R. Drew in the late 1940's. *(Associated Publishers, Inc.)*

have asserted that he quit to protest the racist policies of the program. No record exists, however, of his ever claiming such a motivation. The best evidence is that he returned to Howard because he wanted to become chief of surgery, because his leave of absence had expired, and because his job in New York was essentially completed. Drew frequently stated that surgery was his major interest. In April, 1941, he returned to Howard and was certified by the American Board of Surgery (ABS).

### Surgery and Teaching

Drew took the examinations for certification at the Johns Hopkins University. During his oral exam, he was asked about fluid balance in the human body. Overwhelmed by Drew's sophisticated answer, his examiner called in other surgeons to help in the evaluation, but none knew as much on the subject as Drew. Thus, he was certified, and six months later he became the first African American surgeon to be appointed as an examiner by the ABS.

For the remainder of his life, Drew stayed at Howard, focusing on surgery and teaching more than on research. He was an exceptional teacher. In December, 1948, the first class of residents he trained went to Johns Hopkins for examination by the ABS. Drew fretted over how well his students would do against white students from more privileged backgrounds—until he learned that the top two scorers were his students.

### Honors

Drew received numerous honors, including the SPINGARN MEDAL of the NATIONAL ASSOCIATION FOR THE ADVANCEMENT OF COLORED PEOPLE (NAACP) and an appointment as surgical consultant to the surgeon general of the United States. Nevertheless, he was never allowed to join the American Medical Association (AMA). The AMA left membership decisions up to its local chapters, and the District of Columbia chapter was one of many that refused to accept African American members. Drew continued to seek admission to both the AMA and the American College of Surgeons (ACS) without success. A year and a half after his death, the ACS issued Drew a posthumous certificate of membership.

Like his plasma work, Drew's death has been the topic of much comment. Both became sources of myth despite the efforts of family and friends to correct false rumors. Early in the morning of Saturday, April 1, 1950, Drew and three other doctors were on their way to a free clinic in Tuskegee, Alabama. Near Burlington, North Carolina, the group's car ran off the road, and Drew was seriously injured. Rushed to the nearest hospital, he received prompt and competent care, but he was too

critically injured to survive. Rumors began that Drew was refused admittance to a white hospital and was allowed to bleed to death. Though refuted by all witnesses and by Drew's wife and children, the story persisted and even appeared in reference works. It might, however, be argued that he was nevertheless a casualty of racism. For it was due at least partly to the fact that African Americans could not count on finding overnight accommodations while traveling that Drew and his associates were undertaking a dangerous all-night automobile trip.

*—Linda O. McMurry*
*See also:* Medicine; Health care professionals.

Suggested Readings:

Hardwick, Richard. *Charles Richard Drew: Pioneer in Blood Research.* New York: Charles Scribner's Sons, 1967.

Jenkins, Edward S. *To Fathom More: African American Scientists and Inventors.* Lanham, Md.: University Press of America, 1996.

Lichello, Robert. *Pioneer in Blood Plasma: Dr. Charles Richard Drew.* New York: Julian Messner, 1968.

Love, Spencie. *One Blood: The Death and Resurrection of Charles R. Drew.* Chapel Hill, N.C.: The University of North Carolina Press, 1996.

Mahone-Lonesome, Robyn. *Charles Drew.* New York: Chelsea House, 1990.

Wynes, Charles E. *Charles Richard Drew: The Man and the Myth.* Urbana: University of Illinois Press, 1988.

**Driskell, David C.** (b. June 7, 1931, Eatonton, Georgia): Painter, art historian, art consultant, and educator. A professor of art and former department chair at the University of Maryland, Driskell saw his artworks displayed in many public and private collections. He served as curator for several significant art exhibitions and wrote several art catalogs and

Artist David C. Driskell in his Maryland studio. *(© Roy Lewis Archives)*

art history books, including *Two Centuries of Black American Art* (1976). His writings emphasize traditional African art and the works of black American artists. Among his responsibilities, Driskell served as a consultant to the National Endowment for the Arts, to museums, and to private individuals. Driskell's artwork, writings, and speeches call for greater recognition of black art in America.

*See also:* Painters and illustrators; Visual arts.

**Du Bois, Shirley Graham** (Shirley Graham; November 11, 1896, Evansville, Indiana—March 27, 1977, Beijing, China): Writer and THEATER figure. Shirley Graham Du Bois married CIVIL RIGHTS organizer and writer W. E. B. DU BOIS late in her life, so she was known as Shirley Graham for most of her career.

The Graham family had a legacy of resistance which characterized much of Du Bois's later life. Shirley was born in her great-grandfather's house, which had once served as a station on the UNDERGROUND RAILROAD for runaway slaves on their way to Canada. Her

father, the Reverend David A. Graham, was an AFRICAN METHODIST EPISCOPAL CHURCH minister. He and his wife, Etta Bell Graham, reared their family in varied parsonages in the United States and, later, in western Africa. After graduating from Lewis and Clark High School in Spokane, Washington, Du Bois went on to business college. After marrying Shadrach T. McCannes in 1921, she worked at various jobs, including clerk, organist, and singer, while simultaneously caring for the couple's two sons. The couple was divorced in the mid-1920's, leaving Du Bois as the primary caregiver of the children.

In 1926 Du Bois studied music at the Sorbonne in Paris, France. Her additional exposure to Senegalese music and that of blacks from Martinique who had emigrated to Paris left an African imprint upon her later musical compositions. In the early 1930's, after having taught music for two years upon her return to the United States, Du Bois pursued her bachelor's degree at OBERLIN COLLEGE. While at Oberlin, she launched her career by writing the musical *Tom-Tom*, which soon was expanded into a sixteen-scene black opera depicting the African American journey from Africa to the New World and presented at the Cleveland Stadium in 1932. Du Bois continued her studies at Oberlin, completing her A.B. in 1934 and her M.A. in 1935.

Accepting the supervisory position of the Chicago Federal Theater in 1936, Graham revitalized the black unit by directing, writing, and designing productions that brought the company national recognition. Awarded a Julius Rosenwald Fellowship for creative writing, Graham spent two years (1938-1940) at the Yale School of Drama, where she wrote five plays, all exploring racial themes: *Dust to Earth, It's Morning, Track Thirteen, I Gotta Home,* and *Elijah's Raven.*

Du Bois was hired as a theater director at the Army camp at Fort Huachuca in Arizona. She directed theatrical productions and founded a camp magazine, and she was soon embroiled in the evident racial discrimination against black soldiers at the base. She challenged these social injustices on a number of levels, by writing protest letters to Washington and speaking out against discrimination. Labeled a troublemaker, she was dismissed in 1942. She moved to New York City and worked as a field secretary for the NATIONAL ASSOCIATION FOR THE ADVANCEMENT OF COLORED PEOPLE (NAACP). She began writing biographies for adolescent readers, including *Dr. George Washington Carver: Scientist* (1944, with George D. Lipscomb) and *Paul Robeson: Citizen of the World* (1946). *There Was Once a Slave: The Heroic Story of Frederick Douglass* (1947) won her the Julian Messner Award. She was also a founding editor of *Freedomways* magazine.

Although she had been a political activist in the 1940's, her career decidedly was eclipsed when she married W. E. B. Du Bois, the crusading civil rights fighter, in 1951. Their marriage followed his indictment in that same year for his participation in the world peace movement. In 1961, at the invitation of President Kwame Nkrumah, the couple moved to Ghana, where W. E. B. Du Bois died in 1963. Forced to flee Ghana after a coup in 1967, Du Bois relocated to Cairo, Egypt. She made several trips to China to support leftist causes and to seek treatment of the cancer that caused her death in 1977.

**Du Bois, W. E. B.** (February 23, 1868, Great Barrington, Massachusetts—August 27, 1963, Accra, Ghana): Sociologist and CIVIL RIGHTS leader. William Edward Burghardt Du Bois was born in 1868, at the same moment an effort was being made to impeach President Andrew Johnson. He died in 1963 as the MARCH ON WASHINGTON was marking a new stage in the African American struggle for equality. Born and reared in a small, mostly white New England town, Du Bois attended FISK UNIVERSITY, a historically black institution in Nashville, Tennessee, as an undergraduate. He later attended the University of Berlin and Harvard University, from which he received his doctorate. His Harvard dissertation, later published as *The Suppression of the African Slave Trade to the United States* (1896), underscored the importance of the slave trade in the development of the U.S. economy and of capitalism generally.

*Scholarship and Writing*

Du Bois was a heralded sociologist and historian. In the former field, he engaged in pioneering research that led to the publication of *The Philadelphia Negro: A Social Study* (1899) and other works on African American culture. His best-known historical work, however, was *Black Reconstruction* (1935). In this groundbreaking work, Du Bois set out to correct the historical record, which to that point mostly had portrayed the post-CIVIL WAR period known as RECONSTRUCTION as a time of African American misrule, scandal, and corruption. On the contrary, Du Bois demonstrated, Reconstruction was a period of democracy, reform, and wealth redistribution. Du Bois also wrote *The World and Africa* (1947) and other works seeking to establish a more accurate history of the African continent.

In addition to his work as a scholar, Du Bois was a novelist and a skilled essayist. His famous 1903 work, *The Souls of Black Folk,* is a complex exploration of philosophy and ideas, and its analysis of the psychology of African Americans continues to be praised. Du Bois was also a noted memoirist; *The Autobiography of W. E. B. DuBois: A Soliloquy on Viewing*

*My Life from the Last Decade of Its First Century* (1968) is still viewed as a major literary and philosophical work.

### The NAACP

As a political figure, Du Bois initially came to prominence because of his conflict with the policy of ACCOMMODATION to segregation that was espoused by Booker T. WASHINGTON. Du Bois was of the opinion that segregation should be challenged, not accepted, and he disagreed publicly with the politically powerful Washington. The conflict led Du Bois to form the NIAGARA MOVEMENT, a militant forerunner of the NATIONAL ASSOCIATION FOR THE Advancement of Colored People (NAACP), in 1905. Though others were involved in the organization of the Niagara Movement, Du Bois came to symbolize the opposition to Washington's approach.

On February 12, 1909, the centennial of the birth of Abraham Lincoln, the NAACP was founded by a group of socialists and radicals that included Du Bois. It was not merely opposition to Washington that sparked the group's formation: Race riots that had recently scarred African American communities as diverse as ATLANTA, GEORGIA, and Springfield, Illinois, also gave impetus to the organization. It was not surprising that socialists and radicals would be involved with organizing the NAACP (Du Bois had joined the Socialist Party at about this time); notions of black inferiority were widely accepted, and agitation for social equality of the races was considered subversive. Du Bois became the editor of the NAACP's journal,

W. E. B. Du Bois. *(Library of Congress)*

THE CRISIS, which quickly established itself as the leading organ of African American opinion. Under Du Bois's leadership, *The Crisis* commented widely on domestic and international affairs, particularly the plight of colonized Africa languishing under European domination. *The Crisis* also was prominent in fomenting the HARLEM RENAISSANCE, the 1920's burst of creativity by African American artists and writers.

Du Bois's initial tenure with the NAACP came to an end in 1934, when he came into conflict with other NAACP leaders over efforts promoting African American solidarity that some interpreted as a form of self-segregation.

Du Bois left the organization he founded and returned to ATLANTA UNIVERSITY to continue writing and research.

He stayed at Atlanta University until 1944, when the school's administration asked him to retire because of his age. At the time, Du Bois was seventy-six, but he was of the opinion that the request was politically motivated. Du Bois then decided to accept an offer from the NAACP to return to the group's headquarters in New York City to help coordinate the NAACP's work in the international arena, especially the question of the decolonization of Africa.

### Cold War Controversy

After World War II, Du Bois became increasingly critical of the world's leading powers for their failure to free their colonial dependencies fully. His criticisms of U.S. foreign policy also intensified, and he moved more and more to the political Left. The onset of the Cold War and its domestic companion of accelerated anticommunism, though, made Du Bois's political leanings unpopular.

The change in atmosphere worsened Du Bois's already strained relations with NAACP leaders Roy WILKINS and Walter WHITE. Before the Cold War, these personal differences had been overshadowed by a political accord. In 1948, however, as the political climate was changing, Du Bois was fired from the NAACP. He had refused to go along with the leadership's support for Harry S Truman's presidential campaign. Du Bois was an avid supporter of Henry Wallace's third-party campaign for the White House on the Progressive Party ticket. Moreover, he sought to draft a petition bringing human rights violations against African Americans before the United Nations. NAACP board member Eleanor Roosevelt objected strenuously to this initiative, as did White and Wilkins. Du Bois refused to back down and was fired. In 1951 Du Bois married writer and activist Shirley Graham.

### Pan-African and International Activism

After leaving the NAACP, Du Bois helped to found the Peace Information Center, which distributed the antinuclear Stockholm Peace Appeal and campaigned against the KOREAN WAR. This activity led to his being indicted as an agent of an unnamed foreign power—implied to be the Soviet Union. Du Bois toured the country raising funds for his trial and speaking out on the issues that had led to his indictment. Du Bois was acquitted, so the then-octogenarian managed to escape spending his final years in prison.

Du Bois began working closely with Paul ROBESON, the noted activist, singer, and actor, in the COUNCIL ON AFRICAN AFFAIRS (CAA) after leaving the NAACP. The CAA, founded in 1937, was the major organization in the United States pushing for decolonization of Africa and lobbying against apartheid in South Africa. The CAA raised funds for liberation movements, sponsored conferences, published a newsletter, and remained in close contact with Nelson Mandela, Walter Sisulu, Kwame Nkrumah, Jomo Kenyatta, and other African leaders. Yet the CAA soon ran afoul of the U.S. government, which charged the group with being a COMMUNIST PARTY front. The CAA was subjected to investigations and close scrutiny and finally was run out of business in the mid-1950's.

Through most of the 1950's, Du Bois, along with Robeson and other activists, was denied a U.S. passport. Finally, in the late 1950's, Du Bois was accorded a passport, and he traveled to China and Eastern Europe. Despite—or perhaps because of—the attitudes of Cold War America, Du Bois did not renounce socialism; indeed, his commitment to it seemed to heighten. He spoke glowingly of socialism during meetings with Mao Tse-tung (Mao Zedong) and other leaders perceived as hostile to the United States. In 1961 he joined the Communist Party of the United States, but shortly thereafter he left the country for good.

Du Bois emigrated to Ghana, which was then under the leadership of his friend Kwame Nkrumah. There he attempted to coordinate the publication of a massive encyclopedia of African culture until he died in 1963.

—Gerald Horne

*See also:* Africa and African American activism; Du Bois, Shirley Graham.

Suggested Readings:

Bell, Bernard W., Emily Grosholz, and James B. Stewart, eds. *W. E. B. Du Bois on Race and Culture: Philosophy, Politics, and Poetics.* New York: Routledge, 1996.

Byerman, Keith E. *Seizing the Word: History, Art, and Self in the Work of W. E. B. Du Bois.* Athens: University of Georgia Press, 1994.

Du Bois, W. E. B. *The Autobiography of W. E. B. Du Bois: A Soliloquy on Viewing My Life from the Last Decade of Its First Century.* New York: International Publishing, 1968.

———. *The Correspondence of W. E. B. Du Bois.* Edited by Herbert Aptheker. 3 vols. Amherst: University of Massachusetts Press, 1997.

———. *The World of W. E. B. Du Bois: A Quotation Sourcebook.* Edited by Meyer Weinberg. New York: Greenwood Press, 1992.

Horne, Gerald. *Black and Red: W. E. B. Du Bois and the Afro-American Response to the Cold War, 1944-1963.* Albany: State University of New York Press, 1986.

Katz, Michael B., and Thomas J. Sugrue, eds. *W. E. B. DuBois, Race, and the City: The Philadelphia Negro and Its Legacy.* Philadelphia: University of Pennsylvania Press, 1998.

Lewis, David L. *W.E.B. Du Bois: Biography of a Race, 1868-1919.* New York: Henry Holt, 1993.

Pobi-Asamani, Kwadwo O. *W. E. B. Du Bois: His Contributions to Pan-Africanism.* San Bernardino, Calif.: Borgo Press, 1993.

Reed, Adolph L. *W. E. B. Du Bois and American Political Thought: Fabianism and the Color Line.* New York: Oxford University Press, 1997.

Zamir, Shamoon. *Dark Voices: W. E. B. Du Bois and American Thought, 1888-1903.* Chicago: University of Chicago Press, 1995.

**Dudley, Edward Richard** (b. March 11, 1911, South Boston, Virginia): Political appointee. Dudley was educated at Johnson C. Smith University, receiving his bachelor of science degree in 1932. He received his law degree from St. John's University Law School in 1941 and was admitted to the New York State bar that same year. Dudley served as assistant special counsel to the NATIONAL ASSOCIATION FOR THE ADVANCEMENT OF COLORED PEOPLE (NAACP) from 1943 to 1945 and again from 1947 to 1948. He was appointed as U.S. ambassador to LIBERIA and served from 1948 to 1953. Dudley later served as the borough president of Manhattan from 1961 to 1965. He was appointed as an administrative judge of the New York City Criminal Court in 1967, became an administrative judge of the New York supreme court in 1971, and retired from the bench in 1985.

*See also:* Judges.

**Dunbar, Paul Laurence** (June 27, 1872, Dayton, Ohio—February 9, 1906, Dayton, Ohio): Poet. Dunbar was one of the first African American poets to become nationally recognized. As a boy, he was seen as a black prodigy in a white world. The only African American in his high school class, he was popular, achieving positions of editor-in-chief of the school paper and president of the school literary society. After graduation, Dunbar had to take one of the few jobs available to a young man of his race, operating an elevator.

While Dunbar worked, he continued to write poetry. By 1893 he had saved enough money to publish fifty-six poems in a slim volume entitled *Oak and Ivy.* Two years later, he put together a second book of verse, *Majors*

Paul Laurence Dunbar. *(Library of Congress)*

Dunbar's need to survive in the white literary world led him to go against his creative impulse. He wrote DIALECT PO-ETRY and uninspired prose (articles, short stories, and novels) to please this audience. He always believed that his voice was truer and that his emotions were purer in his Standard English poems. Despite his popular success, Dunbar was haunted by disappointment, believing that his greatest poetic gift was not properly appreciated.

When Dunbar succumbed to tuberculosis at age thirty-three, he was considered by the American public as the dean of black poets. Included in his later poetic works were *Lyrics of Love and Laughter* (1903), *Lyrics of Sunshine and Shadow* (1905), and the posthumous *Complete Poems* (1913). He produced four novels and four volumes of short stories over the course of his career.

*See also:* Literature.

*and Minors*, which he also paid to have published. William Dean Howells reviewed this second book in *Harper's Weekly*. The favorable commentary from the illustrious white writer served to verify Dunbar's talent. Howells's praise encouraged Dunbar to take the best poems from his first two books and reissue them under the title *Lyrics of Lowly Life* (1896). Howells wrote a preface for this book, helping it to succeed in the white world of letters. As a result of this book, Dunbar was afforded the means to pursue writing full-time. He was in demand by the most prestigious white magazines, which clamored for his articles, stories, and poems, which he turned out in great volume. In 1898, Dunbar wed activist and poet Alice Moore. Their marriage ended four years later.

**Dunbar Nelson, Alice Moore** (July 19, 1875, New Orleans, Louisiana—September 18, 1935, Philadelphia, Pennsylvania): Journalist, short story writer, poet, literary critic, and teacher. Dunbar Nelson was also a political and social activist.

At age fifteen Alice Moore entered the teacher training program at Straight University in New Orleans; she later earned her M.A. at Cornell University. She published *Violets and Other Tales*, a collection of stories, poems, and essays, in 1895; it was followed in 1899 by *The Goodness of St. Rocque, and Other Stories*. She also edited two volumes of speeches by African Americans. Her diary, *Give Us Each Day*, edited by Gloria T. Hull in 1984, is an intimate portrait of her life. She married poet Paul Laurence DUNBAR in 1898, but after four turbulent years they separated. After a brief second marriage, her third marriage, to journalist Robert J. Nelson, lasted until her death.

Dunbar Nelson's columns in both black and white periodicals forcefully advocated racial equality and women's rights. A friend of many prominent figures of the HARLEM RENAISSANCE, she influenced many younger writers and artists. In Wilmington, Delaware, and Philadelphia, she was an outspoken member of many political organizations. For three years she was executive secretary of the American Inter-Racial Peace Committee, a Quaker antiwar organization. A teacher all her life, Dunbar Nelson was best known as a poet and as the widow of Paul Laurence Dunbar. More recent critics also have high regard for her short fiction.

*—Marjorie Podolsky*

**Duncan, Todd** (February 12, 1903, Danville, Kentucky—February 28, 1998, Washington, D.C.): Opera singer and actor. After obtaining a master's degree from Columbia University Teachers' College, baritone Todd Duncan began teaching voice at HOWARD UNIVERSITY, in Washington, D.C., in 1931. He made Washington his home for the rest of his life. Duncan attained fame in 1935 when he premiered the role of Porgy in the Broadway musical *Porgy and Bess*. He performed the role again in revivals in 1937 and 1942. In 1945 Duncan became the first African American singer to perform with the New York City Opera. That same year he retired from Howard because of his busy schedule.

Duncan traveled the world as a concert singer, giving recitals in more than fifty countries. He also appeared in a few films, including *Syncopation* (1942) and *Unchained* (1955), and maintained a long and influential career as a private voice teacher. Duncan won the 1950 Critics Award for best male performance in a Broadway musical; fifteen years later, he sang at President Lyndon B. Johnson's 1965 inaugural. Duncan's other stage and opera performances included roles in *Cabin in the Sky*, *Lost in the Stars*, *Cavalleria Rusticana*, *Pagliacci*, and *Carmen*. His success encouraged many African Americans to seek careers in the performing arts.

*See also:* Classical and operatic music; Theater.

**Duncanson, Robert** (1817 or 1821, New York State—December 21, 1872, Detroit, Michigan): Painter. The first African American artist to earn international recognition, Duncanson is best remembered for his romantic landscapes. His art career began in 1841 in Cincinnati, OHIO, where wealthy patrons commissioned him to paint portraits, murals, and land-

Robert Duncanson's *Blue Hole, Little Miami River. (National Archives)*

scapes. The Anti-Slavery League sponsored Duncanson's European travels, helping him to gain the attention of art connoisseurs abroad.

*See also:* Painters and illustrators; Visual arts.

**Dunham, Katherine** (b. June 22, 1910, Chicago, Illinois): Dancer and choreographer. Katherine Dunham, an internationally known choreographer, teacher, and anthropologist, introduced and popularized Afro-Caribbean DANCE throughout the world. Her works include *Bal Négre, Choros, L'Ag'Ya, Shango,* and *Rites de Passage.* Throughout her professional life, she was involved with integrating African and West Indian dance forms with cultural anthropology and exhibiting the uses of dance in ameliorating the oppressive conditions of African American and African diasporic peoples. Drawing on her research into the experiences of eighteenth-century Haitian revolutionaries, she focused on the liberating and revolutionary aspects of Afro-Caribbean dance.

One scholar calleed Dunham's use of dance a means of communicating an "alternative ethos . . . to express dissent." Believing that the arts can turn back repression, Dunham maintained that it is necessary for dancers to know the history and culture of the communities out of which they come in order to understand their dancing and its potential to enhance the community. Thus, though Dunham's dance theater and choreography is high art, it also has an important social and political function.

According to Dunham, performers are to be among and of the community rather than detached from it, since their work contains an educative potential important for the survival of all. An important aspect of Dunham's aesthetic, therefore, is self-mastery and empowerment. Of herself, she once said, "I am not a dancer, I am not an ethnologist. I am an evangelist."

*Youth and Education*

Dunham's father was a traveling salesman who later owned a dry-cleaning business. Dunham's mother died when Katherine was very young, and Katherine's father remarried; Katherine's father and stepmother reared her and her six brothers and sisters in Joliet, Illinois.

Dunham received her bachelor's, master's, and doctoral degrees from the University of Chicago in anthropology, specializing in dance. She was introduced to the field of anthropology by Robert Redfield, who directed her toward seeking African origins of American dance. She continued graduate study with another well-known anthropologist, Melville HERSKOVITS, the head of the African Studies Department at Northwestern University, where Dunham also studied. Herskovits, whose own research was seminal in locating African survivalisms in the culture of blacks in the United States, sponsored her for a travel fellowship from the Rosenwald Foundation, which she used to go to the Caribbean and WEST INDIES in 1935 for field work. Based on that research trip, she wrote her first book, *Katherine Dunham's Journey to Accompong* (1946), about the MAROONS (former slaves who escaped into the Blue Mountains) of JAMAICA. In 1947 she published another book, based on subsequent research in HAITI, on the influence of Haitian culture and history on dance. In addition to her anthropological studies, Dunham studied dance with Mark Turbyfill and Ludmila Speranzera, who taught her ballet and modern dance, respectively. She made her dancing debut in 1933 in the ballet *La Guiablesse.*

During Franklin D. Roosevelt's presidency, Dunham worked for the Works Progress Administration as a leader of the Federal Theatre Project. Her ballet *L'Ag'Ya,* based on a fighting dance from Martinique, was accepted by the project and was performed in 1936 in Chicago. A year later, with fifteen dancers, she established her first ensemble company while also serving as director of the New York Labor Stage. She also met her future husband, John Pratt, a costume and set designer and painter. They were married in 1941, following her divorce from her first husband, Jordis McCoo.

### Dance Innovations

Based on her research in both Afro-Caribbean dance and cultural anthropology, Dunham perfected a new dance technique called "dance-isolation," which involves the movement of one part of the body while other parts are kept stationary. Her work also included a considerable element of theatricality, which has been both praised and criticized and which has sometimes been called "primitive"; such criticism perhaps stems from a misunderstanding of what Dunham called her "study of primitive rhythms in dance with percussion as a base." Dunham's philosophy of dance suggests the primal in the sense that she believes everyone needs movement, as in dance, to live. She once said:

Portrait of Katherine Dunham taken by Carl Van Vechten. *(Library of Congress)*

> Dance can free people from some of their oppressions. Just by using the body in its rhythmic patterns, it heightens circulation. Then if you work hard enough, so that water is running off you, there is a purifying process in dancing.

In addition to her career as a performer, Dunham was a teacher. In 1938 she ran a dance school in Chicago, and from 1945 to 1955 she operated the School of Dance in New York City. She gave as her reason for training other dancers her desire "To attain a status in the dance world that will give to the Negro dance student the courage really to study. . . . And to take *our* dance out of the burlesque—to make it a more dignified art."

### Post-Performance Career

Dunham gave her last dance performance in 1965, at the famed APOLLO THEATER in HARLEM, New York, but her career in the arts was far from over. She became the director of the Performing Arts Training Center, which she established at Southern Illinois University in East St. Louis, where she made her home. There, she put into effect her principles relating to the social uses of the dance form. Through her work at the center, she came in contact with the young people of the city, including members of gangs, and she addressed the social and urban ills that confront them and her.

Dunham interpreted the phenomenon of

BREAK DANCING, which started in the inner cities, as an example of appropriate and ameliorating socialization through the arts, harnessing energy in constructive ways when it could be unleashed negatively. She viewed this in the context of the dance of the Haitian revolutionary era, which was, she perceived, a unifying element and an "expression of dissent." When she taught dance to senior citizens in pain from arthritis and the afflictions of aging, it was to show them how to have control once more over their lives by overcoming pain and isolation through dance movements.

### Awards and Activism

Dunham's numerous awards and honors include Kennedy Center Honors (1983) and the Scripps American Dance Festival Award (1986). She mentored the Women's Honorary Scientific Fraternity at the University of Chicago and was a member of the Royal Society of Anthropology in London. Dunham had also become a Mambo, or high priestess, of Voodun (VOODOO), an African-derived religion widely practiced in Haiti. In 1966 Dunham served as cultural adviser to the president of Senegal. Her involvement in international affairs continued in the 1990's. Dunham, who had a home in Haiti and a spiritual connection to the country and its people, used her professional reputation as a culture-bearer and artist to protest the forced repatriation of Haitian refugees by the U.S. government. In 1992 Dunham went on a hunger strike, declaring it her intention to remain on her strike until the refugees were allowed to remain in the United States. When it became clear that the U.S. government policy of returning the refugees would not be changed, however, others persuaded Dunham to end her hunger strike, which had lasted more than forty days.

—*Nancy Elizabeth Fitch*
*See also:* African music and dance.

Suggested Readings:

Aschenbrenner, Joyce. *Katherine Dunham: Reflections on the Social and Political Contexts of Afro-American Dance.* New York: CORD, 1981.

Beckford, Ruth. *Katherine Dunham: A Biography.* New York: Marcel Dekker, 1979.

Coe, Robert. "Katherine Dunham and Her People." In *Dance in America.* New York: E. P. Dutton, 1985.

Dunham, Katherine. *A Touch of Innocence: Memoirs of Childhood.* Chicago: University of Chicago Press, 1994.

Harnan, Terry. *African Rhythm, American Dance: A Biography of Katherine Dunham.* New York: Alfred A. Knopf, 1974.

Wilkerson, Isabel. "A Grand Dame Fasts for Haitians and Suffering City Responds." *The New York Times* (March 8, 1992): A12.

**Durham, Eddie** (August 19, 1906, San Marcos, Texas—March 6, 1987, New York, New York): Trombonist, guitarist, and arranger. Durham was among the first musicians to perform on electric guitar. He developed a reputation in the Southwest, having made musical contributions to the Kansas City JAZZ scene. His early musical activity included performances with his brother as part of the Durham Brothers Band, which played in minstrel shows. Durham performed with Jimmie LUNCEFORD and worked as well with Bennie MOTEN between 1929 and 1933. Durham also toured with the Blue Devils, led by Walter Page.

As an arranger, Durham was associated with Willie Bryant after relocating to New York City in 1934. Durham was responsible for arranging "Pigeon Walk," "Lunceford Special," and "Blues in the Groove" for Jimmie Lunceford. For Count BASIE, he arranged such compositions as "Out the Window," "Topsy," and "Time Out." In 1938 he recorded "Good Mornin' Blues" with the Kansas City Five and "Way Down Yonder in New Orleans" with the

Kansas City Six. Most notably, Durham worked with the big bands of Lunceford and Basie during the late 1930's. Durham's arranging talents were also used by such bandleaders as Glenn Miller and Artie Shaw. For the Glenn Miller Orchestra in 1939, Durham arranged "Slip Horn Jive," "Glen Island Special," and "Wham." Durham demonstrated the versatility of the African American jazz artist who not only performed but also arranged for both black and white bands.

As a leader, Durham was involved in the formation of an all-female orchestra and other types of ensembles. In the late 1960's, he performed with Buddy Tate and was later associated with the Harlem Blues and Jazz Band as well as the Countsmen. As a recording artist, Durham worked with Eddie Barefield and can be heard on the album *Eddie Barefield* (1973). In 1973 he recorded an album in his own name, *Eddie Durham* (1973). As a leader, he recorded *Blue Bone* (1981).

**Du Sable, Jean Baptiste Pointe** (1745, St. Marc, Saint-Dominque [now Haiti]—1818, St. Charles, Missouri): Founder of the city of CHICAGO, ILLINOIS. Details of Du Sable's life prior to 1779 are not well documented. Du Sable was the son of a French sailor and a slave who was born in Africa. He, like many free people on Haiti, may have been educated in Paris. It is believed that he worked in his father's business in NEW ORLEANS, LOUISIANA, in the 1760's.

The first written information about Du Sable is a 1779 report by Colonel Arent de Peyster, a British officer in charge of the area that now includes Chicago. De Peyster detained Du Sable on suspicion of treason, believing that he was acting on behalf of the French. Du Sable escaped but was arrested again.

Du Sable impressed his captors, so much so that the British governor, Patrick Sinclair, re-

leased him and placed him in charge of a settlement on the St. Clair River, as liaison between Native Americans and white officials. Du Sable remained there until 1784, when he returned to what is now Chicago. Probably sometime in the 1770's, Du Sable had built the first house on the banks of what is now called the Chicago River. He had established a permanent settlement there by 1790.

While in Chicago (then called Eschicagou), he built a trading business. He had built several trading posts in the area over the previous decades. His Chicago trading post included a log house of almost 900 square feet in area, a bakehouse, a dairy, a smokehouse, a poultry

The site on which Jean Baptiste Pointe Du Sable built Chicago's first house was designated a National Historic Landmark in 1976. *(Arkent Archive)*

house, a stable, a barn, and perhaps more buildings. He married Catherine, a Potawatomi Indian, in 1788. They had two children, a son, Jean Baptiste, Jr., and a daughter, Suzanne. Du Sable at one time stood for election as chief of the Indian tribes in the Mackinac area. His defeat may have influenced him to sell his holdings in Chicago after sixteen years or so of residence there.

Real estate records indicate that he probably lived near or in St. Charles, Missouri, from 1805 to 1814. He transferred a house, lot, and property to a granddaughter, Eulalie Derais, in June, 1813. He was almost penniless when he died, even though he had sold his Chicago property for $1,200, at that time a considerable amount of money.

In 1912 a plaque was placed on a building at the corner of Pine and Kinzie Streets in Chicago, indicating that Du Sable had built the first house in the city at that spot. Chicago has a Du Sable High School, and Du Sable was one of eight Illinoisians chosen to be depicted on the frieze of the Illinois Centennial Building in 1965. The site of his home was designated a National Historic Landmark on May 11, 1976. *See also:* Exploration of North America; Frontier Society; Urbanization.

**Dutch West India Company:** Trading company founded in 1621. The company was chartered by the government of the Netherlands and was formed by various Dutch merchants. It was given trading and colonizing privileges in the West, particularly in the Americas, Africa, and the West Indies.

In the fifteenth century, the Portuguese were the first Europeans actively involved in trade on the West African coast. By the seventeenth century, the Dutch had joined the Portuguese in West Africa, along with the French, English, Danes, and Swedes. Dutch merchants gradually became more knowledgeable about commerce and eventually emerged as the most commercially efficient in trading. The Dutch West India Company was designed to compete with Spain and Portugal for economic power in the various colonies.

The Dutch followed the Portuguese pattern in West Africa and established permanent settlements along its shores. As a result, Dutch merchants destroyed the Portuguese monopoly and took over trading in coastal West Africa. The Dutch West India Company was granted a monopoly on trade with West Africa and the Americas, and with the area between them. In turn, merchants immediately gave financial support to the Swedish African Company in attempts to weaken the Dutch company's monopoly. The Dutch West India Company continued to carry out trade successfully between Europe, West Africa, and the Americas until 1794, when it was dissolved after the French invasion of the United Provinces.

The Dutch West India Company accrued most of its wealth from slave trading, exporting millions of slaves from Africa in the seventeenth century. It was the Dutch West India Company that brought the first African slaves to the French colonies founded in the Americas. It supplied many of the slaves in the West Indies and South America.

The Dutch West India Company also founded the New Netherland Colony, in 1623. This colony included parts of present-day New York, New Jersey, Delaware, and Connecticut, and had its capital in New Amsterdam (later New York City). The company built several large plantations and supplied each with slaves. Low rates of Dutch immigration and underinvestment made the colony unable to compete with French and English settlements, and it was ceded to Great Britain in 1667.

**Dyer antilynching bill:** Legislation that went before Congress on April 11, 1921. For years, the NATIONAL ASSOCIATION FOR THE ADVANCEMENT OF COLORED PEOPLE (NAACP) had lobbied for just such legislation because of widespread mistreatment, including beating, shooting, torturing, and LYNCHING, of African Americans, especially in the South. Dyer's bill would have assured "persons within the jurisdiction of every state the equal protection of the laws" and would have punished the crime of lynching. Further, any county where a lynching occurred would be assessed a heavy fine, with part of the payment going into a victims' fund to be delivered to the deceased's relatives.

Many southern congressmen opposed the bill, and some became indignant and used delaying tactics to stop a vote in the House of Representatives. The NAACP, however, organized a massive public relations drive to gather support for the bill. On January 26, 1922, the House passed the bill by a vote of 246 to 101. African American celebrations took place all across the United States, but cynics noted that they were premature.

In November, the Senate Judiciary Committee reported favorably on the antilynching bill. A group of southern senators, however, managed to gain the floor and threatened a filibuster. On December 2, Republican leaders withdrew the Dyer bill. An NAACP lobbyist in Washington, James Weldon JOHNSON, later explained what had happened: Republicans who supported the bill had in effect cleared their consciences but could now throw up their hands in surrender; after all,

the southern Democrats forcefully had put themselves on the record and could shoulder all responsibility for the failure to get the Dyer bill through the Senate.

Regardless, the doomed bill may have had positive consequences. Through the 1920's,

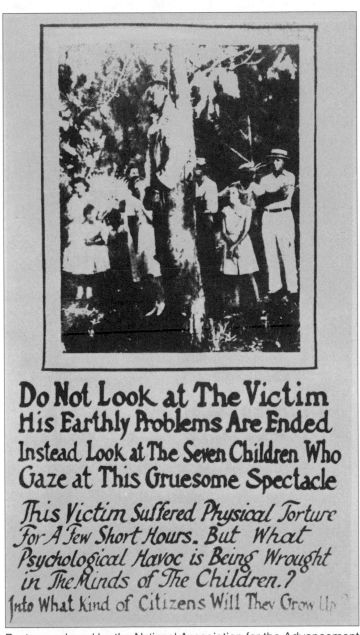

Poster produced by the National Association for the Advancement of Colored People to publicize the horrors of lynching. *(Association for the Study of African-American Life and History)*

lynchings declined in the South because white leaders feared the intervention of the sfederal government, an intervention that would be the first since the RECONSTRUCTION era. To avoid such a dire possibility, many white leaders knew that they must limit the murders of African Americans in the South.
*See also:* Wells, Ida B.

**Dymally, Mervyn** (b. May 12, 1926, Trinidad, British West Indies): CALIFORNIA legislator. A Democrat, Dymally was elected to California's State Assembly in 1962. He became a state senator in 1967, then lieutenant governor of California from 1975 to 1979. He and George L. Brown of COLORADO were the first African Americans elected as state lieutenant governors in the twentieth century. Dymally represented LOS ANGELES in Congress from 1981 to 1992, when he retired. He championed civil rights for Micronesians and Pacific Islanders.
*See also:* Congress members; Politics and government.

# E

**East St. Louis, Illinois:** Predominantly African American city, with a population that was more than 90 percent black in the 1990's. During the last decades of the nineteenth century, East St. Louis grew rapidly as a railroad, meat-packing, and metal-working center. Prior to 1910, it attracted relatively few African American residents. WORLD WAR I changed that, however, and the city's railroads made it a natural destination for southern blacks seeking employment in midwestern industries. As increasing numbers of African Americans poured into the city, white workers reacted negatively. Tensions mounted, and in July, 1917, they burst forth in the worst race riot in American history up to that time. Thirty-nine African Americans and nine white people died in the violence, in which some members of the local police department participated. The EAST ST. LOUIS RIOTS provoked a national outcry, giving the city a negative image that would plague its future.

East St. Louis survived the riots and continued to attract African Americans. During the 1940's and 1950's, the city was at the peak of its prosperity as a rail and meat-packing center. In 1960 its population had reached almost eighty-two thousand, equally divided between blacks and whites. During the 1960's, however, its industries began to decline, and East St. Louis began to experience the urban trends associated with larger cities. WHITE FLIGHT, a declining tax base, a growing poor population, a rising crime rate, and a tradition of fiscal mismanagement that went back to the nineteenth century all contributed to a sense of urban decline. By 1970 the population had fallen to less than seventy thousand.

The city experienced severe fiscal problems. Despite the election of the energetic Carl E. Officer as mayor in 1979, fiscal problems multiplied. By the mid-1980's, the city was almost bankrupt. In 1990, with the city fifty million dollars in debt, the state of Illinois took over its finances. By this time, its population had fallen to just over forty thousand, almost two-thirds of whom were on public aid. Officer had been in office for more than ten years when the election of newcomer Gordon Bush in 1991 raised hopes of a revival. The new mayor cultivated better relations with state and county governments. The primary event that made East St. Louis's revival possible was the fact that the state granted the city a coveted license for newly legalized riverboat gambling.

With tax revenues from the gambling boat, and with a state office still overseeing the city's finances, the city's fiscal situation improved nearly overnight. The city doubled its budget, reduced debt, and cut property taxes. The city quickly put more—and better-equipped—police on the street, reducing the crime rate, bought new fire trucks, and improved other city services. On the other hand, the city still faced serious problems in the late 1990's, and its central areas remained blighted, desolate, and poverty-stricken. Bush won a second four-year term in 1995; he decided not to run for a third, and Debra A. Powell was elected mayor in 1999.

*See also:* Mayors.


**East St. Louis riots:** Two serious riots occurred in EAST ST. LOUIS, ILLINOIS, in July of 1917. The first erupted after a trade union leader led a delegation protesting the employment of African Americans. The precipitating event was a rumor that an African American had murdered a white man. Militia promptly dispersed the rioters.

The second riot was preceded by an incident in which an unidentified automobile sped into the city's black residential section. Its passengers began firing guns, seemingly at random targets. Frightened residents armed themselves and then fired upon a second car, an unmarked police vehicle that had entered the area. The car's two occupants were killed. Rioting again ensued.

The East St. Louis rioting was fueled by police bias and failure to contain disturbances quickly. Police officers actually incited mob violence by parking the bullet-ridden unmarked police vehicle in front of headquarters. The East St. Louis police department numbered only fifty-two officers in a city of about seventy thousand. As a result, militia had to be called in to quell the riot, but efforts were not immediately successful. A militia force of 170 inexperienced men was commanded by a white officer who reportedly refused to call for additional help if mobs "killed nobody but Negroes." A military board of inquiry ultimately did not question militia inaction.

An underlying cause of the riots was African Americans' attempts to gain employment. This was the time of the GREAT MIGRATION, and many African Americans recently had migrated to East St. Louis from the rural South. The city's black population had increased in proportion from 10 percent to 12 percent. Unskilled white workers felt especially threatened by an increasing black presence. Prior to the first July riot, the Aluminum Ore Company labor union lost a strike when black workers replaced the strikers.

Citywide problems also contributed to interracial tensions. In St. Louis, Missouri, population increases had placed stress on housing, public transit, and other urban services. These problems spread to East St. Louis. In addition, white prejudice had resulted in friction when African Americans did not follow the segregated life patterns under which they had lived in the South. Politically, increased tension resulted from black voting, which was perceived to be the deciding factor in several elections.

*See also:* Race riots.

**Ebenezer Baptist Church:** Home church of Martin Luther KING, Jr. Ebenezer Baptist Church in ATLANTA, GEORGIA, has been one of the most prestigious pulpits in the African American religious community since the beginning of the twentieth century. In 1894 King's grandfather, the Reverend Adam Daniel Williams, began with a thirteen-member congregation; he initiated a series of fundraisers and revivals that created a viable and vibrant community of more than a thousand members. A new church was built in 1900, and the present church building was erected in 1922. The charismatic Williams died in 1931 and was replaced by a superb organizer, the Reverend Michael Luther King, later to be known as Martin Luther KING, Sr.

King revolutionized the church's budgetary and fund-raising system and developed new forms of community outreach. The changes revitalized the Ebenezer community, which had declined as a result of the GREAT DEPRESSION. If Williams's accomplishments were impressive, King's were doubly so. King took the community from a membership of two hundred to a Depression peak of more than four thousand. His congregation sent him on a tour of the Holy Land and Europe. On his return, he changed his name to honor the symbolic father of Protestantism, Martin Luther. King had always said that that was the name his father had originally given him.

Martin Luther King, Jr., gave his first sermon at Ebenezer in 1947. Although he would not make Ebenezer his permanent home church until much later, he was, in many ways, always associated with the church. The 1950's were a vital time for Ebenezer. Many prominent African American Atlantans were members, including publisher C. A. Scott and banker Jesse Blayton. King, Sr., negotiated a $150,000 loan in 1956 for yet another expansion of the church. In 1957 one of the first organizing meetings of the SOUTHERN CHRISTIAN LEADERSHIP CONFERENCE (SCLC), the coalition of ministers and churches that was at the forefront of civil rights leadership, was held at Ebenezer. In 1960 Martin Luther King, Jr., became copastor of the church and developed many of his challenging religious and social ideas in Ebenezer sermons. After King's death, the church continued to be an important African American institution in Atlanta. Martin Luther King, Sr., retired as pastor of the church in 1975.

*See also:* Baptists.

Ebenezer Baptist Church in 1968. *(AP/Wide World Photos)*

*Ebony:* Monthly magazine. *Ebony* was launched in 1945 by John H. JOHNSON, the chairman and chief executive officer of JOHNSON PUBLISHING COMPANY. Well-respected author Lerone BENNETT, Jr., served as longtime executive editor. *Ebony* focused on providing an appreciation of the genius, beauty, and potential of African Americans. This focus is in keeping with the ebony for which the magazine was named—a hard, black wood that can be polished to a beautiful metallic luster.

When Johnson published the first issue of the magazine in 1945, he ushered in a new era of journalism in the African American community. The first twenty-five thousand copies of the magazine printed, priced at twenty-five cents each, sold out in hours. Market demand for the first edition of the magazine was so great that Johnson had to print an additional twenty-five thousand copies. The magazine's circulation grew from twenty-five thousand to 2 million; readership also grew, from an estimated 125,000 per issue to 11.9 million per issue.

The magazine covers an array of topics deemed pertinent to people of African descent in the United States and in the rest of the African diaspora. During its first fifty years, *Ebony* successfully chronicled the travails and triumphs of African Americans in economics, politics, arts, humanities, and science. From 1945 to the early 1960's, the magazine not only covered the contributions of African Americans but also chronicled the various laws enforcing segregation in the United States. It presented stories about how American presidents cooperated with African American leaders on CIVIL RIGHTS legislation. It also reported on how the U.S. SUPREME COURT upheld the law on behalf of African Americans and publicized the calls for black power.

From the mid-1960's to the 1970's, *Ebony* was in the forefront in covering the push for civil rights. It showed how the movement was led by a generation of leaders who were educated, articulate, and determined to build on the hard-fought gains of their predecessors. The magazine also reported on how African Americans were playing a larger role in America's cultural activities—from the many talented artists who carried on the traditions of the HARLEM RENAISSANCE to sports teams with outstanding African American athletes. Many African American authors were also interviewed and profiled by the magazine.

In the 1980's and 1990's, *Ebony* reported the sentiments of many African Americans who felt that they were losing ground. The magazine explored, for example, how the Supreme Court was curtailing the effectiveness of AFFIRMATIVE ACTION laws. In 1990 *Ebony* reported that the Department of Education had tried to cut back the number of scholarships that colleges receiving federal funds could give. The magazine presented stories on how African American activists turned their energies to politics to effect change. Articles have also reported on how some African American leaders were moving in the opposite direction, working for separation of the races.

*See also:* Black press; Columnists; *Emerge*; *Jet*; Print journalism; *Sepia*.

**Eckstine, Billy** (b. July 8, 1914, Pittsburgh, Pennsylvania): Singer, trumpeter, valve trombonist, and bandleader. Best known as a fine singer of lush ballads, William Clarence "Billy" Eckstine is most significant as leader of one of the most important bands in JAZZ history. Eckstine was a vocalist with the Earl HINES band from 1939 until 1943, when he gained considerable celebrity with his recordings of "Skylark," "Jelly, Jelly," and "Stormy Monday Blues," the last two of which he cocomposed with Hines. Eckstine established his own band in 1944. He was able to keep it together until 1947 because his suave manner, good looks, and singing ability enabled him to

attract audiences. Although many of the band's numbers featured the leader's singing, including such hits as "A Cottage for Sale," "Prisoner of Love," and "I Surrender, Dear," listeners more concerned with innovative instrumental music than with elegant singing also found much to admire in Eckstine's band.

During the years Eckstine led his band, a musical revolution was taking place. With the end of WORLD WAR II, swing music, which had dominated the 1930's, gave way to modern jazz, known as BEBOP. In its emphasis on new rhythms and harmonies, bebop was more in keeping with the spirit of the time. Eckstine's band was something of an incubator of the new music. The leader employed two of the most adventuresome and accomplished of the younger musicians, saxophonist Charlie PARKER and trumpeter Dizzy GILLESPIE. They were, with a few others, the founding fathers of bebop. Also in the band were trumpeters Fats NAVARRO, Kenny Dorham, and Miles DAVIS, saxophonists Dexter GORDON and Gene AMMONS, and drummer Art BLAKEY. Vocalist Sarah VAUGHAN also performed with the group.

Eckstine continued singing as a solo entertainer, often backed by a band led by Bobby Tucker. In 1959 he recorded an album of vocals with Count Basie's band. He was less prominent after the 1950's but continued to perform as a cabaret entertainer.

**Edelman, Marian Wright** (b. June 6, 1939, Bennettsville, South Carolina): Lawyer and CIVIL RIGHTS activist. Edelman was the youngest of five children born to Arthur Wright, a Baptist minister, and his wife Maggie. In addition to their church work, her parents founded the Wright Home for the Aged in Bennettsville to serve the needs of its elderly black citizens. Edelman's father died in 1954 and her mother cared for twelve foster children in order to put her youngest children through college.

## College Life

Edelman was accepted at SPELMAN COLLEGE in Atlanta in 1956. As a result of her outstanding academic performance, she received a Charles Merrill grant to study abroad during her junior year. She spent the summer of 1959 studying French civilization at the Sorbonne University before continuing her academic studies at the University of Geneva. Edelman received a Lisle Fellowship to travel to the Soviet Union for a two-month study program during her second semester abroad.

Upon her return to Spelman, Edelman was uneasy about the segregated environment she reentered. During her senior year, she participated in a SIT-IN protest at Atlanta City Hall and was one of fourteen students who were arrested for taking part in the protest. This early involvement in the developing Civil Rights movement influenced Edelman's decision to apply to law school. After graduating from Spelman as class valedictorian in 1960, she was awarded a John Hay Whitney fellowship to attend Yale University Law School.

## SNCC and NAACP Activism

During the spring break of her third year at Yale, Edelman joined her friend Robert Moses, field secretary for the STUDENT NONVIOLENT COORDINATING COMMITTEE (SNCC), in traveling to MISSISSIPPI to participate in a massive registration drive to increase the number of African American VOTERS in that state. While in Mississippi, she realized for the first time how outsiders—backed by public opinion and the principles of moral suasion—could change even the most resistant racist practices. After graduating from Yale with her LL.B. degree, Edelman trained in New York with the NATIONAL ASSOCIATION FOR THE ADVANCEMENT OF COLORED PEOPLE (NAACP) before returning to Mississippi as one of the first interns with the NAACP Legal Defense and Educational Fund in 1964.

In the spring of that year, she opened her own law office in Mississippi and accepted several civil rights cases for student activists who were being arrested and sent to jail for their activities. As part of her work as head of the NAACP Legal Defense and Educational Fund office, Edelman lobbied tirelessly for federal funding to support a black community-based Head Start program in Mississippi in 1965. She was the first black woman to pass the Mississippi state bar examination in 1965. During the course of her legal efforts on behalf of African Americans, she was jailed, faced many threats, and was refused entry into a state courthouse.

## Legislative Research and Lobbying

In 1967 she met Peter Edelman, a young Jewish lawyer who was serving as one of Robert F. Kennedy's legislative assistants and was visit-

Marian Wright Edelman in 1996. *(AP/Wide World Photos)*

ing Mississippi on a fact-finding mission for the Senate Subcommittee on Employment, Manpower, and Poverty. Drawn together by their shared commitment to civil rights, they were married in July of 1968. In March of 1968, Marian Wright Edelman received a Field Foundation Grant and moved to WASHINGTON, D.C., where she began to work on creating legislation that would address the problems caused by the extreme POVERTY she had witnessed in Mississippi. As a result of her concern that impoverished people had no voice to represent their needs and interests, Edelman founded the Washington Research Project. She also served as a congressional liaison for the SOUTHERN CHRISTIAN LEADERSHIP CONFERENCE (SCLC) during preparations for the POOR PEOPLE'S CAMPAIGN in 1968.

### The Children's Defense Fund

In 1971 the Edelmans left the nation's capital for BOSTON, where Peter was appointed vice president of the University of Massachusetts at Boston and Marian was appointed director of the Harvard University Center for Law and Education. Marian commuted between Boston and Washington, D.C., in order to continue her work overseeing the Research Project's activities. As an outgrowth of her concern for those lacking a political voice in Washington, she founded the CHILDREN'S DEFENSE FUND in 1973 and served as its president. The fund's goal was to encourage national awareness of the needs of children and to educate people about issues related to children, including teenage pregnancy, child welfare, nutrition, education, child abuse, youth employment, child care, and family support programs. The fund's advocacy of children's rights and family issues made Edelman a vital source for legislators and journalists who were educating themselves and others about these issues. First Lady Hillary Clinton was one among many of the fund's influential supporters in the 1990's.

The Children's Defense Fund sponsored several research and educational campaigns in order to inform the public on children's issues. Its campaign for child-care legislation was credited as the major force behind Congress's passage of a child-care bill in 1991. The legislation supports safe, well-structured, affordable child care, critical in providing the early educational foundation that all children need. Among its other research efforts, the fund documented the rise of child poverty in the United States as compared with other industrialized nations, especially the increase in homelessness among minority children. In her efforts to provide the legislative groundwork for addressing this issue and meeting the basic needs of all children, Edelman believed that the solutions must instill in children a sense of hope and confidence in the future.

During the 1990's much of Edelman's effort was put into the fund's Black Community Crusade for Children and its Stand for Children campaign. She voiced her strong disapproval of the welfare reform legislation of 1996 and her disappointment in the CLINTON ADMINISTRATION's part in drafting and approving the legislation, which she feared would be devastating to poor families. Her campaign to gain popular and government support for high-quality and affordable day care remained unrelenting. In 1998 the Children's Defense Fund held events to celebrate its twenty-fifth anniversary. Edelman was still its president and guiding force.

### Awards and Achievements

Edelman received numerous awards, including a distinguished service award from the National Association of Black Women Attorneys in 1970, a professional achievement award from *Black Enterprise* magazine, a MacArthur Fellowship in 1985, the Albert Schweitzer Humanitarian Award in 1988, and an Essence Award in 1992. Her written works include articles in several professional journals and national magazines as well as books such as *Children Out of School in America* (1974), *Families in Peril: An Agenda for Social Change* (1987), and *The Measure of Our Success* (1992).

Suggested Readings:

Edelman, Marian Wright. *Guide My Feet: Prayers and Meditations on Loving and Working for Children.* Boston: Beacon Press, 1995.

_____."Healthy Start: An Interview with Marian Wright Edelman." *The Christian Century* (July 15, 1998): 682-685.

_____. "Marian Wright Edelman: On the Front Lines of the Battle to Save America's Children." Interview by Norman Atkins. *Rolling Stone*, December 10, 1992, 126-130.

_____. *The Measure of Our Success.* Boston: Beacon Press, 1992.

Guy-Sheftall, Beverly. "Marian Wright Edelman." In *Notable Black American Women*, edited by Jessie Smith. Detroit: Gale, 1992.

Haywood, Richette L. "Marian Wright Edelman: First Mom, Activist Asks America to Stand for Children." *Ebony* (May, 1996): 150-153.

Kaus, Mickey. "The Godmother: What's Wrong with Marian Wright Edelman." *The New Republic* 208 (February 15, 1993): 21-25.

Lanker, Brian. *I Dream a World: Portraits of Black Women Who Changed America.* New York: Stewart, Tabori & Chang, 1989.

"Marian Wright Edelman." *Current Biography* 53 (September, 1992): 3-7.

Tompkins, Calvin. "Profiles: A Sense of Urgency." *The New Yorker* (March 27, 1989): 48-74.

**Edley, Christopher Fairfield, Sr.** (b. January 1, 1928, Charleston, West Virginia): Attorney, fund-raiser, and education advocate. After completing his undergraduate education at HOWARD UNIVERSITY in 1949, Edley earned his law degree from Harvard Law School in

Christopher Edley in 1973. *(AP/Wide World Photos)*

1953. Upon leaving Harvard, Edley worked as an assistant district attorney in Philadelphia from 1954 to 1956, and later became a partner in Moore, Lightfoot & Edley. In 1963 Edley began working as a program officer for the Ford Foundation.

After more than a decade of service with the Ford Foundation, Edley was chosen in 1973 to serve as president and chief executive officer of the UNITED NEGRO COLLEGE FUND (UNCF), a prestigious black philanthropic organization dedicated to promoting and supporting higher education for African Americans. That year the UNCF launched its national advertising campaign to raise money using the slogan "A Mind Is a Terrible Thing to Waste." Edley was instrumental in promoting this campaign and in coordinating fund-raising strategies to increase the annual revenue of the fund.

Under his leadership, the UNCF publicized the financial needs of historically black colleges with award-winning television spots that set new standards in public service advertising. Before health problems forced him to retire in December of 1990, Edley secured a fifty-million-dollar challenge grant from media giant and philanthropist Walter H. Annenberg as part of the UNCF's new "Campaign 2000: An Investment in America's Future." Edley was succeeded as president of the UNCF by former congressional representative William H. Gray III. In 1991 the Congressional Black Caucus presented Edley with the George W. Collins Award in recognition of his contributions to the black community.

**Edmunson, William** (1882, Davidson County, Kentucky—1951): Self-taught sculptor. Edmunson received major recognition in 1938 through a solo exhibition of his works at the Museum of Modern Art in New York. His sculptures prior to this exhibition were intended as gravestones for black patrons. Edmunson's work is characterized by representations of humans and animals, sculpted with fluidity and economy of detail.
*See also:* Sculptors; Visual arts.

**Education:** Throughout their history, African Americans have utilized whatever resources they could command in pursuit of education, both formal and informal. African American history is a testament to faith in education and pursuit of education as a prize with its own value. This pursuit has required great sacrifices, in part because American society long viewed education as a privilege of the elite rather than a right possessed by all citizens regardless of race, political clout, or economic resources.

*Before the Civil War*
During the era of SLAVERY there were significant numbers of both slaves and FREE BLACKS, and their educational opportunities differed markedly. In almost all the southern states, it was illegal to teach slaves (and in some states, free blacks) to read and write. Literacy was seen as inappropriate for slaves. However, some slaves learned basic reading skills anyway, either by being taught by whites or by managing to gain the knowledge secretly. According to many historians, at the outbreak of the CIVIL WAR approximately half of free blacks and about 10 percent of slaves were literate.

Among slaves, household and personal servants enjoyed certain advantages. They were better clothed and sheltered, and they were more likely to be literate than were other slaves. Urban blacks, whether slave or free, were more often literate because the opportunities and stimuli to learn were so much greater than for rural blacks. Free blacks were better educated than slaves, and many were trained in vocational skills. Many free blacks were the offspring of slave women and slaveowners. These mulattoes were sometimes educated and freed out of a sense of guilt or simply because of their white heritage.

Groups of free blacks in the cities started their own schools, usually in private homes. Some black churches maintained schools for children, free and slave. A variety of white organizations, especially churches and religious groups but also antislavery groups, were involved in the education of African Americans. The first schools for blacks were established in New York in the 1700's; the first free secular school was begun in 1787.

The education of slaves was limited and rarely was acknowledged. Education resulted largely from various forms of self-help and from some surreptitious or inadvertent help from whites. Training, when it did take place, consisted primarily of basic skills in reading, writing, and perhaps some arithmetic. A small number of blacks, because of individualistic reasons or unique circumstances, received some of the classical education of the day. More were provided with vocational education or industrial training.

In the South, education for slaves (for those who were fortunate enough to acquire some) usually began on the PLANTATIONS. Industrial training in such crafts as carpentry, blacksmithing, mechanics, and barbering was generally encouraged because the market value of a slave was increased by such skills, raising the owner's prestige and providing an opportunity for additional sources of income. Skilled slaves were often hired out, even though the practice was illegal. For some slaves, the plantation became what Booker T. WASHINGTON called an "industrial school"; for others (primarily house servants), it provided opportunities to learn at least the essentials of reading and writing.

When literacy was useful to the performance of a particular job or to learning a trade, slaves might be taught by the master or some member of the household. There were some whites who argued that slaves should be taught to read the Bible in order to make them more obedient. Religious education for slaves was based on the assumption that they could be trained in obedience. Even without this rationale, developed to accompany the religious ideology of the day, some whites, especially the wives of slave masters, quietly (and often secretly) taught slaves to read and write. It would be misleading, however, to present the education of slaves as the norm. The vast majority of whites were fearful of educated slaves, and punishment was often meted out to those who were caught learning to read or write or who exercised literacy skills without permission.

Slave children, in their roles as both companions and miniature servants to white children, often had opportunities to learn that their parents did not have. Slave children sometimes waited nearby as white children were tutored; they listened and learned as well. In addition, older white children were fond of playing school, with younger children, black and white, as their pupils. These play schools served a very real function for the education of slave children.

### Reconstruction and the American Dream

During and immediately after the Civil War, freedmen's aid societies and missionary societies were founded in the North to begin schools and to send teachers to the South to teach the freed slaves. Historians have characterized the newly freed blacks after the Civil War as wanting to own land and to secure an education, goals very consistent with the American dream of success. Those with even minimal literacy skills were drafted into service as schoolteachers, and all sorts of buildings were converted into schools.

On March 3, 1865, shortly before the end of the Civil War, Congress created the Bureau of Refugees, Freedmen, and Abandoned Lands, later known as the FREEDMEN'S BUREAU. Creation of this agency put responsibility for the protection and welfare of newly freed blacks, including provision of the "foundations of education," on the federal government. The military general commanding the bureau affirmed the importance of education in helping to solve some of the problems created by slavery. "Education," he stated, "underlies every hope of success for the freedmen." During Reconstruction, when leaders of black organizations were given opportunities to express desires for self-improvement programs, education was always first.

Along with founding schools for former slaves, the Freedmen's Bureau coordinated the many programs already in existence. Bureau officials also were called upon to provide protection for the teachers and missionaries who came from the North to establish schools for blacks. Most of the actual work of establishing and operating schools was done by teams representing benevolent and religious organizations. It was a piecemeal effort, with urban blacks contributing through their own churches and organizations. Some southern whites, even some former slaveholders, also helped in the educational effort, if only by advancing money to pay the first teachers until blacks could assume this responsibility themselves.

By the end of 1865, there were between five hundred and six hundred freedmen's schools in the South, most supported by the combined efforts of churches and charity organizations from the North and the South, both black and white. In the years following the Civil War, African Americans made substantial investments in their own schools in the form of small cash gifts, donated carpentry skills and maintenance services, and fund-raisers to buy books and furniture. W. E. B. Du Bois estimated that from 1865 to 1870 African Americans contributed more than $750,000 in small cash gifts to their schools. This sum is particularly impressive given the fact that most African Americans were but a few years removed from slavery. Of the 236 schools in Georgia in 1867, 152 were partially or entirely owned by blacks.

Attention turned to questions of a standardized curriculum to meet the unique needs of black children. As efforts expanded to reach as many black children as possible, the special curriculum designed for them contained not only some of the classical education that white children were getting but also an emphasis on teaching "white ways" to black children.

The establishment of institutions of HIGHER EDUCATION for blacks was a natural outgrowth of the freedmen's schools, in which most teachers were white. At least some whites acknowledged that blacks could and should become their own teachers. Blacks needed institutions to train their own leaders, especially ministers, teachers, physicians, and lawyers. Thus the Freedmen's Bureau began the process of overseeing the establishment of a system of black colleges, a group of institutions later known as HISTORICALLY BLACK COLLEGES and universities. As with the establish-

ment of elementary schools, the bureau largely provided coordination and oversight. Working with the AMERICAN MISSIONARY ASSOCIATION and black citizens, it laid groundwork in 1865 for what was to become the ATLANTA UNIVERSITY complex. Similar cooperative efforts helped to establish FISK UNIVERSITY in Nashville, Tennessee (1866), HOWARD UNIVERSITY in Washington, D.C. (1867), and Talladega College in Talladega, Alabama (1867).

The Reconstruction period ended with only a few liberal arts colleges being established in the South. Because of the almost total absence of secondary schools for black youngsters, all these colleges had to include high schools or academies to prepare their own students for entrance. Most of the early schools for African Americans were designed to train religious leaders. Such was the explicit purpose of Walden College, Shaw University, Morehouse College, Wayland Seminary in Washington, D.C., and Richmond Theological Seminary. The need for religious and spiritual leaders was perhaps the least controversial issue relating to higher education for African Americans during the period of Reconstruction.

This period marked the beginning of a long-running debate as to the proper focus of higher education for blacks, with proponents lined up on the side of either vocational or classical education. HAMPTON INSTITUTE (1868) and later TUSKEGEE INSTITUTE (1881) are examples of the introduction of vocational education into black higher education, fueling an argument that lasted well into the twentieth century about which kind of education was best for blacks. Howard University stood alone among institutions of higher education founded during Reconstruction in building a structure for those who wished "collegiate and professional" training. Five years after the first students were admitted to Howard in 1867, the university had nine departments:

normal and preparatory, MUSIC, theology, MILITARY, industrial, commercial, college, law, and MEDICINE. The structure of a great university was in place.

The classical education that at least some elementary children experienced in the freedmen's schools of the South came to a rather abrupt and premature end in some of the southern states. Whites feared the people who were being educated there and feared the power that education might give them. The governor of NORTH CAROLINA closed that state's freedmen's schools. In 1865 FLORIDA imposed a tax on all black men to pay for "Negro schools." Sentiment grew against the northern teachers who came South to teach the freed slaves. Many freedmen's schools were in jeopardy because administrators, funding, and teachers were northern in origin. The schools became, in the minds of many bitter southerners, a plot to take over the South.

*Segregated Schools*

During Reconstruction, the principle of free public education for all children was written into the constitutions of the former Confederate states, patterned after what was already in place in other states. By 1870 most southern states were willing to permit the education of blacks, or at least had not attempted to make such education illegal. The implementation of free public education for blacks, however, was still in the future.

The states that had not abolished the freedmen's schools eventually inherited these schools. By the end of Reconstruction, there were more than twenty-six hundred such schools in the South. Some states merged the freedmen's schools into their school systems, while others left them intact but made the teachers and administrators answerable to the white superintendent of schools. As power and school governance in the South was returned to the states, the power of the federal government was lessened. Thus began an era of "Negro education" that was segregated and unequal and was based on the assumption that the education needed by blacks was less complex and less expensive than that needed by whites.

By the last decade of the nineteenth century, every southern state had in place segregated educational systems. "Negro education" in the South, with few exceptions, became industrial education, with a clear if unstated goal of preparing African Americans for a place in society that was lower than that of whites. This education was designed to support the economy of white society.

In 1896 the U.S. SUPREME COURT ruled in the case of PLESSY V. FERGUSON that state laws providing segregation on the basis of race were constitutional, so long as the state maintained equal facilities for each race. Although the case dealt with public transportation, it was nevertheless a test of the right of southern states to pass segregation laws. The decision was a victory for states' rights proponents, including those who advocated the right to maintain segregated school systems. *Plessy* established what came to be known as the SEPARATE BUT EQUAL doctrine in a segregated South.

When the separate systems of education were conceived, the dollar expenditures per child were relatively equal for black and white students in some states. Large sums of private money from the North supported black schools, helping to equalize the balance. However, sources of private funds, apparently intended as seed money, began to dry up just as the proportion of black children in school was increasing. By 1910 it was estimated that 45 percent of black school-age children were in school. By 1930 it was estimated that four-fifths of black children over the age of ten were literate, whereas in 1890 less than half had been literate.

Spending on education for African American children decreased, and so did the quality of the education. Black children, on average, attended school for twenty-seven fewer days per year than did white children in 1910. In 1930 there was still a twenty-day difference in favor of whites. An average black child completed grammar school (eight years) having spent about fifty-eight months in the classroom, while a white child had spent sixty-six months in the classroom. The reason was the need for black children to work; their labor was part of a system of white-controlled family labor among tenant farmers and sharecroppers.

The difference in spending on education is another objective measure of unequal education. The difference actually increased between 1910 and 1930, as did the differences in black and white teachers' salaries. In 1930, for example, South Carolina spent ten times as much to educate a white child as it did to educate a black child. Other states, such as Florida, Georgia, Mississippi, and Alabama, spent five times as much. The average white child in the South studied in a structure that cost more than four times as much as the average structure for black children. Until the 1940's, many children in the rural South attended plantation-owned schools, often consisting of little more than one or two rooms in which all grades were taught together. These schools never went beyond the eighth grade and were shut down whenever children were needed to work in the fields.

Facilities such as this Depression-era southern schoolhouse belied the notion of "separate but equal" in education. *(Library of Congress)*

### The Pursuit of Equal Education

The 1930's and 1940's brought changes in lifestyle, worldview, and residency for many Americans, especially blacks. All Americans experienced the GREAT DEPRESSION of the 1930's, and all made certain sacrifices as a result of the United States' involvement in WORLD WAR II. African Americans found it necessary to confront other forces as well. Beginning with the massive mechanization of the cotton industry in the early 1940's, the rural South no longer provided even a poverty-level existence for many blacks. Changes in the South, coupled with opportunities resulting from the war and postwar recovery, caused more than five million African Americans to migrate from the rural South to various urban areas in the North and the South in search of opportunity. As always, many of their hopes and dreams were fixed on education.

The NATIONAL ASSOCIATION FOR THE ADVANCEMENT OF COLORED PEOPLE (NAACP), with the support of numerous individuals and other organizations, most visibly took up the cause of high-quality education for African Americans. Organized in 1909, the NAACP came to represent reasoned, conservative, and legalistic leadership in the battle for equal rights for African Americans. The NAACP enjoyed support, both financial and moral, from whites and blacks alike.

In 1935 Charles HOUSTON, a law professor at Howard University, made a film for the NAACP on segregated schools in the South. Houston used the film, *Examples of Educational Discrimination*, as a teaching tool with his law students and as a documentary for speaking engagements. Houston had earned a law degree and a doctorate from Harvard, where he studied under Roscoe Pound and was heavily influenced by Pound's "sociological jurisprudence." Later, as a professor and vice dean of law at Howard University, Houston recruited the best students, upgraded the faculty, and made constitutional law central to the school's mission. Howard's law school earned accreditation by the Association of American Law Schools.

The NAACP came to greater public attention in the 1940's and 1950's when it began arguing school desegregation cases on constitutional grounds in the federal courts. Beginning early in the 1930's, the organizational leadership made a decision to direct its financial and legal resources toward achieving equality of educational opportunity for African American children. In 1935 Charles Houston took a leave of absence from Howard to head the NAACP legal team. From that point on, he led the NAACP in a long-range, methodical judicial battle for equal education.

Houston's plan was to begin at the highest level of education, in professional and graduate schools, and to litigate the right cases. Houston reasoned that integration of professional and graduate schools would be less threatening to whites than integration of elementary or high schools. Once integration at that level was accepted, he would spread it to secondary and elementary schools. Houston also knew that he could make his most convincing legal arguments at the professional and graduate school level, because the question would not be whether educational facilities were equal but if, in fact, educational facilities and opportunities even existed.

Houston enlisted the assistance of one of his former students, Thurgood MARSHALL. Their first court victory, in 1935, involved the University of Maryland Law School, from which a black student, Donald Murray, had been turned away under a "whites only" admission policy. The Murray case, *University of Maryland v. Murray*, decided by a Maryland state appeals court, was the first crack in the wall of school segregation. Several other victories, involving students and professional education in Missouri, Oklahoma, and Texas, followed over the next fifteen years.

In 1940 Charles Houston left his position as chief counsel with the NAACP. Although he went into private practice, he continued to work on school desegregation cases, without pay, until his death in 1950. Houston's NAACP position was filled by his former student (and future Supreme Court justice) Thurgood Marshall, who continued the legal challenges to segregated and unequal education.

The cases first filed by the NAACP were challenges to the "equal" requirement of the "separate but equal" doctrine set forth in *Plessy v. Ferguson*. Shortly before his death, Houston decided to shift his approach and to attack segregation as unconstitutional. Meanwhile, the NAACP decided to attack segregation on two fronts: by arguing that "separate but equal" was unconstitutional under the Fourteenth Amendment and that schools, in order to be truly equal, must be integrated. The NAACP set about building a case to prove that segregated schools were by nature unequal schools. The Supreme Court gave the

NAACP the opportunity to make this argument when it agreed to hear BROWN V. BOARD OF EDUCATION.

Linda Brown was one of many African American schoolchildren in Topeka, Kansas, who had to travel miles to attend an inadequate all-black school even though there was a white school near her home. The NAACP filed a class-action suit under her name but on behalf of all African American children who were denied access to schools equal to those of whites. The NAACP never worked on only one case at a time, because it could not know which case might make it from one level of the judicial system to the next, finally coming before the Supreme Court.

The NAACP's efforts to ensure that one strong case reached the Court resulted in five very similar cases reaching the Court at about the same time in 1954, originating from Virginia, South Carolina, Kansas, Delaware, and the District of Columbia. The Court combined all five cases under the title of *Brown v. Board of Education*. A unanimous decision was handed down by the Supreme Court in May of 1954, with the finding that separate educational facilities are "inherently unequal." The decision

put an end to legally sanctioned segregated education. The history of public education, and in many respects the history of race relations, can be written as "before *Brown*" and "after *Brown*."

*Post-Brown Education*

The results of the landmark *Brown* decision were mixed. African Americans have not lost faith in education, and education is not without its rewards, but those rewards have remained considerably more limited for blacks than for whites. Bart Landry, in his study *The New Middle Class* (1987), reported that education remained the single most important avenue into the middle class for blacks, even though returns to education might be lower than for whites. Studies have found that academic achievement does not have the same predictable positive effect on later occupational success for blacks that it does for whites. African Americans have not been rewarded in a monetary or tangible way to the same degree that whites have. The fact that they have relentlessly pursued education, even when it was offered for the benefit of a slaveholder, suggests that the black community as a whole values education for its own intrinsic rewards.

The vast research on post-*Brown* education, while not without its inconsistencies and controversies, suggests the following gains: improved black achievement with no detriment to white achievement, some reduction in the cycle of racial isolation, a sharp increase in the level of African American education, and a rising rate of high school graduation among black students. These gains in the post-*Brown* era are often cited as justification for the

Englewood, New Jersey, residents picket a local high school scheduled to be integrated in 1962. *(National Archives)*

decision to desegregate public schools.

Many whites assumed erroneously that blacks wanted school integration only to be in close proximity to whites, or even because blacks wished they could be white. Those who fought the early school desegregation cases were convinced that the only way to ensure that blacks would have the same quality of education as whites was to be in the same schools. At the same time, some blacks lament the fact that the demise of their own schools has been accompanied by a demise in the transmission of the strengths of African American culture and history. There is some basis for their concern. Although progress has been made toward multicultural education, it is still more an ideal than a reality. The culture and values presented in public schools (and in most private schools as well) are still overwhelmingly white, even if the students are racially and culturally mixed. In such an environment, the life experiences of black children are not validated.

Negative effects from this situation have been found to be less severe for black students in integrated schools with integrated curricula and for students living in integrated neighborhoods. Many American schools have remained segregated—not because of law but because socioeconomic classes and housing are segregated. When this is the case, students leave school to go to their separate social worlds, and it becomes difficult for schools to break down social barriers. When school integration is accompanied by residential integration, some evidence suggests that there is a pattern of social contact between the races.

### The 1980's and 1990's

The most frequently cited benefit of post-*Brown* education is the closing of the gap in completed years of schooling between whites and blacks. Except for older generations, the races had almost reached parity in years of schooling by 1990. The percentage of black

Since the *Brown v. Board of Education* ruling in 1954, the educational gap between whites and blacks has gradually narrowed. *(National Archives)*

students completing high school increased steadily in the thirty years after *Brown* and remained close to the white graduation rate despite a slight decline in the 1990's. The percentage of black dropouts (considered persons eighteen to twenty-four not enrolled in or graduated from high school) declined sharply between 1975 (27.3) and 1996 (16 percent), and the annual dropout rate declined at a less dramatic but substantial rate during this period, from 8.7 percent to 6.3 percent.

By the late 1990's, approximately 87 percent of young black adults were reported to be high school graduates, compared with 93 percent of whites. These statistics include those who completed high school by passing the General Educational Development (GED) Test, which blacks are more likely to take than are whites. However, overall black academic performance, as measured by standardized achievement tests, remained somewhat below the performance of whites.

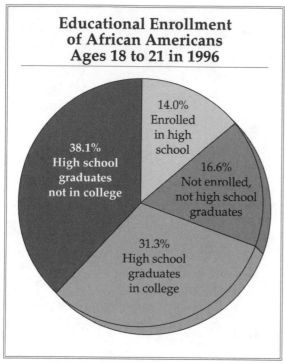

**Educational Enrollment
of African Americans
Ages 18 to 21 in 1996**

14.0% Enrolled in high school

16.6% Not enrolled, not high school graduates

38.1% High school graduates not in college

31.3% High school graduates in college

*Source:* U.S. Bureau of the Census.

Historically low rates of college entry for black high school graduates rose slightly in the late 1980's and early 1990's and fluctuated between 50 and 55 percent for the rest of the decade, while the percentage of white graduates entering college continued to increase. Significantly more black women than men were enrolling in college, however. By the late 1990's, according to Department of Education statistics, black women outnumbered black men in college by 1.5 to 1.

*Theories About Educational Disparities*
A variety of theories have been offered as explanations for why blacks have remained behind whites in education statistics. One type of theory, expressed in varying degrees of sophistication by social scientists and journalists, places the blame with African American culture. Critics of these theories refer to them as "blaming the victim" explanations. Theories of this type use purported facts about African Americans to explain their failure to reach the achievement levels of whites. One such "fact" is a lack of middle-class values, such as delaying gratification in order to pursue education. Another is problems in the African American family that result in children with low self-esteem who are hedonistic, amoral, and negativistic with regard to mainstream culture. A third is a "welfare mentality," or a desire to be taken care of rather than to work.

These types of explanations ignore the fact that the educational system at all levels is but a microcosm of society, reflecting problems and biases of that society. Surveys of parents, regardless of the parents' socioeconomic level or whether they are in two-parent or single-parent households, consistently show that African American parents want the same things for their children as do white parents—a good education and a secure job.

Wealth, power, and privilege are unequally distributed in American society. Educational institutions are one means by which privileges and rewards are distributed. These institutions function daily to weed out some youngsters, thus excluding them from the rewards of education. Some are weeded out on the basis of ability, some because of behavior. Some are

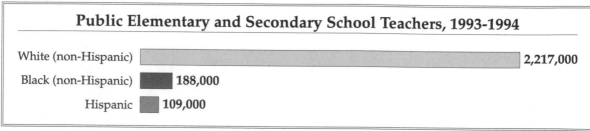

**Public Elementary and Secondary School Teachers, 1993-1994**

| | |
|---|---|
| White (non-Hispanic) | 2,217,000 |
| Black (non-Hispanic) | 188,000 |
| Hispanic | 109,000 |

*Source:* National Center for Education Statistics.

Studies have found that African American parents want the same things for their children that all parents want—especially good educations. (Hazel Hankin)

lost simply because the school seems to them to be irrelevant to their everyday lives. Many of the educational problems or issues identified with African Americans are in reality the problems and issues of all concerned citizens. These are the problems of performance, of teacher expectations and competence, of functionally illiterate high school graduates, and of violence, problems that are exacerbated by race and by low socioeconomic status.

—*Joyce E. Williams*
—*Updated by Michael Burchett*

---

## Adult Education

In 1994-1995, 7.7 million African Americans, or 37% of the African American population, participated in adult education.

| *Reasons for participation* | |
|---|---|
| Personal or social reasons | 45% |
| Job advancement | 48% |
| Train for a new job | 13% |
| Complete degree or diploma | 12% |

*Source:* U.S. Department of Education, National Center for Education Statistics, *1995 National Household Education Survey.*

*See also:* Black studies; Collins, Marva; Head Start; Immersion schools; Independent schools; Intellectuals and scholars; *Journal of Negro Education*; Professors; Secondary education.

Suggested Readings:

Allen, Walter R., Edgar G. Epps, and Nesha Z. Haniff, eds. *College in Black and White*. Albany: State University of New York Press, 1991.

Bowen, William G., and Derek Bok. *The Shape of the River: Long-Term Consequences of Considering Race in College and University Admissions*. Princeton, N.J.: Princeton University Press, 1998.

Bullock, Henry A. *A History of Negro Education in the South*. Cambridge, Mass.: Harvard University Press, 1967.

Fine, Michelle. *Framing Dropouts*. Albany: State University of New York Press, 1991.

Freeman, Kassie, ed. *African American Culture and Heritage in Higher Education Research and Practice*. Westport, Conn.: Praeger, 1998.

Hale-Benson, Janice E. *Black Children: Their Roots, Culture, and Learning Styles*. Rev. ed. Baltimore: Johns Hopkins University Press, 1986.

Jones-Wilson, Faustine C., ed. *Encyclopedia of African-American Education*. Westport, Conn.: Greenwood Press, 1996.

Persell, Caroline H. *Education and Inequality*. New York: Free Press, 1977.

Schofield, Janet W. *Black and White in School*. New York: Teachers College Press, 1989.

"Schooling of Black Americans, The." In *A Common Destiny: Blacks and American Society*, edited by Gerald D. Jaynes and Robin M. Williams. Washington, D.C.: National Academy Press, 1989.

Welch, Susan. *Affirmative Action and Minority Enrollments in Medical and Law Schools*. Ann Arbor: University of Michigan Press, 1998.

**Edwards, Nelson Jack** (1917, Lowndes County, Alabama—November 2, 1974, Detroit, Michigan): Labor union official. Edwards was one of the first African Americans to rise to prominence in the American labor movement. Edwards moved to DETROIT, MICHIGAN, in 1937 and found work in the auto industry. During that time, the United Auto Workers (UAW) union was struggling to organize the auto industry. Using walkouts and sit-down strikes, the UAW organized workers at General Motors, Chrysler, and finally Ford.

Edwards was caught up in this turmoil, becoming an active unionist. His courage and leadership skills won him power and influence in the UAW. As a result, he became the first African American head of a United Auto Workers union local. This was a predominantly white union local. From that post, he rose in the UAW ranks, becoming in 1962 the first African American to sit on the UAW executive board. By then, Edwards was a respected and influential civic leader in Detroit. In 1970 Edwards capped his union career with his appointment to the vice presidency of the UAW. *See also:* Organized labor; Strikes and labor law.

**Eisenhower administration:** Dwight D. Eisenhower served as president from 1953 to 1961, years in which the struggle to secure the constitutional rights of African Americans intensified. Following the president's lead, officials in the Eisenhower administration pursued a cautious course as they dealt with issues involving African Americans.

In June, 1958, President Dwight D. Eisenhower (center) discussed civil rights issues with, from left to right, Lester B. Granger of the National Urban League; Martin Luther King, Jr., of the SCLC; White House administrative officer E. Frederic Morrow; A. Philip Randolph of the AFL-CIO; Attorney General William Rogers; and Roy Wilkins of the NAACP. *(AP/Wide World Photos)*

On occasion President Eisenhower condemned RACIAL DISCRIMINATION, but he did not offer leadership or inspiration to African Americans. His commitment to a narrow definition of the federal government's authority, as well as his personal belief that white acceptance of African Americans was a social problem that could not be solved by legislative action, limited the effectiveness of administration officials in protecting the rights of African Americans.

Eisenhower supported efforts to end segregation in those areas where the federal government held clear responsibility. He called for an end to racial discrimination in Washington, D.C., and he continued the desegregation of the U.S. armed forces military that had begun under the previous president, Harry S Truman. Eisenhower appointed a number of African Americans to positions of authority in his administration, although none held positions of prominence or major importance. Despite these actions, most African Americans in the military or in federal jobs remained victims of discrimination, unable to receive promotions that would have resulted in more authority and better pay.

Eisenhower refused to use the authority of his office in those areas of American life in which he believed that the federal government should not intrude. For example, he believed that public schools were the responsibility of state and local officials, and in 1953 he only reluctantly agreed to allow Attorney General Herbert Brownell to file a brief in the school desegregation case of BROWN v. BOARD OF EDUCATION. When the U.S. SUPREME COURT declared that segregated school systems were unconstitutional, Eisenhower did not offer any praise for the decision.

Administration officials could not avoid responding to southern resistance to school desegregation. In 1957 Eisenhower negotiated with ARKANSAS officials to ensure that a federal court order requiring school desegrega-

President Dwight D. Eisenhower signing the Civil Rights Act of 1960. *(National Archives)*

tion in Little Rock would go into effect. When local authorities failed to stop the violence that occurred when African American students arrived at the high school, Eisenhower sent U.S. military troops to end the conflict. He justified his decision on the grounds that as president he was responsible for enforcing the rulings of the federal court.

Because White House officials saw the ballot box as the best means for increasing African American participation in American life, the Eisenhower administration offered voting rights legislation in 1957. Southern members of Congress weakened the bill, and although he did not approve, the president did little to stop them. As a result of the president's overly cautious stance regarding African American concerns, many black voters who had voted for Eisenhower and other Republicans in 1956 voted for Democratic candidates—including John F. Kennedy, running for the presidency—in the 1960 elections.

*—Thomas Clarkin*

Suggested Readings:

Burk, Robert Fredrick. *The Eisenhower Administration and Black Civil Rights*. Knoxville: University of Texas Press, 1984.

Duram, James C. *A Moderate Among Extremists: Dwight D. Eisenhower and the School Desegregation Crisis*. Chicago: Nelson-Hall, 1981.

Garrow, David J., ed. *We Shall Overcome: The Civil Rights Movement in the United States in the 1950's and 1960's*. 3 vols. New York: Carlson, 1989.

Mayer, Michael. *Eisenhower Presidency and the 1950s*. Lexington, Mass.: D. C. Heath, 1998.

**Elderly:** The elderly population of the United States in 1994 consisted of approximately 33.2 million people. About one in eight Americans was over the age of sixty-five, and persons reaching that age had an average life expectancy of about seventeen additional years. The number of Americans living to age sixty-five and older is steadily increasing, and the African American elderly represent a fast-growing segment of the total African American population.

Persons over sixty-five years of age represent a rapidly growing portion of the African American population. *(CLEO Freelance Photography)*

*Family Ties and Cultural Traditions*

The elderly are generally included in the African American family structure and are accorded respect. They are typically viewed as reservoirs of strength, social and spiritual experiences, knowledge, and skills. They serve as valued links and contributors to cultural traditions. The acceptance by family members of the aging process may stem from the cultural heritage of African values and attitudes toward aging and the aged.

A practice still in existence in Africa, ancestor worship, teaches high regard and respect for the elderly. This cultural tradition of respect continued in African American families. The primary sources of social support for elderly African Americans are family relationships. As the elderly become more frail, family members are inclined to accept them within the immediate family structure.

The family is an essential social unit for the transmission of values, including the care and support of the elderly. Many African American families are multigenerational EXTENDED FAMILY structures that provide strong informal support networks for the elderly. Support takes many forms, including the provision of instrumental and material aid (such as food, money, and transportation) and cognitive aid (such as visitations and companionship). The elastic boundaries found in many multigenerational and extended families include a social network that responds to socioeconomic conditions of poverty and unemployment.

As social problems stemming from drugs and violence in the streets invade family units, many families find themselves faced with additional burdens. Instead of receiving care in old age, grandparents may find themselves fulfilling the role of caregiver when parents can no longer provide for their children. Even African American elderly who are at the point of being great-grandparents may face this situation at a stage in life when their direct child-rearing responsibility should long ago have ended.

### Health

Heart disease is a major problem for elderly blacks. HYPERTENSION (high blood pressure) in the 1990's affected more than thirty-eight out of every one hundred African Americans; they were twice as prone to hypertension as whites were. African American women over the age of sixty-five are at a higher risk for hypertension than are older women of other races. Traditional eating habits contribute significantly to HEALTH risks, and a person's socioeconomic status plays a significant role in determining the types and quantities of food purchased. African American men die from strokes at nearly twice the rate of men in the total population, and they experience higher rates of cancer and arthritis; such conditions may well be diet-related.

Other health conditions affecting elderly blacks, including high blood pressure, lung cancer, and diabetes, are related to lifestyle in varying degrees. Diabetes and the complications of diabetes, such as heart disease, stroke, kidney failure, and blindness, are all more prevalent among African Americans than among whites. African Americans have a 25 percent higher incidence of CANCER, with cancer of the lungs, prostate, stomach, pancreas, and colon being frequent. Breast cancer is also common in African American women.

Efforts of government and community agencies have focused on improving the quality of life for the black elderly; nonetheless, blacks receive less health care than whites, although their needs may be even greater. Blacks are more likely to enter the health-care system at a crisis point—when medical problems have advanced to a critical, even terminal, stage. Generally, blacks have less health insurance coverage to meet the costs associated with obtaining health care than whites do.

Although both Medicare and Medicaid provide valuable protection to the elderly, these programs have crucial gaps in coverage. African Americans are less likely than whites to be able to cover these gaps through private insurance coverage. Rising health care costs thus often force African American elderly to compromise their health care.

### Poverty

Elderly blacks are particularly susceptible to problems associated with societal ills. In the mid-1990's, more than 30 percent of the African American elderly lived in POVERTY, in comparison with about 11 percent of older whites. One-fifth of African Americans live in rural areas, and nearly one out of every two in this group lives in poverty. Economically, African American elderly people, compared with their white counterparts, have less personal postretirement income and are more dependent upon Social Security benefits and other PUBLIC ASSISTANCE PROGRAMS. Among all U.S. residents sixty-five and over, black women have the highest poverty rate.

The median income of African American elderly is considerably less than that of white elderly. In 1996, for example, 25.3 percent of blacks over the age of sixty-five had incomes below the poverty level; for whites the figure was 9.4 percent. A U.S. census study from the early 1990's showed the extremes that existed in 1992: the median income for an elderly white man was $15,276; for an elderly black woman, it was $6,220. Because the African American elderly are more likely to live close

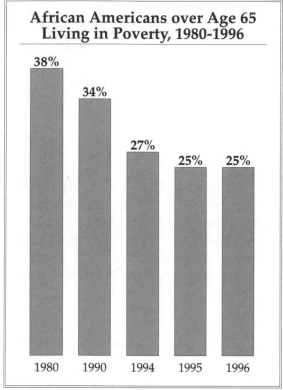

## African Americans over Age 65 Living in Poverty, 1980-1996

38% — 1980
34% — 1990
27% — 1994
25% — 1995
25% — 1996

*Source:* U.S. Bureau of the Census.

to or below the poverty level, they are also more likely to have serious health problems at younger ages and to be more dependent on government-provided health services.

—*Emma T. Lucas*

*See also:* Ancestors; Families; Oral and family history; Parenting.

Suggested Readings:

Billingsley, Andrew. *Black Families in White America*. Englewood Cliffs, N.J.: Prentice-Hall, 1968.

Harel, Zev, Edward A. McKinney, and Michael Williams, eds. *Black Aged: Understanding Diversity and Family Needs*. Newbury Park, Calif.: Sage Publications, 1990.

Lucas, Emma. *Elder Abuse and Its Recognition Among Health Service Professionals*. New York: Garland, 1991.

Nobles, W. W. "African-American Family Life: An Instrument of Culture." In *Black Fam-*

*ilies*, edited by Harriette Pipes McAdoo. Beverly Hills, Calif.: Sage Publications, 1981.

Shrestha, Laura B. *Racial Differences in Life Expectancy Among Elderly African Americans and Whites: The Surprising Truth About Comparisons*. New York: Garland, 1997.

Tate, N. "The Black Aging Experience." In *Aging in Minority Groups*, edited by R. L. McNeely and John L. Colen. Beverly Hills, Calif.: Sage Publications, 1983.

**Elders, Joycelyn Minnie** (b. August 13, 1933, Schaal, Arkansas): HEALTH educator and public official. The oldest of eight children born to sharecroppers, Elders received a scholarship from the United Methodist Church which allowed her to enter Philander Smith College in Little Rock, ARKANSAS, at age fifteen. She worked as a maid to pay her way through the University of Arkansas, where she expanded her experiences and goals through her first encounter with a physician and meeting Edith Irby Jones, the first black woman to attend the University of Arkansas Medical School. Following graduation, Elders joined the U.S. Army to train as a physical therapist. She used her G.I. Bill to attend medical school, graduating from the University of Arkansas Medical School as the only woman in her class in 1960.

Following her residency at the Minneapolis University of Minnesota Hospital, she returned to Little Rock to complete her pediatric residency at the University of Arkansas Medical Center, from which she gained further degrees in biochemistry and completed certification as a pediatric endocrinologist as she rose through academic rank to full professor in 1976. By the 1990's she had written more than 150 articles in her field.

In 1987 Arkansas governor Bill Clinton appointed Elders chief public health director for the state. In this position, Elders supervised twenty-six hundred employees and expanded health-care programs in sex education, contraception, abortion rights, HIV testing, childhood immunization, and prenatal care. Her breast-cancer screening programs and other prevention programs reduced deaths, TEEN-AGE PREGNANCY, and INFANT MORTALITY. Her outspokenness on controversial health issues was established during these years.

When President-elect Clinton nominated Elders to the post of surgeon general, she accepted his offer. Her record in preventive health care led to her serving as a consultant to Hillary Rodham Clinton's health-care task force in February, 1993. Following months of acrimonious debate, Elders was confirmed as surgeon general of the United States on September 7, 1993, becoming the second woman and the first African American to hold that position.

As surgeon general, Elders disseminated information about widespread public health problems. Widespread teenage pregnancy, sexually transmitted diseases, and ACQUIRED IMMUNODEFICIENCY SYNDROME (AIDS) prompted Elders to make public statements encouraging public funding of preventive measures such as condom distribution, sex education, and abortion. Elders's frank discussions and public opinions on these issues stood in direct opposition to conservative opinions. She alienated some members of Congress and portions of the American electorate.

Elders also provoked the anger of the nation's powerful liquor and tobacco lobbies by calling for higher taxes on alcohol and cigarettes. Her support for studying the impact of legalizing drugs also ran counter to political antidrug opinions. Finally, at the 1994 United Nations AIDS Day symposium, Elders's impolitic words about teaching children about masturbation led to a conservative outcry and to her resignation. On unpaid leave from the University of Arkansas for Medical Sciences in Little Rock since her confirmation in 1993, she returned in January of 1995 to teach and pursue medical research.

Suggested Readings:

Elders, Joycelyn M., and David Chanoff. *Joycelyn Elders, M.D.: From Sharecropper's Daughter to Surgeon General of the United States of America.* New York: William Morrow, 1996.

"Dr. Joycelyn Elders Returns to Post as Teacher." *Jet* (January 9, 1995): 26.

"The Talk of the Town: Dr. Elders' Medical History." *The New Yorker* (September 26, 1994): 45-47.

Surgeon General Joycelyn Elders in 1994. *(AP/Wide World Photos)*

**Eldridge, Roy** (David Eldridge; January 30, 1911, Pittsburgh, Pennsylvania—February 26, 1989, New York, New York): JAZZ trumpeter. Eldridge led his own band at age fifteen and played from the late 1920's through the 1970's

Jazz trumpeter Roy Eldridge in 1973. *(AP/Wide World Photos)*

COLN and the subsequent congressional efforts of the RADICAL REPUBLICANS, who fought for RECONSTRUCTION in the South, the Republican Party was seen as the party of emancipation and of support for African American rights.

Southern Republican governments and African Americans' rights to vote and run for office were protected by the U.S. military occupation of the South during Reconstruction. Southern Republicans elected fourteen African Americans from southern states to Congress during the Reconstruction era. MISSISSIPPI Republicans named the first two African American U.S. senators. One of them, Blanche Kelso BRUCE, was the first African American to serve a full six-year Senate term.

in the bands of Fletcher "Smack" Henderson, Gene Krupa, Count BASIE, and others, in addition to appearing at numerous jazz festivals. His hard-driving, strongly emotional style, inspired partly by trumpeter Louis ARMSTRONG, in turn influenced the pioneering BEBOP trumpeter Dizzy GILLESPIE.

However, freeing the slaves proved more popular than granting former slaves the franchise (the right to vote). Reconstruction was losing support among the American people and in Congress, and gradually southern Democrats—the DEMOCRATIC PARTY in the South was virtually all white at the time—were able to join forces with northern politicians to bring Reconstruction to an end after the 1876 election.

**Electoral politics:** African Americans have historically had a unique role in electoral politics in the United States. From the time of the nation's founding to its CIVIL WAR, most African Americans were slaves denied any rights, let alone the right to vote. Among the relatively small number of free African Americans during those years, there were few VOTERS because property qualifications kept all low-income persons from voting.

By 1900 southern state governments run by white Democrats had imposed a wide range of anti-African American legislation, known as JIM CROW LAWS, that resulted in the DISFRANCHISEMENT of African Americans. Blacks would remain disfranchised in the South until the 1960's civil rights revolution and the passage of the VOTING RIGHTS ACT OF 1965.

*From Reconstruction to the 1930's*
After the Civil War ended in 1865, the REPUBLICAN PARTY sought to maintain political control by supporting African American voting rights in the expectation that African Americans would vote Republican. Because of the war leadership of President Abraham LIN-

From the 1870's to the Great Depression of the 1930's, those few African Americans who were able to vote overwhelmingly cast ballots for Republican candidates. Republicans were

The first African Americans elected to Congress under Reconstruction: (left to right) Hiram Revels, Benjamin Turner, Robert C. De Large, Josiah T. Walls, Jefferson H. Long, Joseph H. Rainy, and R. Brown Elliot. *(Associated Publishers, Inc.)*

viewed as the descendants of those who ended SLAVERY under the leadership of Lincoln, and Democrats were seen as supporters of segregation.

In addition to the fact that African Americans were largely excluded from voting in the southern states, they were discouraged from voting in a number of border states. Since few African Americans lived in northern states in the nineteenth and very early twentieth centuries, their impact on national politics was small. From the end of Reconstruction until the changes of the 1960's, only a rare African American, such as Arthur MITCHELL (representing Chicago, the first African American Democrat elected to Congress) or Adam Clayton POWELL, Jr. (representing HARLEM), was elected to the U.S. House of Representatives.

*A Change in Allegiance*

A major shift in African Americans' political orientation began during the GREAT DEPRESSION. The Democratic ROOSEVELT ADMINISTRATION's New Deal policies benefited all low-income persons, including African Americans, who were disproportionally poor. By contrast, the Republican Party opposed government expenditures for the poor and elderly. Black voters began switching to the Democratic Party.

The Roosevelt administration's policies provided government benefits, jobs, and non-discriminatory pay rates—so that African Americans employed on federal programs found that their wages were much better than those paid by private companies or state and local governments. President Franklin D. Roosevelt (president from 1933 to 1945) was not a champion of African American rights; it has been suggested that he feared losing southern white support for his administration. Nevertheless, his policies managed to provide some relief for poor African Americans without alienating whites. Roosevelt's wife, Eleanor, had a highly visible personal commitment to African Americans, and she undoubtedly increased African American support for Democrats.

The African American community was further tied to the Democratic Party because of the policies of Roosevelt's successor, President Harry S Truman (1945-1953), who apparently had a deep commitment to African American rights. He had risked his own political future by opposing the Missouri Ku Klux Klan as a state official. As president, he issued Executive Order 9981, ordering the integration of the armed forces after World War II. He also supported the controversial civil rights plank that Hubert H. Humphrey, Minneapolis mayor and later U.S. senator, introduced at the 1948 Democratic National Convention.

Truman's commitment to African Americans ultimately paid off during his 1948 reelection campaign: African American voters did not desert Truman in favor of a still more liberal Progressive Party candidate when Truman was threatened on both sides in the election—from the strong segregationist appeal of the southern Dixiecrats and the more liberal appeal of the Progressive Party.

*The Kennedy and Johnson Years*
The African American community became even more strongly committed to the Democratic Party during the Kennedy-Johnson years (1961-1969). President John F. Kennedy (1961-1963) was slow to warm to the civil rights cause and often counseled patience to increasingly impatient African American leaders. Eventually, however, he came to the support the Civil Rights movement. National television news programs broadcast dramatic film footage showing the brutality of angry southerners toward civil rights workers in the South. Kennedy finally went on national television to announce his administration's support for civil rights. This announcement made the national government an active partner in the struggle—a marked change from the passive neutrality that the federal government had previously displayed. Kennedy was assassinated in 1963 before his administration could persuade Congress to pass new legislation guaranteeing civil rights.

The African American community benefited more directly from the policies of Kennedy's successor, President Lyndon B. Johnson (1963-1969). Johnson, a southerner from Texas, surprised many when he actively pushed the landmark 1964 Civil Rights Act through Congress. He also strongly supported the Voting Rights Act of 1965 and appointed a number of African Americans to prominent national positions.

Johnson named Thurgood Marshall to the U.S. Supreme Court, making Marshall the first black Supreme Court justice. Johnson's call for the creation of a Great Society and his success in pushing through Congress the legislation cumulatively known as the War on Poverty improved the economic status of low-income Americans and benefited a sizable number of African Americans. The solid legislative achievements of Johnson never earned him the warm feeling in the African American community that they had willingly and generously given to President Kennedy, perhaps because Johnson was a white southerner. Also, in the last years of his presidency he was disliked by many for continuing the Vietnam War, being fought by disproportionate numbers of black soldiers. Nonetheless, the commitment of blacks to Democratic candidates often rose as high as 90 percent of the vote, routinely exceeding the support levels given by any other ethnic or demographic group.

## Conservatives and Republicans

Despite African Americans' generally staunch support of Democrats, they have never exclusively voted Democratic. For many years, the only African American who had served in the U.S. Senate in the twentieth century was a Republican, Edward William BROOKE from Massachusetts. His social and economic views were on the liberal end of the Republican Party, however, and his status as a Republican was something of an anomaly.

The first African American Republican elected to the House of Representatives since Reconstruction was Gary A. FRANKS of CONNECTICUT, who was elected in 1990. In 1994 J. C. WATTS from OKLAHOMA became the second. Watts was elevated to a leadership position in the House Republican hierarchy in 1998. Thomas SOWELL and Walter WILLIAMS became nationally known and strongly conservative social scientists. Ward Connelly stands out as a still comparatively rare African American leader who strongly opposed AFFIRMATIVE ACTION and led popular initiatives to repeal affirmative action provisions in a number of state constitutions and laws. Still, such conservative voices remain a minority in the African American community. Individual conservatives and Republicans running for office usually consider themselves successful if they receive anything close to 30 percent of African American votes in any given jurisdiction.

## The Impact of Redistricting

One chief characteristic of electoral politics since the 1960's has been the changing impact of voting in legislative races as the result of REDISTRICTING and reapportionment.

Once the U.S. Supreme Court had declared that reapportionment was an issue subject to judicial determination or litigation, the Court handed down a series of decisions that led to the almost universal use of single-member, single-election districts for the U.S. House of Representatives, state legislatures, and local governing bodies. Single-member, single-election districts significantly improve the chances for election of minority candidates over other districting systems, such as at-large districts, which tend to submerge African American minorities in much larger white majority areas.

Single-member, single-election districts, coupled with civil rights efforts and the Voting Rights Act of 1965, enabled African Americans to begin winning a wide range of federal, state, and local government positions. From a total of 40 officeholders nationally in 1960, the number had risen to 8,000 African American officeholders by 1994. That year there were 356 African American mayors in the United States and a much larger number of city councilpersons and county commissioners. The increase was particularly important in the South, where discrimination had been the worst. From having no officeholders and almost no voters in 1960, African Americans in Mississippi came to constitute almost 11 percent of all officeholders in the state. These statistics underscore the success of African Americans in local government positions.

A testimony to the impact of the comparatively small single-member, single-election districts on the success of African American candidates is the sizable number who serve in the U.S. House of Representatives compared with the very small number who are able to win statewide races. For example, Republican Edward Brooke and Democrat Carol E. Moseley BRAUN were the only African Americans to serve in the U.S. Senate in the twentieth century, and there were particular factors that influenced the outcomes of each of their races. On the other hand, dozens of African Americans serve and have served in the U.S. House of Representatives.

## Voter Turnout

One major issue affecting the success of African Americans in electoral politics is the question of voter turnout. There are no longer any significant legal barriers to African American voting, and improvement in registration rates have been dramatic. In Mississippi the rate was 6.9 percent before the Voting Rights Act of 1965 but eventually reached a rate that parallels white registration rates. Yet African American rates of registration to vote and voter turnout lag behind whites' rates in most jurisdictions. Statistically, voter turnout generally increases among groups that are older and have higher incomes and higher educational attainment levels. African Americans are generally younger and have lower incomes and lower educational attainment levels. Their rate of participation is not as high as that of whites. Therefore, African Americans are not as effective politically as they would be if they had higher rates of voting.

—*Richard L. Wilson*

*See also:* At-large elections; Civil rights and congressional legislation; Congressional Black Caucus; Congress members; Gerrymandering; Grandfather clause; Jackson, Jesse; Mayors; Mississippi Freedom Democratic Party; Politics and government.

Suggested Readings:
Barker, Lucius J., Mack H. Jones, and Katherine Tate. *African Americans and the American Political System*. 4th ed. Upper Saddle River, N.J.: Prentice-Hall, 1999.
Barker, Lucius J., ed. *Black Electoral Politics*. New Brunswick, N.J.: Transaction, 1990.
Davidson, Chandler, and Bernard Grofman. *Quiet Revolution in the South: The Impact of the Voting Rights Act, 1965-1990*. Princeton, N.J.: Princeton University Press, 1994.
Finkelman, Paul, ed. *African-Americans and the Right to Vote*. New York: Garland, 1992.
Gordon, Ann D., and Bettye Collier-Thomas. *African American Women and the Vote, 1837-1965*. Amherst: University of Massachusetts Press, 1997.
Kousser, J. Morgan. *Colorblind Injustice: Minority Voting Rights and the Undoing of the Second Reconstruction*. Chapel Hill: University of North Carolina Press, 1999.
Lusane, Clarence. *No Easy Victories: Black Americans and the Vote*. New York: Franklin Watts, 1996.
Reeves, Keith. *Voting Hopes or Fears? White Voters, Black Candidates, and Racial Politics in America*. New York: Oxford University Press, 1997.
Walters, Ronald W. *Black Presidential Politics in America: A Strategic Approach*. Albany: State University of New York Press, 1988.
Walton, Hanes Jr. *Invisible Politics: Black Political Behavior*. Albany: State University of New York Press, 1985.
Whitby, Kenny J. *The Color of Representation: Congressional Behavior and Black Interests*. Ann Arbor: University of Michigan Press, 1997.

**Ellington, Duke** (April 29, 1899, Washington, D.C.—May 24, 1974, New York, New York): Musician and composer. Edward Kennedy "Duke" Ellington was one of the foremost composers of the twentieth century. Ellington, known primarily for his major contributions to JAZZ, formed the Duke Ellington Orchestra, a premier touring and recording ensemble that existed for more than fifty years under his direction.

*Early Life*

Born to James Edward Ellington and Daisy Kennedy Ellington, Duke Ellington was reared in the black community of WASHINGTON, D.C. His father, who supported the family through his entrepreneurial activities, was also a blueprint worker in Washington's U.S. Navy yard. Both parents encouraged young Duke's creative leanings, and his mother oversaw his spiritual development by taking him to the Nineteenth Street Baptist Church and the John Wesley AFRICAN METHODIST EPISCOPAL ZION CHURCH.

The black schools in Washington provided Ellington with his early education. He attended Patterson Elementary School, Garrison Junior High School, and Armstrong Technical High School. Young Ellington, who excelled in baseball and the fine arts, was awarded a scholarship to the Pratt Institute of Applied Art in Brooklyn, but he chose instead to pursue music as a profession, having written his first composition, "Soda Fountain Rag," around 1914.

Ellington received some early musical training, but to a great extent he was self-taught. Influenced by James P. JOHNSON, Ellington also came under the tutelage of prominent Washington musicians such as Oliver "Doc" Perry and Walter Dishman. At local theaters and cafés, Ellington heard the popular music of the day. Ellington was dubbed "Duke" by a fashionable associate, Edgar McEntree, who encouraged Ellington's piano playing.

Ellington's developing musical career involved performing at family socials. In 1918 he married Edna Thompson; their son, Mercer, who would take over the Duke Ellington Orchestra after Ellington's death in 1974, was born in 1919. Around 1920, Ellington formed the nucleus of a small group with percussionist Sonny Greer and a fellow Washingtonian, saxophonist Otto "Toby" Hardwick.

### From Washington to New York

In 1922 Duke Ellington, Sonny Greer, and Otto Hardwick ventured to New York, but they returned to Washington without having had much success. As a replacement for Fats WALLER at Barron's, a HARLEM nightclub, Ellington and his associates returned to New York in 1923, when the HARLEM RENAISSANCE was under way. Called the "Washingtonians," the ensemble began to be recognized in New York, securing an engagement at the downtown Hollywood Club in 1923. For the Okeh and Victor recording labels, Ellington composed and recorded such works as "Creole Love Call," "Black and Tan Fantasy," "Black Beauty" (named after the legendary Florence Mills), "The Mooch," and, along with Bubber Miley, "East St. Louis Toodle-oo," which served as the band's signature piece until it was replaced in the 1940's by Billy STRAYHORN's "Take the A Train."

Between 1927 and 1928, the core of the Ellington orchestra was formed. With the assistance of manager Irving Mills, Ellington secured an engagement at Harlem's celebrated COTTON CLUB in December of 1927, and the ensemble became known as "Duke Ellington and His Orchestra" as well as the "Jungle Band." By 1929 the Duke Ellington Orchestra had been heard on nationwide radio and had participated in a film, *Black and Tan*, for which Ellington composed the music.

### The 1930's

During the 1930's, Ellington appeared in such films as Amos 'n' Andy's *Check and Double Check* (1930) and the Marx Brothers' *A Day at the Races* (1937). Ellington furthered his career as composer and arranger by creating his first extended composition, *Creole Rhapsody* in 1931. Ellington's unique arranging and composing conception was also evident in one of his most celebrated compositions, "Mood Indigo" (1930). With the addition of trumpeter Cootie Williams and vocalist Ivie Anderson, the Ellington orchestra grew in renown. In 1933 Ellington became an international figure, making his first trip to England, where the orchestra performed at the London Palladium; there, Ellington was presented to the Prince of Wales.

After returning to the United States, the orchestra embarked on a southern tour by rail and experienced the South's racial segregation. The death of Ellington's mother in 1935 inspired *Reminiscing in Tempo*, one of Ellington's longer compositions, written in his mother's honor. Ellington also composed pieces for the film *Symphony in Black* (1935). By 1939 Ellington had again visited Europe, and the orchestra had undergone a number of changes in personnel, including the addition of saxophonist Ben WEBSTER and legendary bassist Jimmy Blanton. Ellington had also begun his musical association with Billy Strayhorn, who would be his principal musical collaborator for more than twenty-five years.

### The 1940's

The early 1940's has been singled out by many critics as the Ellington orchestra's peak. In 1941 Ellington's *Jump for Joy*, an all-black revue staged in Los Angeles, made a major statement against JIM CROW LAWS and practices and the stereotypical portrayal of African Americans in the entertainment world. In 1943 Ellington appeared in the all-black film *Cabin in the Sky*, and in 1943 *Black, Brown, and Beige*, an Ellington suite, premiered at Carnegie Hall. *Black, Brown, and Beige* was Ellington's fulfillment of his longtime goal to chronicle the history of African Americans. In 1944 Ellington was also in residence at New York's Hurricane Club and performed at the Capitol Theatre. His Carnegie Hall concerts continued during the 1940's, including *New World a-Comin'* (1943), based on black writer Roi Ottley's prose work on the black experience, *The Perfume Suite* (1945), *The Deep South Suite* (1946), and *The Liberian Suite* (1947), commissioned for the centenary of LIBERIA.

### The 1950's

During the 1950's, Ellington weathered changes in musi-cal tastes, as the big band era gave way to smaller group ensemble styles. Many critics have suggested that the orchestra continued to ascend in the 1950's through Ellington's selection of additional virtuoso musicians. Ellington continued to compose longer works, premiering *Harlem* (1951) and *Night Creature* (1955). His collaborative work included the well-known "Satin Doll" (1953), jointly composed with Billy Strayhorn and Johnny Mercer.

The orchestra's 1956 performance at the Newport Jazz Festival represented its reemergence as a stellar ensemble. That year, Ellington was featured on the August 20 cover of *Time* magazine, which addressed his "comeback." In 1957 Ellington and the orchestra were also seen on television in "A Drum Is a Woman," which featured vocalist Joya Sherrill and Ellington's talents as a monologuist. Ellington

Duke Ellington led his orchestra for more than fifty years. *(Library of Congress)*

composed the *Shakespearean Suite* (1957), *The Queen's Suite* (1959), and his first complete film score, for *Anatomy of a Murder* (1959).

### The 1960's

After composing *Suite Thursday* in 1960, Ellington continued to tour and record. In the early 1960's, he recorded with jazz greats Louis ARMSTRONG, Count BASIE, Coleman HAWKINS, Charles MINGUS, and Max ROACH and toured extensively in Europe with Ella FITZGERALD. Ellington also contributed to the CIVIL RIGHTS struggle by producing *My People* (1963) for the Chicago Centennial of Negro Progress Exposition. *My People*, which included a tribute to Martin Luther KING, Jr., was a political statement in music, showing Ellington's solidarity with the Civil Rights movement.

In 1964 Ellington toured Europe, the Middle East, and the Far East at the request of the U.S. State Department. He composed *The Far East Suite* (1964) and *The Virgin Islands Suite* (1965) and began a new direction with the premiere of the first sacred concert at Grace Cathedral in San Francisco in 1965. Ellington also made his first trip to Africa in 1966 for the First World Festival of Negro Arts in Dakar, Senegal, for which he wrote "La Plus Belle Africaine" and acknowledged his link to African music. His longtime collaborator Billy Strayhorn died in 1967.

### The 1970's

The opening of the 1970's was made tragic for Ellington by the death of famed alto saxophonist and longtime orchestra member Johnny HODGES. Ellington's musical activities did not abate, though, and he toured the Soviet Union, Europe, South America, and Mexico. In 1971 he premiered *The Goutelas Suite*, and in 1973 he toured the Far East, Europe, Zambia, and Ethiopia, where he was awarded the Emperor's Star. He also received the French Legion of Honor and published his au-tobiography, *Music Is My Mistress* (1973). At the beginning of 1974 Ellington continued to work, but he succumbed to lung cancer that year, dying on May 24.

In 1999, the centennial of Ellington's birth, numerous concerts and tributes to Ellington were held throughout the United States to honor his major contributions to jazz and to American culture. In Washington, D.C., his hometown, a Duke Ellington Centennial Commission was formed to coordinate the myriad events—concerts, films, reminiscences, a parade, and even a walking tour of "Ellington's Washington"—occurring in the nation's capital.

### Ellington's Composing and Arranging Process

Duke Ellington's compositions, sometimes described as "tone parallels," often contained images of African American life and were frequently the result of the collective contributions of his musicians and collaborators such as Billy Strayhorn. Ellington's unique orchestral colors were derived from the particular musical attributes of his musicians and vocalists, which were blended to create the characteristic Ellingtonian sound. Although Ellington was a remarkable pianist, his true instrument was his orchestra.

—*Joseph McLaren*

See also: Songwriters and composers.

Suggested Readings:

Bigard, Barney. *With Louis and the Duke: The Autobiography of a Jazz Clarinetist*. New York: Oxford University Press, 1985.

Collier, James L. *Duke Ellington*. New York: Oxford University Press, 1987.

Ellington, Duke. *Music Is My Mistress*. Garden City, N.Y.: Doubleday, 1974.

Hasse, John E. *Beyond Category: The Life and Genius of Duke Ellington*. New York: Simon & Schuster, 1993.

Lambert, Eddie. *Duke Ellington: A Listener's Guide*. Lanham, Md.: Scarecrow Press, 1999.

Nicholson, Stuart. *Reminiscing in Tempo: A Portrait of Duke Ellington*. Boston: Northeastern University Press, 1999.

Pinkney, Andrea D., and J. Brian Pinkney. *Duke Ellington: The Piano Prince and His Orchestra*. New York: Hyperion Books for Children, 1998.

Rattenbury, Ken. *Duke Ellington, Jazz Composer*. New Haven, Conn.: Yale University Press, 1990.

Tucker, Mark. *Ellington: The Early Years*. Urbana: University of Illinois Press, 1991.

_____, ed. *The Duke Ellington Reader*. New York: Oxford University Press, 1993.

**Elliott, Robert Brown** (August 11, 1842, Boston, Massachusetts—August 9, 1884, New Orleans, Louisiana): SOUTH CAROLINA politician. Born to West Indian parents and educated in JAMAICA and England, Elliott graduated from Eton with honors. He served on the post-CIVIL WAR South Carolina constitutional convention, won election to the lower house of the state legislature, and served two terms in the U.S. Congress (1871-1874). He served as speaker of the house for the South Carolina legislature for two years, then practiced law in New Orleans until his death.

*See also:* Congress members; Reconstruction.

**Ellis, Trey** (b. 1962, Washington, D.C.): Writer. The son of William Ellis, a psychiatrist, and Pamela Ellis, a lawyer, Trey Ellis grew up amid middle-class affluence. He went to prep school at Phillips Academy and Andover before attending Stanford University, where he was editor of the student humor magazine. He wrote his first novel, *Platitudes* (1988), when he was only twenty-three years old. Ellis began the novel while he was enrolled in a fiction writing class at Stanford taught by Gilbert Sorentino.

During his twenties, Ellis held a variety of jobs—everything from moving furniture to re-searching and reporting for *Newsweek* and for television stations in New York and Atlanta. Despite the opportunities he had to develop a career as a reporter, Ellis continued to concentrate on finishing his novel. Ellis also tried television comedy writing but was unsuccessful. He decided to go to Italy and finish his book.

In Florence, Ellis took four part-time jobs and was able to arrange a schedule that allowed him to write four hours a day. In six months, Ellis had finished a rough draft of *Platitudes*. He sent the manuscript to a friend in New York and then left on a five-month trek, hitchhiking throughout Africa. When he returned to New York, Ellis began rewriting the novel. He supported himself by working as a proofreader for *Rolling Stone* and *Interview* magazines.

Once the novel was finished, Ellis sent it to everyone he knew or could think of in publishing. Eventually an agent took it to Random House, where Vintage Contemporaries made an offer. The novel quickly aroused critical interest.

*Platitudes* is an amusing and intelligent novel that revolves around the themes of love and storytelling. Earle Tyner and Dorothy LaMont are characters in a novel within a novel—the creations of black writer Dewayne Wellington, who is newly divorced and suffering from depression. Finding it difficult to complete his novel, Dewayne invites critical assistance from successful feminist writer Isshee Ayam. The story of the romance between Dewayne and Isshee parallels that of Earle and Dorothy. The intertwined stories are developed into a parody with references to popular TELEVISION SERIES and JAZZ music.

Ellis's second novel, *Home Repairs*, was published in 1993. It follows the misadventures of Austin McMillan, a well-educated, middle-class African American. Both novels illustrate Ellis's commitment to a new style of African American literary art as described in his 1989 article "The New Black Aesthetic."

In the 1990's Ellis began writing for television and film. His script for the HBO production *The Tuskegee Airmen* was nominated for an Emmy Award. *Right Here, Right Now*, Ellis's third novel, was published in 1999. Through protagonist Ashton Robinson, the book satirizes American conformity and a number of other topics. Ellis and his wife, Erika, who is also a novelist, had a daughter, Ava, in 1998. *See also:* Literature.

Suggested Readings:
Brodie, John. "'Inkwell' Scribe Forfeits More than Screen Credit." *Variety* (January 24, 1994): 7-8.
Eisenbach, Helen. "Profile of a First Novelist: Trey Ellis and *Platitudes*." *Writer's Digest* (August, 1987): 56-57.
Ellis, Trey. "The New Black Aesthetic." *Callaloo* 12 (Winter, 1989): 233-246.
Green, Laura. "Right Here, Right Now." Review. *The New York Times Book Review* 104 (February 7, 1999): 16.
Lott, Eric. "Hip-Hop Fiction." *The Nation* (December 19, 1988): 691-692.

**Ellison, Ralph** (March 1, 1914, Oklahoma City, Oklahoma—April 16, 1994, New York, New York): Author. Ralph Waldo Ellison's 1952 novel, *Invisible Man*, won international acclaim and established Ellison's reputation as a major twentieth century American writer.

The atmosphere in which Ralph Ellison grew up encouraged his intellectual and artistic ambitions. Ellison's father, a construction worker who died in an accident when Ellison was three years old, named his son after the nineteenth-century essayist Ralph Waldo Emerson. His mother worked as a domestic in white homes to support her family. She brought young Ralph discarded magazines and books that he eagerly read. Ellison enjoyed listening to jazz in the black section of Oklahoma City and absorbed the stories told by his elders. He and his friends, both white and black, decided to become Renaissance men by mastering all areas of knowledge.

*Education*

Music was young Ellison's major interest. He was the first-chair trumpeter in his high school band and took private lessons, which he paid for by mowing his teacher's lawn. In 1933 the state of OKLAHOMA granted Ellison a scholarship to pay his tuition at TUSKEGEE INSTITUTE. Not having enough money for a train ticket, he hopped freight trains to get to ALABAMA. Ellison majored in music and music theory, hoping to become a professional musician. While at Tuskegee he read widely in modern fiction and poetry and became aware that these books ignored the reality of black life and culture. At the end of his junior year Ellison had difficulty renewing his scholarship. In 1936 he left for NEW YORK CITY, planning to earn enough money to return, but he never did.

Ellison reveled in the rich musical and cultural life of HARLEM. Novelist Richard WRIGHT encouraged him to contribute essays and fiction to the left-wing periodicals he edited. In 1938 Ellison joined the FEDERAL WRITERS' PROJECT, with which he carried out street interviews documenting the urban folklore of Harlem. During WORLD WAR II, he served as a cook in the merchant marine to avoid being drafted into the then rigidly segregated armed forces.

*Publications*

In the short stories that Ellison published from 1938 to 1942, he slowly developed a complex style that combined realistic observation with symbolism and mythic folk motifs. Ellison worked on his novel for seven years before it was published in 1952. *Invisible Man* begins with a prologue in which the unnamed narrator, who has retreated into an underground shelter which he lights with electricity stolen

Author Ralph Ellison is best known for his masterful novel, *Invisible Man* (1952). *(National Archives)*

from the Monopolated Light & Power Company, listens to Louis ARMSTRONG's recording of "What Did I Do to Be So Black and Blue?" To answer that question the narrator recapitulates his experiences for the reader, primarily from the viewpoint of a naïve youth but also including satirical asides from an older, wiser perspective. From his expulsion from a black state college for permitting a white philanthropist to observe unsavory aspects of black rural life, through his exploration of Harlem, where he is rejected by both communists and black nationalists, no one he encounters sees him as a real flesh-and-blood person. In the closing epilogue the narrator meditates on the meaning of his experiences and puzzles over his identity. Every chapter contains symbolic episodes and characters that connect the narrative to major aspects of American and African American life and LITERATURE.

*Invisible Man* was an instant success; most reviews were favorable, and the novel won the National Book Award for fiction in 1953. In 1965 a *Book Week* poll of two hundred authors, editors, and critics selected *Invisible Man* as the most distinguished novel published by an American in the previous twenty years. Critics praised both its symbolic complexity and the sophisticated way Ellison connected black life and culture with such universal themes as the search for identity. In the 1960's, however, Ellison came under attack by black nationalists; they condemned him precisely for the universal nature of his work. Detractors termed this an abandonment of the black protest tradition and a failure to accept his proper racial commitment as a black writer. During the 1980's black critical opinion shifted, and Ellison's use of BLUES and FOLKLORE was praised as a major literary contribution, bringing black culture into the mainstream of contemporary American writing.

Ellison later published two collections of critical essays and interviews, *Shadow and Act* (1964) and *Going to the Territory* (1986), in which he examined black literature and folklore, blues, and JAZZ, and argued that mainstream American culture had been heavily influenced by black culture. Ellison taught at Bard College (1958-1961), at Rutgers University (1962-1969), and at New York University, where he served as Albert Schweitzer Professor in the Humanities from 1970 until his retirement in 1979. He also lectured frequently at other universities. Ellison received many awards and over a dozen honorary doctorates, including one from Tuskegee Institute in 1963.

## Second Novel

From 1955 to the end of his life, Ellison worked on a second novel. He was always a slow and painstaking writer, and the pressure to produce a work that would match the acclaimed *Invisible Man* made Ellison even more cautious and meticulous. A fire at his summer home in 1967 destroyed both copies of more than 350 pages of manuscript. Depressed, Ellison did not begin reconstructing what he had written until three years later. At his death he left several thousand pages of manuscript and some fifty computer disks dealing with the unfinished second novel. Many episodes in the story exist in several versions. Ellison's literary executor planned to sort them out and publish the novel.

After Ellison's death, his literary executor compiled *The Collected Essays of Ralph Ellison* (1995) and *Flying Home and Other Stories* (1997). The first work includes the complete texts of *Shadow and Act* and *Going to the Territory* along with a dozen additional essays. The second book contains thirteen stories, six of which were previously unpublished. Ellison's unfinished second novel was published as *Juneteenth* in 1999, edited by John F. Callahan. It concerns a black minister who takes in and raises a little boy as black even though the boy appears white. The boy runs away and eventually becomes a race-baiting U.S. senator. *Invisible Man* has been translated into fourteen languages, and it and Ellison's two volumes of essays have never been out of print. They are regularly assigned in courses dealing with classical American as well as black literature.

—*Milton Berman*

Suggested Readings:

Benston, Kimberly W., ed. *Speaking for You: The Vision of Ralph Ellison*. Washington, D.C.: Howard University Press, 1987.

Busby, Mark. *Ralph Ellison*. Boston: Twayne, 1991.

McSweeney, Kevin. *Invisible Man: Race and Identity*. Boston: Twayne, 1988.

O'Meally, Robert, ed. *New Essays on Invisible Man*. Cambridge, England: Cambridge University Press, 1985.

Schor, Edith. *Visible Ellison: A Study of Ralph Ellison's Fiction*. Westport, Conn.: Greenwood Press, 1993.

**Emancipation Proclamation:** The CIVIL WAR raged from 1861 to 1865. On January 1, 1863, the president of the United States, Abraham Lincoln, declared that all persons held as slaves within any state whose people had risen up in rebellion against the union should be set free. This declaration, known historically as the Emancipation Proclamation, especially when coupled with the famous Gettysburg Address, gives the name of Lincoln almost mythic qualities in the American psyche. Since he gave freedom to millions of blacks and hastened the end of the Civil War, some call Lincoln a supreme liberator.

In reality, the Emancipation Proclamation was the act of a president caught in the throes of national race prejudice, abolitionist pressure, and, most pressing, a brutal civil war in which expediency was required. Although he had shown interest in the emancipation question ever since his early days in Congress, Lincoln did not make his 1863 proclamation out of particular humanitarian concerns for blacks. It was a war measure, a tactic used by a president who was desperate to bring a horrible war to an end.

*Historical Background*

The Civil War was a logical result of long and bitter sectional strife over the question of SLAVERY and was considered an altercation between whites in which blacks had no business. The emancipation question, however, was crucial to the war efforts from start to finish. Northern Democrats were as determined as southerners were to defend slavery and keep blacks "in their place." Yet those in the ABOLITIONIST MOVEMENT who supported the REPUBLICAN PARTY's antislavery platform in the 1860 election held their victorious party to its pledge to free the slaves.

As a congressman in 1849, Lincoln had introduced a bill calling for a gradual emancipation in the District of Columbia; he later expressed an interest in nationwide emancipation. As president, he even contemplated compensating owners for emancipated slaves, to a maximum of three hundred dollars per slave. When the war began, however, Lincoln gave specific orders that slaves must not be freed and that fugitives were to be returned to their masters. Lincoln needed all the white support he could muster in the North. In order not to give the impression that the war was being fought on behalf of blacks, the president refused to accept black military units from the Hannibal Guards of Pittsburgh, the Crispus Attucks Guard of Ohio, and other groups of free blacks who had responded to his call for volunteers after the fall of Fort Sumter in 1861.

When G. P. Miller, a black physician from Battle Creek, Michigan, sought permission to amass a regiment of about ten thousand blacks to help win the war, he was told that the conflict was a white man's war and that the president was not inclined to alter "the course thus far pursued." In his attempt to please border states, whose slaves the 1863 proclamation did not affect, Lincoln refused to develop a workable policy regarding slaves who had abandoned their masters by the hundreds of thousands and were flocking to the Union lines.

Lincoln even reprimanded General John C. Frémont for issuing a proclamation freeing the slaves of Missouri rebels, and he moved quickly to nullify a similar proclamation of General David Hunter relative to slaves in Georgia, Florida, and South Carolina. For roughly two years, Lincoln maintained his equivocal stance on the slavery question, partially because of Democratic opposition to emancipation.

The Emancipation Proclamation. *(Library of Congress)*

### The Circumstances

The Emancipation Proclamation was predicated on three major developments. First, the determination of the South to maintain and defend its slave economy engendered staying power in its soldiers, who vowed to fight to the death. This determination forced the Union to abandon the naïve notion that the war was a brawl between white gentlemen that would soon be over. The North realized that it was fighting a powerful enemy and that it needed all the support, weapons, and fighting power it could muster. The realization forced Lincoln to contemplate a decisive strike at the "bread and butter" of the South—its economy built on slavery.

Second, southern blacks, by fleeing the PLANTATIONS, flocking to the Union lines, and waving the flag, forced northerners to take them seriously as an entity in winning the war. Generals began using them in support services and referring to SLAVE RUNAWAYS as "contraband of war," a term that was much

African Americans marching through the streets of Richmond, Virginia, to celebrate Emancipation Day around the turn of the twentieth century. *(Library of Congress)*

less explosive on Capitol Hill than "escaped slaves." Finally, in Congress, abolitionists such as Charles Sumner, Thaddeus Stevens, Henry Wilson, and Benjamin Wade seized the opportunity to act on behalf of the slaves. They passed legislation that forbade Union officers to return fleeing slaves to rebels, declared rebel slaves free, emancipated the slaves in the District of Columbia, and gave war powers to the president to use black troops to help bring the war to a swift end. These steps proved advantageous to the abolitionists' cause, and they pushed the president toward emancipation.

*Timing the Proclamation's Release*

In the summer of 1862, Lincoln realized that he had delayed strategic action for too long and that a decisive plan was imperative. On July 22 he called a cabinet meeting and laid a draft of the Emancipation Proclamation on the table. A top adviser prevailed upon the president to delay action further for fear that he would be perceived by critics as collaborating with blacks to win the war. Union generals in South

Carolina, Kansas, and Louisiana, however, ignored such concerns and, rather than waiting for a proclamation they were not sure Lincoln would make, began recruiting blacks to strengthen their regiments. While Lincoln was polishing his proclamation speech in late summer, General Benjamin Butler was already issuing papers for the First Louisiana Native Guard to begin operation as a recognized black regiment in the Union army.

Five days after the Union won the Battle of Antietam in September, 1862, the president announced that he would emancipate the slaves and confiscate southern property on January 1 unless the South changed its rebellious course. On January 1, 1863, Lincoln finally struck his decisive blow against the CONFEDERACY by issuing the Emancipation Proclamation, which declared all slaves in the rebellious states free forever.

*The Results*

The prevailing response in the North to the proclamation was unfavorable, and some white soldiers even resigned rather than fight a war that they believed was being conducted to free blacks. So-called Peace Democrats accused Lincoln of wasting white lives in a bloody abolitionist war. In the black community, however, there was jubilation. Upon closer scrutiny of the proclamation, abolitionists were disappointed that the president had left slavery alive in the border states that had not rebelled against the Union. For a full quarter of the slaves in the United States, therefore, 1863 was less a year of celebration than of mourning. Abolitionists knew that their fight against slavery would have to continue until every black in the United States was freed.

—*N. Samuel Murrell*

*See also:* Lincoln administration; Thirteenth Amendment.

Suggested Readings:

Cox, LaWanda C. F. *Lincoln and Black Freedom: A Study in Presidential Leadership.* Columbia: University of South Carolina Press, 1994.

Franklin, John Hope. *From Slavery to Freedom: A History of African Americans.* 7th ed. New York: Alfred A. Knopf, 1994.

McPherson, James M. *The Struggle for Equality: Abolitionists and the Negro in the Civil War and Reconstruction.* Princeton, N.J.: Princeton University Press, 1964.

Quarles, Benjamin. *Lincoln and the Negro.* New York: Oxford University Press, 1962.

Trefousse, Hans L. *Lincoln's Decision for Emancipation.* Philadelphia: J. B. Lippincott, 1975.

Wesley, Charles H., and Patricia W. Romero. *Negro Americans in the Civil War: From Slavery to Citizenship.* 2d rev. ed. New York: Publishers Company, 1969.

**Emerge:** Magazine. Published for and by African Americans and subtitled *Black America's Newsmagazine, Emerge* was established in 1989 by its founding editor, Wilmer C. Ames, Jr. Based in Washington, D.C., the magazine later came under the direction of editor-in-chief George E. Curry. *Emerge* established a publishing schedule of ten issues a year (combined issues appear in December/January and July/August) by Emerge Communications, Inc., a subsidiary of BLACK ENTERTAINMENT TELEVISION. In addition to feature articles, the magazine developed sections such as "People Watching," "Friendly Fire," "Diaspora Watch," "Capital Scene," "Minding Our Business," "Vital Signs," "Just Jazz," "Cover to Cover," "Speaking Volumes," and "The Last Word."

*Emerge* focused on publishing hard-hitting articles on issues and events concerning the African American community. A number of issues devoted extensive coverage to the subject of African American political prisoners in the United States. In June of 1994, for example, *Emerge* ran a cover story entitled "FBI Cover-Up: How Black Panther Geronimo Pratt Was Framed." An accompanying story, "Other Political Prisoners," discussed the case of journalist and convicted murderer Mumia Abu-Jamal, along with six other cases. In the November, 1995, edition, a lengthy piece chronicled new developments, grassroots support, and celebrity interest in Abu-Jamal's case.

*See also:* Black press; Columnists; *Ebony*; *Jet*; Print journalism.

**Employment and unemployment:** One enduring dimension of the African American struggle for survival in the United States is the struggle for economic equality and justice. Unemployment, underemployment, and discrimination in employment and wages are significantly more pervasive problems for African Americans than for white Americans. Poor health care, high INFANT MORTALITY rates, short life expectancy, inferior educational opportunities, inadequate housing, and high rates of victimization from crime are some of the direct consequences of unemployment and the debilitating POVERTY faced by many in the black community.

*From Slavery to World War II*

From colonial days to the end of the CIVIL WAR, most African Americans were inescapably disadvantaged for the simple reason that they were slaves with no rights and no hope for a better life. The census of 1790 indicated that 19.3 percent of the country's population, approximately 800,000 persons, was African American. Of this population, 59,000 were free blacks. By 1860 the number of African Americans had increased to 4.4 million (14.1 percent of the total American population), and the number of free blacks was less than half a million. At the time of the Civil War, there were nearly 4 million slaves.

Although SLAVERY was abolished in 1865, there was little improvement in the economic conditions of the newly freed African Americans. In 1890 about 3 million African Americans were in the labor force, but the majority were compelled to work as tenant farmers or sharecroppers. Generally, because of the nature of SHARECROPPING, most gained very little in terms of wages or improved living standards. Most were deeply in debt to white property owners at the end of each year.

By 1930 the African American labor force had grown to more than 5.5 million. Large numbers of African Americans had migrated from the South, seeking better opportunities in the industrial areas of the North and Midwest, however overt RACIAL DISCRIMINATION forced them into the lowest-paying, least-skilled, and least desirable jobs. During the 1920's and 1930's, very few African Americans held white-collar jobs. The entry of African Americans into the industrial sector was abruptly ended by the GREAT DEPRESSION in the 1930's. There was no major improvement in the employment patterns or opportunities for African Americans until WORLD WAR II.

Beginning in the 1940's, African Americans began to make considerable progress in gaining access to jobs and occupations that were traditionally reserved for whites. Many ana-lysts attribute this success to a convergence of social forces that caused the United States to address the economic disadvantages imposed upon African Americans. The country's need for workers during various periods of the twentieth century and protest movements by the African American community were among the factors that contributed to employment gains made by African Americans.

*After the Civil Rights Movement*

The Civil Rights movement ushered in a new era of economic and occupational opportuni-

Before the Civil Rights movement era, racial discrimination drove African Americans to the lowest-paying, least-skilled, and least-desirable jobs, symbolized here in Gordon Parks, Sr.'s *American Gothic*. (Library of Congress)

ties for blacks. The Civil Rights Act of 1964 and several other major laws were designed to eliminate discrimination against African Americans and other minorities in the job market. AFFIRMATIVE ACTION laws and policies were implemented, and they enabled African Americans to enter professions and corporations that historically had been closed to them. Voting-rights laws and judicial decisions increased the political power and participation of African Americans. This political power led to greater employment within the public sector for African Americans.

Even though African Americans have enjoyed success in gaining entry into better jobs, they are still less likely than white workers to be employed in the best jobs and more likely to be employed in the worst jobs in every occupational category. For example, in 1990 6.8 percent of African American men and 14.6 percent of white men were employed in executive, administrative, and managerial jobs; 7.5 percent of African American women and 11.6 percent of white women were employed in

## Percentages of African Americans in Employment Categories, 1983 and 1997

| Occupation Category | 1983 | | 1997 | |
| --- | --- | --- | --- | --- |
| | Total Employed, All Races (× 1,000) | African American Percentage of Total | Total Employed, All Races (× 1,000) | African American Percentage of Total |
| Total | 100,834 | 9.3 | 129,558 | 10.8 |
| **Managerial and Professional Specialty** | 23,592 | 5.6 | 37,686 | 7.3 |
| Executive, administrative, and managerial | 10,772 | 4.7 | 18,440 | 6.9 |
| Professional specialty | 12,820 | 6.4 | 19,245 | 7.8 |
| **Technical, Sales, and Administrative Support** | 31,255 | 7.6 | 38,309 | 10.5 |
| Technicians and related support | 3,053 | 8.2 | 4,214 | 9.7 |
| Sales occupations | 11,818 | 4.7 | 15,734 | 8.1 |
| Administrative support, including clerical | 16,395 | 9.6 | 18,361 | 12.8 |
| **Service Occupations** | 13,857 | 16.6 | 17,537 | 17.6 |
| Private household | 980 | 27.8 | 795 | 16.2 |
| Protective service | 1,672 | 13.6 | 2,300 | 18.7 |
| Other service occupations | 11,205 | 16.0 | 14,442 | 17.5 |
| **Precision Production, Craft, and Repair** | 12,328 | 6.8 | 14,124 | 8.1 |
| Mechanics and repairers | 4,158 | 6.8 | 4,675 | 7.9 |
| Construction trades | 4,289 | 6.6 | 5,378 | 7.1 |
| Extractive occupations | 196 | 3.3 | 145 | 8.6 |
| Precision production occupations | 3,685 | 7.3 | 3,926 | 9.7 |
| **Operators, Fabricators, and Laborers** | 16,091 | 14.0 | 18,399 | 15.1 |
| Machine operators, assemblers, and inspectors | 7,744 | 14.0 | 7,962 | 14.8 |
| Transportation and material-moving occupations | 4,201 | 13.0 | 5,389 | 15.2 |
| Handlers, equipment cleaners, helpers, and laborers | 4,147 | 15.1 | 5,048 | 15.5 |
| Farm operators and managers | 1,450 | 1.3 | 1,317 | 1.2 |
| Other agricultural and related operations | 2,072 | 11.7 | 2,030 | 6.6 |
| Forestry and logging operations | 126 | 12.8 | 108 | 6.7 |

Source: U.S. Bureau of Labor Statistics.
Note: For civilian population 16 and over; annual average of monthly figures.

As the main phase of the Civil Rights movement crested, African American residents of Birmingham, Alabama, massed to protest job discrimination at the U.S. Steel plant, a major local employer. *(AP/Wide World Photos)*

these categories. Similar disparities in numbers existed in professional, technical, and sales occupational categories.

Some progress is clearly shown by an analysis of changes in occupation distribution by race from the 1940's to the 1990's. For example, one-third of African Americans were farm workers in 1940, and only 6 percent were white-collar workers. By 1975 only 2.7 percent worked as farm workers, and 37.8 percent were employed in white-collar jobs.

In 1990 28.1 percent of African American women, 40.8 percent of white women, 36.9 percent of African American men, and 61.8 percent of white men were employed in the five occupational groups (executive; administrative and managerial; professional; sales; and precision production, craft, and repairs) that offer the best jobs.

Between 1983 and 1997 African Americans increased their representation in most major occupational categories, according to the statistics and job classification system of the U.S. Bureau of Labor Statistics. African Americans as a percentage of the labor force in general increased from 9.3 percent in 1983 to 10.8 percent in 1997. In managerial and professional employment, black representation increased from 5.6 to 7.3 percent. In technical, sales, and administrative support jobs, representation increased from 7.6 to 10.5 percent. Representation in service occupations rose from 16.6 to 17.6 percent, in precision production, craft, and repair work from 6.8 to 8.1 percent, and in the category of operators, fabricators, and laborers from 14.0 to 15.1 percent.

*African American Women*

From World War II to the 1980's, African American women fared somewhat better in the labor market than African American men. In 1940 73.5 percent of working African American WOMEN worked in domestic and agricultural occupations, whereas only 13.4 percent of white working women worked in these sectors. By 1988 only 13.4 percent of African American women and 2.5 percent of white women worked in these jobs. American women moved from domestic services and agricultural jobs to clerical, managerial, professional, and technical jobs.

In 1988 49.7 percent of working African American women were employed in these occupations—19.6 percent in managerial, professional, and technical jobs and 30.1 percent in clerical positions. The major increase in the number of African American women employed in clerical positions occurred within the public sector. The impact of this increased opportunity was a reduction in the disparity in income between African American women and white women.

*Unemployment and Poverty*

The disadvantage of belonging to a minority group is vividly illustrated by a comparison of the unemployment rates of African Americans to those of non-Hispanic whites. In 1950 the unemployment rate for African Americans was 9.0 percent, compared with 4.9 percent for whites.

In 1992 the unemployment rates for people in the prime wage-earning years of twenty-five to sixty-four were 12.4 percent for blacks and 6.0 percent for whites; in 1997, thanks to the booming U.S. economy of the 1990's, rates had decreased to 8.1 percent for blacks and 3.9 percent for whites. Despite the drop in unemployment, the black unemployment rate was still more than double the white rate.

African Americans between the ages of sixteen and twenty-four are even more severely affected by unemployment. In 1976 the unemployment rate was 28.6 percent for African American youths and 13.1 percent for white youths. In 1997 the rates for youths were 25.4 percent for young blacks and 10.3 percent for young whites.

The impact of these disparities is visible in levels of poverty in the United States. In 1959 9.9 million African Americans and 28.3 million whites were classified as poor. By 1970 these numbers had declined to 7.5 million African Americans and 17.5 million whites. In the 1980's, the number of poor Americans in-

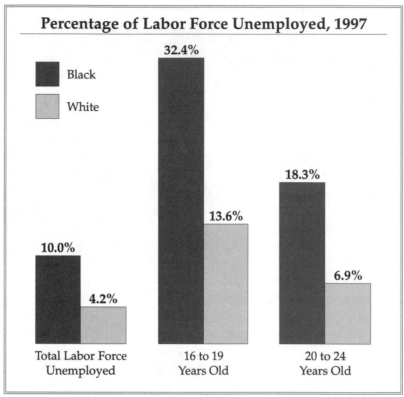

**Percentage of Labor Force Unemployed, 1997**

■ Black
▢ White

10.0%
4.2%
Total Labor Force Unemployed

32.4%
13.6%
16 to 19 Years Old

18.3%
6.9%
20 to 24 Years Old

*Source:* U.S. Department of Labor Statistics.

creased; in 1991 9.8 million African Americans (31.9 percent) and 22.3 million white Americans (10.7 percent) were living below the poverty level. In 1997 about 9.1 million African Americans (26.5 percent) and 24.4 million whites (11.7 percent) were below the poverty level.

—*Richard Hudson*

*See also:* Business and commerce; Comprehensive Employment and Training Act of 1973; Demography; Income distribution; Institutional racism; Job Opportunities in the Business Sector program.

Suggested Readings:

Bailey, Ronald W., ed. *Black Business Enterprise: Historical and Contemporary Perspectives.* New York: Basic Books, 1971.

Berry, Mary F., and John W. Blassingame. *Long Memory: The Black Experience in America.* New York: Oxford University Press, 1982.

Blackwell, James E. *The Black Community: Diversity and Unity*. 3d ed. New York: HarperCollins, 1991.

Foner, Philip S. *History of Black Americans*. Westport, Conn.: Greenwood Press, 1983.

Franklin, John Hope. *From Slavery to Freedom: A History of African Americans*. 7th ed. New York: Alfred A. Knopf, 1994.

Lathan, E. LeMay. *The Black Man's Guide to Working in a White Man's World*. Santa Monica, Calif.: General Publishing Group, 1997.

Roberts, Bari-Ellen, with Jack E. White. *Roberts vs. Texaco: A True Story of Race and Corporate America*. New York: Avon Books, 1999.

Schwartzman, David. *Black Unemployment: Part of Unskilled Unemployment*. Westport, Conn.: Greenwood Press, 1997.

Swinton, David H. "The Economic Status of African Americans: Limited Ownership and Persistent Inequality." In *The State of Black America 1992*, edited by Janet Dewart. New York: Urban League, 1992.

Weiss, Robert J. *"We Want Jobs": A History of Affirmative Action*. New York: Garland, 1997.

**Engineers:** Used in medieval times to identify a person who designed fortifications or military weapons, the term "engineer" evolved to include individuals trained to apply scientific and mathematical principles to design and produce a variety of machines, devices, and structures. African American engineers have made important contributions to civil, mechanical, chemical, and electrical engineering, and many have specialized in applications to fields such as acoustics, aerospace, AGRICULTURE, communications, the MILITARY, mining, traffic control, and water supply technology.

### Sugar Refining Process

Norbert RILLIEUX was born to a Creole family in New Orleans, Louisiana, in 1806. As a young man, Rillieux traveled to France, where he studied engineering at L'Ecole Centrale in Paris and took a post as an instructor there in 1830. Rillieux returned to the United States during the 1840's and began working on a system for improving sugar refining. After patenting a vacuum evaporating pan in 1846, Rillieux was hailed as the creator of the greatest chemical engineering innovation of that time. The vacuum evaporating pan was adopted worldwide and was adapted to improve the production of many other industrial chemicals, including soap and gelatin.

### Innovations in Heat Control

Born in Nashville, Tennessee, in 1898, David N. CROSTHWAIT, Jr., received his scientific education at Purdue University. After graduating with a B.S. degree in 1913 and an M.E. degree in 1920, Crosthwait focused his attention on the investigation of heat transfer processes, including heating, ventilation, and air conditioning. From 1925 to 1930, Crosthwait worked as a research engineer for the C. A. Dunham Company and served as a technical adviser for Dunham-Bush from 1930 until 1971. Before his death in 1976, Crosthwait received 39 patents, including those for a vacuum pump and a number of automotive heating and heat control processes. The best-known application of his industrial heating designs was the heating system installed at New York City's Radio City Music Hall.

### Industrial Research in Materials Engineering

Harry J. Green, Jr., was born in St. Louis, Missouri, in 1911, and attended Ohio State University, where he received his bachelor's degree in chemical engineering in 1932. Green continued his chemical engineering studies at the Massachusetts Institute of Technology (MIT), where he received his M.S. degree in 1938 before returning to Ohio State University to complete his Ph.D. in 1943. Green accepted a position as professor at North Carolina A&T College in 1943 before pursuing a career in industrial engineering with the Stromberg-Carlson Company from 1944 to 1967. Green later worked for General Dynamics from 1967 to 1970 before taking a position with the Xerox Corporation. His research included work on state-of-the-art industrial materials, including polymer applications, telephone transmitter materials, xerographic materials, and microelectronic packaging of thin-film hybrid circuits.

### Practical Applications of Physics

Born in Jacksonville, Florida, in 1919, Robert H. Bragg attended the Illinois Institute of Technology (IIT), where he received his B.S. degree in 1949 and his M.S. degree in 1951 before completing his Ph.D. studies. From 1951 to 1956, Bragg worked as an industrial research physicist at the IIT Research Institute before accepting a research position with the Lockheed Missile and Space Company in 1957. Bragg left Lockheed in 1969 after he was appointed to a post as professor of material science and mineral engineering at the University of California at Berkeley. While at Berkeley, Bragg became chairman and a principal investigator at the materials and molecular division of the Lawrence Berkeley Laboratory. In addition to his many publications and honors, Bragg established himself as a leader in the fields of physics and engineering, holding memberships in both the American Physical Society and the American Institute of Mining and Metallurgical Engineers.

### Aerospace Engineers

Raymond E. Rose and Christine M. Darden are among several black scientists who have established themselves in the field of aerospace engineering. Rose was born in Canton, Ohio, in 1926, and received his B.S. degree in 1951 from the University of Kansas before completing his M.S. and Ph.D. degrees at the University of Minnesota in 1956 and 1966, respectively. Employed by Honeywell, Inc.,

from 1966 to 1976, Rose progressed from the rank of scientist to supervisor of the firm's Systems Research Center. In 1976 Rose joined the National Aeronautics and Space Administration (NASA) as program manager for general aviation. He won the 1980 NASA Spaceship Earth award for encouraging disadvantaged youngsters to improve themselves. Rose's research endeavors include improvements in helicopter aerodynamics, supersonic aircraft data-sensing devices, and design of supersonic parachutes. He held several patents for his designs and wrote many technical publications related to his work.

Christine Darden was born in 1942 in Monroe, North Carolina, and studied mathematics at Virginia State College. After receiving her B.S. degree in 1962, Darden worked as a high school and college instructor while completing her M.S. degree in 1967. Darden began her aerospace career in 1967 when she joined the staff of NASA's Langley Research Center as a data analyst. During her career at Langley as an aerospace engineer, Darden wrote numerous technical reports, published articles in professional journals, and attended George Washington University, where she graduated with a D.Sc. degree in mechanical engineering in 1983.

### Civil Engineering and Academic Excellence

Irving W. Jones was born in Washington, D.C., in 1930, and began his engineering studies at Howard University. He completed his B.S. degree in civil engineering in 1953 before moving to New York to attend Columbia University. Jones received his M.S. degree from Columbia in 1957. After considerable industrial experience, including work at Grumman Aerospace Corporation and a partnership with Technology Associates, Jones completed his Ph.D. degree in applied mechanics at Howard University in 1967. He accepted an associate professorship at Howard in 1969 and became the chairman of the school's civil engineering department in 1972. His teaching skills encouraged many of Howard University's young black students to pursue careers as civil engineers.

*Nuclear Engineering*

Born in Jackson, Missouri, in 1934, Henry T. Sampson chose to attend Purdue University, where he received his B.S. in chemical engineering in 1956. After receiving his M.S. at the University of California at Los Angeles in 1961, Sampson completed his Ph.D. studies in nuclear engineering at the University of Illinois in 1967. After receiving his Ph.D. degree, Sampson joined the technical staff of the Aerospace Corporation. His hard work was rewarded in 1981 when he was named director of planning and operations for the company's space program. In addition to his professional publications, Sampson holds several patents for aerospace propellants.

Early achievements in engineering were difficult for African Americans because they lacked access to the scientific education necessary for a solid grounding in basic engineering. Despite these constraints, many African Americans were drawn to the creative science of invention and provided inspiration to the engineers who followed them. From Norbert Rillieux to Christine Darden, these engineers combined their knowledge of basic science with an interest in its practical applications to various fields of engineering. Many of them produced significant inventions, producing numerous patents on engineering processes that have been essential to several American industries and have had applications worldwide.

—*Sanford S. Singer*

*See also:* Inventors; Science and technology; Professors.

Suggested Readings:

Brody, James M. *Created Equal: The Lives and Ideas of Black American Innovators.* New York: William Morrow, 1993.

Klein, Aaron E. *The Hidden Contributors: Black Scientists and Inventors in America.* New York: Doubleday, 1971.

Sammons, Vivian O. *Blacks in Sciences and Medicine.* New York: Hemisphere, 1990.

Van Sertima, Ivan, ed. *Blacks in Science: Ancient and Modern.* New Brunswick, N.J.: Transaction Books, 1991.

Wharton, David E. *A Struggle Worthy of Note: The Engineering and Technological Education of Black Americans.* Westport, Conn.: Greenwood Press, 1992.

Winslow, Eugene, ed. *Black Americans in Science and Engineering: Contributions of Past and Present.* Chicago: Afro-Am Publishing, 1974.

**Environmental hazards and discrimination:** Residential patterns in the United States are characterized by DE FACTO SEGREGATION along racial and ethnic lines. A majority of people of color are clustered in neighborhoods, urban ghettos, barrios, reservations, and rural poverty pockets. Studies have shown that a high number of polluting industries, toxic waste landfills, and hazardous waste disposal facilities are sited near minority communities. Benjamin F. CHAVIS, Jr., a former chairman of the NATIONAL ASSOCIATION FOR THE ADVANCEMENT OF COLORED PEOPLE (NAACP), referred to this situation as "environmental racism."

Environmental racism is RACIAL DISCRIMINATION in environmental policy making, in the enforcement of regulations and laws, and in the deliberate targeting of communities of color as sites for toxic waste disposal and polluting industries. Consequently, certain environmental issues can be seen as part of the larger struggle against oppression and dehumanization. The poisons in the environment are a social justice issue for African American communities because environmental hazards affect black communities more severely than white communities.

There are several key issues regarding environmental justice for African Americans: lack of official warnings that hazardous conditions are present in or near black communities; the targeting of black communities for the location of locally undesirable land uses (LULU); the notion that there is a conflict between economic growth (jobs) and environmental regulation; the prevalence of lead poisoning among African Americans; and evidence of racial discrimination in the priority given to cleanup and funding for contaminated communities.

## Hazards Without Warnings

The capitalist system of the United States has historically placed business and economic growth above the protection of people's HEALTH. This is particularly evident in the case of noxious industries that produce hazardous conditions. These hazardous conditions may affect all aspects of the environment: air, water, food consumption, housing conditions, and working conditions.

For the most part, members of a community must challenge polluters and must prove that exposure to toxins is damaging to the health of individuals. Not until harm or discrimination is recognized and documented can regulatory action be taken. The burden of proof falls to the members of the community. The evidence that hazardous conditions are present and disproportionately burden African Americans because of discriminatory practices is subjected to denial of intent on the part of the polluters. Regardless, patterns of environmental racism have been well documented. The locations of toxic and hazardous waste sites disproportionately threaten and burden minority communities, particularly black communities. Two important studies found race and class to be highly correlated with LULU.

In the early 1980's, NORTH CAROLINA planned to establish a polychlorinated biphe-nyl (PCB) landfill in Warren County. The residents of Warren County were predominantly African Americans with low incomes. The United Church of Christ Commission for Racial Justice joined with the residents of Warren County to oppose this hazardous waste facility. The protest raised the issue of racism and exposure to environmental hazards. In response to the protests, the U.S. General Accounting Office (GAO) conducted a study in 1983. The GAO studied the racial and socioeconomic makeup of the communities surrounding four hazardous waste landfills in the southeastern United States. The study found that African Americans made up the majority of the population in three of the four communities studied.

Another study was published in 1987 by the United Church of Christ Commission for Racial Justice. This study was national in scope and further showed that race is the single best predictor of where commercial hazardous waste facilities are located, even when household income and average value of homes are considered. This commission was one of the first national civil rights organizations to raise the question of environmental racism and bring it to national attention.

Researchers Robert W. Collins and William Harris, Sr., examined the conflict between environmental issues, the need for efficiency and competing interest, and the claim of environmental racism. These researchers reported on a case study of King and Queen County, VIRGINIA, whose population was 50 percent white and 50 percent African American. A clear pattern of racism in selecting waste disposal sites was revealed. Four of the five county landfills were located in predominantly black neighborhoods. In addition, the response of county officials to protests lodged by white citizens had immediate results: The landfill located in the white neighborhood was the only site closed down. Although the Eastern District Court of Virginia concluded that black residents were disproportionately subjected to landfills, the court also responded that there was no evidence of racial discrimination. The court argued that the board of supervisors of King and Queen County "appeared to have balanced the economic, environmental, and cultural need of the County in a conscientious manner."

The difference in government response to the environmental protests of black and white residents in King and Queen County seems to provide evidence of racial bias that privileges whites over blacks. Sociologists refer to this type of differentiation as a kind of INSTITUTIONAL RACISM. Resistance to institutionalized racism in the struggle for a clean, safe environment is hindered by the lack of systematic notification of the presence of hazardous conditions. Some researchers and industrialists argue that, in a majority of cases, no detrimental effects are adequately documented and that equity issues therefore involve only potential risk or harm.

### NIMBY and PIBBY

The United States produces between 250 and 400 million metric tons of toxic waste per year. There are more than six thousand industrial plants in the United States that produce dangerous chemicals. Major class and race disparities are apparent in the location of the polluting industries and of facilities that store toxic waste. Land-use decisions reveal an institutional bias that favors the needs of whites and the affluent over those of blacks and the poor. Affluent neighborhoods use their economic and political clout to influence land-use decisions and fend off undesirable facilities.

The "not in my backyard," or NIMBY, syndrome has been the usual reaction of white middle- and upper-income groups on the issue of allowing noxious facility sites to be placed near their communities. Critics of public policy coined the term PIBBY principle, for "put in blacks' backyards," to describe the in-

equity of toxic or noxious facility siting. Many of the most noxious industries are located in working-class districts populated by a high percentage of African Americans. Many toxic waste storage facilities are also located in or near black communities.

Researcher Vicki Been explored the possibility that locally undesirable land uses in the communities of minorities and African Americans were actually chosen fairly but that subsequent events produced certain discrepancies. In other words, the process of selecting LULU sites may be a result of market forces rather than racism and classism specifically. Nevertheless, her examination of the communities at the time that LULUs were sited suggests that siting practices are most likely to affect people of color disproportionately. Her study suggests that discrimination in housing and the racism that still exists in market dynamics inhibit environmental justice.

### Economic Issues and Environmental Hazards

It has been commonly believed that nonwhite communities in the United States will accept the risk of possible consequences of hazardous industries and waste storage in exchange for economic incentives. African Americans who are economically disadvantaged, however, are usually not in positions of power and lack control over decisions to make these kinds of economic arrangements. Frequently, when a company presents plans for locating a LULU such as a hazardous waste landfill or a noxious industry in or near a black neighborhood, a white-controlled commission or corporate board downplays the risks associated with hazardous waste landfills and industries while emphasizing the economic benefits. This scenario has been nicknamed "job blackmail."

Job blackmail is the practice of exploiting communities that are economically vulnerable. That is, communities that suffer from chronic unemployment, poverty, and a lack of

Environmental sociologist Robert Bullard equates job blackmail with antebellum slavery. *(© Roy Lewis Archives)*

a sound economic infrastructure are particularly at risk from polluting industries confronted by the white NIMBY syndrome. Robert D. Bullard, an environmental sociologist, sees job blackmail as equivalent to the type of domination techniques practiced by whites in the antebellum South. Bullard describes petrochemical colonialism as a form of slavery in which the executives of these industries fill the roles of master and overseer.

Polluting industries exploit the pro-growth and pro-jobs sentiments among working-class, poor, and minority communities. Many community leaders and workers come to believe that environmental regulations result in plant closings and job loss—such fears, frequently encouraged by the businesses themselves, are essentially another form of job blackmail. The idea that profit is the reward for hard work contributes to the prevalence of job blackmail because of the idea that if one wants to improve one's situation one must "make sacrifices." This concept, although frequently true, is abused when it is applied to polluting industries. Working in, or living beside, a business that is injurious to one's health should not be among the sacrifices that anyone should be expected to make.

Black workers are overrepresented in low-paying, low-skill jobs and are twice as likely as whites to be unemployed. This situation makes black workers particularly vulnerable to job blackmail. The fear of unemployment and the desire to earn a living acts as the driving force to work in jobs that are detrimental to the health of workers and their families.

Communities that are host to hazardous waste disposal facilities receive fewer economic benefits (such as high-paying jobs and community services) than do the communities that generate the waste to begin with. The residents near facilities that produce hazardous by-products are the least to benefit from the products of the industry. The benefits derived from industrial waste production are directly related to affluence.

### Lead Poisoning

Lead poisoning is completely preventable, yet it is one of the most common environmental health hazards in the United States. African Americans at all class levels have a significantly greater chance of being lead poisoned than do whites. Nearly half the African American children residing in inner cities are exposed to dangerous levels of lead, compared with 16 percent of white inner-city children. This disparity also exists outside large urban areas, where 36 percent of African American children are poisoned, compared with only 9 percent of white children. There is clear evidence that lead poisoning is detrimental to the health and development of children. Yet lead paint and lead dust in the home have not been removed in any systematic manner.

The U.S. Department of Housing and Urban Development (HUD) conducted a national study in 1989-1990. HUD researchers found that 57 million of the 100 million housing units in the United States contain lead-based paint on interior or exterior surfaces. While part of the danger comes from children eating peeling lead-based paint chips, paint dust is far more dangerous. Lead paint dust covers a larger surface area and is absorbed more readily in the body. Renovations increase exposure to contaminated dust and can result in poisoning even though exposure takes place only for a short amount of time. A larger proportion of black Americans than white Americans are exposed to lead. One reason is that they are subject to housing discrimination and redlining, which, combined with the fact that many are poor, means that more blacks live in older housing containing lead paint.

—*Lydia Rose*

*See also:* Employment and unemployment.

Suggested Readings:

Austin, Regina, and Michael Schill. "Black, Brown, Red, and Poisoned." *The Humanist* 54 (July/August, 1994): 9-26.

Bryant, Bunyan, and Paul Mohai, eds. *Race and the Incidence of Environmental Hazards: A Time for Discourse*. Boulder, Colo.: Westview Press, 1992.

Bullard, Robert D. *Confronting Environmental Racism: Voices from the Grassroots*. Boston: South End Press, 1993.

_____. *Dumping in Dixie: Race, Class, and Environmental Quality*. Boulder, Colo.: Westview Press, 1990.

Goldman, Benjamin A. *The Truth About Where You Live: An Atlas for Action on Toxics and Mortality*. New York: Times Books/Random House, 1991.

Greve, Michael S., and Fred L. Smith, Jr., eds. *Environmental Politics: Public Costs, Private Rewards*. New York: Praeger, 1992.

Mohai, Paul. "Black Environmentalism." *Social Science Quarterly* 71 (December, 1990): 744-765.

Petrikin, Jonathan S. *Environmental Justice*. San Diego: Greenhaven Press, 1995.

Russell, Dick. "Environmental Racism." *The Amicus Journal* 11 (Spring, 1989): 22-28.

United Church of Christ. Commission for Racial Justice. *Toxic Wastes and Race in the United States: A National Report on the Racial and Socio-economic Characteristics of Communities with Hazardous Waste Sites*. New York: Public Data Access, 1987.

**Episcopalians:** The Protestant Episcopal Church of the United States came into being in the year 1784, when Bishop Samuel Seabury was consecrated in Scotland. As a result of the American Revolution, the Church of England would not recognize the new American branch. To retain the apostolic succession of priests, Seabury went to Scotland for recognition. Later in the year, the Church of England agreed to consecrate an American, Bishop William White, and the rift was healed.

*Origins of Black Congregations*

Shortly after the Episcopal Church in America was instituted, the first black Episcopal church was created by a breakaway group from the St. George's Methodist Episcopal Church in PHILADELPHIA. A famous event led to the founding of the first black Christian denomination and the first black Episcopal church in America: Richard ALLEN and three of his colleagues at St. George's decided to ignore the segregation of black parishioners from white at church services. Custom required black slaves to sit in the church balcony and whites who were not indentured servants to sit downstairs in the nave. Allen and his colleagues were free blacks. To emphasize their free status, they chose to sit with the white worshipers. The ushers of St. George's instructed Allen and his friends to take seats in the balcony. At the time, Allen and the others were kneeling in prayer, and they requested that the ushers leave them alone until prayers were finished. Then Allen, Darius Jennings, Absalom JONES, and William White departed from St. George's. On April 12, 1787, they formed a religious group temporarily named the FREE AFRICAN SOCIETY.

The new African Church sought affiliation with a denomination other than the METHODISTS, with whom they eventually parted company. The deciding factor was the exceptional support and encouragement given to the breakaway church by the Quakers and Episcopalians. A group within the Free African Society decided to join the Episcopal Church and to call their congregation the St. Thomas African Church. Recommending Absalom Jones as their preferred leader, the St. Thomas congregation announced on August 12, 1794, their conditions for alignment with the Protestant Episcopal Church of the United States. First, they wanted to be received as an entire corporate group. Second, they wanted to retain independence and control of their affairs. Third, they felt that one of their number should be licensed as lay reader; the implication was that a member of the church should be prepared for the priesthood as soon as possible. On October 12, 1794, the Protestant Episcopal Church in Philadelphia received the congregation of St. Thomas into full communion.

In the following year, two major events in the history of the black church took place. First, Absalom Jones was ordained as a deacon on August 6, 1795. More than a year later, he became the first black ordained Episcopal priest in the United States. Second, Richard Allen and his followers formed the AFRICAN METHODIST EPISCOPAL CHURCH, the first black Christian denomination in the United States.

### Church Activity in New York

In the early years of the nineteenth century, the second black Episcopal congregation, St. Philip's Church, came into being. It started with support and encouragement from the congregation of Trinity Parish, Wall Street, which had recognized the importance of ministering to the black parishioners of the colony. Trinity Parish undertook the work of preparing able black parishioners to lead their own congregation.

St. Philip's began when a small group of blacks within Trinity Parish met to learn confirmation instructions. As the group grew to become a congregation, they needed larger quarters. The necessary help came from a generous man from New York by the name of George Lorrillard, who leased them land on Collect Street (later called Center Street). The condition of the lease allowed the congregation of St. Philip's to rent the land for $250 per year for a period of sixty-nine years, at which time the land would revert to the ownership of St. Philip's. The church building was erected under the direction of black master craftsmen and was consecrated on July 3, 1819. The first leader of the church, Peter Williams, was ordained as a deacon on October 20, 1819. Seven years later, he was ordained to the priesthood.

George Bragg, one of the earliest historians of black Episcopalians, noted that St. Philip's occupied a special place in the church history of New York as well as of the Episcopal Church. When St. Philip's was founded, the total population of New York was about 160,000. Less than 10 percent of the population was of African ancestry. Only sixty persons of color paid taxes, and only sixteen were eligible to vote.

### Church Leaders

A number of illustrious black church leaders arose by dint of hard work and dedication. Bishop John Payne was consecrated in July, 1851; he was known for his strong emphasis on high intellectual standards for clergy and laity. The Reverend Samuel David Ferguson was the first black man to become a full-fledged bishop in the House of Bishops of the

Episcopal Church. Ferguson, who was born in SOUTH CAROLINA in 1842, later became the bishop of LIBERIA. (The Episcopal Church tended to appoint blacks to head the Episcopal ministries in Liberia.)

Another person who was an outstanding role model for black Episcopalians was the Reverend Edward Thomas Demby, who was born in Delaware and grew up in Philadelphia. In 1918 he was consecrated as a bishop in a famous Episcopal church, All Saint's Church of St. Louis, Missouri. The last of the early black bishops to be recognized was the Reverend Henry B. Delany, who was consecrated on November 21, 1918. The earliest bishops were confined to domestic and international mission work with black Episcopalians. Not until the mid-1960's, when the Reverend John Burgess was consecrated bishop coadjutor—a

The Reverend John M. Burgess became the first black Episcopalian bishop in the United States in 1969. *(AP/Wide World Photos)*

bishop who succeeds the incumbent—in the Diocese of Massachusetts, did black Episcopalians achieve full status in the Episcopal Church of America. In 1989 the Massachusetts diocese consecrated Barbara Harris as the first black woman to be made a bishop suffragan.

Among the most prominent black Episcopalians of the early years of the church was the Reverend Alexander CRUMMELL, who was also associated with the diocese of MASSACHUSETTS. Crummell experienced discrimination within the ranks of the Episcopal Church when he tried to enroll in the General Theological Seminary of New York. When he was rejected by the seminary, the diocese of Massachusetts sponsored his candidacy to the priesthood at a theological seminary in Boston. Crummell was ordained to the priesthood in 1844 and later attended the University of Cambridge, where he obtained a degree in 1853. He later decided to emigrate to West Africa to assist with the development of an independent black church movement. After sixteen years in Liberia, Crummell returned to the United States and settled in Washington, D.C., where he served as pastor of St. Lukes Episcopal Church until 1894.

*Black Episcopal Schools*

Scholarship and intellectual contributions of black Episcopalians were centered at Bishop Payne Divinity School in VIRGINIA until the early 1950's. The Bishop Payne seminary was started as an extension of Virginia Theological Seminary in Alexandria in 1878. Largely through the conscientious efforts of the Reverend John Wesley Johnson, the rector of St. Philip's Church in Richmond, Virginia, the school expanded and trained black men for the priesthood. Historically, several Episcopal-sponsored colleges have served as beacons of intellectual endeavors, two of the most prominent being St. Paul's College in Lawrenceville, Virginia, and St. Augustine's College in Raleigh, NORTH CAROLINA.

*Attention to Black Issues*

Episcopalians of African heritage asserted their leadership in 1968 by forming the Union of Black Episcopalians. Because they account for only about 10 percent of the Episcopal population in the United States (or about 180,000 in the 1990's), many black Episcopalians believe that the church often overlooks their contributions and ministries. To balance the national church's emphasis, the union lobbied to put black issues on the agendas of the General Convention of the Episcopal Church, which meets every three years. The union established its headquarters in Washington, D.C. As a corporate body, the union strives to protect the future of the black Episcopal Church in the United States; Sandra A. Wilson was elected the group's thirteenth president in 1998.

—*Patricia C. Gloster*

Suggested Readings:

Baer, Hans A., and Merrill Singer. *African-American Religion in the Twentieth Century: Varieties of Protest and Accommodation*. Knoxville: University of Tennessee Press, 1992.

Bragg, George F. *History of the Afro-American Group of the Episcopal Church*. Baltimore: Church Advocate Press, 1922. Reprint. New York: Johnson Reprint, 1968.

Frazier, E. Franklin. *The Negro Church in America*. New York: Schocken Books, 1974.

Hoskins, Charles L. *Black Episcopalians in Georgia: Strife, Struggle, and Salvation*. Savannah, Ga.: Hoskins, 1980.

Lewis, Harold T. *Yet With a Steady Beat: The African American Struggle for Recognition in the Episcopal Church*. Valley Forge, Pa.: Trinity Press International, 1996.

Rigsby, Gregory U. *Alexander Crummell: Pioneer in Nineteenth Century Pan-African Thought*. New York: Greenwood Press, 1987.

**Equal Employment Opportunity Commission:** Federal government agency. The EEOC descended from the Fair Employment Practices Commission (FEPC) established by President Franklin D. Roosevelt's EXECUTIVE ORDER 8802, which banned RACIAL DISCRIMINATION in WORLD WAR II defense-industry hiring. The FEPC was to investigate job-bias charges and persuade employers to adopt nondiscriminatory hiring practices. The FEPC's mandate lapsed after the war. Racism in employment practices persisted, however, and in 1964, through Title VII of the Civil Rights Act of 1964, the Equal Employment Opportunity Commission (EEOC) was established.

The mandate of the EEOC was to eliminate discrimination based on color, race, religion, national origin, or age, as that discrimination pertained to employment. The EEOC also promotes voluntary action by employers, unions, and community organizations to make equal employment opportunity a reality. In addition, the EEOC is an oversight body, charged with ensuring compliance with equal opportunity laws, especially those pertaining to federal employees and applicants.

Originally, the EEOC had the power to mediate disputes and to identify deliberate and systematic discrimination, but it could not bring suit in court. It had to refer cases to the attorney general. That changed with the Equal Employment Opportunity Act of 1972, which allowed the EEOC to bring suit. Beginning in 1974, it was allowed to bring "pattern and practice" lawsuits, class action suits that charged employers or unions with widespread discriminatory practices. The agency was granted further powers in 1979 when it took over responsibility for enforcing the Equal Pay Act of 1963 and the Age Discrimination in Employment Act of 1967 from the Department of Labor.

With increased investigative and enforcement powers, the EEOC during the 1960's and 1970's was instrumental in opening job opportunities to minorities and women. Through vigorous enforcement of civil rights laws and

At the root of all civil rights struggles has been the demand for equality of opportunity. *(AP/Wide World Photos)*

the use of class action lawsuits, the EEOC under such administrators as Clifford ALEXANDER and Eleanor Holmes NORTON fought effectively against race and gender job discrimination. It won significant cases against Sears, General Motors, and AT&T.

In the 1980's, during the REAGAN ADMINISTRATION, the EEOC under Clarence THOMAS and Evan Kemp changed its emphasis from class action suits to investigating and litigating on behalf of individuals. Fighting job discrimination against the handicapped was added to the EEOC's mandate. Critics charged that the approach taken by the EEOC during the 1980's was far less effective in fighting racism and sexism in hiring than were earlier tactics. They pointed to the increase in cases dismissed as having no merit and the decrease in settlement amounts as evidence.

The EEOC continued to face difficulties and shrinking budgets in the early 1990's. Inundated by discrimination complaints, the EEOC developed a huge backlog of cases, and its mandate continued to expand. Among the issues the EEOC faced in the 1990's were the acceptable role of religion in the workplace and the issues of accommodating workers with psychiatric disabilities.

In 1994 the EEOC was given the responsibility of processing the job-discrimination claims of federal workers. Another change that had a significant effect on the EEOC was the body of U.S. SUPREME COURT rulings limiting the application of AFFIRMATIVE ACTION policies based on racial preferences. In 1999 the Clinton administration announced that a significant part of the federal government's increase in spending on civil rights law enforcement would go to the EEOC.

*See also:* Employment and unemployment.

**Equiano, Olaudah** (Gustavas Vassa; 1745, probably near Onitsha, Nigeria—April 31, 1797, England): Author and former slave. Equiano is the author of an early and famous slave narrative, *The Interesting Narrative of the Life of Olaudah Equiano, or Gustavas Vassa, the African* (1789). Equiano also worked as an abolitionist, motivated by his own experience in SLAVERY.

The account given by Equiano in his narrative is significant for several reasons. First, he describes his life in Africa before he was captured into slavery. This childhood recollection offers a unique perspective in African American slave narrative: Most other narratives begin with stories of enslavement in the Americas. In Equiano's narrative, readers can see a firsthand account of West African Ibo village life through the experience of a child born into a family of some power but later kidnapped by other Africans and sold into slavery. Equiano eventually was renamed Gustavas Vassa by an English naval officer who bought him soon after Equiano's arrival in VIRGINIA. This renaming signals a familiar theme in African American slave narrative—the importance of naming as an act of identity.

Equiano recounts the horrendous Middle Passage ocean journey from Africa into New World slavery. This also is uncommon in African American slave narratives, since many slave narrators were born in America, not in Africa. Whereas many later African American writers could use the middle passage symbolically or metaphorically, Equiano is able to recount the actual experience in his autobiography, thus confronting his readers directly with the harsh reality experienced by Africans forced out of their homeland.

Finally, Equiano experienced slavery in a wide range of settings, from the British West Indies to North America to England. He traveled extensively, having been purchased several times by naval officers or merchant seafarers. Equiano's narrative thus offers a uniquely cross-cultural perspective on slavery.

Many later literary critics and historians consider Equiano's narrative to be the model for later African American SLAVE NARRATIVES, despite the fact that Equiano spent little time actually in North America. Equiano purchased his freedom in 1766, worked as an abolitionist, and died in England, where he spent his later life.

**Erving, Julius** (b. February 22, 1950, Hempstead, New York): Basketball player. Erving, nicknamed "Dr. J.," was one of professional BASKETBALL's leading career scorers and one of the game's most acrobatic performers. In sixteen professional seasons, he scored 30,026 points.

Like many other African American basketball greats, Erving learned the game on urban

Julius Erving scoring for the 76ers in 1987. *(AP/Wide World Photos)*

playgrounds. By the time he entered Roosevelt High School, he was a skillful ball handler and had grown to six feet, three inches in height. He received a scholarship from the University of Massachusetts and enrolled there in September, 1968. During three varsity seasons at Massachusetts, Erving averaged more than twenty points and twenty rebounds per game.

After his junior year at Massachusetts, Erving signed with the Virginia Squires of the American Basketball Association (ABA). He was an immediate success, averaging 27.3 points per game in his rookie season. Two years later, however, the Virginia team, which was struggling financially, traded him to the New York Nets. Continuing his outstanding play, he led the Nets to ABA titles in 1974 and 1976. In the final series of 1976, he turned in one of the best performances in playoff history, scoring 226 points and grabbing eighty-five rebounds in six games. In the series' first game, during which he scored forty-five points, Erving tallied eighteen points in the final eight minutes.

After the 1976 basketball season, the ABA merged with the older National Basketball Association (NBA), and Erving was traded to the Philadelphia 76ers. Playing before the larger NBA audiences and against the tougher NBA competition, Erving made the basketball world aware that he was among the game's best players. He awed opponents and thrilled fans with his driving, twisting moves to the basket and his spectacular slam dunks.

During eleven seasons with the 76ers, Erving averaged twenty-two points per game, and he was chosen for the all-star team each year. Erving won the NBA most valuable player award in 1981, but his most satisfying season came two years later, when he and Moses Malone led Philadelphia to the NBA championship.

Erving retired from pro basketball in 1987. Shortly afterward, mainly to appear more legitimate when he urged members of African American youth groups to attend college, Erving completed his bachelor's degree at the University of Massachusetts. He was inducted into the Naismith Memorial Basketball Hall of Fame in 1993, and in 1996 an NBA panel named him one of the fifty greatest players of the league's first half century.

In 1999 it was revealed that Erving was the natural father of rising tennis star Alexandra Stevenson, who was born in 1980 to journalist Samantha Stevenson. Married to Turquoise Erving since 1972, Erving initially denied that Alexandra was his daughter but later admitted his parentage. Although he had never developed a relationship with Alexandra, he had supported her financially throughout her life.

**Erwin, Richard C.** (b. August 23, 1923, Marion, North Carolina): Federal JUDGE. Erwin joined the U.S. Army in 1943 and served as a first sergeant during WORLD WAR II. He was discharged in 1946 and completed his undergraduate studies at Johnson C. Smith University in Charlotte, NORTH CAROLINA. Erwin graduated with his B.A. degree in 1947. He attended law school at Howard University and received his LL.B. degree in 1951. He passed the bar examination in that year and became a partner in the law firm of Erwin and Beaty.

In January of 1978, Erwin took office as a judge for the North Carolina State Court of Appeals, becoming the first African American to win a statewide race for elective office in the history of North Carolina. On October 31, 1980, President Jimmy Carter appointed him to serve as U.S. district judge for the Middle District of North Carolina.

**Espy, Mike** (b. November 30, 1953, Yazoo City, Mississippi): Politician. Alphonso Michael "Mike" Espy was the first African American to be elected to the U.S. Congress from MISSISSIPPI since RECONSTRUCTION. Espy, from the Mississippi Delta, represented a district more than half of whose residents were African Americans. He first won his seat in November, 1986, against two-term Republican Webb Franklin by attracting most of the black vote and 10 percent of the white vote.

*Political Career*

Espy represented one of the country's poorest districts but was himself the son of the prosperous owner of a chain of funeral parlors. He received an undergraduate education at HOWARD UNIVERSITY and attended the University of Santa Clara Law School. He joined the state government in 1980 as Mississippi's assistant secretary of state and later served as assistant attorney general.

In his political career, he sought to bridge

gaps across racial and class lines. As a member of the U.S. House of Representatives, Espy worked to represent wealthy white Delta soybean farmers as well as the large number of unemployed African Americans in his district living in substandard housing. His work on the House budget and agricultural committees enabled him to convince the Pentagon to increase its purchase of Mississippi Delta catfish, a major part of the Delta economy, by 65 percent. He later got Congress to declare June 25 as National Catfish Day. He also initiated a bill to create a Delta Commission to study the area's severe economic problems.

In 1988, despite suffering racial harassment, he successfully ran for reelection with the backing of conservative white farmers who also supported Republican presidential candidate George Bush. He may have gotten as much as 20 percent of the white vote, a major accomplishment in a majority-black district that had been disturbed in the past by racial unrest. A cautious Democrat, Espy did not become involved in the Democratic presidential primary race between Jesse JACKSON and Michael Dukakis. In 1993 Espy was confirmed as the secretary of agriculture under President Bill Clinton.

### Achievements as Agriculture Secretary

A visible member of the CLINTON ADMINIS-TRATION, Espy was frequently in the public eye announcing agricultural trade pacts with other countries, national disaster-aid initiatives, and stricter inspection standards for meat and poultry. Espy actively participated in the administration's commitment to "reinvent" government, especially through streamlining programs and bureaucracy and cutting waste. In October of 1994, Espy had a prominent role in designing and successfully guiding through Congress a sweeping plan to reorganize the Department of Agriculture and the federal government's crop insurance program. Under the plan, thousands of jobs

within the department were slated to be cut, its agencies would be nearly halved, and a number of the department's county area field offices would be consolidated or closed. The federal government's expensive disaster relief program was to be confronted in large part by requiring farmers to purchase catastrophic crop insurance.

### Charges of Ethics Violations

Espy's achievements, however, were soon overshadowed by emerging allegations of ethics violations and other improprieties. In August of 1994, Attorney General Janet Reno announced that she had asked for the appointment of an independent counsel to investigate charges that, in accepting gifts from firms regulated by the Department of Agriculture, Espy had violated ethics laws. Espy and Patricia Jensen, an assistant secretary in the department responsible for meat and poultry inspection, were alleged to have received free travel,

Secretary of Agriculture Mike Espy in 1993. *(AP/Wide World Photos)*

meals, and tickets to sporting events from Tyson Foods, Inc. Based in Arkansas, Tyson dominated the U.S. poultry business and was a major contributor to President Clinton's gubernatorial and presidential campaigns. Earlier allegations had been made against Clinton himself, charging that while he was governor of Arkansas he had shown favoritism toward Tyson through lax enforcement of laws affecting the company. Critics accused Espy of intervening to delay implementation of new, stricter poultry inspection rules that would have affected Tyson.

There were further allegations, including a charge that Espy had asked the Environmental Protection Agency to postpone a ban on an agricultural insecticide used by a California agribusiness that had contributed to his previous congressional campaigns (and whose chief lobbyist was a former college friend) and that he had leased a car in Mississippi for some seven months in 1993 for personal use at government expense. The cumulative effect of the ethics charges led Espy, on October 3, 1994, to announce his resignation. Espy left office in December, 1994, succeeded as secretary of agriculture by Dan Glickman, a former U.S. representative from Kansas.

*Acquittal*
Espy began a successful private law practice in Mississippi and was soon in demand as a public speaker. However, for more than four years Espy faced the prospect of his upcoming trial, and he amassed a reported $1.5 million legal bill. The charges against him finally went to trial in late 1998. After a seven-week trial, a jury in federal court found Espy not guilty on all thirty charges that had been brought against him. In 1999 the Clinton administration named Espy to a position on the Secretary of Energy Advisory Board.
—*Updated by Forest L. Grieves*
See also: Congress members; Politics and government.

*Essence:* Magazine. *Essence* was established in New York in 1970 with a monthly publication schedule. It was founded by Essence Communications and placed under the direction of publisher and chief executive officer Edward Lewis and president Clarence O. Smith. Susan L. Taylor became editor-in-chief in 1981.

The magazine developed a content designed to appeal to African American WOMEN, including feature articles, health and beauty tips, FASHION tips, and regular columns on food and lifestyles. No matter what subject is being covered, articles call for African Americans to come together and use their economic power to speak with one voice.

In 1988 the magazine began sponsoring the annual *Essence* Awards, honoring the achievements and accomplishments of noteworthy African American women. The magazine published a special issue celebrating its twenty-fifth anniversary in May of 1995.

**Ethiopianism:** Ethiopianism is a theme that emerged at an early period in the African American experience and that expressed itself as an idea, a symbol, and a movement concerned with African liberation and vindication. As a dominant theme in African American religion, it has been one of the salient traits of African American Christianity. Despite its close association with African American Christianity, Ethiopianism has been a quasireligious movement with a strong black nationalist emphasis.

As an idea, Ethiopianism provided African Americans with a messianic tradition that was uniquely African American in origin. This tradition was not centered exclusively on Jesus, nor was it limited to the story of the Jewish exodus, another dominant theme in African American religion. Ethiopianism became a kind of messianic ancestralism derived primarily from the uniqueness of the African American experience and expressed as an important tradition in African American religion in general and Christianity in particular. It defined the fundamental mission of African Americans as a divine mission in its own right.

### Pre-Civil War Period

The Ethiopian tradition emerged prior to the 1800's. The idea was expressed by various black leaders and others who spoke on behalf of their people, free and slave. Prior to 1830, two important documents, Robert Young's *The Ethiopian Manifesto*, published in 1829, and David Walker's *Appeal to the Colored Citizens of the World*, which followed months later the same year, were widely circulated. The first document established the use of "Ethiopian" as a synonym for black and associated the term with the struggle for freedom. The second argued that Egyptians were Africans or were a racial mixture of Ethiopians and Egyptians—in effect, the same as black people in the United States.

Walker's *Appeal* referred specifically to the "God of the Ethiopians" and alluded to the Bible in an appeal for collective struggle against oppression. This spirit of Ethiopianism pervaded much of the discussion about the black struggle for freedom and justice leading up to the CIVIL WAR. The claim that two great ancient civilizations, Egypt and Ethiopia, were black implied the self-worth of all Africans, and this past greatness was taken to portend future greatness for African people.

### Post-Civil War Period

Immediately prior to and following the Civil War, a different emphasis was given to Ethiopianism. The call for blacks to emigrate from America and return to AFRICA during the early 1800's gave rise to the American COLONIZATION MOVEMENT.

By the 1850's, the concept of Ethiopianism was being used to argue in support of black emigration from the United States, especially to Africa. During this period, it was argued that Ethiopianism meant that African Americans should return to Africa, because they had a responsibility to contribute to the uplift of Africans and Africa. African Americans had the skills needed to develop Africa's potential and enable it to take a place among modern civilizations. At the end of the decade, on the eve of the Civil War, Martin DELANY, a leading black intellectual and activist, and Bishop Alexander CRUMMELL, in association with Henry Highland GARNET, the AMERICAN COLONIZATION SOCIETY, and other church leaders and emigrationists, became strong proponents of the movement to Christianize and civilize Africa.

The Civil War brought an interlude in the call for emigration activity; however, the Ethiopianism trend begun prior to the war continued throughout the second half of the 1800's. Out of this trend came the African American missionary movement, which was closely identified with the concept of Ethiopianism as a Christian movement dominated by the black church. This movement adopted the biblical text Psalm 68:31, "Princes shall come out of Egypt; Ethiopia shall soon stretch out her hands unto God," as its motto. From this movement came an interpretation of Ethiopianism that not only argued for an emigration, or a "return," to Africa but also included a view that accommodated the SLAVERY experience and reconciled it with biblical legend. Edward Wilmot Blyden, an intellectual of international repute, and Bishop Henry McNeal TURNER of the AFRICAN METHODIST EPISCOPAL CHURCH were among Ethiopianism's chief proponents during this phase.

### Between the War Years

While affirming the biblically based tradition of Ethiopianism, Blyden and Turner adopted a more critical position toward the Christian missionary approach and affirmed the inherent values and worth of traditional African culture and religion. They provided the foundation for a more Afrocentered Ethiopianism and an approach to the vindication of AFRICAN HERITAGE that was not limited to biblically based sources.

Blyden foreshadowed the vindicationist tradition associated with twentieth-century pan-African scholarship and writing. He also introduced Islam as a religious option for African Americans and questioned the monopoly of the Christian tradition. Turner introduced a more aggressive approach to the African American Christian's mission that challenged white monopoly in foreign missions and control of indigenous churches, especially in Africa. He was also among the first persons to question the dominance of white imagery and symbolism in Christian liturgy, literature, and art. Turner openly asserted the right of people of African descent to reflect the divine presence in black images and symbols, and he called into question widely accepted white paintings and descriptions of Jesus and God.

W. E. B. DU BOIS and, later, Cheikh Anta Diop, along with other twentieth-century pan-Africanists, continued the vindicationist tradition of scholarship influenced by Blyden. Central to this tradition was the claim that both ancient Egypt and Ethiopia were African civilizations whose people were of the same racial classification as African people in general and African Americans in particular. Marcus GARVEY's nationalist movement was also an expression of twentieth-century PAN-AFRICANISM, but Ethiopianism was a subsidiary emphasis in Garvey's movement. Garvey became the main interpreter of biblically based Ethiopianism; he elaborated on the liturgical issues raised initially by Turner and gave expression to liturgical Ethiopianism.

Like many of the twentieth-century pan-African nationalists, Garvey accepted Ethiopia as representative of African people everywhere and thus as symbolic of the prophecy of Psalm 68:31, which also became the motto for his movement. Garvey's messianic Ethio-pianism encouraged a reinterpretation of New Testament Christianity and followed up on Turner's assertion of the right of blacks to interpret Christianity through black images and symbols. Garvey popularized the concepts of the Black Messiah, the black madonna and child, and black angels. He called for all black churches to replace European images and symbols with black ones. Under his direction, the AFRICAN ORTHODOX CHURCH was established as a link with Ethiopian Christianity and as an adjunct to Garvey's UNIVERSAL NEGRO IMPROVEMENT ASSOCIATION (UNIA).

After Garvey, Ethiopianism as an organized expression with widespread institutional recognition and acceptance declined. Yet the spirit of the Ethiopian tradition remained active in certain aspects of African American culture, even in instances where the term Ethiopianism was not used. Quasi-religious and religious cults and sects became the keepers of the messianic tradition related to Ethiopianism from the 1930's until the 1960's. These non-Christian and not exclusively biblically based groups gave rise to a uniquely Islamic-based movement that embodied the spirit of messianic Ethiopianism but that linked the concept to Islamic religion. Eventually, this movement centered in the NATION OF ISLAM and its leader, Elijah MUHAMMAD.

### The 1960's and Beyond

By the 1960's, the Nation of Islam, whose members are commonly referred to as Black Muslims, played a major role in inspiring the nationalism associated with the BLACK POWER MOVEMENT. Black Muslims also indirectly helped to reawaken the spirit of Ethiopianism among some African American Christians and among nationalists in general. This development was assisted by the black theology movement, which sought to establish liberation as the essential basis for African Christianity in particular and black religion in general. Furthermore, it helped to legitimize a more inclusive view of black religion that was acceptable to many within and outside the black church.

Although the general spirit of messianic Ethiopianism is manifested in varying degrees among African Americans in the United States, two groups in particular were the successors to the more traditional Ethiopianism. The Shrine of the Black Madonna church movement is led by Albert CLEAGE of Detroit. Cleage's church reasserts the traditional, biblically based Christian Ethiopianism while incorporating the Turner-Garvey liturgical emphasis. The other group, the quasireligious-cultural Kemetic Studies movement, is closer to the Blyden approach. It reclaims the ancient Nile Valley cultural and spiritual legacy as an integral part of the African cultural heritage and affirms the values and inherent worth derived from that tradition.

Ethiopianism as a quasireligious movement did not cease to be relevant as a movement with appeal to persons of African descent in the modern world. It has persisted over time and adapted to changing situations and different expressions. On the continent of Africa as well as in the African diaspora, in such forms as the Jamaican-derived RASTA-FARIAN movement of the Caribbean or independent religious movements in Africa and in the United States, Ethiopianism survived in both traditional and modified forms.

—*James Wesley Johnson*

See also: Black nationalism; Diaspora, African; Rastafarianism.

Suggested Readings:

Burkett, Randall K. *Garveyism as a Religious Movement*. Metuchen, N.J.: Scarecrow Press, 1978.

Drake, St. Clair. *Black Folk Here and There*. Vol. 1. Los Angeles: Center for Afro-American Studies, University of California Press, 1987.

_____. *Redemption of Africa and Black Religion*. Chicago: Third World Press, 1970.

Martin, Tony. *Race First: The Ideological and Organizational Struggles of Marcus Garvey and the Universal Negro Improvement Association*. Westport, Conn.: Greenwood Press, 1976.

Moses, Wilson J. *The Golden Age of Black Nationalism, 1850-1925*. Hamden, Conn.: Archon Books, 1978.

Stuckey, Sterling, ed. *The Ideological Origins of Black Nationalism*. Boston: Beacon Press, 1972.

Vinson, Robert T. "African Americans in South African-American Diplomacy." *Negro History Bulletin* 61 (January/March 1998): 7-19.

Wilmore, Gayraud S. *Black Religion and Black Radicalism: An Interpretation of the Religious History of African Americans*. 3d ed. Maryknoll, N.Y.: Orbis Books, 1998.

**Ethnocentrism:** An ethnocentric view of another culture or subculture judges that culture by one's own cultural standards. In other words, ethnocentrism is the application of standards and value judgments from one's own culture when making judgments about the culture or subculture of another.

The ethnocentric approach is often contrasted with cultural relativism, the effort to understand other cultures according to their own ideals and standards for behavior. Anthropologists, for example, generally work to maintain a culturally relative perspective and to avoid biased ethnocentric attitudes. Ethnocentrism can be blatant or subtle. It is apparent, for example, in courses on world civilization that focus on Western civilizations to the exclusion or neglect of African or Asian civilizations. Ethnocentrism has often blinded white scholars to the achievements of African cultures and other world cultures and to the truth about African American subcultures in the United States. One example of white

American ethnocentrism has to do with non-standard varieties of English. BLACK ENGLISH has been judged, ethnocentrically, as a deviant or incorrect form of standard English. However, Black English has its own consistent structures, rules, and conventions.

Ethnocentrism has similarities to racism. One could draw the analogy that ethnocentrism is to perceived ethnic difference as racism is to perceived physical difference. The racist typically compares his or her own group to another, judges the other group according to his or her own standards, and finds his or her own group superior.

—*Christopher A. Reichl*


**Eubie Blake Cultural Center** (Baltimore, Maryland): The Eubie Blake Cultural center was established in 1978 as Gallery 409. Norman Ross, the founder and coordinator of the Urban Services Cultural Arts Program, was instrumental in its development. Later, the center was renamed in commemoration of a native Baltimorean, James Hubert "Eubie" BLAKE, a leading American composer of RAGTIME and stage music. The Eubie Blake Cultural Center consists of three components: Gallery 409, the art exhibition area; a second-floor area where classes and programs are held; and the Eubie Blake National Museum, located on the lower level of the center. A BALTIMORE landmark institution, the Eubie Blake Cultural Center has been visited by people from throughout the United States and the world.


**Europe, James Reese** (February 22, 1881, Mobile, Alabama—May 10, 1919, Boston, Massachusetts): Bandleader, pianist, and violinist. Europe was the second of three children, all of whom had extensive musical training. There is little information about his father. His mother, Lorraine, was a pianist, as were his younger sister, Mary, and his older brother, John.

The family moved from ALABAMA to WASHINGTON, D.C., around 1890. Europe continued to study piano and violin and had composition lessons with Enrico Hurlei. Around 1903, following the death of his father, Europe left Washington for NEW YORK. In 1905 he collaborated with the musical stage personality Ernest Hogan to compose the music for Hogan's musical, *The Memphis Students*. Following his success with that production, Europe became the musical director for several leading musical comedies, including Bob Cole and J. Rosamond Johnson's *Shoo-Fly Regiment* (1907) and *Red Moon* (1909) and Bert Williams's *Mr. Lode of Koel* (1909).

By 1910 Europe had established a reputation as a composer and musical theater director. That year, he and several other well-known musicians formed the Clef Club, a musician's association and management agency that looked after the rights and contracts of other African American musicians. Europe was elected as president and conductor of the Clef Club's orchestra, which gave its first concert in May, 1910. In 1912 he conducted the Clef Club Orchestra at Carnegie Hall, with repeat performances in 1913 and 1914. In 1913 he began a musical collaboration with the famous dance team of Vernon and Irene Castle. That same year, he accepted a recording contract with the Victor company, marking the first time an African American musical ensemble had been recorded. Between 1914 and 1917, he was music director and composer for the Castle dance team. He and his Society Orchestra introduced several dances, including the foxtrot, to the Castles, which they in turn popularized.

After WORLD WAR I broke out, Europe joined the MILITARY as a commissioned officer. He was asked to form a military brass band as part of the 369th Infantry. He introduced JAZZ music to the European continent through his concerts in France. In 1919 the 369th returned to the United States, and Europe began a concert tour with its band. The band recorded for the Pathé label. Among other works, it recorded W. C. HANDY's "Memphis" and "St. Louis Blues." Europe was stabbed fatally in Boston by an apparently deranged band member. He was buried with full military honors in Arlington Cemetery. As the most popular African American bandleader of his day, he was dubbed the "king of jazz."

*See also:* Songwriters and composers.

**Evans, James Carmichael** (July 1, 1900, Gallatin, Tennessee—1988): Engineer, educator, and civilian aide. After receiving his bachelor's degree in 1921 from Roger Williams University in MEMPHIS, TENNESSEE, Evans found that he needed additional preparation before pursuing graduate studies in technical sciences. He was accepted into the undergraduate program at the Massachusetts Institute of Technology (MIT), where he was awarded a bachelor of science degree in 1925 before going on to earn his master's degree in 1926.

Evans served on the faculty of West Virginia State College from 1928 to 1942 and taught at HOWARD UNIVERSITY from 1946 until 1970. In 1942, during WORLD WAR II, Evans began working as a civilian defense manpower aide, coordinating pilot training programs and serving as a technical training specialist for the War Production Board. Accepting a position as a civilian aide to Secretary of Defense Louis Johnson, Evans was instrumental in eliminating restrictions that limited the opportunities and advancement of African Americans in all branches of the armed services. He also helped implement desegregation of the military under EXECUTIVE ORDER 9981. Upon his retirement from this post, Evans was awarded the Meritorious Civilian Service Medal by the secretary of defense in 1970. As an inventor, Evans held a patent for a method of using exhaust gases to prevent icing on aircraft.

*See also:* Engineers.

**Evans, Mari** (b. July 16, 1923, Toledo, Ohio): Poet. Evans gained prominence in the early 1960's. Her verse is concise yet incisive, and startling in its understatement. She combined her life as a poet with a variety of wage-paying jobs. At various times, she worked as a civil servant, a musician, a church choir director, a program director for the Young Men's Christian Association, editor of an industrial magazine, publication director at a Job Corps center, television producer-director for *The Black Experience* (1968-1973), and teacher at Purdue University in Indiana and other colleges.

Poets Sonia Sanchez (left), Mari Evans (center), and Gwendolyn Brooks. *(© Roy Lewis Archives)*

Evans's first poems appeared in magazines, including *Phylon*, *Negro Digest*, and *Dialog*. A number of her poems have been anthologized widely by such collectors as Rosey Pool, Arna BONTEMPS, Langston HUGHES, Walter Lowenfels, Dudley Randall, Margaret Burroughs, and Janheinz Jahn. Books consisting solely of her poetry include *I Am a Black Woman* (1970), *Where Is All the Music?* (1968), and *Nightstar: 1973-1978* (1981).

Turning from poetry, Evans revealed an interest in literary criticism. In 1984 she edited a group of critical essays covering fifteen African American female poets, novelists, and playwrights in an impressive volume called *Black Women Writers (1950-1980): A Critical Evaluation* (1984). Her other works include children's books: *J.D.* (1973), *I Look at Me!* (1974), *Singing Black* (1967), and *Jim Flying High* (1979).

Evans's lean verse is best characterized as witty or restrained in tone. She uses short lines, few rhymes or punctuation marks, and minimal capitalization. Her themes are racial, and she speaks in the vernacular of urban African Americans. In a well-known poem, "Status Symbol," she proclaims, after the 1963 MARCH ON WASHINGTON, that she has reached a new level of achievement in American society, having just been hired for a position previously denied to African Americans. She receives, as a status symbol from her white boss, the key to the locked white bathroom. This ironic view permeates Evans's poetry. Her best-known piece, "Alarm Clock," first appeared in 1966 in *Negro Digest*. In this poem, she takes a relaxed moment devoted to daydreaming at a lunch counter and turns it into a jolting reminder of racism.

**Evans, Melvin Herbert** (August 7, 1917, Christiansted, St. Croix—November 27, 1984, Christiansted, St. Croix): U.S. delegate from the VIRGIN ISLANDS. Evans was born on St. Croix shortly after the Virgin Islands were purchased from Denmark by the United States. After attending school on St. Thomas, Evans enrolled at HOWARD UNIVERSITY, where he received his bachelor of science degree in 1940 and his medical degree in 1944.

After graduating from medical school, Evans worked at several hospitals and medical institutions in the United States and the Virgin Islands. In 1959 he was appointed as health commissioner for the Virgin Islands. He served in that post until 1967. He was appointed governor of the Virgin Islands by President Richard Nixon in 1969. Congress had passed the Virgin Islands Elective Governor Act in August of 1968, granting the territory's residents the right to elect their own governor. Evans ran as the Republican candidate for governor and won the election in 1970. He was defeated for reelection in 1974 but was selected to serve as the islands' representative on the Republican National Committee. Evans also served as chairman of the board of trustees for the College of the Virgin Islands.

In 1978 Evans defeated Janet Watlington in the election for congressional delegate from the Virgin Islands. He took office on January 3, 1979, and served on the House Committee on the Armed Services, the House Committee on Interior and Insular Affairs, the House Committee on the Merchant Marine, and the House Committee on Fisheries. Evans labored to gain federal funds for improving law enforcement and public education in the Virgin Islands, introduced legislation to allow foreign doctors to practice in understaffed medical facilities there, and lobbied for the introduction of flood control measures in the wake of devastating tropical storms and hurricanes. He actively supported the efforts to declare Martin Luther KING, Jr.'s birthday a national holiday. Evans was defeated for reelection in 1980 but was appointed to the post of ambassador to TRINIDAD AND TOBAGO in 1981. Evans served in this diplomatic office until his death.

**Evanti, Lillian** (Annie Lillian Evans; August 12, 1890, Washington, D.C.—December 7, 1967, Washington, D.C.): Coloratura soprano. Evanti came from a privileged background. Among her ancestors was Hiram REVELS, the first African American U.S. senator, elected after the CIVIL WAR. Evanti apparently was exposed to much European music as a child. Her father, Bruce Evans, was one of the founders and the first principal of the Armstrong Manual Training Academy, which Lillian attended. She later received a bachelor's degree in music from HOWARD UNIVERSITY (1917) and married her voice teacher, Roy Tibbs. Her stage name, Evanti, was a combination of her maiden name and the first two letters of Tibbs.

In 1925 she left for Europe, making her first stop in France. Eventually, she sang in Italy with the Nice Opera and in Salzburg at the Mozarteum. Her major success was in Nice, France, in 1927, when she sang the title role in Léo Delibes's *Lakmé*, making her the first African American to sing a lead role with a European company.

After several well-received concerts in Europe, Evanti returned to the United States in 1932 and auditioned for the Metropolitan Opera, but she was turned down because of her race. Evanti faced similar rejections from other U.S. opera companies, although most critics agreed that her talent was world-class. She became a star with the National Negro Opera Company which, in 1943, featured her in the role of Violetta in a production of Giuseppe Verdi's *La Traviata*. The performance attracted a crowd of more than fifteen thousand. Evanti repeated the role in the Verdi opera the following year and in the same production at Madison Square Garden.

After retiring from the stage, Evanti devoted herself to politics, composing, and establishing a publishing company, the Columbia Music Bureau. In the 1950's, she founded the Lillian Evanti Chorale, a female group that sang mostly in the WASHINGTON, D.C., area. Her political lobbying for a national performing arts center bore fruit with the opening of the Kennedy Center.

*See also:* Classical and operatic music.

**Evers, Charles** (b. September 11, 1922, Decatur, Mississippi): CIVIL RIGHTS leader and politician. James Charles Evers received his B.S. degree from Alcorn State University, served in the U.S. military in Korea, and returned to direct family business interests in Philadelphia, MISSISSIPPI. In 1957 he moved to CHICAGO, ILLINOIS, where he was a successful owner of a nightclub as well as a real-estate agent. The assassination of his brother Medgar EVERS in 1963 prompted him to return to his home state and become more involved in politics and civil rights activities.

Evers assumed the leadership of the NATIONAL ASSOCIATION FOR THE ADVANCEMENT OF COLORED PEOPLE (NAACP) in Mississippi, the post held by his late brother, just two days after Medgar Evers's funeral. He explained that he was committed to continuing his brother's work without interruption. Using the NAACP as his organizational framework, he quickly recruited members in parts of the state where there had been almost no civil rights programs. In Natchez, Mississippi, he successfully promoted economic boycotts and enlisted some cooperation from white political leaders. The boycotts spread and black communities in the state successfully challenged segregationist laws. Evers realized the need to exploit this unity through political institutions.

In January, 1968, Evers announced that he would run for a congressional seat from southwest Mississippi. He polled forty thousand votes but lost the runoff election. In 1969 he ran for MAYOR of Fayette, in Jefferson County, and won. He was the first African American mayor in a racially mixed town in the South since RECONSTRUCTION. He was reelected in 1973.

Charles Evers during his campaign for governor in 1971. *(AP/Wide World Photos)*

Evers's successful races for mayor were significant because they were won in a biethnic community. They were also notable because Jefferson County had the lowest per capita income in the state at that time, and one-third of its population was functionally illiterate. As mayor, Evers was committed to economic revival in Fayette. He attempted to reverse the trend of youth leaving the area and struggled to maintain an integrated and biracial community. His programs attracted national attention, as he succeeded in halting the town's economic decline.

A trendsetter among African American politicians in the South, Evers showed how economic power can be translated into political change and how politics could be of eco-

nomic benefit to all ethnic communities. He became president of the Medgar Evers Fund, supporting civil rights activities in the South. He published his autobiography, *Evers*, in 1971.

**Evers, Medgar** (July 2, 1925, Decatur, Mississippi—June 12, 1963, Jackson, Mississippi): CIVIL RIGHTS activist. Medgar Evers was one of the most prominent martyrs of the 1960's Civil Rights movement. The youngest son of James and Jessie Wright Evers, he grew up in a rural MISSISSIPPI community that had a strong influence on his life. His father worked at a sawmill and for a railroad; his mother was a domestic worker.

*Youth and Education*
Evers's upbringing was colored by his family's strong commitment to the CHURCH OF GOD IN CHRIST. His parents encouraged Medgar to develop his entrepreneurial skills and instilled in all their children a sense of responsibility and industriousness as virtues.

Evers's elementary training was received in the Decatur Consolidated School. He graduated from high school in nearby Newton, Mississippi. Although he had planned to go to college, WORLD WAR II forced a delay in his enrollment. In 1943 he was drafted into the U.S. Army, and he served in Normandy.

In 1946 he enrolled in Alcorn Agricultural and Mechanical College (later ALCORN STATE UNIVERSITY) in Lorman, Mississippi. Alcorn was a distinguished HISTORICALLY BLACK COLLEGE and America's oldest African American land-grant institution. As a collegian, Evers was a popular student; he was a member of the school's track and football teams, editor of the student newspaper, junior class president, vice president of the student forum, and a member of the college glee club. He earned extra money by selling snacks to classmates who were studying late at night, and he majored in business administration with the aspiration of becoming a lawyer.

During his college years, he met and married Myrlie Beasley of Vicksburg, Mississippi, a nursing student who left college after marriage to rear their children. After college, the family settled in the African American town of MOUND BAYOU, MISSISSIPPI, where Evers worked as an insurance salesman for the Magnolia Mutual Life Insurance Company. Evers, though, left the insurance company to become more involved in the burgeoning Civil Rights movement.

*Civil Rights Work*

In 1954 Evers became the state field secretary of the NATIONAL ASSOCIATION FOR THE ADVANCEMENT OF COLORED PEOPLE (NAACP). His involvement in the NAACP was a result of his experiences as a child growing up in Mississippi, where he had encountered taunts from local whites and had become familiar with the brutality that was common in the tense racial climate of the state. His early experiences, combined with later adult encounters with racism, led to his active participation in civil rights work.

In 1962 he played a major role in assisting the enrollment of James MEREDITH in the University of Mississippi. After the U.S. SUPREME COURT issued the 1954 BROWN v. BOARD OF EDUCATION decision outlawing segregation in public schools, Meredith had attempted unsuccessfully to enroll in the university. Evers's involvement in the Meredith enrollment process was only one of his many contributions to the early stages of the Civil Rights movement.

In the early 1960's, Evers spearheaded a number of economic boycotts in Mississippi, including boycotts of beverage companies, bakeries, and clothing stores whose owners were supporters of segregation. Along with other civil rights leaders in Mississippi, he helped to organize the "Jackson movement," an NAACP-led coalition of black organizations that sponsored mass meetings, demon-

Medgar Evers during a 1962 television interview. *(Library of Congress)*

strations, and boycotts to challenge the segregationist system in Mississippi.

*The Jackson Movement*

In 1962 the Jackson movement staged a successful boycott of Mississippi's segregated state fair and a boycott of businesses in downtown Jackson. The Jackson movement issued demands to the city's white leaders that included calls for the hiring of African American policemen and school crossing guards, for the removal of segregation signs from public facilities, for the improvement of job opportunities for African Americans on city payrolls, for the integration of public parks and libraries, for the appointment of an African American to the city parks and recreation commission, and for the integration of the public schools. Evers played a major role in resolving an internal conflict in the Jackson movement between conservative, middle-class adult organizations and radical youth organizations. His ability to negotiate with various groups was a hallmark of his leadership; he was able to recognize the importance of a wide base of participation to the Civil Rights movement in Mississippi.

As one of the most prominent African American leaders in Mississippi, Evers was aware of the need to have some native white southerners involved in the political changes occurring in the state. Evers was able to get moderate and liberal Mississippi whites to participate in liberal organizations such as the Mississippi Council on Human Relations.

*Assassination*

On June 12, 1963, Evers was killed by an assassin's bullet as he returned home from a mass meeting of the Jackson movement. Byron de la Beckwith, a fertilizer salesman and a member of an old Mississippi family, was accused of the murder. Beckwith was tried three times for the crime and finally convicted of the murder in February, 1994. Evers's death was a pivotal event in the Civil Rights movement. He was a respected member of the African American middle-class community and a well-known national civil rights leader, and his death showed the extent to which racial violence was tolerated in Jim Crow Mississippi. Reaction to Evers's murder led to increased participation in the Civil Rights movement from a wide segment of the African American community in Mississippi.

Evers was buried in Arlington National Cemetery in Washington, D.C., with full military honors. Afterward, the NAACP honored him posthumously for his contributions to the civil rights struggle with the 1963 SPINGARN MEDAL.

—*Donald Cunnigen*

*See also:* Segregation and integration.

Suggested Readings:
Evers-Williams, Myrlie, with William Peters. *For Us, the Living.* Garden City, N.Y.: Doubleday, 1967.
Massengill, Reed. *Portrait of a Racist: The Man Who Killed Medgar Evers?* New York: St. Martin's Press, 1994.
Moody, Anne. *Coming of Age in Mississippi.* New York: Dell Books, 1968.
Morris, Willie. *The Ghosts of Medgar Evers: A Tale of Race, Murder, Mississippi, and Hollywood.* New York: Random House, 1998.
Nossiter, Adam. *Of Long Memory: Mississippi and the Murder of Medgar Evers.* Reading, Mass.: Addison-Wesley, 1994.
Salter, John R., Jr. *Jackson, Mississippi: An American Chronicle of Struggle and Schism.* Hicksville, N.Y.: Exposition Press, 1979.
Sewell, George A. *Mississippi Black History Makers.* Jackson: University Press of Mississippi, 1977.
Vollers, Maryanne. *Ghosts of Mississippi: The Murder of Medgar Evers, the Trials of Byron de la Beckwith, and the Haunting of the New South.* Boston: Little, Brown, 1995.
Wells, Dean F., and Hunter Cole, eds. *Mississippi Heroes.* Jackson: University Press of Mississippi, 1980.

**Evers-Williams, Myrlie** (b. March 17, 1933, Vicksburg, Mississippi): CIVIL RIGHTS activist. Myrlie Beasley was reared by a grandmother and an aunt, both of whom were teachers. After graduating from high school, she followed their example by majoring in education at Alcorn Agricultural and Mechanical College in Lorman, Mississippi. At Alcorn, she met Medgar EVERS, a veteran seven years her senior, who was returning to complete his education. They were married on December 24, 1951. The couple moved to the historically black community of MOUND BAYOU, MISSISSIPPI, following his graduation in 1952. With her husband's employment as an insurance agent for the black-owned Magnolia Mutual Insurance Company, Myrlie Evers was able to settle down to domestic life rearing three children: Darrell, born in 1953; Reena, born in 1954; and James, born in 1960.

When Medgar Evers became the field secretary for the state chapter of the NATIONAL ASSOCIATION FOR THE ADVANCEMENT OF COLORED PEOPLE (NAACP) in 1954, Myrlie Evers's life began to change. Her husband's commitment to racial justice and equality influenced her vision of activism as she served as his full-time secretary at the Jackson office of the NAACP. Under Medgar Evers's leadership, the Mississippi NAACP publicized the 1955 Emmett TILL murder, aided James MEREDITH's entry into the University of Mississippi, campaigned against racial violence, lobbied for jobs and public access, and organized for voting rights. As Myrlie Evers noted in her book *For Us, the Living* (1967), these activities brought danger and finally death to the Evers family. On the evening of June 11, 1963, her husband was murdered in his drive-

Myrlie Evers-Williams in 1970. *(AP/Wide World Photos)*

way less than twenty-four hours after President John F. Kennedy had given a speech calling for racial equality in the South.

Following her husband's assassination, Myrlie Evers moved from Mississippi. With the help of the NAACP, she settled in the university community of Claremont, CALIFORNIA, where she worked as the assistant director of educational opportunity. In 1968 she graduated from Pomona College with a degree in sociology. She completed her studies while rearing her family, giving public speeches, and commuting to Mississippi to testify in the first trial against Byron de la Beckwith, the man accused of assassinating her husband.

She worked as the director of public affairs for Chevron Oil, campaigned for political office, and worked on many civic projects in California, during which time she met Walter Edgar Williams, a retired longshoreman and civil rights activist whom she married in 1976. Evers-Williams continued working with the NAACP and accepted the appointment by Los Angeles mayor Tom BRADLEY as the city's commissioner of public works, becoming the first African American woman to serve in that post, which she held until 1990.

New evidence brought the retrial of Byron de la Beckwith, who was found guilty of Evers's murder on February 5, 1994, and sentenced to life in prison. With this closure, Evers-Williams donated the Evers family home in Jackson to Tougaloo College as a museum. Her second husband died of cancer in February of 1995, the same month she was elected chair of the NAACP board of directors. With her election to this post, Evers-Williams became the first African American woman to lead the nation's premier civil rights organization.

Suggested Readings:
Bailey, Ron. "Myrlie Evers Williams." In *Black Women in America: An Historical Encyclope-*

*dia*, edited by Darlene Clark Hine. Brooklyn, N.Y.: Carlson, 1993.

Evers-Williams, Myrlie, with William Peters. *For Us, the Living*. Garden City, N.Y.: Doubleday, 1967.

Evers-Williams, Myrlie, and Melinda Blau. *Watch Me Fly: What I Learned on the Way to Becoming the Woman I Was Meant to Be*. Boston: Little, Brown, 1999.

Haywood, Richette L. "Can Myrlie Evers-Williams Save the NAACP?" *Ebony* (October, 1995): 38-42.

Manegold, Catherine S. "She Has a Dream." *Harper's Bazaar* (July, 1995): 58-59.

White, Jack E. "A Matter of Life and Death." *Time* (February 27, 1995): 23.

**Ewing, Patrick** (b. Aug. 5, 1962, Kingston, Jamaica): BASKETBALL player. Ewing first took up basketball in a Massachusetts high school after immigrating with his family from Jamaica when he was thirteen. He earned an athletic scholarship to Georgetown University and led the Hoyas to the NCAA finals three times, including a championship in 1984. That same year he played for the winning U.S. team at the Los Angeles Olympics. During his senior year he was named college player of the year by four different bodies.

The New York Knicks made Ewing first pick of the 1985 National Basketball Association (NBA) draft, and he became rookie of the year. A seven-foot-tall center, he averaged more than twenty-three points and ten rebounds a game and was a perennial all-star selection through fourteen pro seasons. In 1992 he earned a second gold medal at the Olympics as the starting center of the U.S. "Dream Team." In 1996 an NBA panel named him one of the fifty greatest players of the league's first half century. The following year he was elected president of the NBA Players Association and was a hardliner in a labor dispute with the league that delayed the opening of

Throughout his long career, Patrick Ewing has always been a powerful force under the basket. *(National Basketball Association)*

the 1998-1999 season. Midway into the shortened season that followed, he tore an achilles tendon and missed the rest of the season, while the Knicks reached the championship finals. He returned to play midway into the following season, in December, 1999, and led the Knicks back to the play-offs.

**Executive Order 8802:** Presidential order that forbade racial discrimination in defense industries holding government contracts and in government training programs. President Franklin D. Roosevelt issued the order on June 25, 1941. Less than a month later, he created the Fair Employment Practices Commission to investigate complaints. A. Philip RANDOLPH, a longtime labor leader in the African American

Wartime poster celebrating the integration of defense industries. *(National Archives)*

community, had threatened Roosevelt with a large-scale "march on Washington" if steps were not taken to end discrimination. Convinced that racial divisions would harm his military preparedness campaign, Roosevelt gave in and signed Executive Order 8802.

*See also:* Roosevelt administration; World War II.

**Executive Order 9981:** Executive order integrating the U.S. military that was signed by President Harry S Truman in 1948. Truman issued Executive Order (EO) 9981 on July 26, 1948. EO 9981 mandated "equality of treatment and opportunity in the armed

forces without regard to race, color, religion, or national origin." It also established the President's Commission on Equal Treatment and Opportunity in the Armed Forces. Charles Fahy was appointed by Truman to chair the commission.

Integrating the military has been heralded as one of Truman's greatest CIVIL RIGHTS achievements. African Americans had fought for independence in the Revolutionary War and helped preserve the Union while in uniform during the CIVIL WAR. However, as was the case with most institutions in American society, the military remained segregated through WORLD WAR II.

During and after World War II, prominent African American leaders such as A. Philip RANDOLPH and Walter WHITE, as well as African American journalists, advocated integration. Two other timely events caught the attention of the nation and the president, one being the successful cross-country flight by two African American pilots—Dale White and Chauncy Spencer. The other was the many accomplishments of the famous TUSKEGEE AIR-

During the summer of 1948, many African Americans marched outside the Democratic Party Convention demanding an end to racial segregation in the military. President Truman's Executive Order 9981 met their demands. *(Schomburg Center for Research in Black Culture, New York Public Library)*

MEN and NINETY-NINTH PURSUIT SQUADRON, African American fighter pilots who did not lose a single American bomber under their protection during World War II.

It is also believed that President Truman supported integration for political reasons, as he was running for reelection and needed the support of black voters. On the other hand, Truman was known as a strong believer in equality. EO 9981 helped lay the groundwork for the Civil Rights movement of the 1950's and 1960's. Since its passage, African Americans have attained numerous leadership positions in the military, including chair of the Joint Chiefs.

—*Robert P. Watson*

*See also:* Military.

**Exodusters and homesteaders:** Settlers who accepted free land on the frontier in exchange for developing it. Although some western states outlawed SLAVERY before the CIVIL WAR, blacks did not begin homesteading in great numbers until the RECONSTRUCTION era after the war. In 1862 the U.S. government offered free land to people who would relocate to the West. "Homesteading" consisted of planting crops, building a house, and maintaining a residence. According to the Homestead Act, land had to be occupied and cultivated for five consecutive years before ownership was transferred to the homesteader. Many homesteaders failed to meet the requirements because of insufficient capital or training. Much of the land available to homesteaders was of low quality, making their task even more difficult.

The best land had been purchased prior to the Homestead Act.

Because the South failed to grant equality to African Americans after the end of the Civil War in 1865, black newspapers such as the *Nashville Herald* and the *Pilot* encouraged African Americans either to emigrate to Africa or to homestead west of the Mississippi River. Men such as Henry Adams, a young former slave, and Benjamin "Pap" Singleton, a mulatto and former slave, opposed an African exodus and urged a western move. Singleton organized at least four colonies in KANSAS between 1872 and 1878. One of the most important of these settlements, NICODEMUS, KANSAS, attempted to aid migrants who were receiving pay for the first time in their lives. Begun in 1877, Nicodemus claimed more than six hundred homesteaders by 1879, partly because of anticipated railroad construction.

The "Exodusters" were so named because faith, rather than reason, led them to migrate by the thousands, primarily to Kansas, in the "great exodus" of 1879-1881. Despite many obstructions and certain chaotic conditions, these Exodusters saw the West, particularly Kansas, as a land of freedom and opportunity. Kansas, they remembered, was the home of

Tens of thousands of African Americans left the South for the West, particularly during 1879-1881. *(Associated Publishers, Inc.)*

abolitionist John Brown, the state of earlier colonizations, and a state that had never permitted slavery.

Homestead movements prior to 1878 were conducted in an orderly way, but the great exodus of 1879 was massive, unplanned, and controversial. Many of the new immigrants were unable to fend for themselves. Therefore, area organizations, such as the Colored Relief Board, and other groups, such as the Quakers, offered assistance. Quakers purchased four hundred acres of land to build the Agricultural and Industrial Institute, which offered training in farming, building, and domestic chores. Even so, by 1890 only one of three homesteaders was able to fulfill the requirements to claim a homesteaded plot. Although they remained poor, Exodusters believed that their new lives were better than their lives as slaves. One visitor, Sojourner Truth, a former antislavery crusader, arrived in Kansas, announced the exodus as a great crusade, and composed a poem to commemorate the event.

Although life was hard, by 1910 there were a million black settlers west of the Mississippi River. The Black American West Museum and Heritage Center in Denver, Colorado, collected more than thirty-five thousand artifacts, re-creating the role that these exodusters and homesteaders played in settling the American West.

*See also:* Black towns; Colonization movement; Dearfield, Colorado; Frontier Society.


**Expatriates:** The expatriate impulse—the desire to live in another country for a time or to resettle there permanently—has been significant throughout the United States' history. As early as the eighteenth century, the tradition of expatriation flourished. African Americans had some of the same reasons for moving abroad that any Americans did—to study, for example—but they also sometimes left the United States to escape its racism and to advance in fields that were not as open to them in the United States. Some were temporary expatriates, remaining overseas for a few years; others adopted their new country, living there till their death.

They came from many walks of life and included such renowned figures as fighter Jack Johnson, dancer Josephine Baker, writers Richard Wright and James Baldwin, journalist John Russwurm, and political figures W. E. B. Du Bois and Stokely Carmichael (Kwame Toure). They moved to Canada, Great Britain, Scandinavian countries, France, and countries such as Liberia, Sierra Leone, and Ghana in West Africa.

*Early Expatriates*
During the eighteenth and nineteenth centuries African Americans associated Europe, particularly France, with the ideas of freedom and democracy. Escaped slaves composed the earliest group of expatriates. They chronicled slavery from the security of Europe and produced the first black expatriate literature. In the tradition of racial protest, Gustavus Vassa, William and Ellen Craft, Frederick Douglass, and William Wells Brown wrote slave narratives. Other blacks were equally determined to flee the hopeless racial situation in the United States and to seek refuge abroad.

Among those expatriates who went to Liberia were Lott Carey, who emigrated in 1821 and was active in missionary work and the Liberian government, pioneering journalist John B. Russwurm, who moved there in 1829, and Alexander Crummell and Edward W. Blyden, who moved there later in the nineteenth century.

African American entrepreneur Paul Cuffe, though not an expatriate himself, was active in advocating black emigration from the United States in the early nineteenth century. Martin Delany also advocated emigration; he moved to Africa for a time but returned to the United States after the beginning of the CIVIL WAR. The early nineteenth century saw a peak in the African COLONIZATION MOVEMENT, spearheaded by the controversial AMERICAN COLONIZATION SOCIETY. Marcus GARVEY and his UNITED NEGRO IMPROVEMENT ASSOCIATION (UNIA) were the main forces in a new emigration and colonization movement in the first half of the twentieth century.

African American leaders who traveled to Europe for relatively brief periods included Bishop Daniel A. PAYNE, Frederick Douglass, Booker T. WASHINGTON, and Mary Church TERRELL.

African American boxers composed a small group of early nineteenth century expatriates who moved to England. Fighters could earn money there, and the racial climate was more liberal than in the United States. Among the fighters who moved to England were Tom Molyneux, Bill Richmond, Henry Sutton (who was at one point a contender for the British title), Sam Robinson, and Sambo Sutton, who, when he retired, taught boxing at Cambridge.

*Early Twentieth Century*

Painter Henry Ossawa TANNER, frustrated by a lack of recognition in the United States, went to Paris to study in 1891. He lived mostly in Paris thereafter until his death in 1937, partly to escape U.S. racism. He was elected to the French National Academy. Singer Roland HAYES, who gave recitals in which he performed both classical works and spirituals, had a rewarding career in Europe, studying and performing there; Hayes spent much time in Europe, particularly in the 1920's.

As soldiers in WORLD WAR I, a number of African Americans were stationed in France; among them was future historian and writer Rayford LOGAN. There they found democracy for the first time, and some remained abroad after the war.

Among the most famous early expatriates in Paris were fighter Jack Johnson and enter-

Among the most famous African American expatriates was entertainer Josephine Baker, seen here during a return to Broadway in 1951. *(AP/Wide World Photos)*

tainer Josephine Baker. Johnson fled to Paris in 1913 to avoid legal troubles in the United States. He remained there, famous for his flashy lifestyle—including fast cars, wild clothes, jewelry, and beautiful women—until returning to the United States in 1920. Five years later, a French theatrical producer saw dancer Josephine Baker perform in New York and asked her to relocate to Paris. Baker did, and she created an immediate sensation. She made Paris her home from 1925 until her death in 1975. She performed all over Europe and starred in French films of the 1930's. During WORLD WAR II she was active in the French Resistance. Baker was later made a member of the French Legion of Honor. Other entertainers and musicians who became expatriates in the 1920's and 1930's included Mercer COOK, Richard Lambert, Edmond Dede, Ira ALDRIDGE, and T. Morris Chester.

## World War II and After

World War II offered a special chance for blacks to live abroad and to reassess their position in the United States. The war experiences abroad inspired many African Americans to examine anew the dilemmas at home. To some extent, the segregated armed forces served as a microcosm of American life. Black American recruits in both the North and South were generally subject to the most overt kinds of discrimination. Tensions over race relations in the United States were at an all-time high in 1945. Though blacks on the home front gave generous support to the war effort, high unemployment rates among blacks, inadequate housing, riots, racial persecution, and oppression raised anew the difficult issues of black survival in America.

A number of classical, JAZZ, and BLUES musicians either moved to Europe or spent considerable time there beginning in the 1950's and 1960's. Composer Julia Perry moved to Paris for a time in the 1950's and studied with Nadia Boulanger and Luigi Dallapiccola. Bigband singer June Richmond moved there in 1954. Bluesman MEMPHIS SLIM relocated to Paris in the 1960's. Blues guitar virtuoso and songwriter Jimi HENDRIX's time in London was relatively brief in the mid-1960's, but it was crucial; it was there he created a sensation and truly began his career. A number of artists went to Europe as well; one was sculptor and painter Daniel LaRue Johnson, who moved to Paris in 1965 to study with Alberto Giacometti. Two American intellectual and political figures who moved to Africa in the 1960's were W. E. B. Du Bois, who emigrated to Ghana in 1961, and Stokely Carmichael, who moved to Guinea in 1968, changing his name to Kwame Toure two years later.

## Expatriate Writers

In the twentieth century many African American writers not only geographically but also philosophically chose to become expatriates. Claude McKay, Nella LARSON, Willard Motley, Richard Wright, Chester HIMES, William Gardner Smith, James Baldwin, William DEMBY, Ronald FAIR, Richard Gibson, and Frank YERBY all became expatriates after World War II. Varied reasons prompted their exiles—the search for identity, the need for artistic freedom and recognition, the rejection of the dominant values of white America, the racial situation in the United States. The literature produced by this diverse and talented group has been rich and artistically successful. Philosophically, all were united in the convictions that only from a geographical distance could the question of black survival in America be addressed and answered and that the racial situation the United States was such that the black artist could not achieve personal or artistic freedom.

Writers in the 1940's examined the possibilities for literature in a universe of fragmented beliefs: Marxism had long sustained the idealism of Communist Party members as well as many in the noncommunist Left, but it had failed to come to terms with human freedom and human dignity. Naturalism had failed. As a result, many writers—such as Wright and Himes—saw no alternative but to withdraw from the political scene and to turn their attention elsewhere. This radical disunity that characterized life in the 1940's created spiritual and intellectual turmoil.

African American writers addressed the exigencies of the times: Economic crises, social tensions, and political problems. They created a literature of protest. After tours of duty as soldiers abroad, William Gardner Smith and John O. KILLENS settled in Europe. Wright, Baldwin, and Himes turned to Europe as a means of survival, personally and artistically. Countée CULLEN, Claude McKay, and Langston HUGHES recounted their expatriate experiences in their novels. Europe became the refuge of many African American writers during the post-World War II period. Melvin VAN

Peebles, Carlene Polite, Barbara CHASE-RIBOUD, and Hazel SCOTT chose to live in France for a time, as did black power advocate Angela DAVIS and writer William Melvin Kelly. Only through expatriation, many black writers believed, could they recover their individual humanity and view their racial heritage from an accurate perspective.

—*Jacquelyn L. Jackson*

*See also:* Canada; Craft, Ellen, and William Craft.

**Exploration of North America:** African Americans began exploring North America at the same time Europeans did. Christopher Columbus and the Spanish conquistadores brought African slaves to the New World in the late fifteenth and early sixteenth centuries. While most of these black explorers served their masters in Mexico, Central America, South America, and the Caribbean, several found their way into North America.

The best known of these earliest African American explorers was ESTEVANICO (Spanish for Little Stephen). He was so named not because he was small but because he was not: At perhaps six feet, six inches in height, he was huge for the time in which he lived.

*Estevanico*

Estevanico was a member of an ill-fated expedition that sailed from Cuba to Florida in 1528. After being attacked by natives, the group's survivors sailed west along the coast of the Gulf of Mexico. A series of mishaps left Estevanico and three Spaniards enslaved by Indians in Texas. For several years, the small band lived in the present-day American Southwest until rescued by Spanish soldiers in 1536.

During their wilderness ordeal, the Spaniards and Estevanico heard stories of native settlements to the north and west of Texas where the streets were said to be paved with gold. Spanish authorities in Mexico City were,

Ships of Christopher Columbus, whose 1492 crews included at least one black member, a man known as Pedro Alonzo Nino. *(Library of Congress)*

Modern painting of Estevanico (on white horse) helping to lead the Spanish exploration of the Southwest. *(Associated Publishers, Inc.)*

naturally, intrigued about the possibility of finding so much wealth. When the three Spaniards declined to lead a search for the mythical towns, officials chose Estevanico for the task.

In 1539 Estevanico left Mexico City and traveled north into Arizona. Within a few weeks, natives killed him near present-day Zuni, New Mexico. The golden cities he sought did not exist, but Spaniards continued to look for them for years to come. Thus Estevanico's excursions into uncharted regions prompted further Spanish exploration of North America.

### York

The next black explorer whose exploits on the western frontier of North American are well known was YORK, the slave of William Clark. York accompanied Clark and Meriwether Lewis on their famous journey from the Mississippi River to the Pacific Ocean and back in the early nineteenth century. The Lewis and Clark Expedition left St. Louis in May, 1804, wintered with Native Americans in North Dakota and Oregon, and returned to Missouri in September, 1806.

Like Estevanico and other explorers who were slaves, York had no choice but to accompany Lewis and Clark. Nevertheless, his con-tribution to the expedition was more than merely assisting his master. A strong individual, York performed more than his share of the physical labor required to make the venture successful. He was also a skilled hunter and killed several game animals to help feed his fellow explorers. York was also instrumental in negotiating with Indian communities the entourage encountered. Apparently, many Indians admired York because of his strength and the fact that he—like them—was not white.

### James Douglas

The Lewis and Clark Expedition led to American fur trappers and traders moving into the Pacific Northwest. There they competed with Britons who also claimed the area. Eventually the United States and Great Britain divided the Oregon Country at the forty-ninth parallel, with the United States getting the southern half. For many years prior to the division, the British had claimed everything north of the Columbia River, including the present-day state of Washington. One of the primary British traders in that part of Oregon was James Douglas, a man of African descent.

Like many of the men involved in the fur trade, Douglas married a Native American woman. When the United States and Great Britain settled their Oregon dispute, Douglas had the choice of staying in Washington and becoming a U.S. citizen or moving north into the British section. He chose to relocate, and he fashioned a successful political career which included being governor of British Columbia.

### Edward Rose and Jim Beckwourth

Two African American fur traders explored much of the northern Rocky Mountain region in Montana and Wyoming. Both men—Edward Rose and Jim BECKWOURTH—lived among the Crow Indians and married native women. Consequently, the exploits of one are sometimes attributed to the other, and contemporary observers sometimes were confused about which one of these legendary "mountain men" they had encountered.

Rose, however, was several years older than Beckwourth, and he was quite different in demeanor. He had first traveled to the American West in 1810 as one of fur magnate John Jacob Astor's "overland Astorians," the second group (after Lewis and Clark) to cross North America from the Mississippi River to the Pacific Coast. Because of his ability to learn native languages, Rose later worked for the U.S. government as an interpreter. He was less well known than Beckwourth primarily because he avoided publicity.

Conversely, Beckwourth sought to capitalize upon his unique experiences on the western frontier. His autobiography, dictated to a white newspaperman, was published in 1856. Full of braggadocio and exaggerated feats of bravery, the book was dismissed by historians for many years as containing far more fiction than fact. Eventually, however, Beckwourth's narrative was seen as providing valuable insight into nineteenth century Crow culture—even if untrustworthy otherwise.

Beckwourth did much exploring of the North American West. He worked as a scout for the U.S. Army and occasionally led wagon trains of pioneers to their frontier destinations. Most significant of his discoveries was a passageway through the Sierra Nevada for travelers going to California. He lived for many years at the entrance to Beckwourth Pass, guiding settlers through it to their new homes in the Golden State.

Other African Americans besides Estevanico, York, James Douglas, Edward Rose, and Jim Beckwourth lived in and explored the North American West during the frontier era.

These five, however, are the best known of the black individuals whose hard work under dangerous and difficult conditions helped pave the way for settlement of the West.

—*Roger D. Hardaway*

*See also:* Blacks in the American West; Frontier, Society; Henson, Matthew Alexander.

Suggested Readings:

Betts, Robert B. *In Search of York: The Slave Who Went to the Pacific with Lewis and Clark.* Boulder: Colorado Associated University Press, 1985.

Felton, Harold W. *Edward Rose: Negro Trail Blazer.* New York: Dodd, Mead, 1967.

Sage, Walter N. *Sir James Douglas and British Columbia.* Toronto: University of Toronto Press, 1930.

Terrell, John Upton. *Estevanico the Black.* Los Angeles: Westernlore Press, 1968.

Wilson, Elinor. *Jim Beckwourth: Black Mountain Man and War Chief of the Crows.* Norman: University of Oklahoma Press, 1972.

**Extended family:** Family grouping that includes more than two generations or people not in direct lineage. The extended family is a household horizontally or vertically more inclusive than the typical American family, known as the nuclear family. The nuclear family most typically consists of male and female spouses and the children born of or legally adopted by this union. Vertically, the extended family includes living relatives from previous generations. These are commonly the parents or grandparents of the spouses, but they may include aunts, uncles—or great-aunts and great-uncles—and their children. Horizontally, extended families may include sisters, brothers, or cousins of the spouses as well as nieces and nephews. Some definitions include nonrelatives who live in the family home.

Extended families are traditional in most of the world, but today they have decreased substantially in prevalence, especially in the United States and Western Europe. Although nuclear families were the norm among European Americans by the late twentieth century, extended families were still common among Hispanic, Asian, and African Americans. Ethnic groups coming to the United States typically had extended family patterns. Families usually conformed to the nuclear pattern within one to two generations. Asian American, Hispanic American, and African American extended families are dwindling in number.

The decline of extended families has been attributed to a variety of factors, including assimilation of mainstream values, rising incomes that allow people to live independently, URBANIZATION, the spread of family members to different cities in search of work, and housing options that are less conducive to large households.

The advantages of extended families are increased resources, a broader knowledge base, and increased family and community security. For example, children who grow up in a home with a mother and grandmother exhibit fewer of the behavior or academic problems often experienced by children who grow up in single-parent families. Therefore, the decline of the extended family, though it conforms to

A great grandmother with her great granddaughter. (Martin A. Hutner)

the American mainstream, is not necessarily a positive development.

*See also:* Families; Parenting; Single-parent households.

# F

**Fair, Ronald L.** (b. October 27, 1932, Chicago, Illinois): Novelist and poet. Fair's surreal or absurdist fiction is grounded in naturalism. His second novel, *Hog Butcher* (1966), was made into a feature film and subsequently republished as a paperback entitled *Cornbread, Earl, and Me* (1975). Fair has been praised by literary critics, but his experimental novels did not attain a strong public following. His publications include *We Can't Breathe* (1972), an autobiographical novel, and the poetry collections *Excerpts* (1975) and *Rufus* (1977, 1980). *See also:* Literature.

**Families:** The family is the major social institution that passes on culture, socializes CHIL-DREN, and organizes the distribution of available resources among family members. There are significant variations in the forms that the "family" takes and in the roles and definitions of family members. In some societies, families consist of nuclear units only—a father, a mother, and their biological and/or adopted children. In other societies, the concept of the family may be extended to include other blood relatives such as grandparents, aunts and uncles, and cousins. Family structures may also include other persons who are informally adopted into the family; they are sometimes referred to as "fictive kin."

The importance of the family as a social institution varies considerably from society to society as well. In some societies, the family is more important than its individual members. In others, the individual is more important than the family and has little obligation to fulfill family desires or needs.

African American families remain distinctive in the United States for many reasons. These include a cultural heritage descended from West African societies, a long period of enslavement, and particular ways of defining family members and family ties. Debates surfaced in the latter half of the twentieth century as to whether African American families function effectively as social institutions. Some scholars questioned whether family forms held vestiges of African culture or whether modern family life was primarily determined by the lower-class position of so many African Americans.

A typical slave family living on a plantation in the early 1860's. (*Library of Congress*)

A major debate centered on whether particular family patterns, such as the mother-headed family or the EXTENDED FAMILY, represented unhealthy deviations from father-headed nuclear families. Patriarchal nuclear families, in which the father acts as major provider for his wife and their children and the wife acts as a homemaker, have in the past been accepted as the American ideal. Declining percentages of American families fitted this pattern in the late twentieth century. Opinion polls showed a declining number of people who agreed that this form of family actually was ideal.

To gain an overall understanding of family life among African Americans, it is instructive to examine the legacy of family experiences that enslaved Africans brought with them to North America. From this legacy comes an understanding of the cultural background of African American family life. Certain aspects of African family life can be seen among African Americans throughout their history as they adapted to SLAVERY, to freedom, and to the harsh economic realities that tested the resilience of African American families.

*African Roots of African American Families*
Revisionist historians look to West African cultures to explore the possibilities of enduring African features in African American society. Although there has historically been tremendous variation in the political and economic organization of the peoples of West Africa, there are common features in the organization and importance of family life. These include elaborate lineage systems, the importance of work roles for all family members, the significance of the extended family for individuals, and the importance of motherhood.

Lineage systems were a means of organizing African societies politically, economically, and socially. Regardless of whether these were patrilineal, following descent through the father, or matrilineal, through the bloodlines of the mother, they set the basis for social organization. Lines of descent were the basis by which family residential compounds were established. They often determined access to land, political and religious offices, marriages, and occupations as well.

All social life was organized around the lineage system, and lineage determined patterns of responsibility. In patrilineal societies, the father's immediate family was obligated to oversee the welfare of his descendants. In matrilineal societies, the mother's immediate family saw to the welfare of her descendants. Thus children were not the sole responsibility of their parents but instead were socialized and cared for within a larger extended network of kin. Within that network, siblings were significant caretakers for young children.

Individuals were identified through their membership in and activities engaged in for their kin group. Family was defined as extended, with family members working on behalf of their larger kin network and sharing the resources of that kin grouping. Within the family, men, women, and children all carried out important economic and social activities as participants in a complex network of production, distribution, and exchange. Men and women usually played gender-specific work and social roles. These were viewed as complementary to each other. A man was evaluated as a son, husband, and father in terms of his contributions to his lineage system and his devotion to the socialization of his children. Similarly, women were evaluated as daughters, wives, and mothers on the basis of their contributions to the family and their socialization of children.

Conjugal relationships were less important than positions within extended families. Conjugal relationships served to link extended family groups together. Generally, marriages were monogamous, arranged relationships which took place only with the approval of the larger community. There was also some

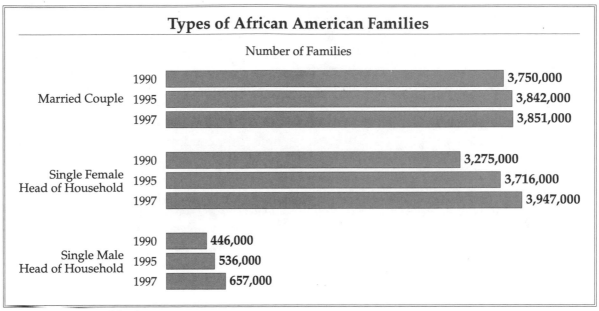

## Types of African American Families

### Number of Families

| | | Number of Families |
|---|---|---|
| **Married Couple** | 1990 | 3,750,000 |
| | 1995 | 3,842,000 |
| | 1997 | 3,851,000 |
| **Single Female Head of Household** | 1990 | 3,275,000 |
| | 1995 | 3,716,000 |
| | 1997 | 3,947,000 |
| **Single Male Head of Household** | 1990 | 446,000 |
| | 1995 | 536,000 |
| | 1997 | 657,000 |

*Source:* U.S. Bureau of the Census.

polygyny, wherein a man might take two or more wives. When a wife joined a residential compound, she was viewed as the wife of all the extended family members in the compound, not just as the wife of her husband.

Residence patterns for families were varied, but two forms predominated. These were either nuclear households, composed of a married couple and their children, or extended family groupings of husband, co-wives, and children; children's spouses and children; and perhaps siblings of the family head, along with their spouses and children.

Generally, women enjoyed high status within their extended families because of the important productive contributions they made to their families. This was particularly pronounced during their childbearing years, because the lineage system was perpetuated through their mothering. As elders, both men and women were entitled to respect and tribute from junior men and women in their extended families.

Children belonged to the lineage system. In a matrilineal society such as that of the Asante, they belonged to their mother's kin group, which was obligated to oversee their development. In such societies, children received inheritance through their mother's oldest brother, not through their father. In patrilineal societies such as that of the Dahomey, children were under the legal authority of their father and received their inheritance rights through him and his line.

In the West African societies from which most African Americans derive their legacy of family values, tribute and obligations were formed through an intricate organization based on kinship. In these systems, men and women derived their worth from their contributions to the family, children were the responsibility of a large network of extended family members, and the elderly occupied the greatest place of reverence. Lines of descent figured prominently in these societies in determining one's social existence.

The introduction of chattel slavery defined Africans as property and tore them from the familiar forms of social organization based on family ties. Many historians argue that although Africans of varying tribes were plucked away from their family groupings, they carried the legacy of family life as they had known it with them to North America. Central to this legacy is a conceptualization of family structure as based on a large kin network rather than on a patriarchal, nuclear family structure.

### Family Life Under Slavery

According to traditional sociologists and historians such as E. Franklin FRAZIER and Stanley Elkins, African family life (and African culture in general) was completely destroyed among Africans who experienced enslavement and among their descendants. In this view, slavery had a devastating effect on African Americans, rendering their family patterns pathological or inappropriate. These scholars argue that chattel slavery destroyed the African values governing marriage, sexuality, socialization, and family obligation. Under the slave system in the United States, marriage between those enslaved was not recognized, parental or kin protection of children could be blocked through the sale of a child or parent, and practice of African customs, including language and religious rites, was forbidden.

According to traditional historians, then, problems associated with mother-headed families, out-of-wedlock births, and social immobility are derived from the traumatic effects of slavery. They further contend that enslavement led to pathological forms of family structure and family formation that endure to this day. Not only was the culture and family system devastated, they argue, but also individuals internalized negative social definitions of blackness.

In contrast to these views, revisionist historians such as Melville J. HERSKOVITS, Eugene Genovese, and Herbert Gutman presented evidence to show that enslaved Africans brought to the Americas a legacy of African cultural institutions, including notions relating to family life. They agree that enslavement certainly involved an attack on traditional cultural institutions insofar as Africans were removed from their communities and were controlled under a slave administration. These historians argue, however, that Africans were resistant to the devastating effects of enslavement and responded by adapting their cultural institutions to the conditions they faced, as far as possible. This view is significant because it departs from looking at slaves as empty vessels who were simply victims of their fate. Instead, this argument promotes an analysis of those who were enslaved as members of communities with particular ways of relating to the world, and with their own notions of social organization.

Furthermore, some argue that particular aspects of African family life have survived enslavement. Traditional practices such as naming customs, rules related to sexuality, marriage proscriptions, and family structures of African Americans have features in common with those of West African families. In fact, African American families are sometimes argued to have more in common with traditional African families than they do with families of white enslavers or with white lower-class families. This argument contends that African American family characteristics are based on a different cultural tradition rather than simply on membership in lower socioeconomic classes.

Revisions of theories of family life among enslaved Africans focus on evidence of vestiges of West African family patterns in slave communities. For example, they rely on evidence that, following their enslavement, Africans continued to place emphasis on relations based on bloodlines rather than relations based on marriage. This is demonstrated by the use of naming practices, in which children are named after blood relatives to carry on the lineage system. Slavery was disruptive of family life, but family life persisted. Although marriage between African slaves was not officially recognized by whites, there is ample evidence that many slaves did participate in marriage rites and lived as married people.

Long-term marriages among those enslaved were recorded in plantation records and in slave narratives. When sales of spouses, children, and other relatives separated family members from one another, enslaved Africans tried in a variety of ways to be reunited. Runaways sometimes made contact with their relatives and tried to secure their freedom as well. Another way in which enslaved Africans continued family traditions was through establishing fictive kin. Adults were designated as aunts, uncles, or grandparents in the absence of blood relatives.

During slavery, certain aspects of African family life were disrupted, such as coresidence by extended family members. The size of slave cabins, for example, dictated the number of relatives who could live together. Some new forms of households emerged, in which women were the heads. In some cases, these household heads were women who did not remarry after the death or sale of a husband. In Africa, widowhood was generally followed by remarriage to the deceased husband's oldest brother. This tradition was not followed among enslaved Africans. In other cases, female-headed households consisted of an unmarried mother and children. Again, this new form was foreign to West African custom, where an unmarried woman and her child would have remained a part of their extended family compound.

Despite the impact of slavery on family life, certain African characteristics endured. These included the importance of kin networks, bloodlines, respect for elders, and reciprocity among family members. These characteristics are found to have existed among enslaved Africans whether they were held as property on large or small plantations, in the upper or lower South, or on owner-managed or absentee-owned plantations.

Although family members tried their best to shield other family members, slavery did not always allow protection. Some slaves responded to the brutality of their treatment by choosing marriage partners from neighboring plantations so they would not have to witness the brutalization of a loved one. Parenting was perhaps the relationship most affected by slavery, for parents were unable to prevent either the sale of their children or the sexual brutalization of their daughters and sons by lecherous overseers and slaveholders. Parental authority was diminished by the fact that African Americans were owned as property, so that the real "head of household" was the slave master. It was he, and he alone, who determined the fate of all family members. Children were often cared for by elderly slaves who could no longer do hard labor, or by older siblings. As a result, children developed more autonomy than they had prior to enslavement.

Some traditional practices that continued through enslavement included naming children for extended family members, prohibiting marriage among members of the same lineage group, and maintaining (where possible) close ties and reciprocity among extended family members. Premarital sexual relations, permitted in West African cultures, were still a norm, as was the ease of divorce in the case of an unhappy marriage. The sense of collective solidarity, traditionally defined in terms of individuals' connections to their extended family and village, was expanded during enslavement. This solidarity was based on the need to bond together against the brutal exploitation of enslavement and on the African heritage shared by enslaved Africans.

### Family Life After Emancipation

Following slavery, African Americans were able to choose to a greater extent the forms their families would take. Thousands petitioned the FREEDMEN'S BUREAU to assist them in registering their marriages and in locating lost family members. Many African Americans paid dearly for a marriage license to legitimate their slave marriages and the children of those marriages. This reveals the value system former slaves held regarding marriage and family relations. Even after a long period of enslavement, the belief predominated that conjugal relations and parental obligation for children should be socially and legally sanctioned.

The constitutional protections given by the Thirteenth, Fourteenth, and Fifteenth Amendments, guaranteeing African Americans their freedom, rights of citizenship, and male suffrage, did not exist for long in practice. The Freedmen's Bureau, which assisted African Americans in reforming families and granted relief to destitute former slaves, was disbanded in July, 1872. RECONSTRUCTION did not integrate African Americans into American society; rather, the aftermath of slavery was marked by the emergence of a strong racist movement which sought to terrorize African Americans and continue the exploitation of African American labor.

One of the types of attacks on the African American family came through the illegal seizure of African American children without parental consent. The children seized were apprenticed to whites as laborers. During its existence, the Freedmen's Bureau was presented with thousands of cases of parents seeking help to petition state courts for the return of their children.

The problems African American parents had in protecting their children following emancipation demonstrate the difficulties of building and maintaining family life. These problems were also related to the desire of African Americans to preserve the dignity of wives and daughters and to end the sexual violence against them. A reign of terror ran rampant through the South following emancipation. African Americans, who primarily worked as sharecroppers for whites after the abolition of slavery, were kept in constant terror to ensure that they would continue to occupy a lowly place in American society. Under the SHARECROPPING system, their labor was exploited and they were overcharged for the use of land, housing, food, and other materials. Those who complained about their treatment, or who tried to protect their wives or daughters from sexual advances by white men, were killed, brutalized, or threatened.

North Carolina sharecropping family returning home after working on a tobacco farm in 1939. *(Library of Congress)*

Despite economic conditions which constrained African Americans to be nothing but farm laborers, and despite the terrorism that emerged with the rise of the KU KLUX KLAN and other white hate groups, African Americans were able to form stable households as free people. The typical household consisted of two parents and their children. Another common form of household was composed of an extended family, in which the core nuclear family of a father, mother, and their children resided with some combination of grandchildren, nephews, nieces, aunts, and uncles. The nuclear household prevailed regardless of the parents' occupations, whether they were farm laborers, sharecroppers, domestic servants, artisans, or middle-class professionals.

Although most families were headed by two parents, a significant proportion of families were headed by women. Typically, female heads of families were older women (over the age of forty) who had been widowed. Young women also had children out of wedlock. In such cases, marriage generally followed the onset of pregnancy or the birth of a child. Young mothers who remained single did not tend to head their households but usually were in an "augmented" family, where their family unit was joined into the nuclear family household of their parents or other relatives.

In the immediate aftermath of emancipation, many African Americans chose to move away from the repressive conditions of the South. Those who migrated during this period of exodus tended to do so as families. In some cases, POVERTY or threat of reprisals prevented some family members from leaving. A large number of those who migrated did so because they were facing brutalization or incarceration. Most left because they sought opportunities for home and land ownership and the possibility of education for their children.

*The Early Twentieth Century*
African American households began to change in composition at the start of the twentieth century. Male-headed nuclear households were still the predominant family form, but extended families were far more common than they had been earlier. This may be a result, in part, of the persistence of difficult economic circumstances, which forced family subsets together for mutual aid. Extended family households were able to combine resources,

share in child care, and work together in the farm labor that continued to be the prevalent source of employment for African Americans.

The prevalence of stable households composed of parents and their children shows that although slavery was a devastating experience, it did not destroy the potential for family life among African Americans. African Americans wanted and had stable families, which were the main source of support for their members. Stable families were defined by long-term marriages, the presence of children, and strong ties to extended family members, who might even share a residence. These features show the persistence of a belief system that valued family life, parenthood, and marriage.

The ability of African Americans to build and maintain families was undermined, but not destroyed, by the political and economic repression that followed slavery. It was only when African Americans had migrated into urban areas, where they were increasingly ghettoized, that family life began to exhibit features that conservative scholars associated with a CULTURE OF POVERTY. Such features include mother-headed families, out-of-wedlock births, and high rates of divorce.

As noted above, African Americans began migrating from the South in large numbers following their emancipation from slavery. The largest migrations occurred, however, during the 1910's and 1940's because of factors associated with WORLD WAR I and WORLD WAR II. During these wars, labor shortages caused by the deployment of troops overseas resulted in an expansion of economic opportunities. In what became known as the GREAT MIGRATION, African Americans flocked to urban areas in the North and South for better-paying factory jobs. The boom periods were short-lived and, aside from wartime economies, African American families have faced unemployment and underemployment in the urban areas of the United States. These conditions, according to many scholars of the African American family, made it difficult for African Americans to put into practice their ideals regarding marriage and family life. The extended family network, which was both an African tradition and a resource during the postemancipation period, diminished in importance following URBANIZATION.

*African American Families After World War II*

African American family structure and family life changed considerably following World War II. One feature that has received much attention is the steady growth of mother-headed households. Although more than half of all African American families in 1990 were nuclear, almost half were headed by one parent, not two. As a result, many African American children were growing up in mother-headed homes. Although surveys indicate that Afri-

can Americans continue to value and desire marriage and family life, a high proportion of marriages end in divorce. Parenthood continues to be highly valued, but since it more often has taken place outside of marriage, the likelihood of poverty has increased.

These features of modern African American families have led some scholars to use a "deficits" approach in their examinations of African American family life. In such an approach, scholars emphasize the weaknesses, or deficits, in African American families. This has been the characteristic approach by mainstream scholars of the family. Other scholars have argued that African American families exhibit considerable strength in supporting their members emotionally and materially, through pooling of resources. They also state that, given the tremendous discrimination and deprivation that have confronted African Americans, it is a sign of the strength of African American families that so many survive. Many scholars agree that African American families are best characterized in terms of both strengths and weaknesses. The persistence of racism in American society and the limited occupational mobility and high unemployment rates among African Americans continue to influence African American families.

African American families vary in structure, location, size, economic status, and nature of relationships among family members. Poverty among African American families increased until the last few years of the twentieth century. By the year 2000 there was still only a small affluent

Based on Louis Peterson's play, the 1958 film *Take a Giant Step* explored the strains within a prosperous African American family whose son, played by singer Johnny Nash (left), felt torn between white and black communities. Beah Richards played his mother. *(Museum of Modern Art, Film Stills Archive)* class among African Americans. Most African Americans continue to hold very traditional values related to marriage, parenting, and the importance of the family, even when they are unable to live up to these values.

The persistence of economic deprivation threatens the stability of extended family networks and of conjugal and parental relations. Some argue that low-income African Americans respond to ghettoization and deprivation by forming "domestic networks." These networks are composed of both kin and "fictive kin" who provide mutual support in finances, child care, transportation, and day-to-day existence. Although this may represent a workable solution to the lack of resources by providing an organization for the pooling of resources, some researchers find that extended family networks or domestic networks may cause marital problems. This happens when the individual's obligation to the network becomes greater than the obligation to the spouse and when the network's needs conflict with those of the spouse. Thus, the extended family or domestic network embodies strengths by providing a larger pool of resources but may weaken particular aspects of family relations within that network.

African Americans continue to value marriage, despite the fact that as a group they exhibit a high divorce rate. The divorce rate does not deter African Americans who have never married from considering marriage as a viable and desirable option. In fact, it may reflect high expectations and high valuation of the marriage relationship. Furthermore, African Americans reveal much more egalitarian values related to sex roles within marriage than do other groups. These include a positive valuation of wives working, equality in decision making, and sharing child-rearing and household tasks.

African American men may feel threatened by their failure to achieve the status of sole provider because of their weak positions in the economy. Some scholars, in fact, argue that women do not receive much economic benefit from marriage because of the low economic status of African American men. In cases where financial security is an important motivation for getting married, if the woman is unable to get economic stability from marriage, she may be less inclined to stay married. Another complicating factor is the numerical imbalance between African American men and women and the resulting limited availability of marriageable African American men. This is related in part to the disproportionate number of African American men who are incarcerated. Perhaps as a result of these problems, the average age at which African Americans marry has steadily increased.

Parenting relationships within African American families reflect the continued cultural importance of children. In surveys, African American women voice a preference for giving birth while young, often by the age of twenty. By 1996, 69.8 percent of African American children were born out of wedlock, reflecting the high rate of teenage pregnancy among African Americans. Statistically the average number of children born to African American women decreased in the 1990's.

As a result of falling marriage rates and high divorce rates, an increasing number of African American children are reared by a single mother. Most children are reared either in a two-parent family or by a single divorced or never-married mother, but a small number are reared by other relatives, typically grandparents or aunts and uncles. Regardless of the family structure, children are central to African American family life. This is reflected both by the proportion of African American families with children and by the high value placed on motherhood by African American women.

The high value placed on motherhood is consistent. African Americans of all ages value their mother figures (which includes grandmothers, aunts, and other women who performed "mothering" functions) most highly of all family members. Many African American mothers are called upon to be both mother and father to their children. This facet of African American family life, coupled with the persistence of ghettoization and youth unemployment, poses special problems for the parent-child relationship. The difficulties that many African American young people encounter in finding positions within the legitimate economy has made it hard for parents to prevent children from seeking illegitimate alternatives.

Families of all types have problems because of the impact of racism on their lives, particularly in its economic manifestation. These problems persist across all status groups of African American families, affecting the young and old, the poor and the middle class. Even college-educated African Americans have significant levels of poverty, as do two-parent families in which both parents work. These facets of economic hardship demonstrate the persistence of racism and illustrate the fallacy of focusing exclusively on family structure as a source of weakness. Again, data on household composition do not reveal the extent to which a particular household may be connected to a larger network for mutual aid.

Although African American families are unable to shield their members entirely from economic problems, they are a primary source of emotional support and happiness. The major role that African American families play in helping their members to survive physically, spiritually, and mentally in a harsh society remains significant. Typically, parents and other family members are the first to teach children about racism and how to deal with it. Because African American children face widespread racism outside the home, they tend to draw their self-esteem largely from within their families. In addition, because family members impart culture to one another, the family continues to be the basis for the perpetuation of a distinct and dynamic African American culture.

—*Sharon Elise*

See also: African heritage; Biracial and mixed-race children; Black matriarchy myth; Community and culture; Parenting; Single-parent households.

Suggested Readings:

Cheatham, Harold E., and James B. Stewart, eds. *Black Families: Interdisciplinary Perspectives*. New Brunswick, N.J.: Transaction Publishers, 1990.

Gibson, William. *Family and Life and Morality: Studies in Black and White*. Washington, D.C.: University Press of America, 1980.

Hill, Robert B., with Andrew Billingsley et al. *Research on the African American Family: A Holistic Perspective*. Westport, Conn.: Auburn House, 1993.

Lewis, Jerry, and John G. Looney, eds. *The Long Struggle: Well-Functioning Working-Class Black Families*. New York: Brunner/Mazel, 1983.

McAdoo, Harriette Pipes, ed. *Black Families*. 2d ed. Newbury Park, Calif.: Sage Publications, 1988.

Toliver, Susan D. *Black Families in Corporate America*. Thousand Oaks, California: Sage Publications, 1998.

Zollar, Ann Creighton. *A Member of the Family: Strategies for Black Family Continuity*. Chicago: Nelson-Hall, 1985.

**Fard, Wallace D.** (Wallace Fard Muhammad; c. 1877—1934): Religious leader. Fard founded the First Temple of Islam, the forerunner of the NATION OF ISLAM (Black Muslims). Few facts are known about Fard's life, except for details pertaining to his activities in DETROIT, MICHIGAN, from 1930 until his death.

Fard claimed that he was born in Mecca, the son of a wealthy member of the tribe of

Koreish. He said he had been educated in England and at the University of California, although no substantiating evidence exists. It is known that Fard, who used a variety of names, appeared in Detroit during the GREAT DEPRESSION and earned a living selling silks and raincoats in Paradise Valley, Detroit's black community at the time. He may have been influenced by Noble Drew ALI, a religious activist who worked in several northern cities from 1913 until his death in 1929. After Ali's death, some of Ali's followers joined Fard's movement. Fard is said to have claimed to be the reincarnation of Ali.

Fard earned a reputation with his sermons denouncing the "white devils." His organization may have had as many as eight thousand members at the height of his popularity. He introduced many of the practices that would become central to the Black Muslim community in the 1950's and 1960's. He established the Fruit of Islam (a men's honor guard), the Muslim Girls' Training Corps, and the University of Islam. He also introduced the practice of claiming an "X" for a last name, in renunciation of the legacy of SLAVERY.

Fard's popularity and his organization declined as quickly as they had emerged. Some scholars have speculated that his insistence upon his own divinity and his infrequent public appearances, coupled with charges by outsiders that followers were disloyal to the United States, led to the group's decline. Fard gradually faded from prominence in the organization he began, and he disappeared in 1934. He greatly influenced Elijah MUHAMMAD, who revived Fard's beliefs and practices and developed a far more powerful and noteworthy Nation of Islam.

**Farmer, Forest Jackson** (b. January 15, 1941, Zanesville, Ohio): Corporate executive. After leaving college to play professional footballl as a linebacker for the Denver Broncos in 1962,

Farmer received a career-ending injury that convinced him to return to Purdue University to complete his bachelor's degree in 1965. Farmer worked briefly as a teacher before deciding to enroll in a training program at Chrysler Motors Corporation in 1968. An energetic worker, Farmer moved up through the ranks at Chrysler from industrial engineer to foreman and up to managerial positions.

Among his leadership positions with Chrysler, Farmer served as plant manager of the Jefferson Assembly Plant in DETROIT, MICHIGAN (1981), as manager of the assembly plant in Newark, Delaware (1983-1984), as director of advanced manufacturing and planning at the plant in Sterling Heights, Michigan (1986-1987), and as general manager of the plant in Highland Park, Michigan (1987-1988). Beginning in 1988, he served as the president of Acustar, an independent subsidiary of Chrysler that produced electronic components for automobiles. In helping to position Acustar as a competitive manufacturer, Farmer was responsible for overseeing the operations of Acustar's three primary divisions. In 1995 he left Acustar to become CEO of Regal Plastics.

**Farmer, James Leonard** (b. January 12, 1920, Marshall, Texas—July 9, 1999, Fredericksburg, Virginia): CIVIL RIGHTS activist. The son of a local METHODIST minister who was also a professor at Wiley College, James Leonard Farmer was to have a long civil rights career. After attending segregated common schools in Marshall, TEXAS, he enrolled at Wiley, where he received his B.S. in chemistry in 1938. Next, he went to HOWARD UNIVERSITY, receiving a degree in divinity in 1941. While at Howard, he became absorbed with his study of India's Mohandas Gandhi and nonviolent activism.

After graduation, Farmer moved to CHICAGO, ILLINOIS, where he took a job as race relations secretary for the Pacifist Fellowship of

James Farmer speaks to reporters after meeting with President Lyndon B. Johnson in December, 1963. *(AP/Wide World Photos)*

Reconciliation. In his spare time, he worked for local labor unions. Farmer was the principal founder of a new organization, the CONGRESS OF RACIAL EQUALITY (CORE), in 1942. Students from the University of Chicago were some of CORE's first members. Soon Farmer was planning boycotts, organizing peaceful marches, and leading sit-ins in Chicago restaurants. Other leaders eventually joined Farmer, and some established CORE branches in other cities and towns.

By 1960, just the time when Farmer became national director of the organization, CORE had begun focusing more attention on the South. CORE began working with the SOUTHERN CHRISTIAN LEADERSHIP CONFERENCE (SCLC), helping plan and lead sit-ins and boycotts throughout the South. In 1961 CORE attracted international attention by sponsoring the FREEDOM RIDES to enforce desegregation in interstate transportation. The first group of CORE volunteers boarded buses in Washington, D.C., and rode them into the heart of the South, facing violent opposition and massive protests that eventually stopped the first 1961 freedom ride short of its destination.

One of the primary civil rights leaders of the early 1960's, alongside such figures as Martin Luther KING, Jr., Roy WILKINS, and Whitney YOUNG, Farmer continued to lead CORE until 1966, when he turned to a teaching career. He taught civil rights courses and African American history at Lincoln University in Pennsylvania and at New York University.

In 1969 President Richard M. Nixon named Farmer assistant secretary of administration in the Department of Health, Education, and Welfare. Farmer was the first nationally prominent African American to be appointed to high office by the Nixon administration, and he was criticized by other black leaders who disapproved of the Nixon presidency. His response was that blacks needed to be involved in government in any way they could. After two years in the post, however, Farmer resigned in protest of lack of progress and resumed his teaching career.

In 1976 he resigned from CORE, unhappy with the group's leftist positions and particularly with its support of the Marxists in the Angolan civil war. His civil rights activities all but ceased after a failed attempt to develop a multiracial civil rights group with Floyd McKISSICK in the early 1980's. Farmer published a memoir, *Lay Bare the Heart*, in 1985, and occasionally taught at Mary Washington College in Fredericksburg, Virginia, until his health failed in the 1990's.

**Farrakhan, Louis Abdul** (b. May 11, 1933, New York, New York): Minister and national religious leader. One of the most controversial public figures of the late twentieth century, Farrakhan was praised for promoting self-reliance among African Americans and for fighting crime and drug abuse but was also condemned for statements interpreted as revealing prejudice against whites and Jews. After joining the NATION OF ISLAM, Farrakhan quickly rose to a position of power within the organization, becoming its most outspoken orator and eventually its leader. His greatest triumph came during the MILLION MAN MARCH, a gathering of African American men in Washington, D.C., in 1995.

### Early Years

Farrakhan was born Louis Eugene Walcott in NEW YORK CITY in 1933. The son of a teacher and a domestic worker, he attended Winston-Salem Teachers College in NORTH CAROLINA in the early 1950's. The public speaking skills he developed in college later proved of vital importance during his career as a religious leader.

Farrakhan studied music in his youth, learning to sing and to play the violin and guitar. While living in Boston in the late 1950's, he supported himself as a musician. Using the stage name Calypso Gene, Farrakhan accompanied himself on guitar while singing in a Caribbean style. The lyrics to his songs often dealt with political themes. Farrakhan's experience as an entertainer contributed to his ability to hold the attention of an audience while delivering a powerful message.

### Nation of Islam Leader

Farrakhan was recruited into the Nation of Islam (Black Muslims) in 1955 by MALCOLM X, the group's most important speaker of the late 1950's and early 1960's. He soon became close to Elijah MUHAMMAD, the founder of the sect. By the early 1960's, Farrakhan was the leader of the organization's Boston mosque. After

Malcolm X left the group in 1964 over political and religious differences, Farrakhan replaced him as the leader of the HARLEM mosque, and he soon was known as the group's leading orator.

After Elijah Muhammad died in 1975, his son, Wallace D. MUHAMMAD, moved away from his father's belief in the inherent wickedness of whites, the superiority of African Americans, and the separation of the races. The organization, now known as the American Muslim Mission, was dissolved in 1985. Many of its members became part of the worldwide religion of ISLAM. Meanwhile, Farrakhan remained true to the beliefs of Elijah Muhammad and became the leader of a new organization that retained the name of the Nation of Islam. He established a new Nation of Islam newspaper, *The Final Call*.

### National Prominence

Farrakhan argued that African Americans should remain separate from white America as much as possible. He believed that blacks would never rise if they continued to rely upon whites to help them. While blaming whites for racist economic and social policies

Louis Farrakhan in early 1995. *(AP/Wide World Photos)*

883

Louis Farrakhan (right) and Benjamin Chavis at a planning meeting for the Million Man March. *(© Roy Lewis Archives)*

his support of Libya and other Middle Eastern nations that were enemies of Israel.

Despite such controversy, Farrakhan won respect for his efforts to fight crime and drug abuse with unarmed groups of Nation of Islam members. Although these groups sometimes came into conflict with police, many African American churches and other organizations praised their success at reducing violence in African American neighborhoods. Farrakhan was also lauded for his promotion of self-respect, self-improvement, and economic development for African Americans. In 1985 he created People Organized and Working for Economic Rebirth (POWER), a group designed to aid African American business endeavors.

In January of 1995, Qubilah Bahiyah SHABAZZ, the daughter of Malcolm X, was arrested for attempting to arrange the murder of Farrakhan, in the belief that he had been involved in the 1965 assassination of her father. Farrakhan publicly defended Shabazz, claiming that her arrest was the result of entrapment. Shabazz avoided prison by accepting responsibility for the plot against Farrakhan's life, but she was later ordered to seek psychiatric treatment and to undergo treatment for drug and alcohol abuse.

*Million Man March*
Farrakhan's most successful project was the Million Man March, which took place in Washington, D.C., on October 16, 1995. This event brought a huge number of African American men together in a rally to promote reconciliation and empowerment. (The actual number of people attending the event has been debated, with some observers saying at-

that led to current social problems, Farrakhan promoted self-help and black separatism as prerequisites to advancement. He upheld individual responsibility and chided the black community for much self-destructive behavior. He preached against the use of alcohol, tobacco, and illegal drugs and promoted black education. He linked religion, learning, morality, and family as central to a program of change.

Farrakhan came to national attention while working with Baptist minister and CIVIL RIGHTS activist Jesse JACKSON during the 1984 presidential campaign. Jackson, the first African American to make a serious attempt to run for U.S. president, won the support of Farrakhan and his followers, but because of this he suffered the effects of Farrakhan's controversial beliefs and statements. Among other remarks, Farrakhan was widely quoted as referring to Judaism as a "gutter religion." Although he insisted that his words were misrepresented by being taken out of context, many critics of Farrakhan found clear evidence of racism and anti-Semitism in his speeches and writings. Farrakhan was also criticized for tendance was over one million and others insisting that it was significantly less.) The event was referred to by its leaders as a "rights and responsibilities" rally.

Other than Farrakhan, speakers included Jesse Jackson, Benjamin F. CHAVIS, Al SHARPTON, Rosa PARKS, and Dorothy HEIGHT. Farrakhan led the vast assembled group in a mass pledge to "never raise my hand with a knife or a gun to beat or cut or shoot any member of my family or any human being." When violent crime was reported to have dropped by about 5 percent the next year, according to statistics from the FEDERAL BUREAU OF INVESTIGATION (FBI), Farrakhan took credit for the reduction. Each year after the Million Man March, thousands of Nation of Islam members and their supporters gathered together on the anniversary of the march in an event known as the World's Day of Atonement.

In 1996 Farrakhan began a tour of eighteen nations in AFRICA and the Middle East. He was widely criticized for visiting Iran and Libya, nations that the U.S. government held responsible for international terrorism. He was also condemned for making statements against the United States while in these countries. In 1999 he announced he was taking a leave of absence for several months because of ill health, and it was unclear at that time whether he would return to active leadership of the Nation of Islam.

—Rose Secrest

See also: Religion.

Suggested Readings:

Alexander, Amy, ed. The Farrakhan Factor: African American Writers on Leadership, Nationhood, and Minister Louis Farrakhan. New York: Grove Press, 1998.

Gardell, Mattias. Countdown to Armageddon: Louis Farrakhan and the Nation of Islam. London: Hurst, 1996.

Levinsohn, Florence Hamlish. Looking for Farrakhan. Chicago: Ivan R. Dee, 1997.

Magida, Arthur J. Prophet of Rage: A Life of Louis Farrakhan and His Nation. New York: Basic Books, 1996.

Singh, Robert. The Farrakhan Phenomenon: Race, Reaction, and the Paranoid Style in American Politics. Washington, D.C.: Georgetown University Press, 1997.

**Fashion:** The Civil Rights movement enabled black Americans to gain access to areas of mainstream America that previously were closed to them. One of these areas is the fashion industry. Black designers, for the most part, were virtually excluded from the fashion scene in New York and elsewhere. Similarly, black models, regardless of their poise and beauty, neither walked down the runways nor appeared as models or cover girls in white magazines.

*Black Efforts in Fashion*

The exclusion of African Americans from the mainstream world of fashion and design did not discourage black creativity and business ventures in the fashion industry. African American designers found outlets for their talents within the black community. Many sold their creations in boutiques, designed and sewed for both white and black patrons, and showed their wares in black-sponsored fashion shows. Moreover, just as influential African Americans promoted black talent in other areas, they promoted black designers and models. For instance, in 1950 the National Council of Negro Women sponsored the National Association of Fashion and Accessory Designers, a professional organization for black women in the fashion industry. One of its charter members, Lois K. Alexander, later founded the Harlem Institute of Fashion and the Black Fashion Museum in the late 1970's.

Before the 1970's, African Americans in fashion received their greatest support from

(continued on page 887)

# Notable Fashion Designers

**Brown, Carl** (b. 1969, Queens, N.Y.), **Daymond John** (b. c. 1970, Queens, N.Y.), **J. Alexander Martin** (b. 1970, Queens, N.Y.), **Keith Perrin** (b. 1970, Queens, N.Y.). Partners in FUBU (For Us By Us). In 1992 chief executive officer John launched the FUBU line, with vice president and head designer Martin and cofounders Brown and Perrin. The line included baseball caps, hockey jerseys, rugby shirts, and T-shirts. The designers subsequently introduced lines for women and boys.

**Burrows, Stephen Gerald** (b. Sept. 15, 1943, Newark, N.J.). Burrows attended the Fashion Institute of Technology from 1964 to 1966. In 1970 he was hired to work for noted designer Henri Bendel. Burrows started his own firm, Stephen Burrows, Inc., in 1973. In addition to his regular line of clothing, he launched a knitwear line and offered a line of fragrances. Burrows  won Coty Awards for fashion design in 1973 and 1977 and was given a special Coty for loungewear design in 1974.

**Chanticleer, Raven** (b. Sept. 13, 1933, New York, N.Y.). Progressive fashion designer Chanticleer opened his House of Fashion in 1969. He designed clothes for celebrities including Della Reese and Eartha Kitt and had numerous theater, television, and film credits.

**Haggins, Jon** (b. Sept. 5, 1943, Tampa, Fla.). Haggins began designing in the mid-1960's, producing clinging jersey dresses. At age twenty-two, he opened his own design studio in New York City. It closed in 1972 for lack of capital. Eight years later, Haggins made a comeback with his Jungle Fever collection, featuring animal patterns and rain-forest motifs.

**Hankins, Anthony Mark** (b. Nov. 10, 1967, Elizabeth, N.J.). Bold colors and ethnic prints are signatures of Hankins's work. His styles have appeared in department stores such as J. C. Penney and Sears. In 1994 he started his own company, Anthony Mark Hankins Designs, which became a $40-million concern. His book *Fabric of Dreams: Designing My Own Success* was published in 1998.

**Hayatt, Lester** (b. 1948). In 1980 Hayatt incorporated his own wholesale company, Lester Hayatt Sportswear. Six years later, he opened two retail outlets called "Hayatt" in New York City. In 1984 Hayatt was among the ten African Americans honored for their impact on the fashion scene in the sixth annual Tribute to the Black Designer gala, held at Lincoln Center in New York City.

**Jones, Carl** (b. c. 1955, Tenn.) and **Thomas "T. J." Walker** (b. c. 1961, Toomsuba, Miss.). Partners in the Cross Colours clothing line, founded in 1990, Jones and Walker are noted for helping to bring African American fashion into the mainstream. Throughout the early 1990's, Cross Colours expanded, distributing jeans designed by Karl Kani and adding children's clothing and other divisions. Eventually, orders for their products proved overwhelming as Jones and Walker struggled to finance the manufacturing required to meet demand. In 1994 they were forced to restructure as a licensing firm.

**Kani, Karl** (Carl Williams; b. 1968, Costa Rica). Kani appointed himself chairman and chief executive officer of his own $60-million clothing company, Karl Kani International. His line included his trademark jeans, jerseys, jackets, and T-shirts as well as a children's line and a leather collection for women. Kani launched a collection of men's suits in the fall of 1999.

**Kelly, Patrick** (Sept. 24, c. 1954, Vicksburg, Miss.—Jan. 1, 1990, Paris, France). Kelly moved to Paris in 1979 to pursue fashion design. In 1988 he became the first American elected to the Chambre Syndicale du Pret-a-Porter, an association of fashion's elite in Paris, France. Until the exclusive boutique Victoire provided him with a workshop and showroom in 1984, he sold his fashions in flea markets. Three years later, Kelly launched a special line as part of a multimillion-dollar deal with Warnaco, a major apparel firm. Kelly's designs are notable for their references to African American culture.

**Lars, Byron** (b. 1965?, Oakland, Calif.). Upon completing his studies at the Fashion Institute of Technology, Lars worked for several fashion designers and earned awards in national design competitions. He established his own design business in 1990. As a result of his success as a designer, Lars was named rookie of the year by *Women's Wear Daily* magazine in April of 1991.

**Lowe, Ann** (Dec. 14, 1898, Clayton, Ala.—Feb. 25, 1981, Queens, N.Y.). Lowe's most famous creation was the wedding gown worn by Jacqueline Bouvier for her marriage to John F. Kennedy in 1953. She later created designs for department stores, including Neiman Marcus and I. Magnin, as well as sold her own designs. She opened her own Madison Avenue shop in New York City in 1968.

**Malone, Maurice** (b. Sept. 26, 1964; Detroit, Mich.). In the 1990's Malone was considered one of the most promising young designers by the Council of Fashion Designers of America. His first collection was a mix of athletic apparel, jackets, and logo-cuff jeans; he subsequently debuted a collection of men's suits. Malone also launched women's and boys' lines.

**Smith, Willi** (Feb. 29, 1948, Philadelphia, Pa.—Apr. 17, 1987, New York, N.Y.). Smith started his own line of clothing, WilliWear, in 1975. He received the 1983 Coty American Fashion Critics Award in Women's Fashion for his designs. Smith designed for everyday people, keeping his clothes affordable. After a slump in sales in the early 1980's, WilliWear gained renewed popularity after Smith designed the wedding dress for Caroline Kennedy, the daughter of former president John F. Kennedy. Smith's WilliWear line did not survive his early death.

the black media, notably the BLACK PRESS. Founded in the early 1940's, the Johnson Publishing Company of Chicago promoted black cover girls, models, and designers through its publications. Early issues of EBONY, the company's most successful family-oriented magazine, featured pioneer black models such as Dorothea Towles and Sara Lou Harris. In addition, JOHNSON PUBLISHING COMPANY made it a point to picture African American models in advertisements and urged other publications to do the same.

*The Ebony Fashion Fair*
Johnson's promotion of black designers and models was not been limited to its publications. In 1963 Eunice Johnson, wife of the company's founder, John Harold JOHNSON, began producing the Ebony Fashion Fair. In choosing fashions for this extravaganza, Johnson visited the most prestigious fashion houses in Europe—Cardin, Ungaro, Valentino, Armani, and others—in search of selections for her shows. She also chose from America's finest

designers. Even more important, Johnson featured in her shows creations from talented African American designers, among them Patrick Kelly, Willi Smith, Gordon Henderson, C. D. Greene, Byron Lars, and Eric Gaskins.

Described as a traveling extravaganza, the Ebony Fashion Fair promoted the careers of black models and has confirmed that women of color can wear bright colors. Its displays of colorful clothes on models of various degrees of blackness dispelled the once-prevalent idea that women with black skin should wear drab, dark colors and avoid colorful hues such as yellow, red, green, pink, and gold. Moreover, the shows brought high fashion to audiences of predominantly black women in the big cities as well as remote towns and villages across the United States. For many women in these audiences, the fair afforded the only opportunity to see the fashions of prestigious designers or to see any high-fashion clothes being worn by professional African American models. Undoubtedly, both models and designers in the shows have encouraged many African

Americans to explore the world of fashion.

The doors of the fashion world gradually began to open to black designers. By the early 1990's, black fashion designers, many of them in their twenties and thirties, were showing their works at major New York and Paris shows.

### Black Designers

One of the most successful of a group of black designers who showed their creations in New York City in the 1990's is Byron Lars. Audiences in the fashion business—consisting of department and specialty store buyers, fashion editors, writers, photographers, and celebrities—are critical, but Lars's designs were well received. According to the president of one boutique chain, Lars's collection was the hit of the 1992 New York collections. Some

Designer Byron Lars at a New York show of his fall 1994 womenswear collection. *(AP/Wide World Photos)*

fashion critics believed that Lars's first full-scale New York show in 1992 was the "hottest event" of the fashion season.

By the 1990's, other young African American designers had also arrived on the New York fashion scene. Among those staging shows were Gordon Henderson, Tracy Reese, C. D. Greene, Michael McCollom, and Kevin Smith. At least one collaborative show featured nearly a dozen black designers.

If retail sales provide an indication of a designer's success, some of the young artists were well on their way. During the 1991-1992 seasons, Lars's "streetwise garments" quadrupled in sales. They were sold in prestigious stores including Nordstrom, Neiman Marcus, Saks Fifth Avenue, and Victoire in Paris. Tracy Reese experienced a rather bumpy career in the 1980's, but in 1990 she became the primary designer for the Japanese-based Mogaschoni collection. Her line of designs had grossed more than $3 million in sales for the company by the end of 1992.

### Black Models

By the early 1990's, black women were being seen on the fashion runways of European salons as well as on the covers and throughout the pages of fashion magazines. Black fashion models, like black designers, had once had very limited access to the world of beauty and fashion. During the 1950's, for example, Dorothea Towles and Sara Lou Harris found that despite their beauty, their opportunities as models were limited in the United States. Accordingly, both women went to Europe in order to enjoy the success denied them in the United States.

Several factors contributed to the success enjoyed by black fashion models during the 1980's and 1990's. First, black-owned publications and black-sponsored events, such as the Ebony Fashion

## Notable African American Models

**Banks, Tyra** (b. Dec. 4, 1973, Los Angeles, Calif.). At the age of twenty, Banks became the first African American "cover girl" for Maybelline cosmetics. In 1996 she was the first black model to grace the cover of *Sports Illustrated*'s swimsuit issue. Banks appeared in numerous advertising campaigns and on the covers of several magazines in the 1990's. She also appeared in television and film roles.

**Beckford, Tyson** (b. Dec., 1971, New York). In 1993 Beckford was hired to represent Ralph Lauren's Polo Sport line exclusively after initially appearing in a series of advertisements for Lauren's sport, fragrance, and body lines. By 1995 he was on the cover of major magazines, including *Essence*, and was being featured in multipage layouts in *GQ* and *Vogue*.

**Campbell, Naomi** (b. May 22, 1970, London, England). Campbell started modeling at the age of sixteen. In 1989 she became the first African American model to appear on the cover of the French edition of *Vogue* magazine. She maintained her standing among the industry's elite models through the 1990's by gracing the cover of every major fashion magazine and remaining one of the highest-paid models in the world. Campbell appeared in some guest-starring roles on television and had several small roles in films.

**Houston, Whitney.** *See main text entry.*

**Iman.** *See main text entry.*

**Johnson, Beverly** (b. Oct. 13, 1951, Buffalo, N.Y.). In 1974 Johnson became the first African American fashion model to appear on the cover of *Vogue* magazine. The following year she was named outstanding U.S. model. Johnson continued to model into the 1990's and ventured into acting by appearing in small film roles and music videos. As an author, Johnson shared many of her beauty secrets and ideas in books written specifically for African American women.

**Sims, Naomi.** *See main text entry.*

**Tyson, Cicely.** *See main text entry.*

---

Fair, allowed black women to acquire experience in the world of modeling. Moreover, both the magazines and the fashion shows allowed more Americans to see beautiful women of color. The emphasis in the 1960's and 1970's on blackness as a positive and beautiful attribute influenced many in the beauty business to question and to expand their concepts of beauty. Gradually, a more cosmopolitan and sophisticated concept of beauty—one that included more than white skin and straight hair—emerged.

Some practical considerations also aided black models in becoming more successful and in demand. A number of manufacturers discovered that sales were boosted by using black models to appeal to black consumers and to influence their purchasing decisions. The exposure that models of color received from the media and in fashion shows indicated that women of color were ideally suited to wear colorful fashions. In the particular case of swimwear, warnings by the American Cancer Society against exposure to the rays of the sun caused some swimsuit manufacturers to employ more women of "natural" color in their advertisements.

Several African American women became "household faces" of the modeling world. By the 1970's, Beverly Johnson, a black woman with exotic features, was cited as one of the beauties of the age. She became one of the most photographed faces in the fashion and beauty world. Johnson was the first black woman to appear on the cover of *Vogue* and was featured on more than five hundred magazine covers. She also appeared in countless advertisements for beauty and cosmetic products aimed at both white and black consumers. Johnson revealed her beauty secrets and

Iman modeling a swimsuit designed by Patrick Kelly at a Paris show in 1989. *(AP/Wide World Photos)*

gave tips in several mainstream fashion magazines.

During the 1980's, many black women were modeling and appearing in fashion magazines as well as in catalogs for exclusive shops, boutiques, and department stores. Somalia-born IMAN became one of the most popular models in the world. By the early 1990's, British-born Naomi Campbell had become one of the most highly sought runway models of any ethnic group. Campbell's exotic looks enabled her to earn as much as $15,000 per day as a model, and she appeared on the covers of several magazines.

During the mid- to late 1990's, major cosmetics companies finally began to award contracts to African Americans, including Halle

BERRY and Vanessa WILLIAMS—the former was signed by Revlon, the latter by L'Oréal. As the century ended, African American models Tyra Banks, Tyson Beckford, Alex Wek, and others enjoyed lucrative contracts with designers such as Ralph Lauren.

African American designers such as Fubu and Karl Kani earned millions of dollars in the fashion industry by capturing not only a share of the African American dollar but also the business of white and Latino consumers. Many entertainment luminaries, such as Sean "Puffy" Combs, Spike LEE, and Russell Simmons, also branched out into the fashion industry by creating lines directed at a youthful, urbane market.

—*Betty L. Plummer*
—*Updated by Andrea E. Miller*

*See also:* Visual arts.

Suggested Readings:

Alexander, Lois K. *Blacks in the History of Fashion*. New York: Harlem Institute of Fashion, 1982.

Boston, Lloyd. *Men of Color: Fashion History Fundamentals*. New York: Artisan, 1998.

Hageney, Wolfgang, ed. *Black Africa Impressions: Graphic and Color and Fashion and Design*. 2d ed. Rome, Italy: Belvedere, 1983.

Myers, Walter D. *Crystal*. New York: Viking Kestrel, 1987.

Salley, Columbus, ed. *Accent African Fashions*. New York: Col-Bob Associates, 1975.

Starke, Barbara M., Lillian O. Holloman, and Barbara K. Nordquist. *African American Dress and Adornment: A Cultural Perspective*. Dubuque, Iowa: Kendall/Hunt, 1990.

Summers, Barbara. *Skin Deep: Inside the World of Black Fashion Models*. New York: Amistad Press, 1998.

**Father Divine** (George Baker, later Major J. Devine; May, 1879, Rockville, Maryland—September 10, 1965, Philadelphia, Pennsylvania): Religious leader. Little is known of Father Divine's early life, partly because he deliberately obscured his past. Early scholarship usually gave his birthplace as Hutchinson's Island, Georgia. He was an active preacher in Sunday schools in East Baltimore, MARYLAND, in the early part of the twentieth century. He probably was influenced by religious activists Sam Morris ("Father Jehovah") and John Hickerson, both of whom were active in the first decade of the century.

He began to act as an informal employment agent in New York City, helping new arrivals to the North from the South. Gradually, he created the persona of Father Divine. He established a meeting place in Sayville, Long Island, New York, in 1919, and referred to it as heaven. Many of his followers began to see him as God incarnate. His reputation grew when a judge who had convicted him on public nuisance charges died suddenly and unexplainably soon after Father Divine's incarceration.

Father Divine's Peace Mission movement relocated to Manhattan in New York City and to PHILADELPHIA, PENNSYLVANIA, following legal difficulties at the Long Island location. In the 1930's and 1940's, news of the ministry was communicated through a weekly magazine called *New Day*. Father Divine taught that this magazine was to be considered as the bible for his followers, that races should be integrated, that heaven was on Earth, and that all things were to be forsaken for him, as God. Some scholars have estimated that he had as many as fifty thousand followers in the mid-1930's, although there are few reliable records.

In 1953 Father Divine moved his community, the Kingdom of Peace, to Woodmont, a 73-acre estate in Merion Township, Pennsylvania. He may have had as many as half a million followers by the time of his death. He owned nothing, but his followers provided him with access to a fortune that may have been as large as ten million dollars. The minis-

try collapsed after his death, unable to operate effectively without his leadership.

Much of Father Divine's appeal to his followers was the role that the provision of food and shelter played in his ministry, especially during the GREAT DEPRESSION. Unlike other religious leaders, who primarily preached moral reform and biblical devotion, Father Divine recognized the need to meet an individual's basic survival needs. Some scholars and religious leaders have argued that he took advantage of his followers. The Kingdom of Peace was more a cooperative economic service agency than it was a ritualized religious community, and in some ways it can be seen as a predecessor of the NATION OF ISLAM. Although Father Divine became more conservative after WORLD WAR II, when his ministry had built up significant assets, his theology was always a combination of the Protestant work ethic with the reform-minded concerns of the Social Gospel approach.

**Fauntroy, Walter** (b. February 6, 1933, Washington, D.C.): WASHINGTON, D.C., politician. Fauntroy graduated cum laude in 1955 from Virginia Union University with the B.A. degree, and from Yale University Divinity School in 1958 with the bachelor of divinity degree. An ordained Baptist clergyman, Fauntroy was awarded honorary degrees from Georgetown University Law School, Yale University, and Virginia Union University. He also won the National Urban Coalition's Hubert Humphrey Humanitarian Award in 1984.

Fauntroy was named pastor of New Bethel Baptist Church in Washington, D.C., in 1958. In 1960 he became the director of the SOUTHERN CHRISTIAN LEADERSHIP CONFERENCE (SCLC) in the District of Columbia. He was the local coordinator for the 1963 MARCH ON WASHINGTON. He also helped organize the SELMA TO MONTGOMERY MARCH in Alabama in 1965, was vice chairman of a White House

Walter Fauntroy represented the District of Columbia in the House of Representatives for two decades. *(Archive Photos)*

conference geared toward formulating legislation guaranteeing black rights, and was appointed vice chairman of the Washington City Council in 1967 by President Lyndon B. Johnson. He successfully enlisted clergy and laity in social and political rights organizations from his pastorate at New Bethel Baptist Church.

In March, 1971, Fauntroy won the race to represent the District of Columbia in the House of Representatives by nearly forty thousand votes. He remained in that position until 1990. He was chair of the CONGRESSIONAL BLACK CAUCUS from 1981 to 1983. His district was characterized by major social problems, including poverty, crime, overcrowded housing, and unemployment. Fauntroy was recognized for his intimate style with constituents, attempting to resolve problems personally, and for his constant communication with the population through regular radio and tele-

vision programs. While in the House of Representatives, he was successful in increasing funding for the district, in preventing additional sales taxes on basic commodities such as food, in providing rent control legislation for Washington, and in obtaining funds to fight diseases such as sickle cell anemia that affect African Americans.

Fauntroy's civil rights and political commitments originated in his religious background. He was a prototype for African American clergy who continued the tradition of the black church's involvements in addressing social problems in order to benefit the larger society.

**Fauset, Crystal Bird** (June 27, 1893, Princess Anne, Maryland—March 28, 1965, Philadelphia, Pennsylvania): Politician. Crystal Bird Fauset was the first African American woman elected to a state legislature. She won a seat in PENNSYLVANIA in 1938. Fauset was also a social worker and educator, and she served as a member of the Franklin D. ROOSEVELT ADMINISTRATION's "black cabinet."

**Fauset, Jessie Redmon** (April 27, 1882, Camden New Jersey—April 30, 1961, Philadelphia, Pennsylvania): Novelist and editor. One of the people credited with bringing the HARLEM RENAISSANCE into existence, Fauset was also an author in her own right.

The youngest of seven children, Fauset grew up in PHILADELPHIA and attended the city's public schools. She entered Cornell University in 1901, after not being accepted at Bryn Mawr, and graduated in 1905. The previous year she had been elected to Phi Beta Kappa as possibly the first African American to receive this prestigious award. After graduation, she taught briefly in NEW YORK CITY and BALTIMORE before accepting a position at M Street (later named Paul Laurence

DUNBAR) High School in WASHINGTON, D.C.

In 1919 Fauset was named the literary editor of THE CRISIS, the magazine of the NATIONAL ASSOCIATION FOR THE ADVANCEMENT OF COLORED PEOPLE, (NAACP). In this capacity she introduced the literary world to the works of writers Jean TOOMER, Countée CULLEN, and Nella LARSEN, and she published the works of others already known, including Claude McKAY and Langston HUGHES. In his autobiography, *The Big Sea* (1940), Hughes identifies Fauset as one of three people who "midwifed the so-called New Negro literature into being." In 1920, when W. E. B. DU BOIS began the *Brownies Book*, a magazine for African American children, he selected Fauset as its managing editor. Fauset's own short stories, poetry, and nonfiction frequently appeared in *The Crisis* and *Brownies Book*.

To counter the image of the black middle class that was presented in T. S. Stribling's novel *The Birthright* (1922), Fauset began writing. In 1924 her first novel, *There Is Confusion*, was published. The story of two middle-class families, the novel traces the lives of three characters, Joanna Marshall, Peter Bye, and Maggie Ellersley as they attempt to follow their aspirations in a world that limits them because of their color.

In 1926 Fauset left *The Crisis* and returned to teaching, but she continued to write. Her second novel, *Plum Bun*, was published in 1929, the year that she married Herbert Harris. The story of Angela Murray, a young African American woman who decides to "pass" for white in order to achieve her career goals, *Plum Bun* is considered Fauset's best novel. In 1931 *The Chinaberry Tree* was published; it is the story of two cousins, Laurentine Strange and Melissa Paul, who learn to live their own lives by defying community prejudices regarding their family background. Fauset's final novel, *Comedy: American Style* (1933), relates the story of Olivia Cary, the wife of a physician and mother of four who destroys

her marriage and family. These works rank Fauset as the most frequently published novelist of the Harlem Renaissance.

After her husband died in 1958, Fauset returned to Philadelphia, where she died three years later at age seventy-one. Decades later, the significance of Fauset's own contributions as a Harlem Renaissance writer came to be seen as equal to that of her role as literary midwife. During the 1990's her work enjoyed renewed attention when the Northeastern Library of Black Literature reprinted *There Is Confusion* and *The Chinaberry Tree*.

—*Paula C. Barnes*

*See also:* Literature.

**Federal Bureau of Investigation:** The Federal Bureau of Investigation (FBI), the national police force of the United States, has historically had a controversial relationship with African Americans, especially in the area of CIVIL RIGHTS.

The FBI was formed, as the Bureau of Investigation, in 1908. It was not until the 1920's, however, that it took on its modern form under the leadership of J. Edgar Hoover. Hoover, raised in segregated WASHINGTON, D.C., would strongly influence the nature of the FBI's relationship with African Americans. Until the 1960's, as far as the FBI was concerned, African Americans were either victims, criminals, suspects, or subversives. The FBI did not have any African American agents until 1962 (it did have a few African American employees), when it was pressured to change its recruitment practices by the Kennedy administration. Hoover frequently listed his black servants as members of the FBI in order to deflect criticism that there were hardly any black FBI employees.

In the 1960's, the FBI's relationship with African Americans became increasingly strained. The Civil Rights movement was a major source of conflict. The FBI, reflecting the racial attitudes of its leader, Hoover, was not a proponent of civil rights. In fact, leading proponents of civil rights and improved conditions for black Americans, including Martin Luther KING, Jr., and MALCOLM X, were subjects of extensive surveillance by the FBI.

Believing the Civil Rights movement to be inspired by the Communist Party, Hoover had the FBI do little to aid the cause during the Kennedy administration. There was strong animosity between Hoover and Martin Luther King, Jr, in particular. Because one of King's advisers actually was a communist, Attorney General Robert Kennedy eventually gave Hoover permission to use electronic surveillance against King. The FBI discovered marital infidelities and sent this information to King through an anonymous letter that urged the civil rights leader to step down—and even indirectly suggested that he commit suicide.

Under the JOHNSON ADMINISTRATION, which began in November, 1963, the FBI finally took a more important role in aiding the Civil Rights movement. Specifically, it directed its resources against the KU KLUX KLAN. The shift in focus began in the aftermath of the murder of three civil rights workers in 1964 in Mississippi, when President Lyndon B. Johnson announced that the full powers of the state would be directed against the secretive and racist organization. Operations against the Klan drastically reduced its power by the end of the 1960's.

Before the 1960's were over, however, the FBI would again be at odds with many black Americans. Black power, especially as personified by the BLACK PANTHERS, became a target of the FBI's COUNTER INTELLIGENCE PROGRAM (COINTELPRO). The FBI did everything that it could to weaken the unity of the BLACK POWER MOVEMENT, frequently trying to sow discontent among members. The FBI also aided other American police forces in their battles against the Black Panthers.

With the death of Hoover in 1972 the FBI modernized, and tensions between the agency and African Americans declined. In the 1980's and 1990's, however, the FBI remained controversial for its role in the United States' "war on drugs." A disproportionate number of black Americans faced arrest and imprisonment for nonviolent drug offenses, leading to charges of racism being leveled against the entire American justice system.

—*Steve Hewitt*

*See also:* Black Panther Party; Crime and the criminal justice system.

Suggested Readings:

Blackstock, Nelson. *COINTELPRO: The FBI's Secret War on Political Freedom.* New York: Vintage Books, 1976.

Friedly, Michael, and David Gallen. *Martin Luther King, Jr.: The FBI File.* New York: Carroll & Graf, 1993.

Powers, Richard Gid. *Secrecy and Power: The Life of J. Edgar Hoover.* London: Hutchinson Ltd., 1987.

**Federal Theatre Project:** Performing arts division of the Works Progress Administration (WPA), one of the New Deal programs of the Franklin D. Roosevelt administration. The project created, nationally, African American THEATER units such as the Federal Negro Theater, the African Dance Unit, the Lafayette Theater, and the Negro Youth Unit. These groups gave African Americans a chance to express and interpret their own culture artistically and allowed them to be part of the American cultural scene. The Federal Theatre Project trained African American directors, technicians, and actors, organized writers' workshops, produced plays by unknown African American playwrights, and found audiences for those plays. The project was dissolved by Congress in 1939.

*See also:* Performing arts; Roosevelt administration, Franklin D.